ASSESSING YOUNG CHILDREN WITH SPECIAL NEEDS

An Ecological Perspective

SUSAN M. BENNER

UNIVERSITY OF TENNESSEE

Longman

New York & London

Assessing Young Children with Special Needs

Longman, 95 Church Street, White Plains, N.Y. 10601

Associated companies:
Longman Group Ltd., London
Longman Cheshire Pty., Melbourne
Longman Paul Pty., Auckland
Copp Clark Pitman, Toronto

Executive editor: Naomi Silverman
Production editor: Till & Till, Inc.
Cover design: Susan J. Moore
Cover photos: Tinah Utsman
Text art: CIRCA 86, Inc.
Photograph on p. 288 courtesy of Bobbie Beckman. All other photographs courtesy of
Tinah Utsman. Photographs taken at the following locations: Child Development
Laboratories, Department of Child and Family Studies, University of Tennessee,
Knoxville; Little Tennessee Valley Cooperative, Birth to Three Program, Blount County,
Tennessee; Maryville City Schools, Preschool Program; Maryville, Tennessee; Pediatric
Language Clinic, Department of Audiology and Speech Pathology, University of
Tennessee, Knoxville.
Production supervisor: Richard Bretan

Library of Congress Cataloging-in-Publication Data
Benner, Susan M.
    Assessing young children with special needs : an ecological
perspective / Susan M. Benner.
        p.   cm.
    Includes bibliographical references and index.
    ISBN 0-8013-0488-1
    1. Behavioral assessment of children.   I. Title.
RJ503.5.B46   1991 1992
155.45'1—dc20
                                                        91-12132
                                                        CIP

1 2 3 4 5 6 7 8 9 10-HA-9594939291

This book is dedicated to
Carol and Amy, who actually got tired of fast food
but realized that it was better than no food
and
David

Contents

Acknowledgments

First and foremost, my gratitude goes to the families depicted in the case studies found in the appendix at the end of this book. Through extensive discussions with the mothers of the children highlighted in these case studies, I developed a deep appreciation for the range of emotions they were subjected to during the earliest months of their children's lives. I am thankful for their willingness to share openly their own experiences, and I hope that students studying from this text can develop an understanding of the need for family-centered care through these illustrations. Additionally, I wish to express my appreciation for the administrators, teachers, parents, and children of the four centers who allowed me to use photographs in the text. Tinah Utsman, the photographer for all but one photograph, was readily available and helpful throughout the photography sessions.

I am grateful to the authors of Chapters 4 and 7 for their contributions to the text. Kathleen Warden and Tricia McClam provide a clear presentation of the psychometric properties of assessment instruments and a straightforward discussion of market-driven variables in test construction. Vey Nordquist and Sandra Twardosz present a unique chapter, emphasizing the interactive nature of behavior and the environment.

I wish to express my appreciation for the assistance of several graduate assistants who helped me gather the resources necessary to complete this text, including Michael Story, Lynn Brown, and Jan Barton. Additionally, the graduate students in my early childhood special education assessment class over the past three years have provided essential critiques of early drafts for which I am grateful. I also wish to acknowledge the support and encouragement for this project from my department chair, Larry Coleman. A word of thanks and appreciation goes to my secretary, Vicki Church, who always extends beyond the call of duty when deadlines come.

Finally, I wish to express my gratitude for those persons involved in the review and editorial process. The reviewers, who provided essential critique of previous drafts along with many positive suggestions for content expansion and formatting, included Merith Cosden, James V. Kahn, Barbara Lowenthal, Mark Wolery, and Mary Kay Zabel. I am grateful for the continual words of encouragement from Naomi Silverman, editor of the text. I also wish to thank the editorial staff of Longman and Russell Till, who did a thorough job in the copy editing process.

Introduction

The importance of intervention in the early years in preventing developmental delays and reducing the effects of disabling conditions on a child's development, as well as reducing the cost of housing and educating the child through the rest of her life, is no longer in question. Determining which children should receive early intervention requires child assessments coupled with information about the families and the communities in which they live. The meaningful determination of what a child is capable of doing must be conducted within the context of each child—his family and community, background, and experiences. This text covers techniques and tools available to gather data about infants and young children with special needs and their families using this contextual, or ecological, perspective.

Although assessment of child functioning in traditional developmental domains represents a significant portion of this volume, that alone would be incomplete. The need for individuation and sensitivity to child and family variables (e.g., handicapping conditions, cultural heritage) is emphasized, even though it is impossible to describe detailed information about the best practices for assessment of every type of child in a single text. Examples drawn from actual case histories illustrate key points. Each chapter concludes with highlights of the key issues related to the ecological perspective.

The text comprises four parts with a total of 14 chapters. Part One sets the theoretical and philosophical tone for the text, outlines the purposes and stages of assessment, describes various techniques of assessment, and reviews basic terminology and statistical concepts. Part Two focuses on family and environmental issues, including the identification of family strengths and needs as well analysis of the home environment. Analysis of preschool environments can determine how environmental features influence child behavior. Part Three begins with a chapter outlining an ecologically valid model of assessment. For children with a different cultural and/or linguistic heritage, the examiner using this model can acknowledge and account for the child's background. It is better to have no test results than test results reflecting biased, unfair testing practices. The Ecologically Valid Assessment Model also distinguishes child functioning across settings. The remaining chapters provide details of assessment procedures in specific developmental domains. Part Four covers child assessment as an element of program evaluation and other timely issues such as drug-exposed babies, AIDS, and advancing medical technology.

The decision to identify a child as disabled or even at high-risk for becoming disabled must be made with extreme caution. Failure to identify children who should receive early intervention can result in delays in providing them with needed services. Premature identification and labeling of children as needing services, when they are developing within normal expectations, can have lasting negative effects as well. Approaching child assessment from an ecological perspective can reduce the errors made in the identification process. The interpretation of test results reflects information provided by children, their families, and the communities in which they reside.

Once the decision is made that a child would, in fact, benefit from early intervention, determination of what to teach and how to teach is the next task. Again, using an ecological perspective is crucial in gaining enough information to provide effective intervention. Knowing about the family and community are as important as knowing about the child. The organization and rationale of this text is predicated on this ecological perspective. Included in the appendix at the back of this text are two case studies, which are cited throughout the text to illustrate points and provide actual examples of assessment reports and test results.

Several chapters include appendixes that provide brief descriptions of assessment tools relevant to the topic of the chapter. I have included information on the psychometric properties of those instruments for which I could locate such information.

I have chosen to alternate the use of gender-specific pronouns by paragraph unless a specific person is referenced. Illustrations of positive or negative behaviors are not linked to sterotypic gender characterizations.

PART ONE

Foundations of Ecologically Valid Assessment

Part One of this text is designed to achieve several purposes. It presents the theoretical perspective of the text, the purposes and stages of assessment, techniques used in assessment, and the statistical tools used to interpret assessment results. The first chapter addresses the theoretical underpinnings of the ecological perspective of the text, the work of Brofenbrenner on ecological experimentation, and Thurman's view of ecological congruence. In 1975, McReynolds identified three trends in psychological assessment consistent with this ecological perspective. The trends he identified are (1) extension of assessments beyond individual persons to include couples, families, and small groups; (2) assessments of both social and physical environments in which persons live and behave; and (3) an increasing emphasis on assessments in naturalistic settings. However, Willems's comment on the state of affairs of psychological study made in 1977 is still descriptive of typical child assessment reports.

> We say that systems concepts, complex dependencies, reciprocity and extended time-related cycles must be entertained as descriptive and explanatory terms, but they almost never show up in the actual reports of our research. By and large, we continue to study behavior as though its important phenomena were simple, single-file and relatively short-term. (1977a, p. 12)

Willems's example of a woman who was effectively taught to reduce her nagging behaviors toward her noncompliant son makes the point all to clearly. She actually reduced her commands toward her son from 100 per hour to an average of 15 per hour. However, her rate of eating increased, as did her anxiety and tension. Finally, she abandoned the child and left town. The interventionist expressed no remorse, but rather noted that this departure caused a troublesome interruption of the treatment that had been so successful.

An ecological perspective is particularly significant when assessments are focused on young children with disabilities or those who are at a higher than normal risk of becoming disabled. Young children with special needs are especially dependent upon the adults in their environment to ensure their developmental progress. In discussing the environmental forces on physically disabled children, Schoggen (1978) noted how physical features interact with the environment in a reciprocal manner as the person develops. Disability is viewed as a phenotypical phenomenon that has no simple, direct relation to behavior and personality but that does have potential for modifying behavior in two important ways. First, disability can modify the instrumental value of physique; that is, it can change the adequacy of a person's physique for carrying out important activities leading to significant goals. Second, disability can modify dramatically the social stimulus value of physique; that is, it can change the way in which the person is seen by others and by the person himself. Who the person would have been without the physical disability is not known to us. An interweaving between the person and the social and physical settings surrounding that person cannot be separated. Thus, any meaningful assessment of an individual must incorporate information far beyond a simple view of that individual's capacities on one instrument at one moment in time.

Chapter 2 covers the purposes and stages of assessment. Clarity as to the reasons for an assessment is critical to its usefulness and should be clearly defined during the planning stage. Adjustments can be made as the assessment progresses and new areas of interest or concern emerge. When an examiner doubts her ability to add any new information or obtain the type of information sought through the tools she has at hand, she should acknowledge these limitations to those who have requested the assessment.

Effective assessment techniques vary according to the purpose and subjects involved. Chapter 3 contains a description of seven strands that reflect the variety of available techniques. Persons conducting assessments need to employ a variety of these techniques, avoiding the formation of comfortable habits, which can result in neglecting the careful planning of each assessment as a new problem to be solved. Assessments that include multiple types of data from multiple sources are characterized by a richness of information not available in the simple one-shot routine use of the examiner's favorite test.

The final chapter in Part One, by Kathleen Warden and Tricia McClam, covers the interpretation of assessment results. The statistical information incorporated in the chapter provides test users and consumers of assessment reports with the knowledge needed to critique the psychometric properties of the tools used. Additionally, the chapter contains information addressing the reliability and validity of assessments based on observational data. The final section of the chapter raises some serious concerns related to the testing industry. All professionals using or consuming reports based on these instruments should be aware of the profit-making aspects of testing. The tests are designed to sell, not just to assess children with accuracy. Unless test users and report consumers demand high quality in terms of psychometric properties, reasonable costs, and relevance to children with various disabilities and cultural backgrounds, these concerns will not be a top priority of the testing industry.

An Ecological Perspective on Assessment

CHAPTER OUTLINE

QUESTIONS ANSWERED IN CHAPTER 1

- What are the primary components of PL 94–142, PL 99–457, and PL 101–476?
- How does the federal legislation relate to an ecologically based view of child assessment?
- What is the theoretical foundation for ecologically valid assessment?
- What are the general characteristics of infants and young children who are at-risk, developmentally delayed, or who evidence one or more of the disabling conditions defined in PL 94–142 and PL 101–476?
- What are the basic constructs of ecologically valid assessment?

CHAPTER OVERVIEW

This book is about assessing infants, toddlers, and preschool children with developmental delays, disabilities, and those at-risk for developing disabilities. Conducting such an assessment without regard to the child's family and community circumstances will produce incomplete results at best. Removing the child from his "context" for purposes of assessment can be compared to taking a few words from an entire passage, thereby changing the meaning of the words. Therefore, this book is also about identifying strengths and needs of the child's family and analyzing the environments in which he functions. Ultimately, the information gained from these sources must be integrated to form a complete picture of the child.

   The perspective of this book is an ecological one, which incorporates a child's total environment, including her family and community life. Ecologically valid assessment acknowledges the impact of these elements on child functioning across all developmental domains. This chapter begins with a brief review of PL 94–142, PL 99–457, PL 101–476 and a discussion of the nature of conditions that necessitate early intervention. The remainder of the chapter centers on the ecological perspective, including a rationale, theoretical underpinnings, and basic constructs.

FEDERAL LEGISLATION: PL 94–142, PL 99–457, AND PL 101–476

Federal legislation has played a critical role in the provision of services to children of all ages who have disabilities. In 1975 PL 94–142, the *Education of All Handicapped Children Act* (retitled *Individuals with Disabilities Education Act* in 1990) mandated that all school-age children with disabilities receive a free appropriate education in the least restrictive environment. The law stipulated that schools provide the children with needed special education and related services. Related services include such things as transportation, physical therapy, occupational therapy, adapted physical education, and psychological assessments. States could serve children 3 to 5 years of age through this legislation and were required to do so equivalent to the services provided for nonhandicapped children. For example, a state with mandatory kindergarten was expected to provide services to kindergarten-age children with handicaps as well. Additionally, school systems could apply for grants to support early intervention.

   The basic components of PL 94–142 are the following:

- Free appropriate education in the least restrictive environment for all children, regardless of the severity of their disability
- Provision of related services as needed to enable children to profit from their education
- Educational decision making by a multidisciplinary team, which includes professionals and parents

- Development of Individual Education Plans, stipulating annual goals of the child's educational program
- Due process for parents or schools when agreements regarding educational and related services cannot be reached through the multidisciplinary team process

The *Individuals with Disabilities Education Act Amendments of 1986* (PL 99–457) extend the mandate to provide all of these services to the 3- to 5-year-old population (Part B), and offer states additional incentives to provide early intervention for the birth through 2-year-old population (Part H). Part C of the amendments of 1986 reauthorizes funding of models of service delivery for young children previously known as Handicapped Children Early Education Projects (HCEEP).

Part H (Programs for Infants and Toddlers) is intended to provide a system of family-focused intervention. The objective of this part of the legislation is to establish a new state grant program for infants and toddlers, ages birth through 2 years (up to the third birthday), in order to do the following:

1) Develop and implement a statewide, comprehensive, coordinated, multidisciplinary, interagency program of early intervention services for infants and toddlers with disabilities and their families;
2) Facilitate the coordination of payment for early intervention services from federal, state, local, and private sources (including public and private insurance coverage); and
3) Enhance the states' capacity to provide quality early intervention services and expand and improve existing early intervention services being provided to infants and toddlers with disabilities and their families. (Sec. 303.1)

In order for a state to receive Part H funds it must participate in a 5-year sequence culminating in full implementation of intervention services. Within the first 2 years the governors of participating states must designate a lead agency for overall administration of the program. The governor is also responsible for establishing an Interagency Coordinating Council (ICC) composed of representatives of appropriate state agencies, higher education, service providers, and parents. The ICC is expected to assist in the development and implementation of state plans and facilitate interagency agreements designed to create a comprehensive network of services throughout the state, including 14 components of the law. These components include defining developmental delay, interagency collaboration, development of Individual Family Service Plans and case management systems, multidisciplinary assessment systems, timely reimbursement policies, designation of a lead agency, assurance of qualified personnel, provision of personnel development, public awareness, child-find activities, a statewide central directory of services, and data collection.

Early intervention services as defined in PL 99–457 (Sec. 303.12) refer to a wide array of services, including audiology; case management services; family training, counseling, and home visits; health services; medical services only for diagnostic or evaluation purposes; nursing services; nutrition services; occupational therapy; physical therapy; psychological services; social work services; special instruction; and speech-language pathology. A child referred to a public agency must receive a multi-disciplinary assessment within 45 days to be deemed eligible under the state's definition of developmental delay. The assessment must be conducted by personnel trained to utilize appropriate methods and procedures. It must include a review of pertinent records related to the child's current health status and medical history and an evaluation of the child's level of functioning. The developmental areas that should be included are (1) cognitive; (2) physical, including vision and hearing; (3) language and speech; (4) psychosocial; and (5) self-help skills.

Each child who receives early intervention services through Part H is required to have an *Individualized Family Service Plan* (*IFSP*). PL 99–457 stipulates that assessment of family strengths and needs be incorporated into each child's program planning, including parental instruction whenever appropriate and to the extent desired by the parents. Identification of the strengths and needs of the family as related to enhancing the child's development must always be conducted on a voluntary basis, to ensure that no child is denied services because his family preferred not to participate.

Although IFSPs are not mandatory for 3- to 5-year-olds, a committee report accompanying the legislation strongly recommended that similar procedures be implemented for that age group as well, rather than traditional Individual Education Plans. Never before has the importance of the family unit in early intervention been made as clear as it is in this piece of legislation. It is based on the assumption that if maximum progress is to be made with young children, the family unit must be considered. The idea behind the IFSP is family intervention rather than child intervention.

In October 1990 additional amendments to PL 94–142 (PL 101–476) were passed by the Congress. The changes include the title revision, expansion of the categories of disabling conditions (autism and traumatic brain injury), and the addition of rehabilitation counseling and social work services to the list of related services. Other changes emphasize the importance of planning transition into the workplace and the need to address minority concerns at all levels of programming.

DEFINING THE POPULATION

Young children who are at-risk for becoming disabled or who have a disability present are a diverse group, including infants, toddlers, and preschool-age children with genetic disorders present at birth; preschool-age children showing slight developmental delays in speech and language; deaf or blind children; children with emotional and behavioral problems; and many others. Some children's conditions are readily identified and diagnosed, whereas others may go for years without a clear diagnosis. Sorting and labeling such young children can be difficult, inappropriate, and sometimes impossible. Nevertheless, criteria for eligibility for federally supported programs need to be clear. The categories of disabilities associated with PL 94–142 are specifically delineated, while PL 99–457 employs the broad concepts of developmental risk and developmental delay for eligibility.

Disabling Conditions

The use of a label such as mental retardation for a very young child seems to bring with it an element of finality. However, school systems need such labels and categories to receive reimbursement of funds spent on special education. Children with special needs exhibit a wide variety of disabilities ranging from mild learning or adjustment problems to severe multiple handicaps accompanied by retardation, sensory impairments, an inability to speak, and an inability to walk or care for themselves. The legally accepted definitions for educational purposes are those found in the regulations accompanying PL 94–142 (*Federal Register* [1977, August] *42* [163]. 20 U.S.C. 1401 [1], [15]). The regulations stipulate that children with a variety of specific conditions are considered disabled and therefore eligible for special education. These conditions, or categories, are identified and defined in the following list from PL 101–476. (Definitions of these categories as used in other professional fields may differ.)

> *Children with disabilities* means those children evaluated in accordance with the regulations as being mentally retarded, hard of hearing, deaf, speech impaired, visually handicapped, seriously emotionally disturbed, orthopedically impaired, other health impaired, deaf–blind, multihandicapped, autistic, or as having specific learning disabilities or traumatic brain injury, who because of those impairments need special education and related services. The terms used in this definition are defined as follows:

Autism is a condition of unknown cause related to a variety of symptoms, including (1) disturbances in the rate and appearance of physical, social and language skills; (2) abnormal responses to sensations; (3) absent or severely delayed speech and language development; and (4) abnormal ways of relating to people, objects, and events. (Federal definition was not available at press time.)

Deaf means a hearing impairment which is so severe that the child is impaired in processing linguistic information through hearing, with or without amplification, which adversely affects educational performance.

Deaf–blind means concomitant hearing and visual impairments, the combination of which causes such severe communication and other developmental and educational problems that they cannot be accommodated in special education programs solely for deaf or blind children.

Hard of hearing means a hearing impairment, whether permanent or fluctuating, which adversely affects a child's educational performance but which is not included under the definition of "deaf" as defined above.

Mentally retarded means significantly subaverage general intellectual functioning existing concurrently with deficits in adaptive behavior and manifested during the developmental period, which adversely affects a child's educational performance.

Multihandicapped means concomitant impairments (such as mentally retarded–blind, mentally retarded–orthopedically impaired, etc.), the combination of which causes such severe educational problems that they cannot be accommodated in special education programs solely for one of the impairments. The term does not include deaf–blind children.

Orthopedically impaired means a severe orthopedic impairment which adversely affects a child's educational performance. The term includes impairments caused by congenital anomaly, impairments caused by disease, and impairments from other causes.

Other health impaired means limited strength, vitality or alertness, due to chronic or acute health problems, which adversely affects a child's educational performance.

Seriously emotionally disturbed is defined as follows: The term means a condition exhibiting one or more of the following characteristics over a long period of time and to a marked degree, which adversely affects educational performance:

(A) An inability to learn which cannot be explained by intellectual, sensory, or health factors;

(B) An inability to build or maintain satisfactory interpersonal relationships with peers and teachers;

(C) Inappropriate types of behavior or feelings under normal circumstances;

(D) A general pervasive mood of unhappiness or depression; or

(E) A tendency to develop physical symptoms or fears associated with personal or school problems.

Specific learning disability means a disorder in one or more of the basic psychological processes involved in understanding or in using language, spoken or written, which may manifest itself in an imperfect ability to listen, think, speak, read, write, spell, or to do mathematical calculations. The term includes such conditions as perceptual handicaps, brain injury, minimal brain dysfunction, dyslexia, and developmental aphasia. The term does not include children who have learning problems which are primarily the result of visual, hearing, or motor handicaps, of mental retardation, or of environmental, cultural, or economic disadvantage.

Speech impaired means a communication disorder, such as stuttering, impaired articulation, a language impairment, or a voice impairment, which adversely affects a child's educational performance.

Traumatic brain injury is a wound or injury to the cortex or cerebellum portions of the central nervous system, resulting in a loss of functioning or abnormal functioning, so as to require special education and/or related services. (Federal definition was not available at press time.)

Visually impaired means a visual impairment which even with correction, adversely affects a child's educational performance. The term includes both partially seeing and blind children.

Developmental Risk and Developmental Delay

Risk factors present in the young child and/or her environment contribute to cause developmental delays. As the child matures, the nature of these observable delays may become apparent, resulting in a specific diagnosis, such as one of the disabilities stipulated in PL 94–142. On the other hand, the developmental delay may disappear, and the diagnosis of the child as having one of the specific conditions can be avoided. Although 3- to 5-year-olds must meet the criteria for one of these categories for funding purposes, they can be identified as developmentally delayed until the use of a specific category is more appropriate. Part H of the *Individuals with Disabilities Education Act Amendments of 1986* includes funding to serve infants and toddlers from birth through 2 years who are developmentally delayed or at-risk of becoming developmentally delayed. Individual states are responsible for establishing their own definitions of these terms and appropriate eligibility criteria.

Developmental Risk.   Developmental risk relates to the vulnerability of infants, toddlers, and young children. The terms *developmental risk, high-risk,* and *at-risk* are used by a variety of professionals, each of whom gives the terms their own meanings (Rossetti, 1986). Kopp (1987) uses the term *developmental risk* simply to indicate that the "well-being of children is in jeopardy" (p. 881). Risk incorporates several subcategories of infants and children whose chances of experiencing normal development are in danger. Medical personnel tend to use the term *high-risk* in regard to neonates whose ability to survive is in question (Rossetti, 1986). Other professionals who become involved with the infants once their survival is established are concerned with them being *at-risk* for delays in specific developmental domains such as language or cognition. Educators use the term *at-risk* in reference to the child's future school achievement being jeopardized. High-risk neonates who survive may retain their at-risk status for several years, until they demonstrate an ability to achieve in school.

Risk Factors. Prenatal indicators of risk include radiation, mutant genes, nutritional deprivation, maternal infection, metabolic disorders, and harmful drugs.

Disorders of labor and delivery, neonatal medications, prematurity, cardiopulmonary problems, congenital malformations, metabolic disorders, and infections pose danger during the perinatal period. Postnatal risks include acute illness, chronic disease, accidents and poisoning, malnutrition, poverty, onset of genetic disorders during early childhood, family dysfunction, and sociocultural disadvantages (Ramey, Trohanis, & Hostler, 1982).

A multitude of circumstances can contribute to the risk an infant or young child faces. Tjossem (1976) defined three categories of risk factors—*established risk, biological risk,* and *environmental risk*. Children who have genetic conditions or other medically diagnosed disorders known to cause developmental disabilities would be considered to have an *established risk*. For example, a child with a birth defect such as myelomeningocele (spina bifida) will inevitably face disabilities related to motoric functioning. The extent to which any specific child will be affected by genetic or other medically diagnosed disorders is impossible to predict.

Children with biological histories or conditions associated with a high probability for handicaps developing are considered to be at *biological risk*. Birth trauma, prematurity, infections such as encephalitis, maternal difficulties, or complications during pregnancy all put a child at biological risk. It is possible no long-term effects will be evident from such conditions or incidents, but probabilities indicate that these children will have special needs. The two case studies presented in the appendix to this book are both examples of biological risk. Elizabeth Armstrong suffered from a traumatic birth and Eduardo Manzolis was premature.

An environment that fails to provide adequately for a child's multitude of needs, ranging from proper nutrition, warmth, and clothing to emotional and psychological security, can result in a child becoming disabled. Children experiencing such *inadequate environments* are at-risk for becoming mentally, emotionally, or physically impaired. Such inadequate environments can be characterized as neglectful, harmful, or both. Children who are raised in such environments may have parents who experienced poor caretaking by their parents, have limited educations, are teenagers, have no support systems available, suffer from emotional problems or developmental disabilities, and/or have inadequate economic resources (Ensher & Clark, 1986).

An overlapping relationship exists between the risk categories. For example, children who are facing environmental risk will be more likely to experience biological risk as well. Mothers may be unable to obtain adequate prenatal care for themselves, may be unaware of the nutritional needs of infants and small children, and/or may be unable to meet the emotional needs of their young children. The interrelatedness of these at-risk categories will be evident for most children who experience any one of them. The relationship between biological and environmental factors and the determination of an infant's risk for abnormal development has been emphasized by Sameroff and Chandler (1975). They put forth a transactional model of development in which the child's genotype and his experiences with the environment become inseparable as he moves from conception to death. This transactional model has been used in the development of intervention programs for premature infants (Ramey, Zeskind, & Hunter, 1981).

The interplay among the multiple factors contributing to the infant's risk does make the determination of who is at-risk a complicated matter. Evidence of a child's individual resilience and protective factors (e.g., genetic predisposition and nurturance by an extended family member) further complicate the determination of which children are at-risk (Werner, 1990). Targeting children for whom intervention may prevent potential damage is one of the professional's greatest challenges. When does a home environment constitute such a grave danger to the child that she should be removed from the home? How much risk or deprivation can a particular child tolerate? At what point is the medical status so tenuous that the value of survival is questioned? These questions raise some of the most challenging dilemmas and ethical considerations for professionals working with this population.

Developmental Delay.   The educational community has no universally agreed upon definition of the term *developmental delay*. Typically, it is used in reference to young children who are showing delays in one or more areas of development, including communication, cognition, social-emotional development, and motor development. Determining when a child is showing a significant delay in contrast to normal fluxations and ranges of development can be difficult. Developmental delay is used in describing young children who exhibit general delays across all or most developmental domains and in reference to delays in specific developmental domains (e.g., developmental delay in language). The story of David Griffin (box) illustrates this difficulty.

RATIONALE FOR THE ECOLOGICAL PERSPECTIVE

Careful diagnosis and evaluation of the child in isolation might produce very accurate and informative details about the child's current functioning under specific conditions, in a particular setting. It may not reveal *why* a child is unable to perform certain tasks or whether she can perform similar tasks in different settings. Confusion and misinterpretations can result from missing information and divergent priorities and conflicting values systems between professionals and families. For instance, the child may be asked to use a pair of scissors. She refuses to even hold the scissors, despite assurances and support by the examiner. What might appear on the record sheet after such child-focused assessment is, "Child cannot cut, refuses even to hold scissors." The missing information may be that last week the child got into her mother's sewing basket and was playing with the scissors. Upon discovering this situation, the mother spoke sharply to the child, thus startling her, causing the scissors to drop onto the child's leg resulting in a painful cut. The mother, while dressing the wound, continued to berate the child for playing with the scissors and made her promise never to do such a thing again. The child's behavior during the assessment, in fact, might demonstrate an obedience to her mother and avoidance of pain more than a lack of cooperation with the examiner or inability to perform the task.

Recommendations based on isolated clinical assessments can be directly counter to the family's wishes for the child. For example, developmental specialists may believe a child is ready to be toilet trained, but the mother has no interest in such a project. Previous attempts have failed, and the father abused the child when accidents occurred. Another child in the home is still in diapers, so the mother has decided that working with them together in about six months is the best approach.

Is This Child Developmentally Delayed?

When an infant starts to fall behind in achieving motor milestones, parents and physicians must decide when to be concerned and when to take action. Many parents of children whose developmental delays become clearly apparent as time passes are frustrated by the pediatrician's failure to respond to the developmental lags during infancy. Parents often report that the pediatrician assured them that their child would soon outgrow the present delays and that all was well. First-time parents with limited knowledge of normal child development are particularly vulnerable to these assurances by the pediatrician. When the child fails to mature out of his developmental lags and a referral is finally made, the parents must deal with the child's problems and the seemingly unnecessary delay in beginning intervention as well as their own emotions toward a medical system that let them down. As the child grows older and reaches school age, the parents continue to wonder what benefits were forever lost to their child because intervention was delayed. However, many children who have similar developmental lags do mature, and soon these parents realize that their child is doing just fine—the doctor was right. The anxiety and concern for the child's development during infancy fade into a seemingly ridiculous reaction of nervous parents. The pediatrician is praised for her calm assurances that all would be well. The telltale signs of brain damage, however, although apparent to professionals accustomed to working with infants with brain damage, have no meaning to the unsuspecting parent. Often developmental lags are subtle and of uncertain outcome. The following case illustrates how some children with significant lags do catch up.

David Griffin was born weighing 8 pounds, 13 ounces, after a term gestation. There were no perinatal complications, and he had no significant medical complications during the first few months. At 4 months of age his pediatrician referred him to a neurologist because his head size was at the 98th percentile and was continuing to increase rapidly. The neurological examination revealed no abnormalities or evidence of hydrocephalus, but close monitoring of the head circumference was recommended. When the child was 13 months of age the pediatrician expressed concern about the child's delayed motor development and referred the parents to a therapeutic early intervention center. A comprehensive examination was completed, which included administration of a comprehensive battery of tests. The tests and scores are noted below.

Battelle Developmental Screening Inventory
More than one standard deviation below the mean (which triggered the complete assessment)

Battelle Developmental Inventory

Personal–Social	8 months
Adaptive	9 months
Gross motor	6 months
Fine motor	10 months

Motor total	7 months
Receptive language	8–9 months
Expressive language	8 months
Communication total	8 months
Cognitive	11 months
BDI total	9 months

Milani-Comparetti Neuromotor Screening Test
Approximately 7 months

Bayley Test of Infant Development

Motor	8.3 months (PDI 58)
Mental	10.1 months (MDI 78)

Hawaii Early Learning Profile (fine and gross motor profiles)
Gross motor—6 months with scatter skills to 9 months
Fine motor—11 months with scatter skills to 13 months

These test results appeared to verify the pediatrician's concern about David's motor development. It was recommended and the child began receiving physical therapy once a week. He was enrolled in a regular day care setting at the time of evaluation. After observing David in day care, staff at the therapeutic early intervention center noted that the placement was appropriate for the present time, but reevaluation should occur in 6 months' time. Verbal reports to the parents from the staff at the center left them with the impression that their child was severely developmentally delayed, with serious motor and communication delays. The impact of this news on the family was tremendous. However, shortly after this assessment, David experienced a substantial developmental spurt in both language and motor development. The physical therapy sessions were reduced and stopped completely after four months' time. Had the pediatrician been slower to respond to David's motor lags, the assessment and ensuing recommendations and interventions might have been avoided. Instead the initial assessment hangs over David's head, worrying his parents and coloring the perceptions of professionals. Even when physical therapy ended, the recommendation of an 18-month reevaluation was made. It will be some time before the impact of this assessment dissipates.

The professional who is unaware of the mother's view can easily judge her as lazy and uninterested in her child's development.

Cultural mores may dictate that certain speech and language patterns are preferred over standard English. The parents and community may not want a child to speak in the manner the examiner thinks the child ought to speak. Respect for and appreciation of the family beliefs are crucial for successful communication with parents. If the ultimate goal of assessing young children is to improve their lives and help them to reach the highest quality of life possible, professionals must be willing to go beyond the standard of practice that limits itself to the simple, the straightforward, the traditional clinical approach to assessment.

THEORETICAL BASIS FOR THE ECOLOGICAL PERSPECTIVE

The works of Bronfenbrenner (1976, 1986), Thurman (1977), and Thurman and Widerstrom (1985, 1989) provide a theoretical basis for ecologically valid assessment. Bronfenbrenner proposed that an ecological perspective be used in educational experimentation, as contrasted with contrived, or laboratory, experimentation. Thurman developed a theoretical model of ecological congruence to serve as the foundation for program planning for young children with handicaps. These complimentary theoretical perspectives have implications for assessment, which are embedded into five basic constructs of ecologically valid assessment.

Ecological Experimentation

According to Bronfenbrenner (1976), experimentation using an ecological structure must reflect the natural environment, including the microsystems, mesosystems, exosystems, and macrosystems affecting subjects involved in the experiment. The *microsystem* includes those factors of place, time, activity, and role found in a particular setting. A child's home environment and the developmental preschool he attends are two examples of microsystems. The *mesosystem* incorporates all of the major settings of a particular learner and the interrelationships of the settings. Thus, a child's mesosystem might include his home, preschool, church, doctor's office, park, and relationships across each of them. The *exosystem* includes social structures (e.g., public school system and health care systems), and the *macrosystem* represents the broad culture and subcultures (e.g., regional or ethnic customs and values). The positive correlation between unemployment rates and incidence of child maltreatment is one illustration of the influence of these systems (external to a child's immediate settings) on child development. When the Oregon lumber industry developed unemployment rates in the double digits, a 46% increase in child maltreatment was reported (Birch, as cited in Garbarino, 1990). The importance of these systems to the developing child is also apparent in the relativity of what materials are considered necessities and how we choose to use monetary resources versus time and energy. Garbarino uses the reliance on disposable diapers to illustrate this point. Even families well below the poverty line consider disposable diapers a necessity—and well they might be if no laundry facilities are readily accessible.

Bronfenbrenner postulated 20 propositions regarding the nature of ecological experimentation in education. The basic principles found in them are useful in the development of an ecologically valid model of assessment. These principles focus on the increased validity of experimentation that occurs in real-life or natural settings as compared with laboratory or contrived experimentation, which can be paralleled with the contrast between assessments in the natural setting versus clinical assessments.

Microsystem Level Principles.   The first set of principles deals with experimentation in relation to microsystems. *Ecological validity* requires that all the elements of an experimental setting including place, time, roles, and activities accurately reflect reality. Therefore, educational experimentation should be conducted in a context that is realistic. For example, the effectiveness of a behavior management system within a preschool program cannot be validated through clinical experimentation using a one-on-one teacher–child ratio in a laboratory setting. Participant understanding of and perspectives toward the experimental setting also need to be addressed. The interventionist who feels that the proposed behavior management system "will not work in her situation" is a biased participant and will influence the experimental outcome.

Setting analysis is the second principle in Bronfenbrenner's model of ecological experimentation. It addresses the need for experimenters to attend to the properties of physical setting and social structure in addition to participant behaviors. An experiment focused on child behaviors, exclusive of the physical and social setting in which they occur, offers limited applicable information for classroom teachers.

The principle of *reciprocity* refers to the idea that reactions and behaviors of one person will be related to and influence the reactions and behaviors of others. Social systems are not unidirectional, rather they are reciprocal in nature. An experiment designed to study the effects of teacher behavior on student performance cannot ignore the influence student behavior has on teacher performance. Children do not simply react; they act, react, and are reacted to. Each interaction has an influence on the next one, thus the reciprocal nature of real social systems.

As well as these *direct* influences, there may be *indirect* influences affecting behavior, such as the presence of another person in the room. The expansion of this idea can be continued to include a multitude of possible relationships and interactions. The natural environment of a preschool setting includes any number of children (depending upon the size of the preschool) and several adults, who may be parents, aides, teachers, the program director, volunteers, program monitors, or other visitors.

Direct or indirect influences of the *physical and temporal environment* can become particularly significant when assessing a child's competence in performing a specific task. If the light switch is 4 feet off the floor and the child can only reach 3½ feet, he is unable to perform the task of turning the light on and off. Bringing a short stool into the setting will change the environment sufficiently, so that the child will now be able to perform the task. There is no change in the child, except that he was incompetent and is now competent through manipulation of the environment.

The final principle related to the microsystem addresses the need for ecological experimentation to include *conceptualization and analysis of the setting as a system*. The preschool setting can be viewed as a system, including such components as employment policies, daily scheduling, and philosophical and theoretical bases for program development. Components of the setting can exert significant influence on the outcomes of child assessment. For example, an excellent preschool teacher might be stymied by a mandatory curriculum that eliminates her opportunities for creativity and results in her developing a poor attitude.

Mesosystem, Exosystem, and Macrosystem Level Principles.   Moving into the level of mesosystems, Bronfenbrenner takes the propositions and principles related to microsystems and expands them. The need to incorporate analysis of *interactions between settings* in experimental design is included. Results of the hypothetical study on the effectiveness of a behavior management system within a preschool setting would be influenced by recent events in other settings, including the homes of all the children, teachers and aides, the buses used to transport children to the center, and even the home of the bus driver. The child who has been rewarded and praised throughout the day for cooperative play, good manners, resting at nap time, and drinking all of her milk comes home in a pleasant mood, ready to interact positively with siblings, friends, and adults. The adult who may have faced multiple stressing events that day is unable to cope with a hostile child appearing on her doorstep. The *reciprocal* nature of these interactions is another key concept to be incorporated into ecological experimentation. Events in the home influence behavior in the preschool, which, in turn, influences home behavior.

Assessing children across a variety of settings in which they are expected to function is important, but further analysis of how settings influence behavior in other settings must also be addressed. When the exosystem is incorporated into the ecological experimentation model, features of the community and surrounding environment must be taken into account. The final level of expansion is that of the macrosystem, which addresses global institutions and ideologies. The importance of macrosystem influences is demonstrated through the observable differences in child development seen in cross-cultural studies. For example, 2-year-olds in China are able to sit quietly for extended periods of time, while in America we refer to this age as the "terrible twos." Bronfenbrenner has used these ecological concepts in further study of the child and family (Bronfenbrenner, 1986; Bronfenbrenner & Crouter, 1982; Bronfenbrenner, Moen, & Garbarino, 1984). Further discussion of the levels of systems as related specifically to risk in early childhood is provided in Garbarino (1990).

Ecological Congruence

Thurman's model of ecological congruence is directly related to the development of individualized programming. The environmental context in which behavior occurs and will be occurring needs to be included as the teacher plans educational interventions. When an individual's behavior is considered to be appropriate or at least tolerable within a particular setting, he is experiencing *ecological congruence*. Thurman uses three constructs to define ecological congruence. The first of these is *deviancy/nondeviancy*. Behaviors cannot be determined as deviant or nondeviant apart from the setting in which they occur. For example, behaviors that are perfectly normal for a young child to exhibit outside in his own yard (e.g., running around, climbing, and shouting) might be considered deviant inside at a preschool, church, or neighbor's living room. Setting includes the social context as well as the physical environment. To say that a child had a temper tantrum during morning group time, with no additional information available about the situation, is of little or no value. Perhaps the tantrum began because the child had already heard the story three times that morning, the child was not called on first to answer a question, or another child leaned into him and tried to move into his space. The construct of deviancy/nondeviancy implies that a set of standards for the system exists, from which deviancy or the lack of it is measured.

The second construct used in defining ecological congruence is that of *competency/incompetency*. Rather than focusing on system values, this construct is concerned with an individual's ability to perform certain tasks within environmental settings. Assessment of a child's ability to perform skills that are needed in a particular setting based on a list of the tasks required in the settings offers the most accurate information about her potential success to function within that setting. A child unable to complete required tasks would be considered incompetent within that context. Thus, a child with motor impairments that prohibited her from bringing her hand to her mouth would be considered imcompetent at a traditional dinner table with a plate of food and a typical place setting. However, given appropriate adaptive utensils and proper positioning, it may be possible to make that child able to feed herself.

The final construct of ecological congruence relates to the *tolerance for difference*. The tolerance for difference which any social system will allow directly influences what is considered deviant or nondeviant behavior. This tolerance can range from teacher acceptance of the high energy level of a 3-year-old to biased social attitudes toward groups holding unique religious beliefs. The implications of this construct for persons engaging in assessment of children are significant. For example, the use and interpretation of an assessment technique such as observation of a child at play can be subject to an individual observer's tolerance for difference if precautions to prevent such influences are absent from the observational procedures being employed.

ECOLOGICALLY VALID ASSESSMENT

Defining Ecologically Valid Assessment

Ecologically valid assessment refers to a system of child assessment, environmental analysis, and the identification of strengths and needs of the child's family. It should not be confused with ecological assessment, which refers to assessment of the physical, social, and psychological of behavior settings a child operates within. Ecological assessment is a critical component of ecologically valid assessment, but the equivalent to it. All assessment components are designed with ecological validity in focus. Thus, assessment of a child's language development in a clinical setting with standardized instruments done by an examiner who was previously unknown to the child must be acknowledged as not necessarily representative of the language that same child might display on the playground surrounded by familiar peers or in his own home.

The concept of *synergism* should be ever present in an examiner's mind as she plans and implements ecologically valid assessment procedures. Willems described synergism as "the combined action of discrete agents such that the resultant effect is greater than or different from the sum of the effects of the agents taken singly or independently" (1977b, p. 47). Using an ecological perspective as an overriding factor, an examiner is better able to bring the whole child into view. Assessments are planned comprehensively, and collaboratively, rather than as isolated individual elements. The child and her environment are analyzed collectively and systematically. The awareness that behavior changes from one setting to another and that an individual's psychological identity is not determined by the setting in which she exists (Barker, 1968) dictates to an examiner that the whole child be viewed from an ecological perspective.

Constructs of Ecologically Valid Assessment

Five constructs synthesize the primary elements of ecologically valid assessment.

Construct One. Naturalistic versus Clinical Settings. *Assessments of young children in their natural environments provide information that can be used to determine actual functioning of the child. Dissonance among values, expectations, and priorities of the child's various environments may cause fluctuating performance.* This first construct is related to the ecological validity of naturalistic settings as contrasted with clinical settings. When children are asked to perform tasks alien to their socioeconomic status, ethnic or social milieu in a clinical setting, the equity of such assessments must be investigated through additional assessment in natural environments. The use of language can reflect such a dissonance. The child may perform well below language standards set for his age, but observation of his ability to communicate using nonstandard language patterns in natural environments reveals effective communication. Seen within the context of his environment, the child is capable of learning the language structures to which he has been exposed.

Construct Two. Assessing the Natural Environments of Children.   *Analysis of the settings in which behavior occurs provides essential information when interpreting assessment results.* The issue of ecological congruence has direct application for this construct. It is of limited value to make determinations about deviance and competence of a child's behavior without an awareness of the settings in which the behavior is occurring and the extent to which differences are permissible. Setting analysis should include both the physical setting and the social structures within that setting. Clinical assessments of a child might indicate that a child is unable or unwilling to perform a certain task. When surrounded by a group of peers engaging in the same task, the child might readily participate. In contrast, a child might refuse to perform tasks that she is competent to do when asked to do them in front of her peers. For example, a child may be willing to speak to an adult in privacy or to her parents at home, but be nonverbal in a group setting. The whole picture of the child is incomplete without both pieces of information.

Construct Three. Dynamic Reciprocity of Relationships in Child Assessment.   *Settings in which child assessments are conducted directly and indirectly influence the behaviors of all persons involved in the setting.* Child functioning varies across settings, including place, time, activities, and persons. Even in clinical assessment, the person conducting the assessment can influence the outcomes. An examiner who is sensitive to the emotions and attitudes of the young child is more effective in finding the child's highest potential than one who is more concerned with administering the test efficiently and quickly. Those persons who wish to assess young children with disabilities need to build in an analysis of the child's ability to generalize across settings, with a sensitivity to the many changing variables in a child's environment. For example, a child who is progressing nicely in his ability to separate from his parents while attending a center-based program may suddenly regress by whining and displaying strong resistance to the separation. Looking at the child's changing environment, one discovers that his grandmother has recently left after an extended visit with the family. The regression is probably a display of appropriate temporary anxiety about separations, rather than an attention-seeking behavior or developmental regression. Another child may separate with no difficulty for one parent and not the other, or to one teacher, but not another. It is of limited value to simply note: "The child displays difficulty in separation from parents."

Construct Four. Perceptions Create a Reality.   *Each person's perspective of the child's functioning is a reality regardless of discrepancies between these perspectives and the child's actual behavior.* Perceptions of what a child can and cannot do may be as important as what she can actually do. When there appear to be significant discrepancies between perception and reality, the cause for the discrepancy needs to be explored. Variation in performance across variables (as discussed in Construct Three) might be a contributing factor, inability of parents to face the truth about their child may be another, or misunderstandings in communication could be the source of the discrepancy. Persons conducting assessments need to keep in mind that perceptions hold value regardless of whether or not they hold true.

Construct Five. Interrelatedness of Child Functioning and Mesosystems. *Each child represents a unique set of mesosystems of which he is a participant.* The temptation to categorize and stereotype children based on certain characteristics needs to be avoided in order to appreciate each child as an individual. Socioeconomic status, religious beliefs and affiliation, family dynamics, handicapping conditions, and neighborhoods of residence are some of the many subsystems that interact to create each child's personality and competence. Using a narrow view of the child can lead to the conclusion that a child from a severely impoverished background has very little potential. An ecologically valid assessment directly confronts the functioning of this child from a broader perspective. It acknowledges the entire ecology of the child's environment, rather than encouraging the assumption that everything is just fine in this child's life, except that he is unable to perform as expected for his chronological age. When there is no running water in the home, when nutritional and emotional needs of the child go unmet, and when chaos and instability characterize the home, the child cannot be fairly judged according to standards that assume a nurturing home environment has been provided for the child.

When young children are assessed, they are usually assessed in parts, by developmental domain. Their functioning on certain tasks, in certain settings, with certain people needs to be determined. The parceling out of the child and her environment into manageable units of information is a necessary step in ecologically valid assessment. The key feature of ecologically valid assessment, however, is in the analysis and synthesis of these individual units of information, which provide a complete picture of the child who is operating across systems.

SUMMARY

This chapter introduced the concept of ecologically valid assessment and offered a perspective from which to understand the remainder of the text. The summary of federal legislation related to the education of children with disabilities and/or developmental delays included a discussion of risk factors. Categories of risk include established, biological, and environmental risk. The various disabilities recognized in PL 94–142 have specific definitions, whereas *developmental delay* is a broad term appropriately used with very young children. The concepts of ecological experimentation and ecological congruence provide the theoretical framework for ecologically valid assessment.

THE ECOLOGICAL PERSPECTIVE

- No single source of data can accurately represent a child's abilities.
- How children behave is context-related.
- The values and customs surrounding individuals influence how they develop.
- Environmental nurturance and stimulation enable children to become competent.
- Behavior settings can change a child's abilities.

CHAPTER 2

Purposes of Assessment

CHAPTER OUTLINE

QUESTIONS ANSWERED IN CHAPTER 2

- What are the various purposes of assessment?
- What are case-finding and screening, and when should they be conducted?
- When are diagnostic procedures appropriate?
- What components should be included in assessments for program planning?
- Can we use child assessments in program evaluation?
- What is multipurpose assessment?
- What are the sequential stages of the assessment process?

CHAPTER OVERVIEW

Before assessments are planned and conducted, it must be clear why they are being done. The information sought and how that information will be used form the foundation of any well-developed assessment plan. Interventionists find diagnostic labels of little value when planning developmentally appropriate activities. However, such information can be crucial when placement decisions are made or when a teacher selects basic teaching methods. The hyperactive, aggressive nonverbal 4-year-old suddenly is seen in a different light when it is discovered that he is deaf. While the diagnostic information might explain the child's behaviors, it still does not give a teacher sufficient information to begin intervention.

The purposes of assessment, which can be addressed through an ecologically valid process, are presented in four broad categories:

1. *Identification and diagnosis*
2. *Program planning*
3. *Program evaluation*
4. *Multipurpose assessment*

Identification and diagnosis includes *case-finding, screening,* and the *diagnostic process* that infants, toddlers, and young children typically proceed through on their way to receiving early intervention. *Program planning* incorporates *competence assessment, identification of family strengths and needs, environmental or ecological assessment,* and *mastery motivation*. Traditionally, the primary source of information associated with program planning has been assessment of the child's ability or inability to perform certain developmental or academic skills, coupled with a brief family history. Ecologically valid assessment for program planning requires that the examiner go beyond these traditional components, synthesizing multiple data sources. The third purpose of assessment, *program evaluation,* is aimed at the determination of program efficacy. Finally, assessments can be designed to achieve multiple purposes. Table 2-1 summarizes these purposes of assessment and the type(s) of information each provides.

Regardless of the intended purpose of an assessment, a well-designed process incorporates four fluid stages: planning, assessing, interpreting, and evaluating. As the assessment process is implemented, adjustment can and should be made to ensure that useful data are obtained. Further discussion of these stages follows the sections on the purposes of assessment.

IDENTIFICATION AND DIAGNOSIS

Case-finding and screening are closely connected and sometimes appear to be somewhat synonymous. While there is significant overlap between the two, they can be distinguished. The diagnostic phase of assessment involves a much deeper investigation into the causes of a child's condition than seen during the screening phase.

TABLE 2.1. Purposes of Assessment

Category	Information Obtained	Sources of Information
Identification and Diagnosis		
Case-finding	Identification and referral of at-risk children for assessment	Pediatricians, day care workers, parents, health department, the community
Screening	Division of children into groups: those needing further diagnosis and those who appear to need no follow-up	Screening instruments, developmental checklist, sensory screening, medical observations
Diagnosis	Cause and/or condition that child has and whether additional services are needed	Diagnostic instruments, physicians, psychologists, audiologists, therapists; process-oriented approaches
Program Planning		
Competence assessment	Developmental and educational assessment to determine what skills child has mastered	
Current performance	Previously obtained skills and knowledge that the child consistently demonstrates	Developmental scales, criterion-referenced scales, observation
Performance monitoring	Continuous track of the child's abilities and performance on designated objectives	Curriculum-based assessment, task analysis, observation
Identification of family strengths and needs	Awareness of current family functioning, through identification of strengths and needs of family, particularly as related to coping with handicapped child	Needs and strengths scales, family attribute scales, parent–child interactions
Environmental assessment	Characteristics of the environments child most frequently is in (home, preschool, community)	Naturalistic observation, environmental rating scales
Mastery motivation	Task persistence and pleasure child expresses in achieving mastery of a task; emphasizes how child approaches task rather than competence in performing task	Mastery motivation tasks
Program Evaluation	Effectiveness of program on child progress and accountability of teachers	Stated goals of program dictate design of program evaluation, child progress, parent satisfaction
Multipurpose Assessment	Description of environments and children; placement decisions; prediction of future functioning; and prescription for programming	Multidomain, assessment instruction, curriculum-based assessments, observations

Case-Finding

A comprehensive search for children to be screened within a select geographic area is *case-finding*. Case-finding in and of itself might not necessarily be considered assessment. For example, a community might decide to screen all 2-year-olds for hearing impairments. Case-finding would simply involve locating all 2-year-olds within the specific geographic region. Case-finding can also involve some elements of a screening. The pediatrician who is asked to watch for children between the ages of 2 and 5 with significant language delays for a new community program is engaged in selective case-finding.

Case-finding requires that the target population sought be defined according to geographic restrictions of eligibility for follow-up services. The age range of eligible children should be clearly delineated as well as the purpose of the case-finding. It is possible that all children meeting geographic and age criteria be included in the case-finding, only those children within the population who have demonstrated certain characteristics be included, and/or those who are at high-risk to demonstrate specific characteristics be identified. Case-finding is a mandated component of PL 94–142 and PL 99–457.

Peterson (1987) has described four commonly used approaches taken for case-finding. The first of these involves *building community awareness* and is characterized by public announcements of screening clinics, presentations to community groups, and the formation of an advocacy group designed to increase visibility and local support of the early intervention activities taking place.

The second approach is *setting up a system for referral and eliciting referrals.* Contact should be made with community agencies such as health clinics, social services and welfare offices, local preschool and day care programs, any agencies serving children with handicaps, and private practitioners serving families and young children with special needs. The creation of a central referral system, as mandated in Part H of PL 99–457, can ease the confusion parents often experience when they begin the search for appropriate community services.

Canvassing the community for children who need screening is the third approach suggested by Peterson. Strategies included in this approach are direct observation of children in community programs, consultation with staff of community programs, door-to-door canvassing to provide information and seek referrals, and distribution of informational flyers about screening clinics or other early intervention services to school-aged children, Head Start children, and/or children attending other preschool programs.

Maintenance of local publicity and contacts with referral sources is the final approach. The emphasis in this approach is on continuing contacts and relationships that have been established.

Screening

Screening is a procedure used to distinguish those children who need further study and possible intervention from those who appear to have no need for follow-up. Based on the work of Frankenburg and Camp (1975), Lillie (1977) identified six major principles of screening, which are summarized in the following list:

1. Screening assumes that the condition can be improved through intervention.
2. Early intervention will improve the condition more than would intervention at a later date when the problem becomes more obvious.
3. The condition screened for can be specifically diagnosed through further application of measurement procedures.
4. Necessary follow-up procedures for next steps are available.
5. The condition(s) screened for is relatively prevalent or the consequences of not discovering a rare problem or condition are severe.
6. Measurement procedures for screening are available.

Errors.   Two possible errors that can occur in the screening process are the identification of *false positives* and *false negatives*. When children who are screened and identified as needing follow-up are actually progressing normally, they are considered to be *false positives*. Screenings that result in high numbers of false positives create an overidentification of children who need follow-up diagnostic examinations. *False negatives* occur when children who were not targeted for follow-up at a screening have future developmental progress indicating that they should have been. Screenings that result in high numbers of false negatives lead to the underidentification of children needing diagnostic follow-up and possible intervention.

The most significant problem associated with false positives is the unnecessary anxiety, time, and expense caused for the parents as they pursue diagnostic follow-up. In spite of all additional diagnostic workups indicating that a child is developing normally, the parents may carry anxiety about that false-positive screening for many years. Additionally, if the results of the screening are included in a permanent record for the child, she may be repeatedly required to disprove them. Another problem is the time involved in conducting follow-up diagnostics with the false-positive child. That time is time taken away from diagnostic work on children who really need it and who may have to wait unnecessarily to receive proper attention.

When a child goes through a screening and is not targeted for follow-up, parents and professionals alike presume that the child is progressing within normal limits. Concern for the child may be falsely reduced or eliminated. The opportunity for early intervention may be missed. Probably one of the most dramatic of such errors would be if an infant was screened as not having a high blood phenylalanine level when, in fact, he did. All appears well for the happy parents. They feed the baby a normal diet, resulting in serious damage to the infant since he really has phenylketonuria. By the time a correct diagnosis is made and the baby's diet changed, irreparable damage may have been done to his central nervous system, leaving him mentally retarded. Holtzman, Morales, Cunningham, and Wells (1975) in summarizing research on the critical age at which to begin the diet reached the conclusion that treatment must begin within the first month of life, before the critical age of 3 to 4 weeks of age, to avoid mental retardation. In this example, had the screening for a high blood phenylalanine level been correct, the parents would have sought help in determining whether the baby had phenylketonuria and provided the adjusted diet as needed. With the adjusted diet, he could grow into a normal, healthy child and adult, with no loss of functioning. The false-negative result at the screening could cost this child his normal mental ability.

Use of Parent Knowledge.   Use of parent-completed developmental questionnaires for child-find and screening can be a low-cost means of obtaining reasonably accurate information about children's current functioning levels (Squires, Nickel, & Bricker, 1990). Tools that Squires et al. recommend for parent completion are (1) Communication Development Inventory (short form) (Dale, Bates, Reznick, & Morisset, 1989); (2) Infant/Child Monitoring Questionnaires (Bricker, Squires, Kaminski, & Mounts, 1988; Bricker & Squires, 1989); (3) Language Development Survey (Rescorla, 1989); (4) Minnesota Child Development Inventory (Ireton & Thwing, 1974); (5) Revised Denver Prescreening Developmental Questionnaire (Frankenburg, Fandal, & Thorton, 1987); and (6) Revised Parent Developmental Questionnaire (Knobloch, Stevens, Malone, Ellison, & Risemberg, 1979). However, not all parents are reliable sources of information (e.g., drug-addicted mothers, parents with mental health problems, poor readers responding to written questionnaires, and mentally retarded parents).

Parent knowledge of a child's functioning can be balanced with a professional's awareness of warning signs and risk factors. For Elizabeth Armstrong, whose case is presented in the appendix, although her delivery was traumatic and complications developed immediately after her birth, her mother had no way of knowing the impact of those problems on her development. The mother had heard the physician say that her daughter was fine and, therefore, explained away all conflicting behaviors that she began observing in her daughter. She thought that she was taking home from the hospital a child who would soon be sucking on a nipple just like her two big brothers. She had no clue that her child had brain damage with resulting cerebral palsy, accompanied by gagging and projectile vomiting. The telltale signs, although apparent to professionals accustomed to working with infants with brain damage, had no meaning to the unsuspecting parent. A sensitive parental interview as a part of a follow-up screening procedure could have revealed this child's disabilities to both the physicians and the parents much sooner. Instead, after a prolonged delay, the mother learned from an insensitive social security physician, who merely glanced at her daughter's chart, that the child had brain damage without ever examining the child. The parent felt rather foolish for having harbored visions of normal development when so many telltale signs were available.

Accuracy of Instruments.   The ability of a screening instrument to select children without false positives or false negatives is determined by the test's *detection accuracy, base rate,* and *hit rate* (McCall, 1982). The *detection accuracy* includes the percentage of abnormal children who were detected as well as the percentage of normal children incorrectly identified as abnormal. *Base rate* is the real (although unknown) percentage of abnormal children present in the population to be screened. The *hit rate* is the percentage of abnormal children who are identified by the screening instrument. The higher the percentage of abnormal children present in the population to be screened, the better the hit rate will be. Thus, prescreening by pediatricians, referrals for screening from nurses, and other selective case-finding procedures can reduce errors because many normal children are already eliminated.

Conducting a Screening.   Some screening procedures require specially trained professionals and expensive equipment. Others can be conducted by volunteers after a brief training session. Expense versus benefit is always a consideration. Additionally, the dangers of overidentification and underidentification can be so serious that no screening program may be better than one with a high error rate.

For infants and toddlers routine *medical screenings* play a crucial role in the early detection of conditions warranting further investigation and possible intervention. The well child model, developed by the American Academy of Pediatrics, routinely monitors for each of the following: adequate nutrition; adequate patterns of physical and emotional health; achievement of milestones in motor, communication, social, and cognitive development; protection against preventable disease and injury; absence of illness; and correction of correctable abnormality. When a child is known to be at a high risk for developing special health needs due to a handicapping condition, the well child model should be expanded to a pathophysiologic/medical model. This model includes additional areas for possible assessment and intervention: therapy and special care routines, medications, prevention of complications or secondary handicaps, special equipment, and safety (Zelle & Coyner, 1983).

Diagnosis

Diagnosis involves a more in-depth look at individual children than does screening. Cross (1977) has defined diagnosis as "a process designed: (1) to confirm or disconfirm the existence of a problem, serious enough to require remediation, in those children identified in a screening effort and (2) to clarify the nature of the problem (is it organic, environmental, or both?)" (p. 25). A child targeted during a screening as having a hearing loss needs to undergo a diagnostic evaluation to determine the cause of the hearing loss. After a thorough examination of the child, the apparent hearing loss could be attributed to emotional problems with no biological cause or a temporary loss due to a middle ear infection. It could be a conductive hearing loss, the impact of which could be reduced through the use of amplification. However, if the loss was a result of neurological dysfunctioning, amplification would be of less value. Thus, the diagnosis serves as a follow-up to screening and provides useful information as to the appropriate nature of intervention. The thoroughness of a diagnostic analysis needed to learn the cause of a condition will vary from child to child. In this illustration, a determination that the hearing loss was actually the manifestation of an emotional problem would require the most comprehensive diagnostic workup, in which all biological causes must be ruled out. The middle ear infection could be detected through a simple medical examination of the ear canal. If treatment of the infection eliminated the functional hearing loss, no further diagnostic work would be required as to the cause of the hearing loss.

Ecologically valid diagnostic evaluations involve data gathering from multiple sources across time. Information from parents and/or primary caregivers and former and/or current teachers or day care workers can be synthesized with data gathered from naturalistic observations and child performance on standardized tests. It is, however, possible to conduct a comprehensive diagnostic assessment and still fail to determine the exact cause of a child's condition. Such a failure can be

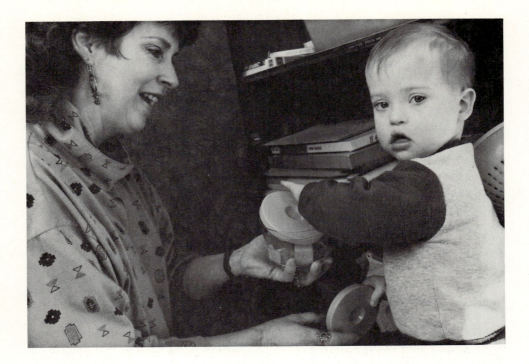

most frustrating to diagnosticians, parents, teachers, and the children involved. Nevertheless, there will come a point in the assessment process where it is more productive to move on to the program planning assessment than it is to continue seeking the answer to an apparently unanswerable question. The results of ecologically valid child and environmental assessments coupled with the identification of family strengths and needs related to enhancing the child's development should provide guidance in the development of goals for intervention.

PROGRAM PLANNING

An effective assessment for program planning includes four components: *competence assessment, identification of family strengths and needs, environmental or ecological assessment,* and *mastery motivation*. Initial program planning assessment should address each of these components, while such would not be necessary throughout the year for ongoing instruction. The emphasis of all program planning assessments needs to be linkage with the curricula (Bagnato & Neisworth, 1981; Bagnato, Neisworth, & Munson, 1989). For example, an early intervention program that has targeted language development as its focus would not include extensive program planning assessments of other developmental domains. However, programs that were designed to meet a child's needs across all developmental domains must have the assessments of each domain prior to specific curricular planning.

Competence Assessment

Assessment of a child's abilities in specific developmental domains is often referred to as educational assessment. However, the term *educational* does not accurately represent the assessment of preschool and younger children. It is more accurate to describe an assessment of a 2-year-old's ability to walk up and down stairs and feed and dress himself as an assessment of competence rather than that of education. Education-related skills, such as concept development, prereading skills, or fine motor skills, do fit under the umbrella of competence assessment, as well as developmental and play skills. Competence assessment can be divided into two categories. The first, *current performance,* is used most frequently for an initial assessment or when a change in placement or services is anticipated. The second, *performance monitoring* (Peterson, 1987), provides a continuous record of the child's performance on targeted objectives for daily planning purposes.

Current Performance.   The purpose of a competence assessment is to gain an accurate picture of a child's present functional abilities in multiple domains across settings. As indicated previously, the extent of the assessment can be somewhat controlled by the anticipated curriculum or program goals that are available to the child. Domains that would be included in a comprehensive assessment are (1) cognitive development, (2) communication and language development (production and comprehension), (3) motor development (gross and fine), (4) physical and sensory development, (5) social and emotional development and mastery motivation, and (6) self-care and adaptive behaviors.

An examiner may wish to examine the current functioning of a child in just one or two specific domains. Screening and/or diagnostic examination of the child might reveal the need for intervention in such focused areas. Thus, programs might be designed to offer intervention programming in only one or two of these domains. Assessment for planning in programs with a limited curriculum need not incorporate extensive assessment of child functioning across all domains. However, functioning in one domain can influence functioning in all others; therefore it is essential that some information about the child's functioning across domains be available to the interventionist.

Performance Monitoring.   Ongoing assessment of a child's competence should become a frequent and routine component of an intervention program, which can be used to determine the effectiveness of the present intervention. Analysis of a child's progress across and within domains can identify areas of uneven gains made by the child, areas of most rapid gains, and those areas in which little or no progress has been made. Performance monitoring can provide a continuous record of the child's status in regard to achieving stated goals in her individualized program. Evaluation of the effectiveness of specific teaching techniques can also be achieved through the use of performance monitoring.

Performance monitoring involves four basic steps:

a.   Planning and designing data collection procedures (including preparation of data collection forms) to monitor each learning objective for each child

b. Collecting data on a systematic basis (daily, every other day, or weekly) in the targeted areas
c. Summarizing and analyzing data regularly to derive some judgments about each child's progress and about the effectiveness of the instructional approach
d. Using that information to make decisions about subsequent instructional strategies (Peterson, 1987, p. 307)

Multiple sources of information are needed in ongoing performance monitoring. On a daily basis, recording child performance of specific skills and collecting anecdotal records are most helpful. To ensure the ecological validity of the performance monitoring, the interventionist should note factors associated with peak performance and those associated with poor performance (e.g., time of day, other children present in the group, person teaching, and materials used). Adjustments in curricula and procedures used can be made rapidly when data collected about child performance reveal such a need. Developmental checklists and behavior rating scales are useful for performance monitoring on a monthly or quarterly basis. They can provide a mechanism for monitoring the child's progress against a background of normal developmental sequences and age expectations.

Models. A number of models of intervention are available for performance monitoring. The *prescriptive teaching model* (Peter, 1967; Gearhart & Litton, 1975) is one that has been applied in school-aged special education classrooms with success. This model is designed to provide information about individual students' progress on specific objectives on a daily basis. The child's progress on each objective is then measured and plotted. *Precision teaching* is a similar method of continuously gathering assessment data during instruction (see Mercer & Mercer, 1985, or Howell, Kaplan, & O'Connell, 1979). A *task analytic model of assessment* is described by Browder (1987) as a useful method of ongoing assessment for persons with severe handicaps. For further discussion of these techniques, see Chapter 3.

Identifying Family Strengths and Needs

Traditionally, information about family strengths and needs, as related to enhancing the child's development, has not been included as a part of the data gathering for intervention planning. However, the establishment of priority goals for the child is most effectively done within the context of the family system. Information obtained about the family should lead to the identification of family priorities in intervention, be reflective of the types of services that are available, and incorporate reevaluations on a routine basis (Bailey & Simeonsson, 1988).

Environmental or Ecological Assessment

It is impossible to determine accurately a child's competence or incompetence to perform any task or developmental skill apart from the setting in which it is performed. An *environmental or ecological assessment* of the child's behavior settings should include not only an evaluation of the child's surroundings, but also analysis of conditions that seem to increase the child's competence. For example, language samples might be obtained from a language-delayed 4-year-old in a clinic setting during structured lessons, during free play outside, and during a family-style lunch time as well as at home with only family members present, with a home-based interventionist, and so forth. Although the number of language samples collected could go on indefinitely (and actually can for purposes of performance monitoring), it is the responsibility of the person planning an environmental assessment to select a reasonable number of representative samples of behavior settings. Additionally, characteristics of the child's most common behavioral settings can be identified and can provide guidance for program planning. For example, a child's preschool has one hour per day of free choice time, and one child consistently wanders aimlessly about the room. Program planning can involve a reduction in the time allotted to free choice time, a simplification of the choices, and/or peer or teacher partnerships.

Mastery Motivation

On of the most powerful determinates of a child's potential to learn new skills in his motivation to master new skills (Brockman, Morgan, & Harmon, 1988). The infant who has the motivation to learn to stand can easily tolerate the frustration and failure that is inevitable as he attempts to pull himself up only to find himself suddenly back on the floor, having fallen down over and over again. A child who is following a normal developmental sequence in a nurturing environment will experience a balance of successes and failures that enables him to maintain a high level of motivation. The child who is physically or mentally unable to achieve a balance of successes to offset the many failures, or one who is constantly criticized, may lose his motivation to master tasks. Such a child may actually have more potential than another, but be unable to accomplish as much. His motivation to achieve has been destroyed or diminished. An ecologically valid assessment for program planning should include a component to determine a child's willingness to persist on a new task. Chapter 12 includes a discussion of techniques in assessment of mastery motivation.

PROGRAM EVALUATION

Program evaluation is most often thought of in terms of program outcomes for the children receiving services. While factors such as parent satisfaction and professional perceptions may be included as elements of an evaluation, they are not necessarily at issue. For example, a program that has satisfied parents without demonstrating that the children are making reasonable progress would not be an effective one. Moore (1977) has defined evaluation in the following manner:

> The process of determining whether or not the educational program produced the desired results in the development of the children who entered and completed the program. The process includes *analyzing* activities against some *standards* so that *decisions* can be made about the effectiveness of the activities in helping the children reach some predetermined end. (p. 53)

Much has been written regarding the effectiveness of early intervention programs. The data have been difficult to analyze and interpret for a number of reasons. Populations used in efficacy studies have been inadequately described or described using ambiguous terms. The most effective age to initiate intervention is still debated as are the most effective intervention techniques. These debates likely will never end since the most effective intervention age and technique is an individual question requiring an ecologically valid investigation rather than mass programming decisions. Nevertheless, interventionists are obligated to determine the effectiveness of their programs for the children and families served by them and attempt to follow the best practices.

Outcomes used to measure whether a program has been effective often reflect the stated goals of the program. For example, pre- and posttest IQ scores would not accurately measure the effectiveness of a program that had a goal of enhancing a child's social skills and ability to interact positively with other children. Determining a reasonable expectation of developmental gain for young children with wide-ranging disabilities can be challenging for the interventionist. How much progress is reasonable to expect in a 3-year-old with a developmental age of 9 months? How can a determination that a program has been "effective" be reached for such a child? Often interventionists rely on goal attainment, assuming that the goals were a reasonable estimate of what the child should be able to accomplish within a given period of time. At some point the stated goals must also be evaluated to determine how reasonable they actually were. It is possible that a teacher concludes that her program was ineffective for a child, when the stated goals were never realistically within the child's developmental ability. However, a teacher who writes goals for the child underestimating the child's true potential might claim to have offered an effective program. Use of multiple sources of data, such as a change in rate of development index, curriculum-based assessments, task analysis, and parent satisfaction surveys eliminates some of the difficulties associated with program evaluation based on single criteria. Chapter 13 focuses on child assessment for program evaluation.

MULTIPURPOSE ASSESSMENTS

When it is possible to conduct multipurpose assessments, it is advantageous to do so. They can be designed so as to address description, placement, prediction, and prescription questions (Neisworth & Bagnato, 1988). LINK: A Developmental Assessment/Curriculum Linkage System for Special Needs Preschoolers developed by Bagnato and Neisworth (1981; Bagnato et al., 1989) integrates assessment into the curriculum as a single concept of developmental intervention. The linkage model is designed to be used in conjunction with curriculum-based assessment in a four-stage process, each of which involves administrative and clinical appraisals. The stages are (1) screening/identification, (2) perscriptive developmental assessment/curriculum linkage, (3) programming/intervention, and (4) progress evaluation/monitoring. The LINK model employs a variety of forms used to summarize data obtained from the various instruments or procedures included in a

child's Prescriptive Developmental Assessment Battery (PDAB). The PDAB is developed after screening has been done and should include at least four types of assessment, including norm-based, curriculum-based, judgment-based, and ecological (Bagnato et al., 1989). The information gathered through the PDAB is then converted into curriculum and activity planning through the use of task analysis, environmental analysis, and the development of prescriptive linkages. A summary form includes a brief description of the program guidelines along seven parameters: instructional setting, instructional methods, grouping pattern, adaptive arrangements, auxiliary therapies, behavioral strategies, and parent participation. Program evaluation involves the use of the Intervention Efficiency Index (Bagnato & Neisworth, 1981), which is a measure of the rate of growth as compared with that expected in normal child development.

STAGES OF THE ASSESSMENT PROCESS

An assessment for any purpose needs to follow a sequence that ensures it provide the information sought. The basic stages of the process are planning, assessing, interpreting, and evaluation. During the *planning stage,* which must include parents as well as professionals, the group pinpoints the purpose(s) of the assessment and identifies specific information that is needed. It also includes details, such as where and when assessments will take place. The group also makes initial decisions about which instruments and procedures are going to be used.

The *assessment* is the second stage in the process. Child assessments, environmental assessments, and the identification of family strengths and needs, as related to enhancing the child's development, occur during this stage. When the data gathering is completed, those involved in the assessment make *interpretations* of results and formulate recommendations. Again, the inclusion of parents in this stage of the process is critical. Parental perceptions of child performance can be most helpful when a professional is analyzing a child's behavior. Parents and extended family members observe children for signs of normal development and anxiously await the emergence of developmental milestones from the first smile to toilet training and so forth. It is the interpretation of their observations that can become the bridge of communication between parents and professionals. Since their interpretations are based on previous experience and knowledge of child development patterns, use of specific behavioral descriptions provides more information than generalized comments (e.g., "He talks about the same way his brother did, so I guess he's doing fine"). Discrepancies between parental report and professional observation need to be clearly identified before assessment results can be fully interpreted.

The final stage of the assessment process is *evaluation*. Both professionals and parents must be included in the review of the process and analysis of the quality of the information obtained. Parents need to be given the opportunity to discuss the process and recommend changes, if warranted. Professionals also need an opportunity to reflect on the process, identifying areas of needed change.

These stages represent a fluid system that can be adjusted as needed. Even a well-designed assessment plan usually requires revisions based on the initial assessment results. As professionals learn more about a particular child through assessment, they become better able to target additional areas of concern.

SUMMARY

This chapter covered the various purposes of assessment and the stages of the assessment process. The purposes include four broad categories: identification and diagnosis, program planning, program evaluation, and multipurpose assessment. Identification and diagnosis include case-finding, screening, and diagnosis. Program planning includes four key components. The first of these, competence assessment, involves current performance as well as performance monitoring. Identification of family strengths and needs and environmental assessments are also critical to effective program planning. The final component of program planning is mastery motivation assessment. The awareness a teacher has concerning the motivation with which a young child approaches tasks is critical to appropriate planning. A child who is experiencing frustration but who still displays a strong motivation to try needs a program directed at maintaining that high level of motivation without continued frustration. The program for another child, who might actually have higher skills than the first but who has lost her motivation, must be designed so as to restore her motivation to ensure future learning.

The third category of assessment is program evaluation, which can include a review of a child's progress on various outcomes, parent satisfaction surveys, or long-term measures, such as future educational placements and progress made by program participants. Program evaluation should be linked with the effectiveness with which a program met each individual child's needs as well as its overall effectiveness.

Multipurpose assessment is the final category of assessment. There can be a substantial overlap of the purposes of assessment. Screening can overlap with diagnostic testing, both of which can yield information useful in program planning. The linkage between program planning and program evaluation should always be strong. Results of competence assessments can easily be incorporated into program evaluation.

The final section of this chapter addressed stages of the assessment process. These stages are planning, assessing, interpreting, and evaluating. The process is both fluid and circular in nature.

THE ECOLOGICAL PERSPECTIVE

- Knowing what information is sought through an assessment is a prerequisite to obtaining meaningful results.
- All of the systems in a child's life influence test results. The impoverished, the malnourished, the drug-addicted from birth, the homeless, the child of a single teen parent—all children must be assessed with consideration given to their ecologies.
- Effective planning incorporates family systems information and the child's motivation to learn new tasks in the assessment process.
- Identification and assessment of primary behavior settings should become a routine element in the assessment process.

CHAPTER 3

Approaches and Techniques Used in Assessment

CHAPTER OUTLINE

QUESTIONS ANSWERED IN CHAPTER 3

- What theoretical perspectives have influenced assessment of infants and young children?
- What are formal and informal assessment procedures?
- What are norm-referenced, criterion-referenced, and curriculum-based assessments?
- What is standardized assessment, and how does it differ from adaptive-to-handicap assessment?

- How do team approaches to assessment—unidisciplinary, multidisciplinary, interdisciplinary, and transdisciplinary—differ?
- What are direct and indirect assessments?
- How can observational techniques in naturalistic and clinical settings be used in assessment?
- What is the difference in product-based assessment and process-based assessment?

CHAPTER OVERVIEW

Just as there are many purposes for conducting an assessment, there are many valid approaches and techniques to use. The effectiveness of any of them hinges on an examiner's ability to establish rapport with the child and family members. This chapter begins with a section addressing how theoretical perspectives toward child development can influence the assessment process, followed by a section covering a wide array of assessment techniques organized into seven strands. The strands are (1) formal to informal assessment, (2) norm-referenced to criterion-referenced assessment, (3) standardized to adaptive-to-handicap assessment, (4) unidisciplinary to team approaches, (5) direct to indirect assessment, (6) naturalistic to clinical observation, and (7) product-oriented to process-oriented assessment. The final section addresses important considerations specifically related to assessing very young children.

THEORETICAL INFLUENCES ON ASSESSMENT

Early intervention programs for young children with special needs differ from one another in program philosophy, mission and goals of the program, intervention strategies, and assessment and evaluation procedures employed. These differences can often be traced back to the theoretical view of development taken by the program developers. There are four primary theoretical perspectives that influence early childhood assessment practices today. They are developmental, cognitive stages, behavioral, and adaptive-transactive. How a person planning an assessment believes children develop and learn will influence: (1) what needs to be known about the child, (2) techniques used to obtain that information, and (3) analysis and interpretation of results. Developers of commercially available instruments may claim to base their product on a particular theoretical perspective toward child development and learning. However, instruments based on differing theoretical perspectives often have similar test items (Fewell, 1983). The difference may be reflected more in the scoring procedures and analysis of test outcomes or in style of item presentation than in content. An examiner may choose to integrate test results from more than one of these perspectives into a comprehensive assessment.

The Developmental Perspective

The *developmental perspective* is based on a *maturational theory of child development*. According to this theory, maturation of the nervous system governs a child's physical, psychological, cognitive, and social development. Using developmental data gathered on thousands of infants and children, Gesell (1925) identified the ages at which normal children reach motor milestones such as rolling over, creeping, crawling, sitting independently, standing, walking, and stacking three blocks in a tower. Examiners consider children who are unable to perform such tasks at the expected ages to be experiencing developmental delays. Anastasiow and Mansergh (1975) have described programs based on the developmental perspective as aiming to get children ready for school. The emphasis is placed on comparisons of a child to norms established by other children. The child's age serves as a reference point in assessing his functioning.

The developmental perspective is the foundation for checklists that have age ranges within which normal children demonstrate certain skills. The oldest developmental checklist, the *Gesell Developmental Schedules* (Gesell, 1925; Gesell & Amatruda, 1947), has served as a basis for most other more recent developmental scales. Knobloch and Pasamanick (1974) developed an updated revision of the scales. The *Cattell Infant Intelligence Scale* (Cattell, 1960) is based on the Gesell scales. Other instruments with a developmental perspective include the *Bayley Scales of Infant Development* (Bayley, 1984) and the *Battelle Developmental Inventory* (Newborg, Stock, Wnek, Guidubaldi, & Svinicki, 1984), which permits adaptations for children with handicaps.

Early childhood experts have criticized developmentally based assessment instruments for their heavy reliance on motor performance across all domains. Children who have advanced scores on such scales do not necessarily go on to excel in school achievement, nor does poor performance mean a child is retarded. There is also a high incidence of false positives and false negatives when developmental scales are used in screenings, due to the wide range of normal development and the naturally occurring developmental spurts and plateaus in child development.

The Cognitive Stages Perspective

Early childhood educators associate the *cognitive stages perspective* with the work of Piaget and his identification of hierarchical stages of development. These stages and the abilities associated with each are summarized in Table 3.1. There are approximate age levels associated with each of the stages a child goes through. However, the emphasis is on the sequence of stages and the abilities associated with each, rather than on the age of skill acquisition. According to Piagetian theory, a child develops as a result of her interactions with the environment coupled with natural physical and neurological maturation. Therefore, the quality of the child's environment can directly influence her cognitive, psychomotor, and social development. Additionally, the theory includes the premise that the stages of development through which children pass are invariant, sequential, and qualitatively different.

An assessment tool directly based on the Piagetian theory of cognitive development is the *Infant Psychological Development Scales* (IPDS) (Uzgiris & Hunt,

TABLE 3.1. Piagetian Stages of Development

Developmental Stage	Developmental Accomplishments	General Characteristics
A. Sensorimotor Period (0–2 years) I. Use of reflexes (0–1 month)	Learns to use reflexes in new behavior patterns (e.g., sucking nipple, expands to sucking other objects) Cries when another infant is crying	Predominated by reflexive behavior—blinking, sucking, startled by loud sounds, motor reflexes
II. Primary circular reactions (1–4 months)	Hand-to-mouth coordination Visually attempts to follow objects as they move outside visual range Repeats own sounds and movements after adult imitations Plays through continual repetition of patterns of movement and/or sound	Trial and error explorations repeated until they become habits Focus of attention is on infant's own body Integration of sensory and motor behaviors for beginning interaction with the environment
III. Secondary circular reactions (4–8 months)	Repeats patterns of behavior that produce pleasurable effects Restores visual contact when objects move out of sight by anticipating reappearance or removing material covering object Imitates sounds and simple gestures that infant is capable of producing Plays through repetition of interesting actions using objects in the environment	Awareness that his own behavior can have an effect on the environment Repetition of actions that produce pleasurable effects on the environment
IV. Coordination of secondary schemes (8–12 months)	Creates series of behaviors to achieve goals Touches adult's hands in order to initiate or continue an interesting activity Studies objects in a manner reflecting appreciation of three-dimensional attributes Obtains objects that he has watched be hidden Imitates novel sounds that are similar to previously produced sounds Imitates novel movements that include actions similar to previously accomplished ones	Behavior becomes goal directed Application of previously learned behaviors to new situations

(continued)

TABLE 3.1 (*continued*)

Developmental Stage	Developmental Accomplishments	General Characteristics
V. Tertiary circular reactions (12–18 months)	Seeks novel ways to desired goal Locates objects hidden in a series of observable displacements Hands objects to adult to initiate or repeat a desired action Imitates novel sound patterns and words not previously heard Imitates novel movements not previously performed Substitutes objects during play (e.g., toy dishes for real ones)	New behaviors learned through trial and error Actions and thoughts are flexible Many cognitive and motoric alternatives used in problem solving
VI. Combination of new means through mental combinations (18–24 months)	Uses foresight to invent new behaviors (purposeful problem solving) Locates objects that are hidden (object permanence) Able to infer a cause when only the effect is seen and to understand the effect when just the cause is known (cause-effect relationship) Imitates complex verbalizations; reproduces previously heard sounds and words from memory (vocal imitation) Imitates complex motor movements and reproduces previously seen actions from memory (motor imitation) Plays using one object to represent another (e.g., box for a cash register) (symbolic play)	Use of insight rather than trial-and-error problem-solving strategies Use of symbolic language to refer to absent objects
B. Preoperational Thoughts (2–7 years)	Initially speaks in collective monologues (in the presence of others but not addressed to them for communicative purposes; thinking out his actions aloud)	Ability to function primarily in the conceptual-symbolic mode rather than sensorimotor mode

Developmental Stage	Developmental Accomplishments	General Characteristics
	Advances to socialized inter-communicative speech	Socialization of behavior as seen in verbal exchanges and play in games with rules
	Thought processes character-ized by centration (fixing at-tention on a limited percep-tual aspect of an object)	Behavior and thinking are ego-centric (child cannot see viewpoint of another)
	Lacks reversibility (following a line of reasoning back to where it started) in thought processes	Unable to understand or con-ceptualize transformations of objects (just sees an ini-tial and final element when objects are transformed)
	Gradually develops a begin-ning understanding of con-servation (conceptualization that the amount or quantity of matter stays the same re-gardless of changes in shape or position)	Initially thought is slow, plod-ding, inflexible, dominated by perceptions, and remains irreversible; gradually as egocentrism diminishes de-centering and attendance to simple transformations in-crease reversibility of thought, skills in conserva-tion developed sequentially: Number (age 5–6) Mass (age 7–8) Area (age 7–8) Weight (age 9–10) Volume (age 11–12)
C. Concrete Operations (7–11 years)	Becomes a social being Decenters perceptions	Reasoning processes become logical—makes cognitive and logical decisions as opposed to perceptual deci-sions
	Attends to transformations Attains reversibility of operations Improves operations of seriation and classification	Egocentrism diminished as child uses social interaction to verify or deny concepts
D. Formal Operations (11–15 years)	Able to deal with complex ver-bal problems, hypothetical problems, or problems in-volving the future	Cognitive structures reach maturity

1975). Other instruments based on Piagetian theory include the *Albert Einstein Scales of Sensorimotor Development* (Escalona & Corman, 1966) and the *Piagetian Infancy Scale* (Honig & Lally, 1970).

The usefulness of Piagetian-based scales with handicapped populations has been debated, with some strongly supporting them and others challenging their usefulness (Fewell, 1983). Those in favor of the approach cite the freedom from age

scores and the emphasis on a process-based approach, since examiners observe children as they interact with the environment in play situations. Those opposed point out that individuals with severe or profound disabilities may be operating in the sensorimotor stage throughout their lives. The theory neither satisfactorily addresses such individuals' development, nor was it intended to do so. Without appropriate intervention, domains such as cause-and-effect relationships may be perpetually delayed for children with severely limited abilities to act on the environment. Piagetian-based scales have proved useful in the assessment of minority and bilingual children (de Avila & Havassy, 1974, 1974b).

The Behavioral Perspective

Behavioral learning theory, which is founded upon the premise that all behavior is learned, is the basis for the *behavioral perspective*. It is not simply the result of maturation, but rather comes about as a child engages in behaviors that result in consequences. If the consequences reinforce a behavior frequently enough, it becomes a learned behavior. For example, the infant who randomly swats at brightly colored objects dangling near his face and happens to produce a pleasing sound and motion from the object eventually comes to control the voluntary muscles and coordinate eye-hand movements to make intentional swats at the object. The ages at which learning takes place are not of significance to the theory. Behavioral theory is applied extensively in programs for children with mental retardation, autism, and those exhibiting behavior disorders.

The emphasis in behaviorally oriented assessment is on what skills the child has acquired and which ones remain to be learned. Criterion-referenced (e.g., *Brigance Diagnostic Inventory of Early Development*) or curriculum-based assessments (e.g., *Learning Accomplishment Profile*) take this functional approach to child assessment. Other techniques that are associated with the behavioral perspective include task analysis and applied behavioral analysis. These techniques avoid comparison of children to norms and are most useful in assessment for program planning.

The Adaptive–Transactive Perspective

Assessment techniques associated with the developmental, cognitive stages and behavioral perspectives have limitations in their usefulness with children with limited response repertoires. The need for alternative approaches to assessment that do not rely on voluntary muscle control or speech production is readily apparent to the examiner facing the challenge of assessing a nonverbal 2-year-old with severe motor impairments whose parents are convinced is of normal intelligence. The result of testing such a child in a nonadapted manner can and often does yield results that depress the estimate of the child's cognitive ability. When caregivers and interventionists are presented with these results, they assume lower expectations for the child, which may, in turn, lead to a depressed performance by the child. Such a prognosis, which can lead to a "syndrome of learned incompetence" (Kearsley, 1979), is known as *iatrogenic retardation*. An iatrogenic condition is one that is the result of treatment. For example, a visual impairment that is the result of prolonged administration of oxygen to a premature infant is an iatrogenic condition (Salvia & Ysseldyke, 1978). Kearsley used the term *iatrogenic retardation* is his work with a number of high-risk infants who were diagnosed as mentally and motorically retarded. Cognitive assessments of these children using adaptive–transactive techniques raised serious concerns about the accuracy of the previously made prognosis. Chapter 9 contains further discussion of these techniques.

ASSESSMENT TECHNIQUES

While each of the seven strands of assessment techniques represents a continuum of options of assessment, it would be impossible to discuss every point along each of the seven strands. Therefore, what is presented are the two extremes along the continuum of each strand and the relationship between each strand and the purposes of assessment.

Strand One: Formal to Informal Assessment

Formal Assessment.   When an examiner sets out to gather data about a specific child—that child's family and/or behavioral settings—she will establish a plan for assessment. The purpose of the assessment will be screening, diagnosis, program planning, effectiveness of intervention, or some combination thereof. The techniques used might include standardized norm-referenced testing, systematic observations in naturalistic settings, systematic observations of contrived situations, structured interviews, and environmental and interactional assessments. Formal assessment primarily involves the administration of standardized tests and the use of structured observational and interview procedures. The examiner has an intentional assessment plan in place with specific structured techniques to be employed.

Informal Assessment.   Informal assessment techniques are used when an examiner explores a child's ability to perform certain tasks using nonstandardized test administration of norm-referenced tests, interventionist-designed tests that are criterion-based, and unstructured developmental tasks in play activities. Informal assessment is often the most effective link between assessment and daily program planning.

Some informal assessments come about in a less-structured or preplanned manner. A teacher might notice during an activity with a small group of children that one child persistently has difficulty understanding the directions and is frequently turning his head to the left. Having noticed this behavior, the teacher might alert all the other adults who will be working with the child over the remainder of the day to be on the lookout for this behavior. No formal plan has been created with a systematic observation system. There is no clearly established purpose for the observation. Nevertheless, all the adults working with that particular child are informally gathering information about a particular behavior. At the close of the day, the adults can compare their observations and make decisions about the appropriate plan of action as a result of the informal assessment. Such informal assessments can trigger the development of a formal assessment.

Strand Two: Norm-Referenced to Criterion-Referenced Assessment

Norm-Referenced Assessment.   Assessment instruments based on comparisons of samples of other children within specified age levels are *norm-referenced*. The emphasis of norm-referenced tests is on how children compare with other children rather than on which specific skills they have mastered. Norm-referenced instruments produce age scores, developmental quotients, grade equivalents, standard scores, percentiles, or some other standardized scoring procedure. They can provide information that may be useful when making diagnostic assessments, placement decisions, and evaluations of child progress. They are of limited value for program planning and development of specific intervention strategies.

The group of children used to establish the level of difficulty of each test item is known as the *norm group*. The test is supposed to be used with children who match (were represented by) the norm group. Three factors should be considered when an examiner is matching a test's norm group to a particular child (Sattler, 1988). These factors are (1) the representativeness of the group, (2) the number of cases in the group, and (3) the relevance of the group. *Representativeness* is the extent to which the characteristics of the norm group correspond with those of the child to be tested. The *size* of the norm group influences the stability and accuracy of the test scoring. The norms are more stable the larger the norm group is. The norm group should include at least 100 subjects for each age or grade level (Sattler, 1988).

The final factor, *relevance,* is critical to the appropriate unbiased testing of special needs children. In actual practice the norm group is not always relevant to the child tested. Many tests, which are primarily used to assess children with disabilities, had norm groups that specifically excluded such children. Norm-referenced tests can screen out infants and children whose development appears to be lagging; however, examiners must consider that handicaps might cause an interference in performance. For example, a spastic child may be unable to stack three 1-inch blocks to form a tower, although she has the cognitive understanding required of the task. The determination of a deaf child's intelligence based on an instrument normed on a hearing population will unquestionably set that child at a disadvantage. Fuchs, Fuchs, Benowitz, and Barringer (1987) have, in fact, concluded that many of the norm-referenced tests used in special education may not be valid with a handicapped population for this reason.

Criterion-Referenced Assessment.   *Criterion-referenced assessment* focuses on what specific skills a child has mastered rather than group or norm comparisons. When criterion-referenced testing is used, the examiner presents the child with a variety of tasks to perform and notes his skills. The results of such testing may not be helpful in determining a diagnosis, but are essential to appropriate individualized program planning.

Criterion-referenced tests can be teacher-made informal instruments as well as commercially available skills checklists. When an examiner selects a commercially available instrument, there are several dangers of which she should keep in mind. First, if the particular instrument used does not accurately reflect a child's experiences, a child's potential to learn the skill is unknown. For example, the test might include assessment of the child's ability to place objects appropriately according to prepositions (e.g., "put the block in the cup, under the cup, behind the cup"), but the intervention program that the child has been participating in has not included such concept development. In this example, testing the child with the instrument before intervention and after intervention might indicate that the child has gained no new skills when the child has actually mastered numerous skills. The criterion-referenced test failed to match the curriculum that the child received. Such inaccurate test results can lead examiners and interventionists to the erroneous conclusion that an intervention program is inappropriate or ineffective.

The second danger of criterion-referenced testing also relates to the match between test items and the curriculum, where the test becomes the curriculum. It is an easy temptation for interventionists to select a commercially available criterion-referenced test and let that instrument dictate the curriculum. While the problem of testing the child on skills that he has not been exposed to has been eliminated, the individualized planning of an appropriate program may have also been lost. While criterion-referenced tests have much to offer early interventionists, they should be reviewed carefully before the content of the test is adopted wholesale as "the program."

An alternative form of criterion-referenced testing designed to avoid these dangers is *curriculum-based assessment.* The primary objective of curriculum-based assessment is success of the students (Hargis, 1987). Accordingly, there two steps to follow. First, it is necessary to find the level of the curriculum at which the child can succeed. Second, daily teaching activities should have assessment components incorporated into them (i.e., program monitoring). Assessment is embedded in instruction as an essential part of the program.

Task Analysis. Another related procedure particularly useful in the assessment of children with severe disabilities is *task analysis*. Task analysis involves the division of a skill into smaller subskills. The procedure is used in assessment as well as instruction. For assessment purposes, examiners can use task analysis to determine which subskills of a task a child has already mastered. From such an assessment it is easy to know what skills to target for the child. There are two approaches that can be taken in task analysis: *skill sequencing* and *chaining of responses* (Browder, 1987). Skill sequencing involves the identification of a sequence of skills that lead to mastery of a more advanced skill. For example, independent toileting involves skills related to muscle control, the ability to anticipate and take action, dressing and undressing, sitting balance, ability to follow a multiple step process without distraction, and general hygiene. Chaining of responses involves the identification of specific behaviors as they occur during the completion of a task. In the toileting example, the following describes a task analysis based on chaining of responses:

1. Become aware of the physical need to urinate.
2. Locate and go to an appropriate bathroom.
3. Remove clothing as necessary.
4. Sit or stand in the appropriate location.
5. Release muscle tension of bladder and urinate.
6. Wipe excess urine off (for females).
7. Stand up (for females).
8. Get dressed.
9. Flush toilet.
10. Find sink and wash hands, using soap.
11. Dry hands.
12. Exit bathroom.

Each of the subskills identified in this example could be further analyzed into additional sub-subskills. The task analysis should be as detailed as needed to isolate specific subskills a child is unable to perform.

Browder (1987) identified a four-step procedure to be used when conducting task-analytic assessment based on chaining of responses. This procedure is presented in Figure 3.1. Figure 3.2 depicts a sample data collection sheet as mentioned in Figure 3.1. In this example, the skill "pour a thermos" is divided into eight subskills. The interventionist collects data during the child's first pouring attempt at lunch and codes the child's behavior relevant to each subskill. In this example the child gets a single opportunity to perform the task. The first failure ends the test. Other procedures, which provide multiple opportunities with cuing or task variation, are also possible. In Figure 3.1, the interventionist assessed the child on her first attempt to pour on October 4 and found that she was able to complete the first three subskills. During her next two attempts, the teacher provided instructional

Figure 3.1. Steps to Task-Analytic Assessment

Step 1. Plan the task analysis
* Consider the student's current performance
* Consult resources on the best way to perform the task
* Identify simple motoric responses
* Simplify the task further with adaptations
* Enhance stimulus control

Step 2. Write the task analysis
* Write the sequence of steps using action verbs
* Clarify steps as necessary
* Try the task following the written steps
* Write the steps on a data collection sheet

Step 3. Plan the assessment
To plan probes:
* Decide how to secure attention, enhance motivation
* Identify the discriminative stimulus to begin the task
* Decide the latency for responding
* Plan how to handle errors
* Plan how to end the assessment
* Write these plans and scoring key on data sheet or the instructional plan

To plan instructional data collection:
* Decide what will be scored
* Plan when to record data during instruction
* Write these plans on the data sheet or plan

Step 4. Conduct the assessment
* Follow the assessment plan
* Schedule reliability observations when possible

Source: D. M. Browder (1987). *Assessment of Individuals with Severe Handicaps.* Baltimore, MD: Paul H. Brookes. Reprinted by permission.

assistance and recorded her performance when given gestural, verbal, or physical prompts. On October 5, the teacher again used the first attempt for assessment and the second and third attempts for instruction.

Strand Three: Standardized to Adaptive-to-Handicap Assessment

Standardized Assessment.   Most norm-referenced tests and some criterion-referenced tests have specific procedures that must be followed for test results to be considered accurate. Some tests provide the examiner with exactly what to say throughout the test. Some tests require the presentation of subtests in a specific order with specific restrictions (e.g., timed portions). Many have specific instructions for establishing starting and stopping points. The starting point usually involves establishing a *basal point,* the point below which it is assumed the child can perform all items. The *ceiling* is the stopping point beyond which it is assumed that no item could be performed.

Since all of the standardized procedures of test administration are used in the

50

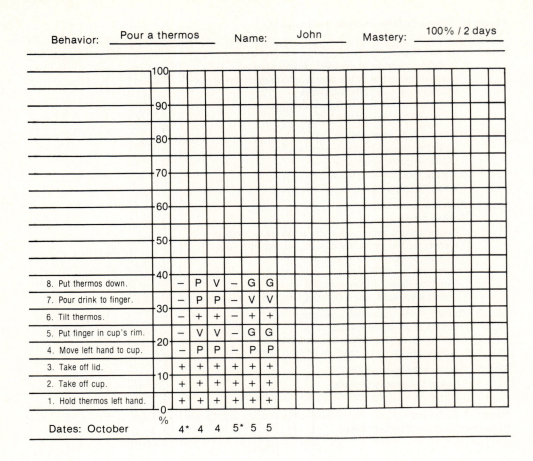

Behavior: Pour a thermos   Name: John   Mastery: 100% / 2 days

		4*	4	4	5*	5	5
8. Put thermos down.	40	−	P	V	−	G	G
7. Pour drink to finger.		−	P	P	−	V	V
6. Tilt thermos.	30	−	+	+	−	+	+
5. Put finger in cup's rim.		−	V	V	−	G	G
4. Move left hand to cup.	20	−	P	P	−	P	P
3. Take off lid.		+	+	+	+	+	+
2. Take off cup.	10	+	+	+	+	+	+
1. Hold thermos left hand.	0 %	+	+	+	+	+	+

Dates: October   4*   4   4   5*   5   5

Probe Data

Schedule: First attempt to pour at lunch on Monday
Attention/motivation: No special procedures
Discriminative stimulus to begin task: John picks up thermos
Response latency: 3 seconds to begin each step
Error treatment: Single opportunity method
Ending the test: Stop at first error and begin task again with instruction
Scoring: + = correct, − = incorrect

Instructional Data

Schedule: First instructional trial each day
Coordination with instruction: Score entire TA after last step
Scoring: + = correct without help, G = correct after gesture (touch or tap),
          V = correct after verbal prompt, P = correct with physical guidance

Figure 3.2. Sample Data Collection Sheet for Task-Analytic Assessment
Source: D. M. Browder (1987). *Assessment of Individuals with Severe Handicaps.* Baltimore, MD: Paul H. Brookes. Reprinted by permission.

establishment of test norms, an examiner must adhere to them for proper test administration. If he deviates from them, the results are no longer comparable to those obtained from the norm group and the scores are not valid. However, following standardized procedures for some children with disabilities can produce equally invalid test results. Some such procedures are obviously inappropriate. If a test requires that a child look at a picture and point to some specific part of it, a blind child simply cannot do it. A nonverbal child cannot recite a nursery rhyme, even if he is familiar with it and has the words memorized. Other testing procedures that present difficulties for these children may be more subtle. For example, timing the speed at which a performance item is completed for a child with motor impairments can result in an unfair and inaccurate assessment of his cognitive potential.

Some examiners do deviate from standardized procedures when testing children with disabilities. Sattler (1988) points out that some deviations appear to be minor and would not preclude the use of standardized norms. For example, children who are physically unable to point can use eye gaze to indicate choices, and examiners can read test items to a child with visual impairments. Even modifications of this nature must be done with extreme caution. Hoffmeister (1988) addressed how such modifications in testing for deaf children fail to take into consideration the developmental differences that they may experience. The tests, based on a norm group of children with intact hearing, may assess cognitive functioning as reflected by auditory, visual, and motor skills, whereas the deaf child develops her cognitive understanding primarily through visual and motor skills. Simply using sign language throughout the test will not improve the poor match between the child being tested and the norm group. Children who do not present a close match to the norm group simply should not be given a test other than for the purpose of comparing the child with the norm group.

For example, a blind child might be viewed as motorically delayed when compared with a sighted population, but when compared with other blind children the motor delay is not apparent. Proper interpretation of the child's performance is that he is delayed in motor development, as typically seen in visually impaired children; this does not indicate a significant motor impairment in addition to the visual impairment. While we should provide intervention to reduce the motor delay, it would be a misdiagnosis to indicate that the child had a motor impairment separate from the visual problem.

A technique known as *testing-of-limits* can be used to explore a child's abilities beyond those exhibited during a standard test administration (Sattler, 1988). The examiner should not use testing-of-limits until the entire test has been given using the standardized procedures. There are five procedures that examiners can employ as a part of this technique.

1. *Provide additional cues:* The examiner can return to failed items and let the child attempt them again with additional help, such as providing the first step in problem solving or increasing the structure.
2. *Change modality:* The examiner can change the modality that is involved in problem solving. For example, moving from oral to written problem solving or from written to oral might change the level of difficulty of the task for some children.

3. *Establish methods used by the child:* Learning how the child went about solving the problem can provide as much information as the fact that she missed it or passed it. Ask the child to explain how she got her answer. If she is unable to explain it, she might be able to show how she found her solution to the problem.

4. *Eliminate time limits:* For those children whose performance was hampered by the time limits on a test, eliminating time limits can give the examiner needed information about the child's ability to accomplish specific tasks.

5. *Ask probing questions:* If a child gave responses that the examiner wanted to explore further but could not while following a standardized testing procedure, he might want to return to those items upon completion of the test. This gives the child an opportunity to tell more about his response.

One drawback to using testing-of-limits procedures is the possible invalidation of any future retesting of the child using the same instrument.

Adaptive-to-Handicap Assessment. Today tests are developed that can be altered for use with disabled children. Adaptive-to-handicap scales allow a child to use alternative senses and responses to attempt test items. Many adaptive approaches can be used. Scales that give the examiner the responsibility of determining if and when modifications of items and procedures are appropriate are now available. Some tests provide guidelines for the alteration of test items or the response required. Such modifications are similar to Sattler's suggestion that an examiner wishing to test-the-limits change the modality required. The use of an instrument specifically designed for such modifications, however, has the advantage of producing a valid score. Another adaptive-to-handicap assessment technique involves the use of instruments specifically designed for and standardized on groups of children with specific disabilities. The following are some additional adaptive assessment strategies:

- Modify the stimulus properties of objects and materials used during testing (e.g., increase size, brightness, number of dimensions, and/or texture).
- Adjust the response modes available (e.g., permit directed eye gaze to communication board or employ the use of microswitches).
- Exclude all tasks that bias performance and prorate score (e.g., putting together a puzzle within a time limit for a child with cerebral palsy).
- Use multidimensional scoring methods (0, 1, 2) to tap performance quality (instead of wrong or right).
- Rearrange the order of presentation of tasks.
- Use tasks from multiple scales that are targeted to the same functions.
- Use a dynamic test-teach-test approach to evaluate learning rate of the child. (Bagnato, Neisworth, & Munson, 1989)

Strand Four: Unidisciplinary to Team Approaches

Unidisciplinary Approach. The *unidisciplinary approach* involves assessment by a single professional. Some young children present problems that are very specific in nature and can be treated by a professional from a single discipline. The child may have no need for a comprehensive program of intervention. When such is the case, the professional from that discipline may work in isolation, involving no other professionals from related fields. If intervention is to be offered by a single discipline, assessment may also be limited to the discipline reflective of the problem. A single professional is often the only one involved in assessments in rural and isolated areas where comprehensive services are not available. Although unidisciplinary assessment and intervention is not the preferred approach for serving children with multiple problems or general developmental delay, it can be of some benefit if it is the only option available. In some instances it is possible to create a *miniteam* approach, wherein professionals from more than one discipline work together, even though they do not represent a comprehensive team.

Team Approaches.   Today many early childhood special educators base programs on a team approach. Young children with disabilities often present a variety of problems requiring knowledge and expertise from multiple disciplines. Motorically impaired children may need physical therapists for treatment as well as training of all adults in proper handling and positioning techniques along with occupational therapy, speech and language intervention, and cognitive development. Meeting the nutritional needs of young children and their families may require the expertise of a nutritionist. The determination of who needs to be included in the team of professionals for early intervention is best made on an individual basis. While the basic composition of teams may be fairly consistent for children with similar disabilities, every child presents a unique picture with needs originating out of their home and community environments. The case studies presented in the appendix illustrate the number of professionals with whom a family must interact. Both Elizabeth Armstrong and Eduardo Manzolis have received services from physical therapists, occupational therapists, speech and language pathologists, nutritionists, special educators, and social workers, as well as a variety of medical specialists. The three models of the team process seen in early intervention are *multidisciplinary, interdisciplinary,* and *transdisciplinary.*

Multidisciplinary Teams.   The *multidisciplinary team* approach emerged from the medical model, in which specialists who have expertise in the areas suspected of causing medical difficulties examine patients. In a multidisciplinary child assessment the relevant professionals each perform separate examinations. Each team member sees the child individually, writes up a report, and makes recommendations for the child in regard to her area of expertise. No discussion, debate, comparison of results, analysis or interpretation of findings, or mutual development of recommendations across disciplines takes place in the multidisciplinary process (Bennett, 1982; Fewell, 1983). One of the problems inherent in this model of assessment for young children is that it can leave parents with multiple, even conflicting recommendations. In one such case, a 4-year-old hearing-impaired child from a rural community received services from an oral/aural therapy program and a separate comprehensive development center (where the child was encouraged to develop signing skills). This child was put on a bus at 6:00 A.M. and returned home after 5:00 P.M. three days a week. She also received intervention in the home, based on a total communication program.

Even when the team channels all of the assessment results to one professional, who then summarizes the findings and makes recommendations for the parents, there are flaws in the multidisciplinary model. The biases of the person responsible for summarizing the results will influence his interpretation of the findings (Hart, 1977). Additionally, this person might be put in a position of trying to help the parents interpret medical test results and make decisions about their child's future without an adequate background.

Interdisciplinary Teams. The composition of an *interdisciplinary team* might be identical to that of a multidisciplinary team. The difference between the two lies in the formality of communications and group decision making (Fewell, 1983). Members of an interdisciplinary team come together informally during the assessment process and formally when the process is complete and it is time to make decisions regarding services. The interdisciplinary model may be hampered by communication difficulties across disciplines. Professionals who are familiar with the language associated with their particular area of expertise may have difficulty understanding and being understood by professionals from other disciplines. Professionals might also disagree as to what are the priority areas for intervention. Thus, the inclusion of a formal system of communication into the model does not assure that cooperative group decisions will be reached regarding the recommendations for a child and his family.

Transdisciplinary Teams. As with the interdisciplinary model, team membership on the *transdisciplinary team* is similar to the multidisciplinary team. How the team functions, however, is very different. While some initial assessments and ongoing medical procedures will always necessitate separate clinical evaluations, a significant portion of the assessments typically conducted on young children with disabilities can be performed using transdisciplinary teams. Such assessments are often conducted as *arena* assessments. The actual handling and interaction with the child are limited to one or two individuals while other professionals observe the child. The professional who is interacting with the child conducts an assessment of the child in her own discipline as well as asking the child to perform tasks relevant to other disciplines. Professionals from the various disciplines involved can observe the child's performance and ask the one conducting the assessment for additional information regarding unobservable characteristics.

In order for the transdisciplinary model to be successful, the team members need to reach agreements in five areas: (1) acceptance of differences in skills, (2) acceptance of differences in approach, (3) willingness not to try to know everything, (4) an ability to call on others for assistance and ongoing knowledge, and (5) nonthreatening opportunities for discussion of these areas (Howard, 1982). Without such commitments, transdisciplinary teams face the same limitations found in the interdisciplinary model. However, the greatest drawback of the transdisciplinary approach is the time commitment that may be required of numerous professionals. The model requires that all involved professionals attend a team meeting, plan the assessment, participate or observe throughout the assessment, and attend a final meeting to summarize results and determine recommendations. Such an approach can be expensive as well as time-consuming. However, it can pay for itself through improved communication and formulation of recommendations regarding needed services for children and their families.

The advantages of such a model of intervention are particularly evident when children present problems that overlap traditional boundaries for service delivery. For example, a child with prespeech and feeding difficulties can profit more when a speech and language therapist works with an occupational therapist and a physical therapist to plan an intervention than when each works in isolation. Transdisciplinary programming can be helpful in reducing the gaps in a child's services if no one person feels adequately trained to address an area of need. As team members, professionals can assist each other in the pursuit of solutions to problems that the children and/or families are facing. The types of information that can be obtained through arena assessments of infants include behavior and style (e.g., appearance, rhythmicity, frustration tolerance, and attention); object interaction and cognition (e.g., symbolic object use, planned problem solving, and discrimination); social and emotional nature (e.g., reaction to strangers, affective range, attachment/ separation behavior, and play style); communication (e.g., frequency/duration, quality of speech, and mode of communication); sensorimotor development (e.g., tactile responsivity and sensitivity, primitive reflexes, tool use, and sucking, drinking, and chewing); and self-help (e.g., feeding, dressing, and toileting).

The arena assessment model used at Child Development Resources (CDR) in Lightfoot, Virginia, incorporates family members as a part of the assessment team. Before the actual assessment, one team member is designated as the facilitator, and another serves as the coach. The role of the facilitator is to interact with and handle the child, while the coach offers assistance and provides reminders or additional suggestions from other professionals observing the assessment. All team members participate in the assessment. "The facilitator serves as the 'hands' for the 'brains' of the observing participants. The facilitator is not the person who 'does' the arena assessment" (Garland, nd). Figure 3.3 depicts one possible arrangement for conducting arena assessments as done at CDR.

Linder's transdiciplinary play-based assessment model (1990) includes an adjustable six-phase process. The first phase is unstructured facilitation, lasting about 25 minutes, where the child takes the lead. The facilitator for the assessment interacts in response to the child, attempting to move the child to higher skill levels through modeling. The second phase, structured facilitation, involves the cognitive and language activities that did not occur during the first phase. The facilitator takes a direct approach with specific requests made to the child, while maintaining play as the vehicle for assessment. Depending on the age, functioning level, and cooperation of the child, this phase should last between 5 and 15 minutes. The third phase entails child-to-child interaction in an unstructured situation. It is preferred that the other child be familiar with the child being assessed, slightly older, of the same sex, and nonhandicapped. The developmental level, however, should be reasonably close to the other child. This phase should last between 5 and 10 minutes. The fourth phase, parent–child interaction, provides the parents with an opportunity to play with their child as they routinely do at home. After a few minutes of this unstructured play, the parents leave for a few minutes and return,

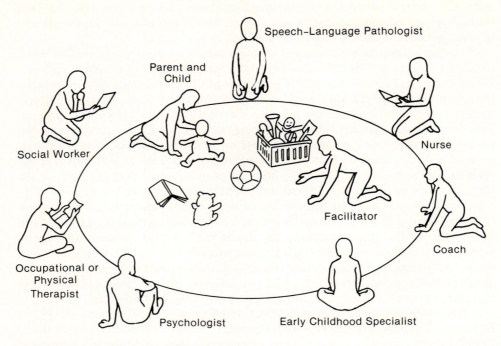

Figure 3.3. Transdisciplinary Assessment.
Source: Adapted from Adrienne Frank, Project KAI (Brighton, MA), Transdisciplinary Model of Service Delivery. Lightfoot, VA: Child Development Resources, 1989. Reprinted with permission.

affording the opportunity for team members to note separation and greeting behaviors. When the parents return, they engage the child in a unfamiliar, slightly challenging task. The fifth phase involves motor play and should last approximately 10 to 20 minutes. Both unstructured and structured activities occur. The sixth and final phase is snack. It is appropriate to allow the other child used in the assessment to rejoin the group so examiners can observe additional social interactions. Linder provides observational guidelines for cognitive, social and emotional, communication and language, and sensorimotor development.

Strand Five: Direct to Indirect Assessment

Direct Assessment.   When an examiner goes about the task of assessing a child by having face-to-face contact in a testing situation (whether it is formal or informal testing) or observing the child first hand, it is direct assessment. Even when the observation is done through videotape, if the examiner is personally watching the tape and making certain determinations about the child's behaviors it is considered to be direct assessment. Some direct assessment should be a part of any complete child assessment.

Indirect Assessment.   Often examiners need information about how a child performs in a variety of behavioral settings. Direct assessments of the child under all of these circumstances are not feasible. In such cases, the examiner can use information available through an intermediate source. Most often indirect assessments involve obtaining information from parents about the child's abilities through interviews or questionnaires. Such indirect assessment procedures can also provide valuable information about the parents' perceptions of the child's functioning. As discussed in Chapter 1, perceptions can create their own reality. Knowledge of how the parents view the child can be as useful as is gaining the information about the child. Early childhood special educators should explore any wide discrepancies between direct assessment of the child's abilities and indirect assessment through a parent interview as a part of an ecologically valid assessment.

Strand Six: Naturalistic to Clinical Observation

Observation is an essential technique of assessment, which involves gathering qualitative and quantitative data about a child's behavior. Brandt (1975) has identified four perspectives used in research involving observation. The *ecological psychology perspective* places an emphasis on the study of naturally occurring behavior in everyday settings. The observer begins the observation with as few preconceptions as possible, hoping to discover the "stream of behavior" that may have been previously unrecognized. *Ethological research* is similar to ecological research in that the emphasis is on observation in a natural setting with relatively few preconceptions; however, it is restricted to those behaviors that are clearly observable—motor patterns and discrete actions. This research approach has grown out of animal studies and does not permit the exploration of the full range of human behaviors. The third perspective, *interaction analysis,* involves the categorization of behaviors observed during interactions. These categories might be predetermined if the observer is using a checklist or rating sheet for the observation or if the observer can create his own categories based on data analysis. The final perspective, that of *behavior modification,* typically focuses on the specific behavior of a child who is the target of the observation. Observers hope to determine what elements of a behavior setting serve as reinforcers for the child and the effectiveness of adjusting those reinforcers to increase desired behaviors and decrease undesired behaviors.

These same four perspectives used in research have direct application to observations that are used for assessment purposes. The intended purpose of an observation influences those behaviors that need to be observed and the appropriate perspective for the observer to take. For example, if a physician is concerned with the effectiveness of a medication that has been prescribed to reduce hyperactivity, an ethological approach to observation would be appropriate—recording the frequency and duration of motor movements. However, the parent might be concerned with the impact the medication is having on the child's social development. In such a case, an ecological approach or an interactions approach would be appropriate.

Examiners using observations for assessment need to focus on the actual events and behaviors, rather than subjective interpretations of those behaviors. For example, an observer witnesses one child kick another. An inappropriate interpretative recording of such a behavior might read as follows:

> Joe and Jack were enjoying the time they have together playing with blocks. They are good friends. When the teacher announced that it was time to clean up both boys became angry because they were disappointed that play time was over. Jack showed a lack of responsibility and immaturity by leaving the play area. This behavior made Joe so mad that he lost all control and started abusing Jack. Jack and Joe will never be allowed to play together again since they treat each other so badly. Joe has been unable to adjust in this setting and needs a program designed to serve emotionally disturbed children.

The underlined portions of the passage are unobservable interpretations of the behaviors that the children displayed. The last two sentences are conclusions drawn by the teacher based on her subjective interpretation of the situation. An appropriate objective recording of the same scene depicting what was actually observable might read in the following manner:

> Joe and Jack were playing with the wooden blocks. They were smiling and talking quietly together. The teacher announced that it was time for the boys to clean up the blocks. Jack walked away from the block area. Joe ran after Jack, grabbed his shoulder, and shouted to him, "Come back!" Then he kicked Jack in the shin and ran back to the block area.

This recording of the scene includes no interpretations of child behavior. It leaves room for investigation into the possible causes for each child's behavior rather than offering up final interpretations. Observers can give the children an opportunity to clarify their behaviors and discuss how they were feeling during the interaction, enabling the observer to make a more accurate analysis of the witnessed events. Even when observers are careful to record actual behaviors there can be disagreement among multiple observers. Further discussion of the dependability of data gathered through observation is included in Chapter 4.

Observations that exclusively target the child, ignoring the ecology of a behavior setting, can lead to confusing and inaccurate conclusions. An observer of a child might carefully note that when asked to draw a picture, the child drew the entire picture in black, indicating the child's overemphasis on the dark side of life and depression. The reality might have been that (1) he was only given black and brown crayons; (2) the black crayon was newest, still having a sharp point, while all the others were worn down; or (3) recently the child had participated in an art workshop in which one of the activities had been to draw an entire picture in one color, and she was simply recreating this experience.

Cautions should be made to distinguish *emic,* or insider, views from *edic* observations, that is, those from an outsider's view. While an outsider may be unaware of certain dynamics or the characteristics of an ongoing relationship, the insider may be unable to free himself to observe from an unbiased perspective.

Naturalistic Observation.   The observation of children in their naturally occurring play interactions under normal routines is *naturalistic observation*. Naturalistic observations can involve the observation of an entire behavior setting and all that occurs within that setting over a given period of time. Such a comprehensive observation could include the observation of all individuals and aspects of the behavior setting or be restricted to certain individuals and aspects of the setting. Analysis of a general observation can lead to the development of focused observations, which provide more detailed information about critical issues.

Through naturalistic observations an observer can look for very specific exchanges or types of behaviors. For example, a child who has been having an unusually high number of temper tantrums might be observed in a naturalistic setting over the course of the day. The behavior that is the focus of the observation is the tantrum. The observer would make note of the times when a tantrum occurred, what preceded each of them, how long they lasted, what followed them, and their nature. The examiner can combine such information with other data available about the child and her micro- and mesosystems for analysis and intervention planning. Elizabeth Armstrong's tantrums in the middle of her kindergarten year were traced to a change in a behavioral setting. During story time an assistant held Elizabeth in her lap on the floor with the other children. One day she abruptly changed this routine and started doing work outside the room during story time. Elizabeth had to remain in her wheelchair on the edge of the circle. Since Elizabeth is unable to speak, she expressed her feelings through the tantrums. After about a week, her mother was able to pinpoint a change in routine as the source of the disruptive behavior.

The techniques used to gather data in a naturalistic observation depend upon the stated purpose and desired outcomes of the observation. Each is described along with appropriate uses and possible drawbacks.

Running Records.   When an observer records everything that occurs within a given time period by taking notes or video taping, it is called a *running record*. It is useful for the teacher to get pictures of what is happening generally and the sequencing of events. Such an observation technique is of most use at the initial stages of assessment. When the purpose of the observation is to make a placement decision about a specific child, to conduct a program evaluation, to identify areas of child functioning that warrant further study, or to initiate an environmental assessment, the running record is an appropriate technique.

Once the observation is complete, the observer has a large volume of information that is not organized in meaningful fashion. The observer must convert the information into another form for analysis and interpretation. The decisions about how to organize the information can have significant influence on the meanings of the information. The observer can study the data in order to form categories, or he can analyze the data using previously identified categories.

The formation of categories that accurately reflect actual behaviors is critical to the meaningful interpretation of the data. The use of a psychometrically validated and reliable coding system can reduce the likelihood of misinterpretation. For example, the *Behavioral Coding System* (BCS) (Jones, Reid, & Patterson, 1975) contains 28 observable behavioral categories, which can be noted during an observation. When more than one behavior is occurring simultaneously, the observer can distinguish between first order and second order behaviors. Each category of behavior is defined for the observer. The following are examples of the behavior categories used in the BCS (from Jones, Reid, & Patterson, 1975):

Verbal

Command: This category is used when an immediate and clearly stated request or command is made to another person.
Command Negative: A command which is very different in attitude from a reasonable command or request.
Humiliate: Makes fun of, shames, or embarrasses the subject intentionally.

Nonverbal

Destructiveness: The person destroys, damages, or attempts to damage any (nonhuman) object; the damage need not actually occur, but the potential for damage must exist.
Ignore: When person A has directed behavior at person B and person B appears to have recognized that the behavior was directed at him, but does not respond in an active fashion.

Either Verbal or Nonverbal

Approval: A person gives clear gestural or verbal approval to another individual. Must include some clear indication of positive interest or involvement.
Play: A person is playing either alone or with other persons.
Noncompliance: When a person does not do what is requested of him.

Jones, Reid, and Patterson established reliability of the BCS through investigation of its generalizability and stability of scores. Interobserver agreements across observations were high. They found that agreement increased as observer skill increased over time. In addition, the complexity of the categories influenced how rapidly observers became skilled. To establish content validity, Jones, Reid, and Patterson asked mothers of preschool-age children to rate 28 behaviors on a nine-point scale of aversiveness. Observations based on the BCS were compared with clinical reports to establish concurrent validity. Use of the BCS in planning interventions and detecting behavioral change following treatment provided the basis for construct validity.

Event Sampling. *Event sampling* involves the measurement of specific behaviors as they occur through *frequency counts* or through *duration recording.* Observers should note environmental variables such as time of day, physical setting, other persons present, and physical condition of the child during event sampling. Observers can use frequency counts for the observation of behaviors that are relatively short in duration (e.g., number of times child hits, number of toileting accidents, and number of verbal outbursts directed to peers) during a specific period of time. Comparisons of behavior frequencies across times and behavior settings can offer additional information. When a teacher's perception of a child's behavior is that the child is constantly engaged in an undesirable behavior (e.g., she is constantly pinching the other children; she cannot keep her hands to herself; or the child never speaks to anyone), frequency counts help determine the accuracy of the perception. If the perception is accurate, she can immediately implement interventions that are designed to reduce the frequency of the behavior. If the perception is an exaggeration of how the child is actually behaving, the teacher can gain new insights into the child as well as plan an intervention program to reduce the troublesome behavior. Ongoing use of frequency counts can provide data necessary to determine the effectiveness of the interventions. A sample form that can be used to record frequency counts for individual children is presented in Figure 3.4.

Duration recording is useful for the measurement of behaviors that vary in length (e.g., length of time child plays alone, number of minutes child cries each day, amount of time on task, time spent wandering aimlessly around room, time engaged with specific toys, and time spent in the imaginary play area). Observers can use this technique to determine patterns of child behavior and to set target goals for intervention. For example, a child has been observed over a one-week period for 2 hours per day to determine the number of minutes he wanders aimlessly around the room and the amount of time spent engaged in appropriate play. Over the 10-hour time period, the child was observed wandering aimlessly for a total of 150 minutes and actively engaged in appropriate play for 75. Three weeks later an observation might reveal that over a comparable time period the child wandered a total of 100 minutes and played appropriately for 100. We see the substantial progress only through comparison with the original observation. A sample form for duration recording is presented in Figure 3.5.

Category Sampling. An examiner interested in a broad category of skills encompassing many different behaviors can employ *category sampling*. For example, recording the number of times a child initiates interactions with peers might involve observing eye contact, smiles, speaking, and touching. Examples of other categories include physical contact, number of times the child displays helping behaviors, and child-demonstrated creativity and originality. Defining the behaviors that fall within the category may not be an easy task for the observer. Disagreement among observers can complicate information gathered through category sampling. The use of established coding systems such as the BCS reduces this problem, however, no existing coding system can account for all the unique behaviors that occur. If an observer chooses to create her own categories, clear definitions that are consistently identifiable during observations by several independent observers should be established.

Naturalistic observations can provide the most ecologically valid assessment of a child's actual functioning and real behavioral changes. Sometimes, however, a spontaneous naturalistic observation is not possible or does not offer the best source of data. In such cases a *structured observation within the natural environment* might be of use. The observer can "arrange" the environment as he needs to and monitor areas of concern. The use of imposed structure enables the observer to create situations that may not otherwise happen during a scheduled observation and

Figure 3.4 Frequency Count Observation Recording Form

Child's Name _____   Time Period of Observation _____

Setting of Observation _____   Observer's Name _____

Behaviors Observed   Time and Date of Observation

1.					
2.					
3.					
4.					
5.					
6.					

make comparisons of child behavior as he manipulates the setting. A structured observation allows the observer to target specific circumstances for observation, whereas an observer might wait weeks for a specific behavior to occur in the natural environment.

Structured observations can involve (1) *simulated or staged situations,* or (2) *role-play situations*. Structured observations that employ simulated or staged situations involve the arrangement of a behavior setting that creates opportunities. For example, a teacher desiring to observe how a child will react when all the materials needed to complete an activity are not immediately available might set out everything needed except one item. The child might ask to borrow from another child, grab from another child, use physical gestures to get assistance from the teacher, begin shouting that she needs the missing item, and so forth.

Figure 3.5 Duration Recording Observation Form

Name of Child _____   Observer _____

Time and Date of Observation _____   Behavior Observed _____

Behavior A				Behavior B			
Comments	Start	Stop	Duration	Comments	Start	Stop	Duration
TOTAL							

Use of role-play for a structured observation gives the child an opportunity to show an observer how he would behave in a specific situation, such as if another child asked him to play house, or if his best friend damaged his favorite toy. Role-playing does require that a child think about the behavior he will exhibit and therefore does not have the spontaneity of a naturalistic observation. While set-up or role-play observations may not offer the ecological validity of naturalistic observation, they do provide the opportunity to target a specific condition for observation. Role-playing can also be designed to target behavior settings for which naturalistic observations are impossible (e.g., grandmother's house 500 miles away, the doctor's office, or the sanctuary at church). They can be manipulated and controlled so as to include those elements of interest to the observer at the moment.

Clinical Observations.   Often formal assessments of children occur in clinical settings rather than natural environments. Manuals of standardized instruments usually stipulate that the proper environment for test administration is in a quiet room free from distractions. The manual typically calls for the examiner to note certain child behaviors occurring during the testing, such as ease of separation from mother, distractibility during test administration, motivation to perform well, and cooperativeness. Early childhood special educators seeking to determine whether a child can perform a skill when removed from the distractions and chaos of a preschool room can conduct informal clinical observations. The teacher can work with the child in a separate room that offers a quiet, distraction-free setting. Such clinical observations are particularly useful when child performance is erratic or seems below expectations.

While such clinical observations can be of great value, particularly in monitoring how a child responds to a new environment or the effort she expends to cooperate with a new adult, they do not necessarily represent behaviors typical of that child in the naturalistic setting. Comparisons between clinical observations and those done in naturalistic settings can be of help in trying to understand a child's functioning. The child who never speaks in naturalistic settings such as day care, around the neighborhood, at the park, but who demonstrates age-appropriate speech and language skills in the clinical setting appears to have a socialization problem rather than impaired speech. The naturalistic observational data alone would have resulted in a misdiagnosis. On the other hand, if the examiner relied solely on the clinical assessment, she would have missed the significant dysfunction that characterizes this child's ability to communication with peers. Examiners need both clinical and naturalistic observations to obtain accurate results.

Strand Seven: Product-Oriented to Process-Oriented Assessment

Product-Oriented Assessment.   A *product-oriented* approach to assessment involves giving the child a battery of tests that produce scores or other final products. Screening and diagnosis procedures are typically product-oriented assessments. Testing of this nature can give parents and professionals information about how the child compares with other children his age (helpful in placement decisions) and can help determine initial instructional levels. The results of product-oriented test assessments are easy to communicate but are at-risk of being meaningless and misleading if used inappropriately or with biased instruments.

Process-Oriented Assessment.   In contrast to product-oriented assessment, *process-oriented* assessment involves the study of the child's interactions with the examiner and/or others as well as responses to environmental stimuli. Examiners find process-oriented assessment particularly useful in estimating the abilities of children with severe impairments. It provides a focus on changes in child behaviors, such as smiling, eye gaze, heart rate, surprise, or other emotional indicators. Piagetian-based assessment measures, such as the Uzgiris-Hunt *Infant Psychological Development Scale,* involve a process-oriented approach. Dynamic assessments (e.g., Feuerstein, 1979), modeled from Vygotsky's concept of *zone of proximal development* (1978), follow a test-teach-test format. Vygotsky focused on the concepts of *actual developmental level* coupled with the *level of potential development.* Actual developmental level is that which is typically measured by tests. It consists of those things a child can do on her own. However, children may have many skills that are in the process of maturation. The child cannot accomplish a task independently, but with some prompting or assistance, she can complete or partially complete it. The distance between a child's actual developmental level and her level of potential development is the zone of proximal development. Minick (1987) cites additional works by Vygotsky in which he makes an analogy to a garden. If a garden's productivity were measured by only those fruits or vegetables that had reached full maturation and no partially developed items could be counted, an inaccurate picture might result. Routine assessments of children are conducted in a parallel fashion. Unless the child can complete a task independently, free from practice, prompts, modeling, or other clues, most tests give the child no credit for the item. Vygotsky (1978) puts forth an illustrative example to make his point clear. Two children both earn a mental age of 8 years on cognitive assessments.

> These children seem to be capable of handling problems up to an eight-year-old's level, but not beyond that. Suppose that I show them various ways of dealing with the problem. Different experimenters might employ different modes of demonstration in different cases: some might run through an entire demonstration and ask the children to repeat it, others might initiate the solution and ask the child to finish it, or offer leading questions. . . . I propose that the children solve the problem with my assistance. . . . it turns out that the first child can deal with problems up to a twelve-year-old's level, the second up to a nine-year-old's. Now, are these children mentally the same? (p. 86)

Vygotsky's view is that learning precedes development and is what creates the zone of proximal development. This theory has led to the development of several divergent systems of dynamic assessment discussed in Chapter 9.

The process-oriented approach to assessment can be time-consuming, both in terms of assessment time and in time spent analyzing and interpreting the results. However, for the infant or very young child with physical impairments, it may be the only method available that is truly fair to the child. *Portfolio assessment,* which

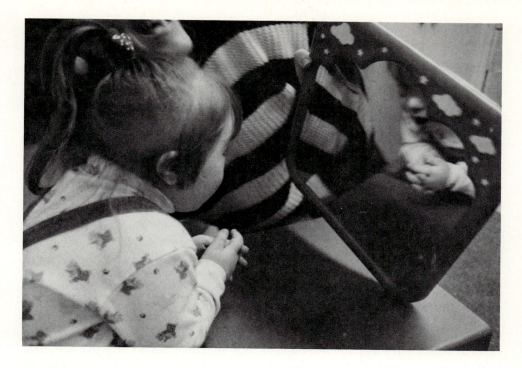

involves the compilation of samples of student work, offers another alternative approach. The student's progress over time across a variety of activities is the focus of assessment rather than single administration formal test scores.

CONSIDERATIONS FOR ASSESSING YOUNG CHILDREN

Assessment of infants, toddlers, and young children requires specific knowledge and skills. A knowledge of child development can prevent misinterpretation of behaviors and/or overemphasis on any one observation of a child. For example, a 6-month-old who routinely babbles may not utter a sound in an unfamiliar setting or while actively engaged in visual and motor tasks. An examiner might observe such behavior during the administration of the *Bayley Mental Development Scale,* resulting in no points earned for language skills, which the child, in reality, does possess. Parental reporting and naturalistic observation can provide a more accurate picture of the child's language abilities than performance during the test.

Four specific characteristics of young children that examiners should be sensitive to are activity level and distractibility, variable states and attention span, wariness of strangers, and inconsistent performance in unfamiliar environments (Bailey & Rouse, 1989). Because young children display these characteristics, examiners need to have the skills to deal with them. Effective infant and toddler assessment requires the following:

1. The ability to handle infants and display affection and enjoyment; appropriate communication skills
2. The ability to follow infant's cues for readiness to interact
3. The ability to maintain a comfortable balance between physical distance and physical closeness, and physical touch
4. The ability to establish rapport with the child's parents (Rogers, 1982)

Examiners of preschool-age children need these abilities as well.

SUMMARY

Theoretical perspectives influence our decisions about what and how to assess children. The most influential perspectives related to the assessment of young children with special needs are the developmental, cognitive stages, behavioral, and adaptive-transactive. These perspectives are evident in the wide array of techniques used in assessment. In this chapter these techniques were organized into seven continuous strands. The strands can be overlapped and used simultaneously to achieve the goal of ecologically valid assessments.

Best practices do not necessarily dictate that one method or perspective be adopted to the exclusion of all others. It is the responsibility of the examiner to be familiar with all of them and use them as tools that increase his effectiveness. The more tools an examiner has available to him, the better he can be in conducting accurate, meaningful assessments.

THE ECOLOGICAL PERSPECTIVE

- Assessment results based on more than one theoretical perspective are more useful than those restricted to a single perspective.
- The best technique to use for assessment is dependent on the purpose of the assessment.
- Comparison and analysis of assessment results across settings, sources of data, and techniques used are keys to obtaining meaningful results.
- Recommendations for action should synthesize all information and be context-specific.
- Examiner effectiveness is a crucial element of the behavioral setting in which assessments occur.

CHAPTER 4

Interpreting Assessment Results

Kathleen Warden
Tricia McClam

CHAPTER OUTLINE

QUESTIONS ANSWERED IN CHAPTER 4

- What does a score really mean?
- How can we compare an individual's score to other scores?
- Can we use a test score to predict behavior or future performance?
- How much confidence can we have in specific assessment instruments?
- How well do scores from one instrument correspond to those of another?
- How can we interpret observational data with confidence?
- What influences do test publishing companies exert on the use of assessment instruments?

CHAPTER OVERVIEW

Approximately 400 to 500 million standardized tests are given every year in the United States, almost enough to give 2 standardized tests per year to every man, woman, and child in the country (Strenio, 1981). Based on test scores, individuals are selected for jobs, admitted to schools and colleges, promoted, placed in special academic classes, and given a label such as "high achiever," "mentally retarded," or "average." Tests are potentially valuable tools in special education. Whether their value can be realized, however, depends largely on the skill of those who are selecting, administering, scoring, and interpreting tests. With over 400 companies in the testing industry today, there are many good tests available for purchase and use as well as many that do not fulfill their promise.

Children undergo more rapid changes in the early years than they will at any other time in their lives. Their performance can be highly variable from day to day, even hour to hour. Any assessment of a child is only a *sample* of that child's behavior, and any score on an assessment instrument is only an approximation rather than a precise indication of performance. Therefore, some criteria are necessary to decide how close we are to a true picture of child functioning. The purpose of this chapter is to describe the psychometric tools necessary to utilize assessment instruments effectively. Much of this chapter focuses on the statistical concepts used in normative assessment, such as levels of measurement, measures of central tendency and variability, and correlation. The chapter also covers the concepts of validity, reliability, derived scores, and discussion of observational data. The final section relates to the influence the testing industry exerts over assessment practices by the field.

STATISTICAL CONCEPTS USED
IN NORMATIVE ASSESSMENT

Statistics, the language that translates numerical facts into meaning, includes both techniques to describe data and techniques to test probability or chance. The focus of this section is on the use of *descriptive statistics* to give meaning to test scores.

This type of statistical analysis summarizes and describes data and includes *measures of central tendency, variability,* and *relationship* comparisons.

Levels of Measurement

Level of measurement is a basic concept in statistics involving the assignment of numerals according to rules. Levels of measurement enable the examiner to record observations in a structured manner. The level of measurement of the data in question dictates appropriate statistical procedures for data analysis. The four levels of measurement are *nominal, ordinal, interval,* and *ratio.* The nominal scale names variables by categorizing them. For example, if the data concern the gender of a group of participants, then male and female constitute the two categories. Events, people, or objects may be classified categorically. Hair color, political party, or disabilities are examples of nominal scale data. Nominal scale data may be subjected to only a limited number of statistical analyses. Its numbers are used to designate categories and are not appropriate for a comparison of magnitude. The second level of data is the ordinal scale. This scale both names and orders variables, representing a series of relationships. Characteristics of things or people, such as socioeconomic status or class rankings, may be expressed by an ordinal scale. Typically, ranks express comparisons such as "greater," "slower," or "more intelligent"; however, the difference between the ranks is not known. Ordinal data may be analyzed by using statistical procedures such as the Spearman Rank Order correlation formula, which is based on ranks.

The interval scale names, orders, and has equal intervals between the ranking points on any part of the scale. The distance between any two points is constant on such a scale. Temperature is an example of the interval scale: the difference between 20° and 40° is equal to the difference between 60° and 80°. This scale also has no real zero point. For example, a temperature of 0° indicates a temperature reading; it does not indicate an absence of temperature. Typically, test scores are measured on the interval scale. Suppose that Jane and John score 110 and 90, respectively, on an intelligence test. It is correct to state that John earned a "lower" score than Jane and that the difference between their scores is equal to the difference between the scores of Jane and Joe, who scored 130. Addition and subtraction as well as statistical procedures based on these arithmetical operations may be performed on interval data. Most data gathered for the purposes of assessing children with disabilities represent the ordinal or interval scale.

The final level of measurement is the ratio scale. Essentially it is the same as the interval scale, but with a true zero point. Height, weight, and other physical characteristics are examples of the ratio scale.

Frequency Distributions

The range and distribution of individual differences in mental and physical characteristics may be depicted by a *frequency distribution,* which provides a means for organizing data in a systematic fashion. A list of scores, usually from highest to

TABLE 4.1. Amount of Time per Week That 20 Children Are Read Aloud to by Parents

Minutes	Frequency
0–10	5
11–20	2
21–30	4
31–40	6
41–50	1
51–60	1
61–70	0
71–80	1

lowest or vice versa, with the frequency or number of times each score appears in the distribution is a frequency table. Table 4.1 provides a hypothetical example of a frequency distribution representing the amount of time per week that the parents of 20 children read to them. The amounts of time are listed in the left column and the frequencies in the right column. This is one of the simplest ways to summarize data.

Frequency distributions may also be represented graphically. For both nominally and ordinally scaled variables, the *bar graph* or *bar chart* is the graphic device.

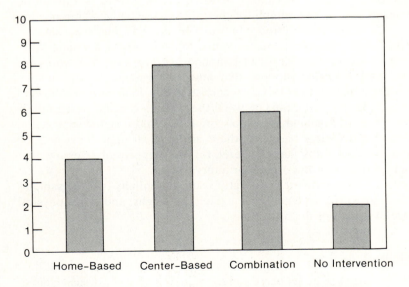

Figure 4.1. Preparation of 20 Handicapped Children for Kindergarten

A vertical or horizontal bar is drawn for each category in which the height (or length) of the bar represents the number of members in that category. No order is assumed for nominally scaled data, and bars are separated so there is no implication of continuity among categories. Figure 4.1 represents the results of a survey of parents of 20 special education kindergartners regarding their child's preparation for kindergarten. Four categories of preschool intervention were identified: home-based, center-based, a combination of home- and center-based, and no intervention. These nominally scaled data are displayed on a bar graph. Ordinally scaled variables are treated the same way except that categories are placed in their naturally occurring order. The hypothetical rank in family of 27 preschoolers who have siblings is displayed in Figure 4.2. Each child is identified as youngest, middle, or oldest. Because these data are ordinal, only the position or rank is known. There is no way of knowing the difference in ages of the siblings in one family. For both interval and ratio data the graphic device is the *frequency polygon,* which is easy to construct and very simple to interpret. Using the *x* and *y* axes, the midpoints of each interval are plotted and the dots connected with straight lines. Figure 4.3 visually presents the data from Table 4.1

A pattern of normal distribution is theorized for many frequency distributions. For example, if a frequency distribution of the height of all 3-year-olds were plotted

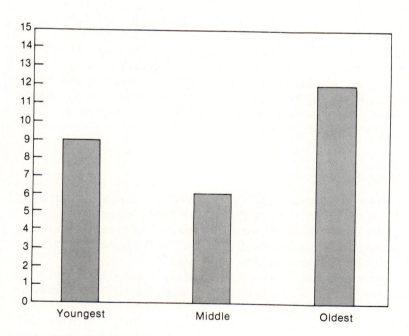

Figure 4.2. Rank in Family of 27 Children in a Kindergarten Class

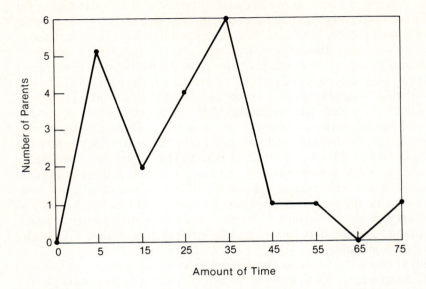

**Figure 4.3. Distribution of Amounts of Time 20 Children Are Read Aloud
to by Their Parents**

using horizontal and vertical axes, it would theoretically form the shape of a bell that encompasses 100% of the recorded heights (scores). In actuality, no such curve exists; however, the conceptualization provides a helpful mechanism to understand and compare assessment results. Theoretically, if a person studies enough subjects on any one trait, such as height or intelligent quotient (IQ), and then plots the results for that trait on a graph, the graph will resemble a bell-shaped or *normal* curve.

Measures of Central Tendency

There are three measures of central tendency which each give a single value that is most characteristic or typical of a set of scores. The most common and reliable measure of central tendency is the *mean,* the arithmetic average of a set of scores. It is calculated by totaling the scores and dividing the sum by the number of scores in the distribution. The mean is represented by the symbol $\bar{X}$.

There are two other measures of central tendency that are more representative for some distributions—the median and the mode. The *median,* the middle score in a distribution or the number representing a point in the middle, is more appropriate for distributions with extreme scores. The median is the value above which 50% of the cases fall and below which 50% fall in a distribution. The *mode* is the score that occurs most frequently in a distribution. On a normal curve it is the highest point on the curve.

In the theoretical normal distribution, the three measures of central tendency

Descriptive Statistics

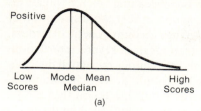
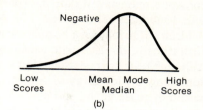

Figure 4.4. Positively and Negatively Skewed Distributions.
Source: Figure from *Reading Statistics and Research* by Schuyler W. Huck, William H. Cormier and William G. Bounds, Jr. Reprinted by permission of HarperCollins Publishers.

TABLE 4.2. Central Tendency Distribution of Number of Books Belonging to 4-Year-Olds in a Kindergarten Class

Child	Number
Craig	0
Jim	5
Tricia	5
Bob	5
Dana	5
Marianne	10
Charlotte	11
Wayne	20
Jack	25
Dawn	25

Mean = 111 ÷ 10 = 11.1.
Median = Between 5 and 10 or 7.5.
Mode = 5.

are identical and any one of them can be appropriately used as the measure of central tendency. In actuality, however, no distribution is perfectly normal. Figure 4.4 presents two *skewed* distributions. Notice that the mean in Figure 4.4(a) is pulled toward extreme positive scores, reflecting a positively skewed distribution. In Figure 4.4(b), the mean is pulled toward the negative scores, representing a negatively skewed distribution. Table 4.2 is a hypothetical distribution of 4-year-old children and the number of books they have in their rooms at home. The mean, median, and mode for the distribution are also provided. Parents wondering how many books should be available to their 4-year-old may not want to purchase the number of books indicated by calculating the arithmetic mean. The two children who have 25 books each are not at all typical in this hypothetical illustration. These are extreme scores that inflate the total so that the mean, 11.1 books, is too high to be representative of the distribution as a whole. In this particular case, the median of 7.5 books may a fairer indication of central tendency, but the mode (5 books) may be the most convenient.

Cautions in the Use of the Mean.   Measures of central tendency within a distribution are a mainstay of data interpretation that can be misleading when populations with disabilities are involved. For example, the assumption that the distribution of children's IQs follows a normal curve does not take into account genetic disorders, birth trauma, diseases, and accidents, all of which can result in severe retardation. Although tests are constructed to simulate a normal distribution, the actual distributions show a wide array of patterns. For example, distribution of IQ has an unexpected increase at the end of the curve. Three errors in interpretation that can be associated with the mean are use of mean scales, learning curves based on the mean performance of many subjects, and use of the mean of one group when the one group may be more properly divided into subgroups (Lewis & Wehren, 1982).

Consider a researcher observing six children as they are allowed into a play room, one child at a time. The researcher is noting the interest shown by each child for a toy that is in the room. Children's interest is rated on a five-point scale as "most interested" (5) to "not interested" (1). At the conclusion of the observations, half of the children were rated 5, the other half rated 1. The mean of their scores is 3.0. If only the mean is reported, it may be interpreted that all children showed average interest in the toy when, in fact, no child in the sample was rated at 3.0. A better way to present these data would be to report the percentage of subjects who obtained each rating. The mean score did not accurately reflect what actually happened in the study.

A second example of misuse of the mean is shown in the way a standard learning curve is often represented. The curve is based on the mean scores of many individuals and looks as if learning takes place as a gradual acquisition of information. If one inspects *individual* learning curves, however, it appears that learning takes place in an all-or-nothing manner, resulting in a sharply rising curve. Using mean data to construct a learning curve or as a basis for a model of learning results in a model that is at odds with actual individual learning curves.

The third example of misuse of the mean involves using the mean of one group when, in fact, the one group may be more properly divided into subgroups. To return to the example of "interest in the toy" study, consider the responses of 30 children, 2 to 3 years old, who enter a room. The questions of interest now are (1) if the child approaches the toy, how much time passes between entering the room and touching the toy; and (2) how long does the child play with the toy? The researcher does computations and reports mean approach time and mean playtime. A second researcher reanalyzes the data, finding that the children fall into 2 natural subgroups. Group A took a long time to approach the toy and then played with the toy a long time. Group B quickly approached the toy and played with it a short time. A single mean may not always adequately describe a group's behavior.

Use of the Mean in Reporting Scores of Children with Handicaps.   Normally developing children, given tests on motor skills and perception, by definition, will probably score within the normal range. A mean score for a normal child probably represents a fairly accurate picture of the child's functioning. In contrast, it is often the case that the skills of a special needs child may vary widely. For example, a child who has an orthopedic impairment may score below the norm on a test of motor skills, but within the normal range on a test of perception. If the scores for motor skills and perceptual skills are averaged and the mean reported, the child may appear below normal in both areas. In addition to the unrepresentativeness of the mean score, it fails to provide any specific information about the intervention strategies that should be developed (Lewis & Wehren, 1982).

Measures of Variability

Another index that describes a distribution is *variability.* Measures of variability are the *range, interquartile range,* the *variance,* and *standard deviation.* These can be used in conjunction with measures of central tendency to provide more information about a large number of scores. Variability means that scores differ from each other to some degree. If all children earned the same score on a test, and did so repeatedly, it would have no variability. A measure of variability indicates how spread out or scattered the scores are. Scores that are similar have little variability, and scores that are widely dispersed have greater variability.

The simplest measure of variability is the range, which is the difference between the highest and the lowest scores in a distribution. For example, a preschool teacher needs to know if the range of communication skills levels in her class is from a low of 2 years to a high of 4 years or 1 year to 5 years. Even though the mean of each distribution might be the same, obviously the second situation would require a greater diversification of activities than the first situation. It is important to keep in mind that the range is based on only two scores; it does not tell anything about the relationships of all the scores between the highest and lowest scores. This limitation is apparent in a distribution with age equivalents ranging from 2.5. to 4.5 where the second highest score may be only 3.6. Therefore, the range is considered a simple measure of variability.

The interquartile range (IR) is the measure of variability that is most often used when the median is the preferred measure of central tendency. It provides a means for measuring skewed distributions or describing distributions that include extreme scores. This range is based on quartiles of the distribution. Just as the median divides a distribution in half, quartiles divide a distribution into four equal parts. Using the formula $IR = Q_3 - Q_1$, the range of the middle 50% of cases is identified and called the interquartile range. Q_1 is the point below which 25% of the cases fall, and Q_3 is the point below which 75% of the cases fall. This type of variability is represented in Figure 4.5.

Two other measures of variability, the variance and the standard deviation, are more sophisticated measures. Standard deviation, an average of individual deviations from the mean, is the most representative measure of variability because it is not unduly influenced by extreme scores. To calculate the standard deviation of a distribution, the following formula is used:

$$S = \frac{\Sigma(X - \overline{X})^2}{n}$$

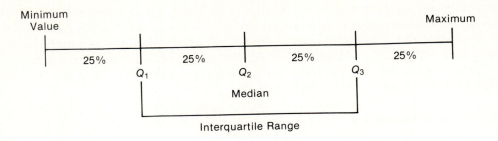

Figure 4.5. Interquartile Range

(where Σ stands for "sum," $(X - \overline{X})^2$ stands for the deviation of each score from the mean squared, and n stands for the number of cases in the distribution). Table 4.3 shows how the standard deviation is computed. The first step in the process is to calculate the mean of the distribution by adding the scores and dividing by the number of cases. The mean is then subtracted from each score resulting in a deviation score for each person. Each deviation score is squared, and a total is calculated. To find the average of the squared deviations, the total is divided by the number of cases and the resulting statistic is called the *variance* of the distribution. The square root of the variance is the standard deviation.

The normal curve helps explain the statistical concept of standard deviation (see Figure 4.6). The standard deviation lines are indicated by the Greek letter sigma (σ). These lines are always a standard distance from the mean ($\overline{X}$). In a normal distribution of scores, 34.13% of the scores will be plotted on the curve within 1 *SD* of the mean. This means that 34.13% of the scores fall within 1 *SD* to the right of the mean on the graph or 1 *SD* to the left of the mean.

Mathematical relationships exist among the variance, the standard deviation, and the range. The standard deviation is equal to the square root of the variance; thus, if the variance is 9 points, the standard deviation is 3 ($SD = \sqrt{9}$), and the range is usually 5 times the standard deviation, giving a range of 15 in this example (Huck, Cormier, & Bounds, 1974). If 1 *SD* of a distribution contained 34.13% of the scores, it would be a perfectly normal distribution.

Measures of Relationship

The measures of central tendency and variability that have been discussed provide information about only one variable. When dealing with the measurements of human traits, there are many situations where it is important to be able to answer questions such as the following:

- To what extent did those students who did well in one area also do well in another?
- How consistently does test A measure whatever it is measuring?
- What is the relationship between two different measures of a certain trait?

TABLE 4.3. Computation of the Standard Deviation for a Distribution of Activity Changes of Five Preschool-Age Children during a 20-Minute Play Period

Child	Play Period Activity Changes	Deviation from Mean	Squared Deviation
John	4	$4 - 6 = -2$	4
Anne	4	$4 - 6 = -2$	4
Ralph	6	$6 - 6 = 0$	0
Linda	7	$7 - 6 = 1$	1
Ken	9	$9 - 6 = 3$	9
	30		18

Mean = $30 \div 5 = 6$.
Variance = $18 \div 5 = 3.6$.
Standard Deviation = $3.6 = 1.89$.

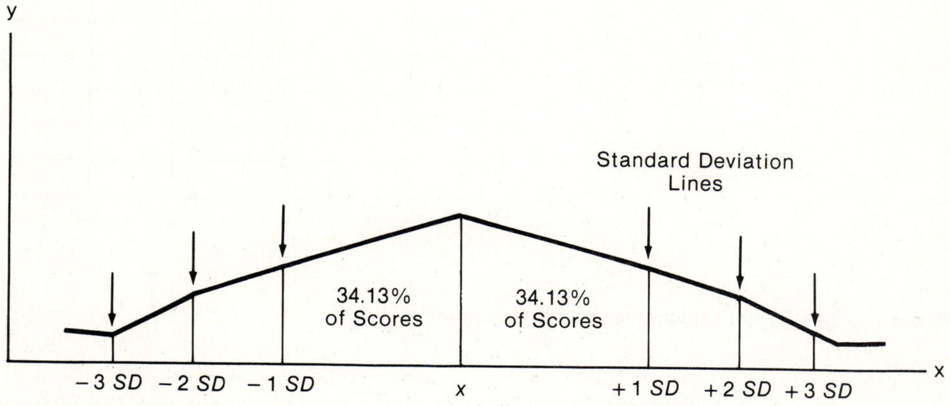

Figure 4.6. Normal Distribution with Mean and Standard Deviations

We may answer these questions by calculating a measure of relationship between two variables or sets of scores.

Correlation Coefficient.   The statistic that represents the degree of the relationship calculated is the *correlation coefficient* (r). Providing information about the strength and the direction of the relationship, the scatterplot or scatter diagram visually displays the relationship.

Direction.   The direction of a relationship is indicated by the use of a plus (+) or a minus (−) before the correlation coefficient. A positive relationship means that individuals who score high on one variable tend to score high on the other variable, and those scoring low on one, score low on the other. For example, the relationship between the time spent studying and the grade on a test should be positive, whereas amount of time spent watching television and the test grade is expected to be

Children	Test A	Test B
Bill	10	20
Kathleen	50	40
Marie	40	40
Wendell	30	20
Michelle	10	10

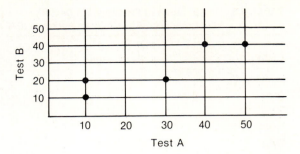

Figure 4.7. Scatterplot of Positive Relationship Scores

Children	Test X	Test Y
Susan	10	40
Chuck	20	50
Kathy	40	10
Larry	50	30
Roger	10	50

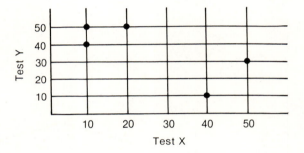

Figure 4.8. Scatterplot of Negative Relationship Scores

negative. Figure 4.7 illustrates the scatterplot of two sets of scores that have a positive relationship. Observe the relationship between the two scores for each individual.

A negative or inverse relationship means that individuals scoring low on one variable tend to score high on a second variable, and conversely, those scoring high on one tend to score low on the second variable. Consider the amount of gas in a car and the distance driven. The more miles traveled, the less gas there is in the car. This situation represents a negative relationship. The negative relationship between two sets of scores is visually displayed on the scatterplot in Figure 4.8.

Strength. The value of a correlation coefficient varies between +1.00 and −1.00. Both extremes represent perfect relationships. As the coefficient approaches zero (0.00), the relationship between the two variables becomes weaker. Coefficients between −.20 and +.20 are almost negligible. Those with strengths of ±.20 to ±.40 are considered small. Correlations of ±.40 to ±.70 are indicative of moderate relationships, and ±.70 to ±.90 are strong relationships. Those with correlations greater than ±.90 are very dependable relationships.

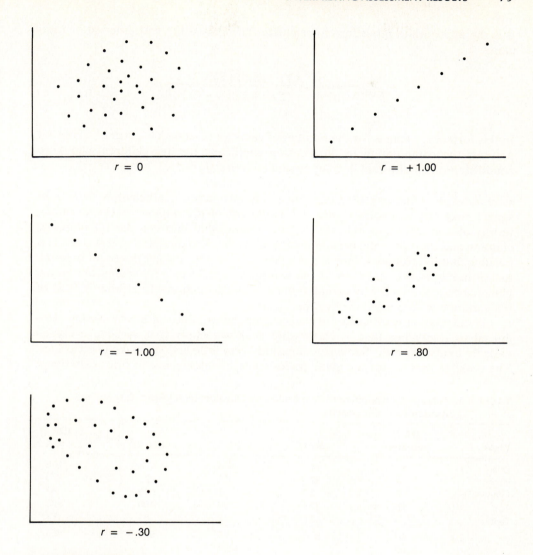

Figure 4.9. Scatterplots

The more nearly related two variables are, the closer the scatterplot resembles a straight line. Figure 4.9 illustrates the scatterplots of various relationships. Think about the direction and strength of each relationship as you examine the graphs. Scatterplots present a vivid but rough illustration of a relationship, and it is often necessary to refine the meaning of the correlation coefficient. Calculation of the correlation coefficient using a precise mathematical formula gives it more precision. There are several formulas that yield a correlation coefficient; however the Pearson Product Moment Correlation Coefficient is the one used most frequently.

It is the appropriate procedure to calculate the relationship with interval or ratio data.

$$r = \frac{n\Sigma XY - (\Sigma X)(\Sigma Y)}{\sqrt{[n\Sigma X^2 - (\Sigma X)^2][n\Sigma Y^2 - (\Sigma Y)^2]}}$$

In this formula, n stands for the number of cases and Σ stands for "sum." Table 4.4 presents the computation of the Pearson coefficient for five children who were administered two different developmental measures.

Interpretation. One way of interpreting the correlation coefficient is to find its square root (r^2) in order to find the *coefficient of determination*. For example, results of a study might indicate that the relationship between the IQ scores of children and their parental occupational level is .30. The direction of this statistic is positive, but its strength is low. If it is squared ($r^2 = .09$), the coefficient of determination indicates that only 9% of the variation in children's IQ scores can be explained or accounted for by variation in parental occupational level; that is, 91% of the variation is accounted for by other factors.

A correlation coefficient only represents the presence of a relationship. It is crucial to remember that a relationship does not imply that variable *a* caused variable *b* or vice versa. Some students study very little and yet make good grades. The possible reasons for the good grades could be intelligence or prior experience

TABLE 4.4. Pearson Computation of Five Children's Developmental Ages (DA) on Two Assessment Instruments

Child	DA 1 (months)	(DA 1)²	DA 2	(DA 2)²	(DA 1) × (DA 2)
Dick	12	144	14	196	168
Terry	18	324	15	225	270
Lynn	6	36	7	49	42
Tim	15	225	20	400	300
Betty	9	81	9	81	81
	60	810	65	951	861
	3600		4225		

$$\frac{5(861) - (60)(65)}{\sqrt{[5(810) - 3600][5(951) - 4225]}}$$

$$\frac{4305 - 3900}{\sqrt{(4050 - 3600)(4755 - 4225)}}$$

$$\frac{405}{\sqrt{(450)(530)}} = \frac{405}{\sqrt{238500}} = \frac{405}{\sqrt{488.36}} = .83$$

with the course content, not the time spent studying. Correlation is a necessary feature of causality, but it is not sufficient proof that a causal relationship exists.

Correlation procedures are valuable tools that have enabled the study of relationships in order to learn more about how people think and behave. They have also been necessary for the development of psychological tests to measure human traits. By analyzing these relationships, it is possible to explore the consistency of tests as well as what a test actually measures.

RELIABILITY OF AN INSTRUMENT

Individuals who use tests and test scores, including educators, examiners, or consumers, need a working knowledge of how tests are constructed and how they should be judged. Two primary considerations in constructing, selecting, administering, and interpreting tests are reliability and validity. Reliability assists in answering how consistently a test measures whatever it measures, and validity helps to establish that a test actually measures what it claims to measure. An instrument can be reliable without being valid, but must be reliable if it is to be valid. A useful analogy can be seen with the automobile. A car that cranks every morning, no matter what weather, is reliable. Until the driver steers it to the proper destination, a reliable car is of no use. Likewise, instruments that miss their destinations are not valid, even if a child earns the same score every time he takes it.

If a student takes the same test several times and the scores do not fluctuate unreasonably, then it is probable that the test used is reliable. Classical test theory assumes that a person's score has two components. The first component is the *true score,* a score that represents a person's real ability. The second is *measurement error,* the seemingly random way a score varies. Having the flu at the time of test administration may prevent a child from doing her best, illustrating random variance. That the child is ill is an unpredictable random event. Theoretically, if the tests were readministered after the child recovered, the score would change, due to measurement error, not a change in her ability. Measurement error is also called *error variance.* For each child's score, part of the score is true variance and part is error variance. Factors influencing error variance in one situation might be considered a part of true variance in another situation. For example, if it were important to know how a child functioned when ill, then the illness would be considered an influence in the true variance.

In addition to the physical health of the child, other sources of error variance, which are not accounted for in common estimates of reliability, are the motivation and stamina of the child. The examiner or scorer can also influence test scores by giving extra help, pointing out errors, and allowing additional time. Situation-induced factors such as ventilation, noise level, lighting, and overcrowding can also influence reliability.

It is only possible to estimate the amount of error any one score has. Two statistics, the *reliability coefficient* of the test and the *standard deviation* of the test, provide estimates of the amount of error associated with the test score and the individual's true score. The estimated reliability of a test as well as the method used to obtain the reliability coefficient should be reported in the manual. The coefficient itself is an indication of how comfortable individuals can be in accepting a score on a test. The lower the reliability coefficient for a particular test, the more caution is needed to be exercised in interpreting the scores. An arbitrary standard of a correlation coefficient of .70 or higher is accepted for individual student evaluation (Feldt & Brennan, 1989).

Types of Reliability

There are four methods used to establish reliability. The first, *test–retest reliability,* yields a stability coefficient that indicates the consistency of a test over time. It is determined by administering a test to the same group of individuals on two separate occasions and correlating the paired scores. Tests that are not subject to practice effect lend themselves to test–retest methods of establishing reliability. Periods of time between tests should be kept to a minimum to avoid allowing time for the development of new skills.

The best estimate of reliability of academic and psychological measures is *equivalent forms reliability.* Also known as alternate forms or parallel forms reliability, this method correlates the results of two equivalent forms of a test that are administered to the same individuals and reflects variation in performance from one set of items to another. The two forms of the test should contain the same number of items, which should be expressed in the same form, covering the same information. The most demanding and rigorous measure is the coefficient of stability and equivalence, which is obtained when the same subjects are tested with one form on the first occasion and with another form on the second occasion. This measure provides scores on two forms correlated over time.

Split-half reliability, also known as internal consistency reliability, is appropriate for long tests. It is obtained by administering the test to only one group. Items are divided into two comparable halves and a Spearman Brown correlation is calculated. This method of establishing reliability is particularly useful with long tests and when no other method seems feasible. A fourth method of establishing reliability is actually an estimate of split-half. Using a Kuder-Richardson formula, reliability is estimated by determining how all the items on a test relate to all other items and to the test as a whole. This method is appropriate when measuring only one trait.

Reliability coefficients are estimates of a test's dependability, and the examiner should evaluate this information carefully, especially when comparing two tests. To facilitate the evaluative process, the examiner must be aware of factors that influence the reliability estimate. Higher reliability coefficients are usually found with longer tests and with tests when reliability is established using groups that are more heterogeneous in ability. With test–retest reliability, shorter times between testings yield higher reliability coefficients. Finally, the type of reliability estimate used will produce coefficients that differ. For example, equivalent forms testing tends to result in a lower estimate than either test–retest or split-half approaches. A reliability of .90 based on equivalent forms is harder to achieve than .90 using test–retest methods.

Standard Error of Measurement

A reliability coefficient gives an estimate of the accuracy of a group of scores. The reliability coefficient also helps to determine the reliability of an individual score. Theoretically, if an individual takes the same test 100 times, the scores would fall within a normal distribution around the individual's true score. The true score would be the mean of the distribution and approximately 68% of the scores would be within ± 1 *SD* of the mean. This means that the chances are 2 to 1 that the score will vary ± 1 *SD* around the mean. If the mean score is 50 and the standard deviation is 5 points, then 68% of the time the individual's score will be between 45 and 55.

The *standard error of measurement* (SE_M) is the reliability of an individual score. It is an estimate of the amount of error that is part of an obtained score. The SE_M is not affected by the variability of the group scores. If the reliability coefficient of a test is known, it is possible to compute the SE_M. It is equal to the standard deviation of the test divided into the square root of 1 minus the reliability coefficient of the test. This procedure is represented by the following formula:

$$SE_M = \frac{\sqrt{1 - r}}{SD}$$

The reliability coefficient should be used to compare the reliability of different tests. To interpret individual scores, the SE_M is the appropriate measurement.

Because an individual's true score is not known, SE_M assists in determining the probability that the obtained score reflects the true score. *Confidence intervals* are ranges of scores where a high probability exists that the true score is included. For example, a 90% confidence interval represents the range in which an individual's true score will be found 90% of the time. The possibility that the true score is outside this range is 10 times in 100. The limits of a confidence interval are established by multiplying the Z score (see section, Standard Scores) associated with the confidence interval in question by the SE_M, which may be found in the test manual or calculated using the formula above. This figure is then added to and subtracted from the obtained score.

Confidence Interval = Obtained Score $\pm Z$ (SE_M)

The following are Z scores for five levels of confidence:

68% level, $Z = 1.00$
85% level, $Z = 1.44$
90% level, $Z = 1.65$
95% level, $Z = 1.96$
99% level, $Z = 2.58$

This information is sufficient to construct the confidence interval for an obtained IQ score of 90 on a test that has a standard error of measurement of 5. The upper limit of the 90% interval is calculated in the following manner:

$$\begin{aligned} \text{Confidence Interval} &= 90 + 1.65(5) \\ &= 90 + 8.25 \\ &= 98.25 \end{aligned}$$

The lower limit of the confidence interval is established by subtracting the same amount from the obtained score (90 − 8.25 = 81.75). The 90% confidence interval ranges from 81.75 to 98.25 and means that the chances the true score is within this range are 90 out of 100. The range at a 68% confidence level is 85 to 95. When an examiner reports an obtained test score, he should include the confidence intervals to reflect that the score represents a range of possible scores.

VALIDITY OF AN INSTRUMENT

Validity is the most important consideration in the construction and use of tests. Its importance is based on the need to determine exactly what a test measures in order for the examiner to know the meaning of a test score. Unless this information in known, it is possible for the examiner to make wrong assumptions about an individual's score, which may result in poor decisions and costly mistakes.

Validity is the extent to which a test measures what it claims to measure. The title of a test may not always accurately reflect the content of a test. Scores that tests produce can be misleading as well. For example, the original version of the *Peabody Picture Vocabulary Test* generated a mental age that could be converted to an IQ. The test actually measured receptive vocabulary, but many professionals interpreted it as a measure of intelligence simply because of the name of the derived score. The revised version of this test corrected this misnomer, and the score is now known simply as a standard score.

Establishing what a test measures is a long and complex process. In the past, defining what a test intended to measure and then collecting data to show how well it did the job were sufficient. This verification was accomplished by correlating scores on the test with a criterion measure obtained in a real situation. For example, a measure of shyness would be correlated with the number of peer interactions in a 30-minute period. Today, there is recognition that establishing the validity of a test is more than simply determining that it correlates with one criterion measure. Rather it is important to assess the actual content of the test and to analyze correlations with a variety of criterion measures in order to answer what a test measures.

Types of Validity

There are several methods that are useful in establishing validity. *Face validity* is the least important type of validity and can be claimed by almost any test. It simply means that the test items appear to measure what the test says it measures. Certainly the examiner should be cautious in using tests with just face validity. The other three types of validity are more rigorous and deserve the examiner's attention.

Content validity involves the subjective analysis of test content. It is concerned with how well the items on a test represent the universe of items that could be covered in that particular domain. Usually test content is drawn from what children are expected to do or learn by a certain age. Sources to evaluate the universe of items are textbooks, child development experts, previously established tests, theories of child development (e.g., Piagetian-based tasks), and developmental scales.

The third type of validity, *criterion-related validity,* is established by comparing test scores with an external variable that is a direct measure of the characteristic or behavior that the test claims to measure. The use of a related external criterion for this purpose distinguishes this type of validity from construct validity, which is concerned with the validity of the theory upon which the test is developed. There are two types of criterion-related validity: concurrent and predictive. *Concurrent validity* procedures are used to investigate the relationship between test scores and measures of some related criterion that is obtained at the same time. This type of validity is useful for instruments that are designed to assess an individual's present status. For example, the correlation between scores on a self-concept scale with teacher ratings of peer interactions should be high. *Predictive validity* refers to the extent to which a test can predict future performance and is expressed as the correlation between test scores and measures of an external criterion where there is a time interval between testing and performance on the related criterion. It is essential for predictive tests such as readiness tests.

Construct validity is concerned with the relationship between test scores and a theoretical construct or trait that underlies the test performance. Usually established for tests of intelligence and cognitive functioning, the three types of construct validity provide a check on the theory underlying the test. First, the nature of the trait or construct being measured is logically expected to be related to certain other measures. For example, new tests designed to measure intelligence are frequently correlated with earlier, well-established intelligence tests.

A second type of construct validity, convergent validity, is established when a test correlates highly with variables with which it should theoretically be related. For example, if the instrument in question purports to measure aggression, then it is reasonable to expect that the members of the defensive line of a football team would score highly on the test. Similarly, it is important to show that the test is not related to other variables with which it should not be correlated. This third type of construct validity is known as discriminant validity.

Factor analysis, a statistical procedure, is the fourth type of construct validity. Its purpose is to analyze the intercorrelations of a group of tests in order to determine the number of factors or clusters that suggest common traits. This procedure allows for the simplification of behavior descriptions by reducing multiple categories of variables to a few common factors or traits.

Assessing Validity

Validity coefficients are correlation coefficients that give information about the strength and direction of relationships between a test and other related tests or measures of relevant criteria. Validity coefficients are influenced by factors such as

the length of time between test administrations, the range of the trait being measured, and the examinees themselves. These statistics should not be automatically
accepted at face value. Factors to consider when evaluating the validity coefficient
include the size of the sample, existing group differences, and the nature of the
external criteria that are used to establish criterion-related validity. Many test manuals report multiple validity studies addressing various types of validity. Reports
from more than one type of validity study should be available. Tests are valid for
specific purposes; therefore, an important consideration in evaluating validity information is the use the examiner plans to make of the test. If the purpose is prediction, then predictive validity needs to be demonstrated. If achievement is the goal,
then content validity is important.

DERIVED SCORES

Performance on norm-referenced tests is interpreted by comparing one child's score
to scores based on the normative sample. The child's test performance is first
computed as a raw score. For example, a 24-month-old earns a raw score of 50
points on the Bayley Mental Development Index (MDI), and an 18-month-old
obtained 47 points. What these raw scores mean and how they relate to scores on
other tests are unknown until the scores are converted to standard scores. The
problem with interpretation of raw scores can be compared to the measurement of
liquids in pints, liters, and buckets. The numbers of pints, liters, and buckets are
analogous to raw scores. In order to compare these various measurements, they
must be converted to one standard of measurement. In a similar fashion, raw scores
are converted to a single standard of measurement, a derived score. Converting raw
scores to derived scores allows the examiner to make meaningful interpretations of
test results and to compare test results across tests and/or across children. The
derived scores used in norm-referenced testing are based on developmental levels
and produce standard scores, percentiles, and age and grade equivalents.

Standard Scores

Several types of standard scores are in use today, including z scores, T scores, and
deviation IQs. A standard score is expressed in terms of the score's distance from
the mean of a normal distribution. Derived standard scores, which are expressed as
z scores, have a mean of zero and a standard deviation of 1. Since the total
distribution of most groups extends no more than 3 SD above or below the mean, z
scores are reported to one decimal point to increase distinctions among scores.
Because z scores are reported in plus or minus standard deviations and decimals,
the numbers can become confusing and they are more difficult to use in statistical
formulas. An alternative standard score is the T score. A T score is based on a
normal distribution with a mean of 50 and a standard deviation of 10. The third
standard score is the *deviation IQ,* which is based on a normal distribution with a
mean of 100 and a standard deviation of 15 or 16 points. Both the *Wechsler Preschool and Primary Scale of Intelligence-Revised* (WPPSI-R) and the Bayley (MDI)

use the deviation IQ. The WPPSI-R however, has a standard deviation of 15, whereas the Bayley uses a standard deviation of 16. Figure 4.10 contains formulas for computing various standard scores. Figure 4.11 illustrates the relationship of the normal curve to various types of standard scores.

Percentiles

Percentile ranks are standard scores of relative standing that indicate a person's position as compared with the standardization sample. A percentile rank represents the point at or below which the scores of a designated percentage of individuals fall. For example, if a person answered 30 problems correctly on a math test and 70% of the persons in the standardization sample answered fewer than 30 problems correctly, then a raw score of 30 would represent the 70th percentile. The 50th percentile corresponds to the median. Those who score above the 50th percentile scored above average on that test. Those who score below the 50th percentile scored below average. Percentiles are not the same as percentages. Percentages are based on the number of correct responses divided by the total number of items (i.e., 9 out of 10 correct is 90%) on a test. Percentiles represent the percent of children who achieve at or above specific scores. An example of a test that reports percentile scores is the *Miller Assessment for Preschoolers*.

For simple reporting, percentile scores are straightforward. If an individual

Score	Formula	Mean	Standard Deviation
z-score	$z = \dfrac{X - \bar{X}}{s}$	0.0	1.00
	X = raw score of specific child		
	$\bar{X}$ = sample raw score mean		
	s = standard deviation of sample		
T-score	$T = 10z + 50$	50	10
Deviation IQ	$D\ IQ = 15z + 100$	100	15

Figure 4.10. Computing Three Standard Scores

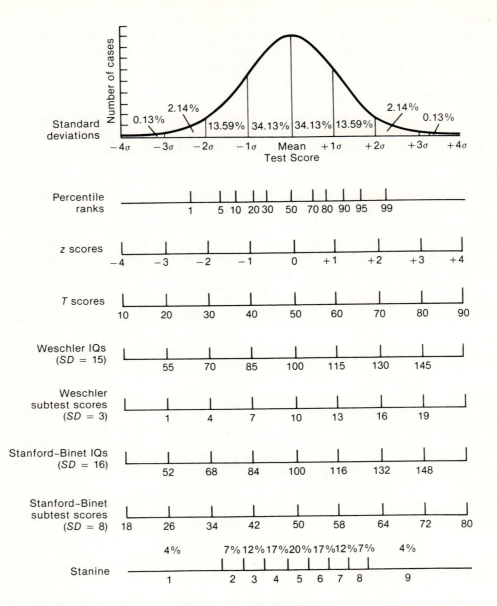

Figure 4.11. Relationship of Standard Scores to Normal Curve.
Source: J. M. Sattler (1988). *Assessment of Children* (3rd ed.), p. 17. San Diego: Jerome M. Sattler.

scores in the 75th percentile, that individual scored as well as 75% of the normative sample. Percentiles do have a drawback, however. Points along the percentile distribution do not represent equal units. (See "percentile ranks" in Figure 4.11.) Near the mean of the distribution, percentile points are closer together than they are at the outer edges of the distribution. Therefore, performing statistical tests on percentile scores requires the conversion of percentile scores to another standard score.

Age and Grade Equivalents

Age-equivalent scores are derived scores based on the average performance of a certain age group. For example, on the Bayley scales, a child who is 24 months old with a raw score of 103 earns a developmental age of 12 months. Similar in concept to age-equivalent scores are *grade-equivalent scores*. Expressed in grades and tenths of grades, these scores represent a level of performance similar to the level of average performance of children at a specific grade level. Sometimes a child performs unlike any children who were in the norm. In such cases the scores must be projected mathematically through interpolation or extrapolation. Interpolated scores are scores that fall within the performance range of the norm group tested, but at a precise point where there were no specific individuals represented in the norm group. However, a child might earn a grade equivalent of 3.0 when, in fact, no child in the norm group was above the second grade. Extrapolated scores are scores falling outside the performance range (higher or lower) of the norm group.

Examiners need to keep in mind cautions related to the interpretation of age- and/or grade-equivalent scores (Anastasi, 1982; Petersen, Kolen, & Hoover, 1989; Sattler, 1988; Salvia & Ysseldyke, 1978). These cautions are presented as follows:

1. The distance between a 1-year-old and a 2-year-old age score is not equivalent to the difference between a 7-year-old and an 8-year-old age score. The developmental difference is 1 year in each case, but does not reflect equal distance.
2. Scores obtained by interpolation or extrapolation are questionable. If an age-equivalent score of 6 months is obtained for a 7-year-old and the norm group did not have any 7-year-olds who fell below an age equivalent of 5 years 3 months, then the score has been extrapolated. That is, no 7-year-old child in the norm group was *actually* tested who functioned as a 6-month-old.
3. Developmental scores encourage us to think that an average 12-year-old or average 5-year-old will perform a certain way. In fact, the average 5-year-old or average 12-year-old does not exist. Averages are created from children who represent a range of performances.
4. Grade-equivalent scores do not mean that a child is functioning at that particular grade level. For example, a fourth grader who has scored at the grade equivalent of 6.0 in reading is not necessarily functioning as a sixth grader. The fourth-grade student shares with the average sixth grader the number of items right on a specific reading test—not all other attributes associated with sixth-grade reading skills.
5. The age equivalents on test A may not be the same as the age equivalents on test B. For example, test A and test B may have items in common, but the items are at different age levels.
6. Grade equivalents assume that curricula are standard throughout school systems. Local variation of curricula influences grade-equivalent scores.

Grade equivalents do not necessarily indicate where a child should be placed in a particular local school organization.

7. Grade equivalents assume that a child's growth throughout a school year or years is constant and linear. In actuality, development follows a sporadic pattern with spurts and plateaus, varying across developmental domains.

8. Small differences in performance on a test between student A and student B may result in one student obtaining a grade equivalent of a year above or below the other student. It is possible, for example, that a raw score on a reading test of 120 will yield a grade equivalent of fourth-grade reading level, whereas a raw score of 110 on the same test will yield a grade equivalent of a third-grade reading level.

9. Age- and grade-equivalent scores are based on ordinal scales. Data from ordinal scales do not permit statistical analysis, such as standard error of measurement.

OBSERVATIONAL DATA

Ecologically valid assessment includes observations of how a child interacts with other people and her environment across many behavioral settings. Observation is considered an objective method of assessment (Taylor, 1989) because samples of overt behavior are thought to "reduce the inferential leap in generalizing from test to nontest performance characteristic of indirect assessment methods" (Kazdin, 1982, p. 5). Yet, direct observational processes may affect observational data. Observations may cause various types of reactivity to occur; as discussed in the following section. In collecting and using observational data, it is critical that data be collected in a systematic and meaningful way and that the data constitute a *representative sample* of the behavior of interest.

Reactivity

Direct observations are often obtrusive; that is, the person or persons being observed are aware of the observation. Obtrusive observation may be *reactive,* which means that the subject's behavior is influenced by knowing that she is being observed. Obtrusive measures are not always reactive, but until an observer knows whether or not reactivity is occurring, the validity of the observational data is in question. The purpose of this section is to describe types of reactivity and the variables that contribute to it. In addition, interpretation of observational data is discussed in terms of validity and reliability.

Types of Reactivity.   There are three types of reactivity relevant to the observation of young children with disabilities (Kazdin, 1982). Type 1 is described as *observing others thereby changing others.* For example, a child has been described to an evaluator as overly aggressive during play situations. After operationalizing the term *overly aggressive* (i.e., identifying exactly what behaviors—e.g., hitting and yelling—are to be counted as overly aggressive), the observer enters the playroom to observe the child who realizes he is being watched. He also remembers that he has been reprimanded for yelling. Because an adult is present, the frequency of his yelling behavior decreases. In essence, the observed "aggressive behaviors" do not provide a respresentative sample of his actual play behavior.

Type 2 reactivity is *observing oneself and changing oneself.* For example, Jennifer, a kindergarten teacher, has been asked to count the number of times she corrects her preschoolers' behavior during the first 15 minutes of class time. "Offering correction" is operationalized (i.e., all requests to stop a behavior are considered a correction), and the teacher keeps a record. It is possible, and even likely, that the teacher may reduce the number of times she corrects her students because correcting students may be seen as a negative strategy by others and Jennifer does not want to be viewed negatively. It is almost impossible to maintain the frequency with which something is done when it is self-observed. Becoming conscious of one's behavior alters that behavior.

Type 3 reactivity is *being observed and changing oneself.* Type 3 alters behavior in the same way type 2 (observing oneself and changing oneself) does, only the observer is another person. For example, if a teacher is being observed by his supervisor, the teacher is likely to be more patient with his students than he would be ordinarily, so that his supervisor will note this positive quality on the teacher's evaluation. Type 1 and type 3 reactivity can be reduced or eliminated if others do not know they are being observed (type 1) or if one does not know he is being observed (type 3). Observing behavior without having it known is often difficult because of the architecture of most settings. Rarely are one-way mirrors built into a naturalistic setting such as a home or playground. Some clinical and school settings may have rooms built for observations, but placing a child in an unfamiliar setting and hoping he will "act naturally" is of questionable validity.

Variables That Contribute to Reactivity.   There are two types of variables that contribute to reactivity (Kazdin, 1982). They are valence, or the social value associated with a specific behavior, and how the characteristics of the subjects and observers interact. The *valence* of a specific behavior may affect the frequency of that behavior. If a behavior is viewed as positive, such as the offering of praise to a child, there is a likelihood that the frequency of a positive valence behavior will increase when a person is being observed. On the other hand, a behavior with a negative valence will decrease in frequency when a person is being observed.

Characteristics of subjects and observers also contribute to reactivity. For example, a female observer is charting the aggressive behavior of a boy and a girl. The behavior has been operationally defined, a time limit set for the observation to begin and end, and the observation is unobtrusive. Theoretically, because of the operational definition, a male child and a female child exhibiting exactly the same behaviors should have identical behavior charts. The charts, however, may not be identical because the observer *perceives* male children to be more aggressive in general, transfers this unconscious perception to the child being observed, and charts behavior that *approaches* the operational definition of aggression. In contrast, the same observer charts only those behaviors exhibited by the female that are defined as aggressive. Similar perceived biases may affect interracial observations, observations across socioeconomic level, among religious or cultural sects, and so on.

One variable of particular import to children with disabilities is the history that they bring with them to any assessment situation. Children with disabilities often have experienced much prodding and poking by professionals and as a result may develop an automatic aversion to any situation that smacks of evaluation, including being observed.

Reliability

Before assessing the reliability of observational data, the quality of the data needs to be examined (Hartmann, 1982). First, were the data gathered in such a way as to be able *to answer the assessment question?* For example, were the observers trained prior to the observations and how is their level of expertise described? Was the coding system used *relevant* to the assessment? For example, coding "staring into space" as off-task behavior may not be appropriate. "Staring into space" could be the behavior a specific child exhibits when thinking about the task at hand. Were behaviors coded at appropriate *times?* That is, if the examiner wants to know how a child functions socially at the beginning of the day, then data collected after lunch are not helpful. Finally, note the *settings* in which data were collected. Observations made and charted while a child is in school may not reflect the way a child behaves at home.

After the quality of data is established, procedures for assessing the reliability of the data may be carried out. Two important forms of reliability for observational data are *observer agreement* and *intra- and interobserver reliability.* One observer watching a situation two or more times (e.g., viewing a videotape several times) who charts the frequency of behavior the same way in all instances is said to have reached *intraobserver agreement.* Two or more observers simultaneously watching the same situation who independently chart the frequency of behavior the same way are said to have reached *interobserver agreement.* Interobserver reliability is reached when two or more observers chart behaviors independently over two or more observation sessions and are in agreement from the first session to the last session. It is possible to have interrater agreement on session A and interrater agreement on session B, without reliability. For example, during the first observation of a 3-year-old child, both observers coded the three categories of behavior: attention seeking, aggression, and anger. During the second observation, the child behaves in exactly the same manner, however, both observers code the behaviors as initiating social interaction, on-task behavior, and regard for self. Although the observers agreed in both instances, they were inconsistent in their interpretation of child behavior.

Estimates of Interobserver Reliability.   Interobserver reliability estimates involve the comparison of scores of two or more observers on one or more observation sessions. The data may be nominal or interval scale ratings. For example, observers may code numbers of aggressive or withdrawn behaviors (nominal scale ratings) or *degree* of aggressive behavior (zero = no aggression to four = very aggressive). When coding degree of behavior, the observer is using an interval scale rating.

Generally, reliability estimates are calculated using correlation coefficients or percentage agreement indices.

Correlation Coefficients. If the data are interval scale ratings and patterns of agreement between or among observers are desired, a product-moment correlation may be used. The product-moment correlation will determine if the observers' measures are linearly related; that is, over time do the observational *patterns* match (e.g., observer A charts a high-low-high pattern and observer B charts a high-low-high pattern)? An intraclass correlation coefficient is used on interval scale data when pattern of agreement and level of agreement are to be measured. "The intraclass correlation coefficient takes into account the extent to which all observers mean exactly the same thing by their judgments" (Sattler, 1988, p. 511).

Percentage Agreement Indices. The kappa statistic (κ) may be used with nominal scale data when correcting estimates for chance agreements. Kappa is used for multiple observers recording multiple categories. The kappa statistic is the "proportion of joint judgments in which there is agreement, after chance agreement is excluded" (Cohen, 1960, p. 46). Kappa's upper limit is 1.00 and the lower limit is between 0 and -1.00. The kappa is a measure of precision, not a measure of validity.

Often an uncorrected percentage agreement is used when it is not important to correct for chance agreements. Uncorrected percentage agreement, usually referred to simply as percentage agreement, is just the percentage of agreement of two or more observers. The most often used percentage agreement methods with interval recording are overall agreement, agreement on the occurrence of the behavior, and agreement on the nonoccurrence of the behavior.

If target behaviors are sampled in more than one setting and on more than one occasion, then test–retest reliability methods will yield a measure of the consistency of behavior across time and settings. To determine an estimate of the internal consistency of an observational instrument, the split-half reliability method is appropriate. An estimate of the consistency on an observational instrument in measuring the same trait or characteristic is the result of a split-half reliability computation.

Validity

Validity, as it applies to direct observational assessment, is a complex issue. It can be argued, however, that direct observational procedures are obviously valid if they measure what they are supposed to measure, that is, if the behavior of interest has been observed, charted, and the data have been subjected to interobserver reliability estimates. It can also be argued that because observations are direct and have not been processed through the filter of a paper–pencil test or a projective test, that validity can be assumed. This assumption is incorrect.

Suppose a child's inappropriate use of toys in a specific setting has been charted. The data included in the report may be accurate, but the validity of the data has not been addressed until there is agreement about how inappropriate use of toys has been operationally defined. The observer(s) of the child has operationally defined "banging on the table" as inappropriate use of toys and, as a result, has charted and reported an accurate count of the child's inappropriate use of toys. The validity question is this: Does "banging on the table" constitute inappropriate use of toys? It is possible that a child is trying to separate two toys stuck together. If the behavior under study is operationally defined in a way that cannot be justified to your satisfaction, the validity of the observational data is in question.

Types of Validity.   Validity is always a matter of degree. Tests and observational instruments "are never valid in isolation from the social system in which they are used" (Sattler, 1988, p. 30). Content, construct, and criterion-related validity are all relevant for observational data.

Content Validity.   Content validity can flow in two directions: from constructs to specific behaviors or from specific behaviors to constructs. Constructs provide the label used to characterize a group of behaviors, such as withdrawn behavior or hyperactive behavior. Instruments based on data from direct observation have some degree of content validity if the theory or construct (withdrawn behavior, for example) is represented by behaviors included on the instrument implied in or listed under a specific theory. To establish content validity (from construct to behaviors), an instrument is judged by persons expert in the theory as to its validity.

The other direction of flow is from a set of behaviors to creation of a construct. For example, a teacher may request that the troublesome behaviors of a particular child be charted and a frequency count recorded. The group of troublesome behaviors may not have a label as yet. The content validity is still an issue even though there is, as of yet, no specific label for this set of behaviors. To establish content validity for an unlabeled set of behaviors, the observational instrument is judged by persons to whom the behavior is important (e.g., teachers, parents, and researchers). Thus content validity may be judged in two ways: (1) if an observational instrument is derived from a theoretical construct, experts in the theory judge content validity; (2) if an observational instrument is derived from a group of behaviors of interest, persons to whom the behavior is important judge content validity (Cone, 1982).

Construct Validity.   Construct validity refers to the extent to which an instrument designed to record behaviors relates to a psychological trait. To establish construct validity for direct observational assessment systems, methods used to establish construct validity for other methods of assessment are appropriate. The observation system must be shown to have both *convergent* and *discriminant validity.*

Criterion-Related Validity.   There are two ways to establish the criterion-related validity of an observational instrument. The first way is to show that a correlation exists between the instrument in question and an instrument that has already been shown to have criterion-related validity. The second way is for the creators of the instrument to validate their categories against the judgment of people in the situation where the behaviors occur (e.g., parents, teachers, and classmates). A simple method might be for an observer to chart a child's aggressive behavior (if this is the behavior of interest) over several days and compare the observer's frequency count with the teacher's rating of how aggressive or nonaggressive a student was at particular times on particular days. If observer's and teacher's ratings agree, then the instrument can be said to have criterion-related validity for that specific teacher (Cone, 1982).

THE TESTING INDUSTRY

One of the purposes of this book is to emphasize that assessment of any type is a socially embedded activity. Assessment is not a neutral activity, producing pure facts about a person's abilities or traits. Rather, it is influenced and changed by the people doing the assessment, by the people being assessed, and by the social context in which these individuals operate. Another influence on assessment is the testing industry itself, which is affected by the politics of American education. Political decisions even influence the creation of knowledge because much research in America is funded through the government or private foundations. The policies of the funding agencies dictate who gets research funds, thereby influencing the creation of knowledge. Research scholars, in turn, have a major influence on state and federal government educational policies, and these policies influence funding decisions. And so the cycle continues.

Test publishing companies are sensitive to the market place just as any industry is, aiming to produce tests what will be bought and used. Many school districts rely on standardized tests to make decisions about students' educational futures. Since standardized tests carry great weight in American culture and are often used as measures of teacher effectiveness, teachers, their supervisors, and school boards will adjust curricula accordingly. "In other words, teachers are very likely to shape their instruction to match a test's specific focus" (Meisels, 1989, p. 17).

Overall the testing industry is one of the participants in what Spring (1988) sees as monolithic conflicts of interest in American education. He distinguishes *external conflict,* which "refers to struggles between individuals and groups outside the administrative structure of education" (p. 23), and *internal conflict,* which "occurs primarily over power and money and involves teachers, administrators and the knowledge industry" (p. 23). Spring goes on to describe conflicts of interest that result from the political power struggles associated with education. Educators permit the industry to "transform testing programs, ideally servants of educational programs, into masters of the educational process" (Meisels, 1989, p. 17).

Ecologically valid assessment for young children with disabilities often has as its goals deciding on appropriate educational objectives and appropriate teaching strategies. If instruction is "measurement-driven" (Madaus, 1988), then educational objectives, teaching strategies, and placement will be affected. For example, young children may have deficits in adaptive and social and emotional behavior; hence educational objectives for these children *should* include educational objectives directed at social and emotional development. Since social and emotional development does not lend itself to mass assessment techniques, it is possible that such a component may receive short shrift in a curriculum that is determined by the publishers of assessment instruments.

Ideally, individual needs of students are the prime determinants of teaching strategies. However, if testing policies constrain interventionists in their decision making, the implication is that they will proceed in a lock-step fashion in order to prepare their children to take tests. It is difficult to assess precisely the impact that the testing industry has on education, but few would argue that there is no impact at all. If the testing industry can have a negative impact on children, then it is an educator's professional obligation to be aware of that impact and to reduce or eliminate, if possible, anything that lessens the probability that children will reach their highest potential.

SUMMARY

This chapter introduced the psychometric tools necessary to utilize assessment instruments effectively. Descriptive statistics summarize and describe raw data and allow for the comparison of test scores. Foundations of descriptive statistics include levels of measurement and the normal or bell-shaped distributions. Measures of central tendency are the mean, median, and mode. Measures of variability are the range, the interquartile range, the variance, and the standard deviation.

Measures of relationship allow the comparison of two variables or groups of scores. A correlation coefficient is the statistic that describes the relationship among or between variables. It expresses the degree of the relationship, providing information about the strength and direction of the relationship. However a relationship does *not* imply cause and effect.

Two primary considerations in constructing, selecting, administering, and interpreting tests are reliability and validity. Reliability assists in answering how consistently a test measures whatever it measures. The standard error of measurement is the reliability of an individual score, that is, an estimate of the amount of error that is part of one's obtained score. Validity is the extent to which a test measures what it claims to measure. An important consideration in evaluating validity information is the use the examiner plans to make of the test.

In order to interpret and/or compare test results, raw scores are converted to derived scores. Derived scores may be standard scores, percentiles, age and grade equivalents, or Deviation IQs. Examiners need to heed cautions related to the interpretation of age- and/or grade-equivalent scores.

The reliability of observational data may be indicated by observer agreement and inter- and intraobserver reliability. Validity as it applies to direct observational assessment is a complex issue. Some argue that if observation is direct then validity of the data can be assumed. The authors suggest this type of validity is confused with accuracy. Validity of observational data rests in part on the operational definition of specific behaviors.

Finally, assessment is not a neutral activity, producing pure facts about a person's abilities or traits. Assessment is a socially embedded activity influenced by the testing industry.

THE ECOLOGICAL PERSPECTIVE

- An assessment of a child is only a *sample* of that child's behavior.
- Decisions about a child or groups of children should never be based solely on a test score.
- There is no average child who represents a diagnostic group; therefore intervention should be planned as a result of individual profiles.
- Assessment is influenced by the people doing the assessment, by the people being assessed, and by the social context in which these individuals operate.
- The testing industry influences what tests are created and how they are given.

PART TWO

The Child in the Context of Family and Environment

In this section of the text the focus is on the family and environmental concerns. Chapter 5 covers the identification of family strengths and needs, and the development of Individualized Family Service Plans. Interview techniques, needs scales, resources and strengths scales, and questionnaires for parents are useful data gathering procedures. However, they must be used with great caution—with an overriding consideration of family privacy. No child should ever be denied services because his parents refused to cooperate in this process. Additionally, identification of family strengths and needs should not be conducted in conjunction with early intervention programs until the program is prepared to incorporate that information into the child's programming and/or assist families in striving to reach family-oriented outcome statements. When an early childhood special educator gathers data about the family, looks it over and then comments, "I'm not sure what I am supposed to do with this information. It won't really change anything I am doing with the child, but I'll keep it in the file in case anyone asks about family assessments," the family has been done a disservice. Data should not be gathered until the examiner has a clear purpose in mind and intends to use it. When families of young children provide information about family strengths and needs, they anticipate that the information will be put to some use for their benefit. When no such benefits are forthcoming, they may become disenchanted with the program and its staff. It is better for a program to delay gathering this type of information until its usefulness is apparent than to have subjected the parents to unjustified anticipation and intrusion of privacy.

The significance of environmental influence on child behavior is most evident in relation to the home environment. Chapter 6 addresses the home environment, including both physical and nonphysical features. Physical features of a child's home environment, such as number of rooms in relation to number of persons living in the home, plumbing and cooking facilities, and number of books in the house, have an impact on a child's development as do nonphysical features, such as parent–child interactions, parental belief systems, parental knowledge of child development, and the social climate of the home. As interventionists begin to determine family strengths and needs, an analysis of the home environment can lead to practical suggestions for the parents that will enable them to meet the needs of their child better. The intertwining of children and their families is described well by Minuchin (1974):

> The individual influences his context and is influenced by it in constantly recurring sequences of interaction. The individual who lives within a family is a member of a social system to which he must adapt. His actions are governed by the characteristics of the system and these characteristics include the effects of his own past actions. The individual responds to stresses in other parts of the system to which he adapts; and he may contribute significantly to stressing other members of the system. The individual can be approached as a subsystem, or part of the system, but the whole must be taken into account. (p. 9)

The final chapter in Part Two, which is contributed by Nordquist and Twardosz, focuses on the analysis of the environment. They discuss the influence the environment can have on child functioning and describe a procedure for problem solving through environmental analysis. Assessment of the environment as one more isolated component in a child assessment does provide useful information, but it lacks the depth of interactive environmental analysis. The environmental analysis conducted in relation to specific children and their responsivity to the environment is more likely to be of significant benefit. This notion returns us to the concept of ecological congruence, so critical to effective early intervention.

CHAPTER 5

A Family-Focused Approach to Assessment

CHAPTER OUTLINE

QUESTIONS ANSWERED IN CHAPTER 5

- What is the rationale for family-focused intervention and assessment?
- What does the Individualized Family Service Plan process involve?
- What components are involved in identifying family strengths and needs?
- What techniques can we use to identify family strengths and needs?
- What are some models for the identification of family-oriented strengths and needs?

CHAPTER OVERVIEW

Assessment procedures used with young children with disabilities should reflect the best practices implemented in intervention programs. Research on the effectiveness of early intervention has consistently led to results that document the importance of environmental influences on child development. Many programs that restricted their efforts to the children and failed to address the needs of the family or conditions present in the home have proved to be of limited value. The shift in programming from child-focused to family-focused intervention is evident in the federally funded Head Start program. The importance of using a family-focused intervention strategy is stressed in PL 99–457. Since programming and intervention are shifting from a child-focused to a family-focused model, then it follows that a system to identify family strengths and needs as related to enhancing child development must become a part of our data gathering.

The child is a part of a family system. There are three implications of viewing the child within a systems context:

1. Intervention with a child is likely to affect the family—effects may be helpful or stressful; family assessment can help professionals gain insight into potential family reactions.
2. Interventions with one family member may have subsequent effects on others in the family—effects may be helpful or stressful; family assessment will help predict the influence of such interventions on others.
3. Families must interact with the larger community—assessment clarifies how families view children and the services provided for them, and how families view and interact with service systems. (Bailey, 1988, p. 3)

The techniques used should identify, build on, and reinforce potential family strengths and resources, leading to enablement and empowerment of families (Dunst, Trivette, & Deal, 1988). The concepts of *enablement* and *empowerment* as used by Dunst et al. include three assertions. First is the assertion that people are competent or have the capacity to become competent. Second, a failure to demonstrate competence is not an indicator of deficits within a person, rather lack of opportunity to display competence. *Enabling experiences* are those that create the opportunities for competence to be displayed. The third and final assertion is that it is crucial that the help-seeker feel a sense of responsibility for any behavior change that leads to improved management of family affairs. When a person has achieved this sense of control, he or she is *empowered*. Early childhood special educators offer a greater influence by assisting parents in the management of their child's needs than by taking charge of the child's needs. For example, a 3-year-old needs an appointment with the eye doctor and the parents never seem to make the necessary arrangements. Finallly, the teacher schedules an appointment and takes the child and mother to the doctor. While the child's immediate needs are met, the long-term benefits are missing. When an eye examination is needed four years from now and the early childhood special educator is no longer a part of the child's life, who will take the child? Unless the parents have assumed the responsibility for their child's needs, those needs may go unmet.

INDIVIDUALIZED FAMILY SERVICE PLANS

With the enactment of PL 99–457 in October of 1986, a family-focused perspective was legally sanctioned through the establishment of required *Individualized Family Service Plans* (IFSPs) for the birth through 2-year-old population who receive services through Part H. The rules and regulations for PL 99–457 provide some guidance as to the content and steps in completion of the IFSP process without requiring that a set federal form be used. The regulations do include information about the content, participants, meetings, and timelines of the process.

Content

There are seven elements included in the IFSP process: (1) statement of the child's functioning; (2) statement of family strengths and needs; (3) statement of outcomes; (4) early intervention plans; (5) dates for services; (6) designated case managers; and (7) a transition plan.

Statement of Child's Functioning.   This first component addresses the present functioning level of the child across multiple domains. Although the emphasis is on the child, the assessments conducted to gather the information regarding the child can and should be done from an ecologically valid perspective. Ecologically valid assessment plans for the child need to be developed that will provide the material for this portion of the IFSP. Examiners should note information regarding the child's strengths as well as his limitations, including diagnostic and functional information.

Statement of Family Strengths and Needs.   A summary of the information obtained through the identification of family strengths and needs as related to the enhancement of child development is the second element of the IFSP. The obligation of any professional gathering data about a family is to identify the strengths as well as the needs. Simply telling a family with serious needs that they can "do it themselves" is not helpful and neither is taking over and doing everything for them. Drawing the careful balance between being helpful to the family and undermining the family's future ability to be functional by taking charge of family responsibilities is the goal.

Statement of Outcomes for the Child and Family.   Goals and objectives are typically behavioral in nature and are required in Individualized Education Plans (IEPs) developed for school-aged special education students. Such behavioral statements are not suitable when interventions are focused on family concerns nor are they required by PL 99–457. Section 677 (d) of the law stipulates that "outcomes expected to be achieved for the infant or toddler and the family" be a part of the IFSP. Outcomes, if they are designed with improved family functioning as a goal, should be written using the words of the family rather than in professional jargon. Outcomes are statements about "the changes family members want to see for their child and themselves" (Johnson, McGonigel, & Kaufmann, 1989, p. 41). Outcome statements should be functionally stated; representative of a family's priorities; accompanied by easily implementable activities that fit within routine family schedules; and focused toward the family's own strengths—their own resources and support networks (Dunst et al., 1988). The following list illustrates examples of appropriately stated family outcomes as contrasted with professionally stated objectives.

Family-Stated Outcomes	**Professionally Stated Goals**
We can work it out so that Beth can make it to the center every day.	Mother will awaken Beth by 7:15 A.M. in order to have her ready for the bus by 8:00 A.M. five out of five days a week.
We will find some way to keep Carl in therapy after the insurance runs out next month.	Parents will file Supplemental Security Income and Medicaid applications within the next week.
The teachers at the preschool will learn how to feed Joanie so I don't have to be there to feed her every day.	Teachers will increase Joanie's food ingestion to 5 ounces per meal when fed by them.

While the objectives might reflect a good plan of action, unless the outcome statements represent the parents' concerns and priorities in language they understand, the IFSP is of little value.

Early Intervention Services to Be Provided.   The IFSP should include a clear statement of the nature of services that will be provided, including the duration and frequency of intervention, where such intervention will take place, and how it will be evaluated to determine its effectiveness. Early intervention is being used in this context in a comprehensive manner and might include any needed therapies or health-related services, such as audiological services, catheterization, tube feeding, medical consultation, nutrition services, physical and occupational therapy, psychological services, social work, and speech and language therapy. Since PL 99–457 is designed as an interagency law, inclusion of needed services on the IFSP does not obligate any one service provider or the designated lead agency to fund everything stipulated on it. Rather, it is intended to be representative of the family's comprehensive needs pertaining to enhancing their child's development. Needs might be identified along with recommended services for which no means of obtaining or paying for them exists (e.g., surgery needed for a sibling, housing difficulties, and needed augmentative communication systems).

Dates for Services.   The IFSP includes when services are to be provided and how long the services should continue. Also included should be the time when the next IFSP planning meeting will take place. Regulations require that meetings to develop IFSPs be scheduled a minimum of once per year with reviews of progress toward stated outcomes at least once every six months.

Identification of a Case Manager.   A case manager, according to PL 99–457 regulations, must be someone from the profession most immediately relevant to the child's or family's needs. The team should designate a specific person who will function as case manager for the family. Responsibilities of the case manager include coordination and facilitation of needed services for the child and family.

Transition.   Since infants grow fast and have rapidly changing needs, just planning for the present time is inadequate and soon outdated. Anticipation of the child's needs and future service delivery options, as well as the family's changing patterns, are all critical components in the development of an effective IFSP. Transition can be defined as pertaining to movement of the child from one program into the next (e.g., moving from a home-based infant stimulation program to a center-based preschool to kindergarten). It can also be conceived of as any significant life event that the child or family experiences (e.g., obtaining an augmentative communication system for a nonverbal child, the birth of a sibling, or a move to a more accessible home). While the first view of transition is easier to anticipate and plan for, the other can be just as significant, if not more so, in the family's life.

The IFSP Process

While the basic content of the IFSP is stipulated in the legislation, no specific format is required other than that it must be a written plan. The emphasis in the development of IFSPs is on *process* rather than completion of a standardized federal form. The National Early Childhood Technical Assistance System has developed 10 guiding principles underlying the IFSP process.

1. Infants and toddlers are uniquely dependent on their families for their survival and nurturance. This dependence necessitates a family-centered approach to early intervention.
2. States and programs should define "family" in a way that reflects the diversity of family patterns and structures.
3. Each family has its own structure, roles, values, beliefs, and coping styles. Respect for and acceptance of this diversity is a cornerstone of family-centered early intervention.
4. Early intervention systems and strategies must reflect a respect for the racial, ethnic, and cultural diversity of families.
5. Respect for family, autonomy, independence, and decision making means that families must be able to choose the level and nature of early intervention's involvement in their life.
6. Family/professional collaboration and partnerships are the keys to family-centered early intervention and to successful implementation of the IFSP process.
7. An enabling approach to working with families requires that professionals re-examine their traditional roles and practices and develop new practices when necessary—practices that promote mutual respect and partnerships.
8. Early intervention services should be flexible, accessible, and responsive to family needs.

9. Early intervention services should be provided according to the normalization principle—that is, families should have access to services provided in as normal a fashion and environment as is possible and that promote the integration of the child and family within the community.
10. No one agency or discipline can meet the diverse and complex needs of infants and toddlers with special needs and their families. Therefore, a team approach to planning and implementing the IFSP is necessary. (Johnson et al., 1989, p. 6)

These principles represent the backbone of the IFSP. The overriding theme of the principles is that families are responsible for their children and that family needs and concerns, as identified by the family, determine the professional's role. PL 99–457 does not require that families participate in the family assessment process in order for their children to receive services. Although family assessments may sometimes be conducted because of a court order or other legal proceedings, the most effective method of obtaining useful information for early intervention is always one in which there is a parent and professional collaborative partnership.

Limitations of the IFSP Process.   Just as special educators have experienced frustration and dissatisfaction with the IEP process mandated in PL 94–142, there is concern about the IFSP process as well. Dunst et al. (1988) go so far as to state, "It is our opinion that the IFSP, as proposed, is *doomed to failure*" (p. 130). There are four reasons they cite. First, since infant and toddlers change rapidly, long-term planning is not possible. Second, many other issues may have priority in a family's life over the specific needs of one child. Third, the implication of the law is that increased frequency and duration are always positive when that may not be the case. And finally, the stipulation that a case manager cannot be the parent undermines the role of the parent.

There are counterpoints to each of these points. First, while the future cannot be seen, various possibilities can be projected so families can anticipate and prepare for the future (e.g., the infant with cerebral palsy might likely need hamstring surgery in the future). The second point, that other issues might have priority in a family's life, should emerge during the assessment phase of the process. Acknowledgment and respect of these priorities do not negate the possibility of providing services to the child and/or family. As to the frequency issue, child development specialists should assist the team in understanding an infant's or toddler's overall needs and avoid overscheduling interventions. The final point related to the restriction of parents serving as case managers for their children need not limit the responsibility any particular parents choose to assume in coordinating their child's care. Beckwith (1990) points out the following:

> Some families are so disordered that basic survival goals—securing adequate nutrition and medical care, providing a safe environment with opportunities for exploration, providing adequate child care, and reducing family violence—must be set before goals of sensitivity, reciprocity, or even security of attachment can be pursued. (p. 69)

In such instances it is clearly evident that the family is struggling with the routine management of a household and would be unable to successfully accomplish the task of coordinating early intervention services without a support system. In other cases the designated case manager might have a minimal role to play in assisting the family with the IFSP. Additionally, legislative proposals to permit parental assumption of this role are currently being considered.

IDENTIFICATION OF FAMILY STRENGTHS AND NEEDS

The determination of what is specifically included in the process of identifying family strengths and needs should be done on an individual basis. The underlying purpose is to identify family strengths, resources, needs, and concerns relevant to an individual family's ability to enhance the development of the child (Johnson et al., 1989). Professionals have a responsibility to gather relevant data in a nonintrusive manner. Only information that can be directly applied to the enhancement of a family's functioning as related to the child's development should be sought. Asking families about personal issues and feelings simply because those questions are a part of a form that has been adopted, when the information will never be put to any real use, is unnecessary and can be harmful to the family. Professionals soliciting information from parents should always begin with an explanation of why the information is needed and how it will be used. Adherence to this procedure can significantly reduce the intrusive questions that the professional may think he needs to know, because he will be unable to clarify the reasons for these questions to the child's parents. Additionally, the professional must always assure parents of their right not to provide information that they consider intrusive. The professional needs to avoid value-laden comments or phrasing of questions, such as, "Are you unable to discipline your child effectively?" Such information might better be obtained through observations or more general questions that do not imply incompetence on the part of the parent, such as, "Tell me what happens when David acts up." No assumptions or valid judgments have been imposed, and the parents are free to give as much or as little information as they desire.

Components of the Process

Identifying the strengths, needs, concerns, and resources of a family as related to enhancement of their special needs child is a substantial task. Mitchell (1983; as cited in Seligman & Darling, 1989) has identified potential problems of families with special needs children according to microsystems, mesosystems, and exosystems. The microsystem level concerns are related to how well parents cope with their child with disabilities, the emotional responses (e.g., depression, guilt, or blame) that may influence overidentification with the child or complete disengagement, parental expectations of siblings, and sibling reactions to the special needs child. The mesosystem incorporates the roles and emotional reactions of extended family members, friends and neighbors, and work and recreation associates, interactions with medical and health care workers, contact with other parents, and other available resources within the local community. Exosystems that influence family functioning include health care systems, social welfare, education, and mass media, which affects public attitudes toward disabled populations. At the level of macrosystems, ethnic and cultural, religious, and socioeconomic factors exert control over how a family interacts with service delivery systems; economic and political elements dictate what resources are available to families of children with handicapping conditions.

The availability of sources of support provides a key to family functioning. The ability of a family to continue functioning effectively regardless of the number of stress factors present, the family composition, and the severity of a child's disability is based on the available social support systems. Three components of social networks that influence effectiveness are (1) network size, (2) network density, and (3) boundary density (Kazak & Marvin, 1984). *Network size* pertains to the number of different types of support available (e.g., spiritual, medical, and psychological). *Network density* refers to the extent members of a support network are known to each other. *Boundary density* is a measure of the number of network members shared by both parents. Reciprocity and dimensionality are two additional network characteristics that may be of interest to persons assisting families in the identification of strengths and needs (Kazak & Wilcox, 1984). *Network reciprocity* is related to the equal exchange of support by network members. For example, taking turns babysitting with a friend might produce a significant imbalance if one of the children is harder to care for than the other. *Dimensionality* addresses the number of functions provided through each relationship. For example, an intimate relationship, such as that of a spouse, should provide support to offset needs across multiple dimensions. For Elizabeth Armstrong's mother, the church proved to be her primary source of support, while she received no emotional or financial support from her family. Eduardo's mother found the most support from her own mother, whereas the religious beliefs of other extended family members impeded her adjustment.

Bailey and Simeonsson (1988) recommend the following five components be included in the process of identifying family-related issues:

1. Child's needs and characteristics likely to affect family functioning (e.g., temperament characteristics, responsiveness, repetitive behavior patterns, presence of unusual caregiving demands, consolability, regularity, endurance, and motivation)
2. Parent–child interactions
3. Family's needs (e.g., babysitting, pediatric care, dental care, financial responsibilities, adaptive equipment, specialized respite care, isolation from friends and family, information about child, future services, strategies, and personal crises)
4. Critical events (i.e., anticipation of events likely to cause stress)
5. Family strengths, including personal resources (e.g., personality, sense of competence and control over life, and religious or philosophical beliefs),

within-family resources (e.g., socioemotional support), and extra-family resources (outside the family)

Guidelines

There are many approaches that can be used for the identification of family strengths and needs. The relationship between parents and professionals throughout the process should be one of *partnership* (Deal, Dunst, & Trivette, 1989), characterized by the following guidelines:

1. Identification of family strengths and needs should not be a mandatory component for delivery of services to children—it should be voluntary.
2. Identification of family strengths and needs should be conducted in a nonintrusive manner.
3. Identification of family strengths and needs should be planned individually with a partnership relationship between parent and professional.
4. Identification of family strengths and needs should be conducted so as to preserve and respect family values and beliefs.
5. Families always have final authority to determine what areas of their lives are open to review.

Assessment Techniques of Data Gathering

We can obtain information about family strengths and needs through interviews, observations, questionnaires, and other test instruments.

Interviews.   Parent interviews can be extremely beneficial in data gathering and in the synthesis of data received from multiple sources. Interventionists use information from interviews to determine the perception parents have about specific events and to identify the priorities for services that they have. A *focused interview* format provides a moderately structured interview procedure (Winton, 1988; Winton & Bailey, 1988). The interview is organized into a five-phase structure and takes place after other assessment procedures have been completed. Table 5.1 depicts the five phases and the stated purposes for each. The ultimate goal of the focused interview is to generate family outcome statements, which are the result of collaborative efforts between the interventionist and the family.

Observations.   Observations can be useful in determining the *rate,* the *quality,* or the *pattern* of behavior (e.g., parent–child interactions). Both naturalistic and clinical observations of families can be helpful in identifying strengths and needs. Observations can be conducted using a coding system designed to measure predetermined behaviors or categories of behaviors (e.g., number of times mother makes a request before compliance, displays of affection, and initiation of interactions with siblings). An alternative approach is to maintain running records of observations. The specific techniques used should be compatible with family functioning style and types of information needed.

TABLE 5.1. A Five-Phase Family-Focused Interview

A Model for Conducting a Family-Focused Interview	
Interview Phase	Purpose
1. Preliminary Identify high-priority needs Identify difficulties in parent–child interaction Specify child characteristics that have potential family impact Note upcoming critical events	Prepare for interview by summarizing assessment data
2. Introduction Explain purpose of the interview Confirm time allotted and format Discuss confidentiality Structure physical environment (if possible)	Reduce parents' anxiety and create appropriate listening environment
3. Inventory Make opening statement Allow parents to do most of the talking	Validate and elaborate information from assessment Identify additional areas of family needs, strengths, and resources Clarify consensus and disagreement between parents
4. Summary, priority, and goal setting Make summarizing statements Explore family's priorities Set goals collaboratively	Agree on definition of family needs Establish priorities and set goals Recognize parents' efforts
5. Closure Express recognition and appreciation of parents' contribution Ask if family members have additional concerns or thoughts about interview	Allow concerns about interview to emerge

Source: D. B. Bailey, & R. J. Simeonsson (Eds.) (1988). *Family Assessment in Early Intervention.* Columbus, OH: Merrill. Reprinted by permission.

Parent–child interactions, often a significant area of interest to the early childhood special educator as well as the parents, can be assessed through naturalistic or clinical observations. Data gathering about interactions via observations should be designed to take into account four principles. First, the *reciprocal nature of interactions* means that both the parent and the child influence each other. Therefore, single exchanges cannot be removed from the context in which they occurred without risking a misinterpretation. Second, the *situational context* of the interaction is critical for complete analysis. The situational context includes what activity is occurring, where it is occurring, whether it is naturalistic or clinical, who is participating, the length of the observation, and how the observation is being recorded (Comfort, 1988). Observations should be arranged so as to address the activity(ies) of most interest to the parents (e.g., bathing, feeding, and playing). Observations should last from 3 to 20 minutes. Going beyond 20 minutes is not appropriate for observations of infants or very young children (Comfort, 1988).

The third principle is that there is a tendency on the part of both the parent and the child to strive for a *homeostatic relationship*. If either the parent or the child changes his behavior, the other will attempt to regain the pattern of interaction with

which he is familiar. The fourth principle is that parents have the ability to behave with a *view toward the future functioning* of the child. For example, all parents talk to and ask questions of newborn babies, although they are perfectly aware that the child is not capable of responding. It is assumed that the baby will develop the skills necessary to respond appropriately some time in the future; therefore the parents behave as if the child has them. Such behavior on the part of parents should not be interpreted to mean a lack of understanding of the child's current abilities or disabilities. Observation instruments that can be used to gather information about parent–child interactions are presented in the appendix to this chapter (see section A.1).

Questionnaires and Test Instruments.   Testing techniques include the use of standardized instruments as well as less formal self-evaluative checklists and scales. Some instruments are specifically designed to identify family strengths, needs, resources, and sources of support rather than assess current functioning. Other instruments are designed to determine current family functioning in specific domains, such as stress, knowledge of infant development, or depression. Those instruments designed to provide helpful information about family strengths, needs, resources, and sources of support are most useful in the IFSP process. The other more specific measures might be identified as a second level of assessment, if, during the identification of strengths and needs process, specific areas of concern emerged. Section A.2 of the appendix lists a variety of instruments that can be useful in the identification of strengths and needs. Instruments designed to assess specific areas of concern, such as stress, are presented in section A.3 of the appendix. Other scales designed to assess sources of support and resources are included in section A.4.

MODELS OF FAMILY-ORIENTED STRENGTHS AND NEEDS ASSESSMENT

There are two comprehensive family-focused models of assessment and intervention that have been developed to facilitate the data-gathering process. Bailey in collaboration with Simeonsson, Winton, Huntington, Comfort, Isbell, O'Donnell, and Helm (1986) developed the *Family-Focused Intervention Model.* The *Family Systems Assessment and Intervention Model* by Dunst, Trivette, and Deal (1988) is the second model. These models are similar in their emphasis on the value and respect that must be afforded to families, and both rely heavily on the interview process.

Family-Focused Intervention Model

The Family-Focused Intervention Model is predicated on the understanding that every family is unique; therefore appropriate procedures must be determined on an individual basis. Additionally, any services to be provided or goals to be established must match the parents' perceptions of what is needed and appropriate. The model consists of a six-step process, which is circular in nature. The first step is conducting the *initial family assessment* and includes data gathering about family strengths, needs, characteristics, and critical events. Initial testing and observations are planned and conducted during this step. The second step, which is the *focused interview,* is used to verify family needs and identify what additional assessments are needed. After the focused interview, *follow-up assessments* should be planned as the third step in the family assessment process. These follow-up assessments can include data gathering pertinent to parent–child interactions, the home environment, child characteristics, family support, transition, or any additional areas of concern identified during the focused interview. The fourth step in this model is the *IFSP meeting,* at which time a multidisciplinary team, including the parents, convenes for the purpose of generating child and family goals and identifying needed services. *Implementation of needed services,* the fifth step, includes case management, programming for the child, and provision of family services identified during the IFSP meeting. The sixth and final step is *evaluation* of the effectiveness of the interventions and services. Such evaluation can include a determination of whether stated goals were attained, parents' satisfaction with the services, and pre–post changes in child and family functioning. The model circles back to the first step as necessary, reflecting the ongoing nature of assessment.

Family Systems Assessment and Intervention Model

The Family Systems Assessment and Intervention Model includes four components with an outcome of empowering the family so they can tap available resources and meet their own needs. In this model the early childhood special educator should do the following:

1. Identify family aspirations and projects using any number of needs-based assessment procedures and strategies to determine the things the family considers important enough to devote time and energy.
2. Identify family strengths and capabilities to emphasize the things the family already does well and determine the particular strengths that increase the likelihood of a family mobilizing resources to meet needs.
3. "Map" the family's personal social network to identify both existing sources of support and resources and untapped but potential sources of aid and assistance.
4. Function in a number of different roles to enable and empower the family to become more competent in mobilizing resources to meet its needs and achieve desired goals. (Dunst et al., 1988, p. 51)

The first element of the model focuses on the *identification of family needs*. It is critical that needs be identified from the perspective of the family rather than from that of the professional. Need identification is influenced by a person's psychological awareness, values and beliefs, ability to recognize available resources as helpful in meeting the need, and an ability to identify solutions to a need. Needs must also be seen in hierarchical arrangements. A family without adequate housing or food is less likely to be worried about a sibling's adjustment to a brother or sister with a disability than is a family with such basic needs already addressed. Dunst et al. (1988) have identified the following 12 categories that can be useful for professionals who are assisting families to identify and prioritize their greatest needs:

Economic	Adult Education and enrichment
Physical	Child education and intervention
Food and clothing	Child care
Medical and dental	Recreational
Vocational	Emotional
Transportation and communication	Cultural and Social

A distinction between *concerns* and *needs* is an important part of this model. A concern is defined as a "worry, problem, dilemma, difficulty, uneasiness, and so forth" (p. 60), whereas a need is seen as an "aspiration, project, goal, desire, and so forth" (p. 60). The professional's task will include assistance in the clarification of concerns so that they can be translated into needs that have solutions.

The Family Systems Assessment and Intervention Model includes interviews and the use of needs-based assessment scales in the process of identifying family needs. Procedures for the interview emphasize the importance of establishing rapport and clearly stating the purpose of the interview. The interview should be seen as the family's meeting—not the professional's. Open-ended questions, which encourage family participation, should predominate the interview session. The following are examples of appropriate open-ended questions:

> What did you know about cerebral palsy (use applicable disability) before your child was born?
> Do you know any other parents whose children have this condition?
> Who is available to help you with child care?
> What do you worry about in regard to your child's future?

A professional's sensitivity to nonverbal messages throughout the process will enhance the success of the interview. The assessment approach that is best suited for this model is that of Little's Personal Projects Matrix, described in section A.2 of the appendix. When data are gathered via needs-based scales, follow-up clarification and prioritizing should occur before any intervention is planned.

In addition to the identification of family needs, the model is designed to *identify family functioning styles and strengths*. The interviewer can obtain this information as well. The emphasis during an interview should be on descriptions of how they "get through the day." Allowing the family to describe their routine interactions and typical activities is more effective than simply asking them to identify their strengths.

The third component of the Family Systems Assessment and Intervention Model is *identification of sources of support and resources*. The seven major sources of support identified by the model developers are nuclear family (household members); kinship (relatives); informal network (e.g., friends); social organizations (e.g., church); generic professionals (e.g., day care workers and family physicians); specialized professionals (e.g., therapists and early interventionists); and policymakers (e.g., school boards and legislators). As was the case with the first two components of the model, interviews and the use of scales are the data-gathering methods. Interviews should focus on the identification of any and all sources of support that the family has relied on in the past and are using currently. The discussion should also draw on the previously identified needs of the family and include an analysis of which needs cannot be adequately met through existing support sources. The identification of new resources, which could provide assistance to the family in addressing those needs, can then become the focus of the discussion.

Information obtained from the *identification of social supports and resources* is then merged with needs and strengths information to develop a "map" of the individual family's personal social network. Figure 5.1 depicts such a map. After the mapping is completed, needs are matched with available sources of support.

The final component of the model addresses the *professional's role as a help-giver* throughout the entire process. Regardless of the specific professional responsibilities, all help-givers should adhere to the guidelines for effective help giving.

Ecological Mapping of the Child and Family
Embedded within Other Social Systems

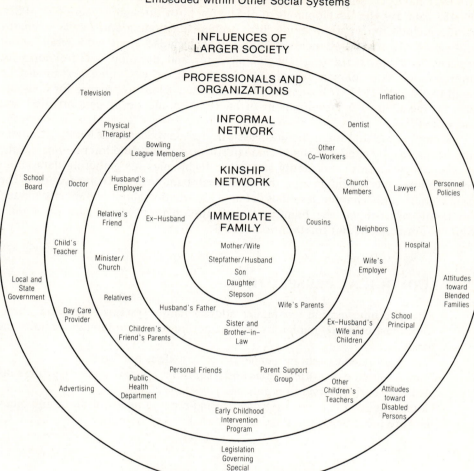

Figure 5.1. Personal Social Network Map from Family Systems Assessment and Intervention Model.

Source: C. J. Dunst, C. Trivette, & A. Deal (1988). *Enabling and Empowering Families: Principles and Guidelines for Practice.* Cambridge, MA: Brookline. Reprinted by permission.

SUMMARY

The rationale for a family-focused perspective for assessment was reviewed along with the roles parents have historically played in early intervention programs. Results of efficacy research consistent support the need to address family issues. Families have a much larger impact on their children's lives than professionals will ever have. In concert with the need to offer family-focused intervention, PL 99–457 calls for the development of IFSPs for birth through 2 years old. IFSPs should include information about current child functioning and family strengths and needs. Outcome statements should also be included along with details about services to be provided (e.g., beginning dates and duration and frequency of intervention). The person responsible for serving as case manager should be identified on the IFSP. If a transition is anticipated, plans to prepare for it should also be included. The development of an IFSP should be process-oriented and individualized.

Components that might be addressed in the identification of family strengths and needs include child needs and characteristics; parent–child interactions; family needs; critical events; and family strengths. Techniques for gathering data about these components are interviews, the use of scales and tests, and observations. The final section of the chapter describes detailed information about two specific models for family assessment: the Family-Focused Intervention Model and the Family Systems Assessment and Intervention Model.

THE ECOLOGICAL PERSPECTIVE

- Effective intervention techniques address family systems issues and, therefore, must be accompanied by data gathering related to family strengths and needs.
- The ongoing consistent influence in a child's life is her family.
- Families are the decision makers and, therefore, are partners with professionals in the early intervention process.
- Comprehensive services that meet broad-ranging needs of all family members are more beneficial than segmented delivery systems.

APPENDIX

A.1. OBSERVATION INSTRUMENTS FOR PARENT–CHILD INTERACTIONS

Title: Dyadic Parent–Child Interaction Coding System
Source: Robinson, E. A., & Eyberg, S. M. (1981). The dyadic parent–child interaction coding system: Standardization and validation. *Journal of Consulting and Clinical Psychology, 49,* 245–250.
Description: Instrument assesses degree to which parent's or child's behavior during play is deviant and can be used to evaluate effectiveness of treatment; parent's direct and indirect commands, labeled and unlabeled praise, positive and negative physical contact, descriptive statements or questions, and child's compliance, whines, and yells. It was normed on children with behavior problems and normal children ages 2 through 7. Mothers and fathers were of low- and middle-class one- and two-parent families with plus or minus 2 children, and parent age was 28 through 32.

Title: Social Interaction Assessment/Intervention

Source: McCollum, J. A., & Stayton, V. D. (1985). Infant/parent interaction: Studies and intervention guidelines based on the SIAI model. *Journal of the Division for Early Childhood.* 9(2), 125–135.

Description: Instrument evaluates parent–handicapped child interaction pre- and postintervention to increase parent's ability to make independent adjustments to child's behavior during play, communicative social interaction, and individualized target behaviors for parent and child (e.g., imitation, vocalization, and turn-taking). It was normed with severely motor-delayed and cognitively delayed children who were 2 through 34 months. Mothers were of lower middle income (one- and two-parent families) with zero to three children. Parent age range was in the twenties to thirties.

Title: Parent Behavior Progression

Source: Bromwich, R. (1981). *Working with parents and infants: An interactional approach.* Baltimore, MD: University Park Press.

Description: Instrument assesses infant-related maternal behaviors to develop short-term goals aimed at changing maternal attitudes and behavior for the purpose of enhancing maternal–infant interaction. There are six levels ranging from maternal enjoyment of infant to mother independently providing developmentally appropriate activities. Behaviors include parent's pleasure in watching infant, physical proximity, awareness of signs of distress, comfort, provides stable caregiver, and provides variety of stimulation. It was used with parents of premature and low birthweight infants at-risk for health or developmental problems who were 9 through 24 months and who had heterogeneous socioeconomic status (SES), maternal age, and family structure. Most were black, Caucasian, and Chicano.

Title: Nursing Child Assessment Teaching and Feeding Scales

Source: Bee, H. L., Barnard, K. E., Eyres, S. J., Gray, C. A., Hammond, M. A., Spietz, A. L., Snyder, C., & Clark, B. (1982). Prediction of IQ and language skill from perinatal status, child performance, family characteristics, and mother–infant interaction. *Child Development, 53,* 1134–1156.

Description: Instrument assesses parent–child behaviors during teaching and feeding as screening device and pre- and postintervention; parent's verbalizations, positioning, and handling; child's gaze and verbal cues. Factor analyzed into six subscales: parent's sensitivity to cues, response to distress, cognitive and socioemotional growth fostering, child's clarity of cues, and responsiveness. It was normed with healthy, normally developing children 1 through 36 months and preterm infants 4 through 8 months. Mothers were of full range of educational status and of one- and two-parent families. Most were Caucasian, but also black and Hispanic.

Title: Interaction Rating Scales

Source: Clark, G. N., & Siefer, R. (1985). Assessment of parents' interactions with their developmentally delayed infants. *Infant Mental Health Journal, 6,* 214–225.

Description: Instrument assesses parental sensitivity to child behavior and reciprocity of interactions during free play; parent's imitating and affect; child's gaze aversion and social referencing; dyadic reciprocity. Behaviors grouped as interaction style, social referencing, and assessment of context. It was normed with heterogeneous group of infants at high-risk and those with Down's syndrome, neurological impairments, and multiple handicaps and their mothers (maternal characteristics not reported).

Title: Teaching Skills Inventory

Source: Rosenberg, S., Robinson, C., & Beckman, P. (1984). Teaching skills inventory: A measure of parent performance. *Journal of the Division for Early Childhood, 8,* 107–113.

Description: Instrument assesses parent's teaching skills with handicapped children pre- and postintervention; parent's clarity of verbal instruction, task modification, effectiveness of prompts; and child's interest. It is normed with heterogenous group of mentally retarded children with mixed and multiple handicaps and mild-to-severe disabilities. Children were 2 through 36 months. Mothers were primarily Caucasian, middle income, and at least high school graduates.

Title: Maternal Behavior Rating Scale
Source: Mahoney, G., Finger, I., & Powell, A. (1985). Relationship of maternal behavioral style to the development of organically impaired mentally retarded infants. *American Journal of Mental Deficiency, 90,* 296–302.
Description: Instrument assesses quality of maternal interactive behavior during play with young mentally retarded children for use in program evaluation; parent's expressiveness, warmth, sensitivity to child state, achievement orientation, social stimulation, effectiveness, ability to give directives; child's activity level, attention span, enjoyment, and expressiveness. It is normed on organically impaired, mentally retarded (primarily Down's syndrome) children who were 1 through 3 years. Mothers were middle class, 60% Caucasian, and 68% unemployed. Most were married.

Title: Parent/Caregiver Involvement Scale
Source: Farran, D. C., Kasari, C., Yoder, P., Harber, L., Huntington, G. S., & Comfort-Smith, M. (1987). Rating mother–child interactions in handicapped and at-risk infants. In T. Tamir (Ed.), *Stimulation and intervention in infant development.* London: Freund.
Description: Instrument describes parent's involvement in play interaction with handicapped, high-risk, or normally developing children; adult's amount, quality, appropriateness of involvement via 11 behaviors (e.g., physical, verbal, responsiveness, and control) and overall impression of affective climate and learning environment. It was normed with mentally retarded, medically or environmentally high-risk children, and those with multiple handicaps who were 2 through 57 months and normally developing children plus or minus three years. Mothers and fathers were of heterogeneous SES, low SES, or mid SES and had varied parental age and number of siblings, were of one- and two-parent families, and were Caucasian and black.

A.2. INSTRUMENTS TO IDENTIFY FAMILY STRENGTHS AND NEEDS

Title: Family Needs Survey
Source: Bailey, D., & Simeonsson, R. (1985). University of North Carolina at Chapel Hill, Frank Porter Graham Child Development Center.
Description: Statements covering six broad areas (needs for information; needs for support; explaining to others; community services; financial needs; family functioning) to which parents respond on three-point scale with "Definitely do not need help with this," "Not sure," or "Definitely need help with this." Form has a total of 35 statements; also has one open-ended question that asks what the greatest needs are currently. Parents are asked to read the statements and respond to the items according to the three-point scale. For the open-ended question, parents can use needs included in the 35 statements and/or identify needs not mentioned on the form. No psychometric information is currently available; however, reliability and validity studies are underway by the authors and other researchers.

Comments: The format is simple and easy to follow assuming that a person can read English. Although the statements could be read to a nonreader or translated for a non-English-speaking parent, the quality of the responses may be affected. The content of the instrument is based on established needs of parents with young handicapped children. The routine collection of this information by an early intervention program when there is no direct usefulness or applicability to the intervention efforts should not occur. The instrument includes an open-ended question regarding parental needs, so parents are free to identify needs not included in the 35 statements. The response choices are limited and do not permit the identification of priority needs; however, the open-ended question does.

Title: Family Needs Scale

Source: Dunst, C. J., Cooper, C. S., Weeldreyer, J. C., Snyder, K. D., & Chase, J. H. In Dunst, C. J., Trivette, C. M., & Deal, A. G. (1988). *Enabling and empowering families: Principles and guidelines for practice.* Cambridge, MA: Brookline Books.

Description: Scale has 41 items organized into 9 categories (e.g., financial, food and shelter, vocation, child care, transportation, and communication). Each item is rated by parents on a five-point scale ranging from "almost never a need" to "almost always a need." Parents are asked to read the 41 items and respond according to the five-point scale or to indicate "not applicable."

Comments: Instrument is dependent on reading skills of parents or must be read to them. It was specifically developed for use in intervention programs and is to be used to prompt discussions about responses to define nature of family's needs. However, intervention programs unable to respond to these needs after they are identified should avoid unnecessary intrusion, which some of these items might cause.

Title: Parent Needs Survey

Source: Seligman, M., & Darling, B. R. (1989). *Ordinary families, special children: A systems approach to childhood disability.* New York: Guilford Press.

Description: Instrument contains 26 statements about needs that parents of young children with handicaps may have. Possible responses to these items are "I really need some help in this area"; "I would like some help, but my need is not that great"; or "I don't need any help in this area." Instrument also includes space for other needs that were not addressed in the 26 items. Parents read the statements and place an "X" by the corresponding response they wish to make to that item. Additional needs can be added at the end of the list.

Comments: Instrument relies on parental reading skills. Introduction and instructions state that the early intervention program might not be able to help in all areas, but that answers can be useful in improving the program—the appropriateness of asking intrusive questions when no real help is offered or available must always be a priority consideration. The form is short and yet permits the addition of new items; however, there is no mechanism for prioritizing needs that fall within the "I really need some help in this area."

Title: How Can We Help?

Source: Child Development Resources, P. O. Box, 299, Lightfoot, VA 23090-0299, 1988.

Description: Instrument has two parts—the first part contains seven open-ended questions, and the second part is a checklist of needs subdivided into six categories (information; child care; community services; medical and dental care; talking about the child; planning for the future and transition). Possible responses include "we have enough," "we would like more," or "not sure." Format includes space for additional items to be added in each of the six categories as well as another open-ended question at the end of the form. Parents complete questionnaire by responding only to those questions that they feel would be helpful for the intervention staff to have the answers to. Open-ended questions appear first and are followed by the checklist, which is responded to by putting a check in the appropriate response column and/or by adding additional items. One final open-ended question follows the checklist.

Comments: Format is structured though nonthreatening and informal. Instructions direct parents to respond selectively, thus reducing intrusive nature of questionnaire. Prioritizing of needs is not provided through form, and parent reading and writing skills are required unless items are read aloud and/or responses are recorded.

Additional Instruments

Title: Personal Projects Matrix
Source: Little, B. R. (1983). Personal projects: A rationale and method for investigation. *Environment and Behavior, 19,* 273–309.
Description: Respondent is asked to list up to 10 personal projects that occupy his time or energy and then to rate each according to its importance, enjoyment, difficulty, stress, positive and negative impact, and progress made toward reaching the goal.

Title: Family Strengths Scale
Source: Family, Infant and Preschool Program, Western Carolina Center, 300 Enola Road, Morganton, NC 28655, ATTN: Community Resource Services
Description: Instrument contains 12 items that assess family pride (loyalty, optimism, and trust in family) and family accord (ability to accomplish tasks, deal with problems, and compatibility). Respondent indicates the extent to which each quality listed is present in her family. Items cover strengths such as trust and confidence, ability to express feelings, congruence in values, beliefs, and respect.

Title: Family Resource Scale
Source: Dunst, C. J., & Leet, H. E. (1987). Measuring the adequacy of resources in households with young children. *Child: Care, Health, and Development, 13,* 111–125.
Description: Instrument measures extent to which households with young children have adequate resources. It has 31 items that address the adequacy of both physical and human resources (e.g., food, shelter, transportation, time to be with family and friends, health care, money to pay bills, and child care). Respondent uses a five-point scale ranging from "not at all adequate" to "almost always adequate" to indicate the adequacy of each resource in his home. Items rated as inadequate can be used to identify household needs; a modified version is available for use with teenage mothers.

Title: Support Functions Scale
Source: Dunst, C. J., Trivette, C., & Deal, A. (1988). *Enabling and empowering families: Principles and guidelines for practice.* Cambridge, MA: Brookline Books.
Description: Instrument measures a person's need for different types of help or assistance. It contains 20 items that cover four types of support needed [financial, emotional, instrumental (e.g., child care), and informational]. Respondent uses a five-point scale ranging from "never have a need" to "quite often have a need." Items rated sometimes often or quite often (have a need) should be followed up with an interview to pinpoint needs.

Title: Family Strengths Inventory
Source: Family, Infant and Preschool Program, Western Carolina Center, 300 Enola Road, Morganton, NC 28655, ATTN: Community Resource Services.
Description: Instrument has 13 items measuring six major qualities of strong families and aspects of interpersonal and intrapersonal relationships. Respondent uses a five-point

scale based on the degree to which the characteristic is present in his family. It yields a total score reflecting overall family strengths; however, analysis of responses to individual items through follow-up interviews provides more useful information.

Title: Family Functioning Style Scale

Source: Dunst, C. J., Trivette, C. M., & Deal, A. G. (1988). *Enabling and empowering families: Principles and guidelines for practice.* Cambridge, MA: Brookline Books.

Description: Instrument assesses 12 qualities of strong families organized into three categories: family-identity measures, information-sharing measures, and coping and resource mobilization measures. The scale contains 26 statements to which responses are made using a five-point scale ranging from "not at all like my family" to "almost always like my family." Scale produces subscale scores for each of the 12 family strengths as well as an overall family strengths score. Scores can be plotted to form a profile of family functioning style.

A.3. INSTRUMENTS DESIGNED TO ASSESS SPECIFIC AREAS OF CONCERN

Stress

Title: Questionnaire on Resources and Stress (QRS)

Source: Holroyd, J. (1974). The questionnaire on resources and stress: An instrument to measure family response to a handicapped member. *Journal of Community Psychology, 2,* 92–94; Holroyd, J. (1986). *Questionnaire on resources and stress for families with a chronically ill or handicapped member: Manual.* Brandon, VT: Clinical Psychology Publishing.

Description: Instrument contains 285 statements organized into three domains and 15 subscales. Respondent indicates true or false for each statement. Scores include 15 subscale scores and an overall score, which can be used to create test profile. The domains are personal problems (e.g., poor health and mood, excess time demands, and overprotection and dependency), family problems (e.g., lack of family integration and financial problems), and problems of index case (e.g., physical incapacitation, occupational limitations, and difficult personality characteristics). A 66-item short form developed by Holroyd and a 52-item version by Friedrich, Greenberg, and Crnic are also available.

Title: Parenting Stress Index

Source: Abidin, R. R. (1986). *Parenting stress index* (2nd ed.). Charlottesville, VA: Pediatric Psychology Press.

Description: Instrument is designed as screening and diagnostic tool to measure the magnitude of stress in the parent–child system. It contains a total of 101 statements divided into 13 subscales representing two broad domains: child characteristics (adaptability, acceptability, demandingness, mood, distractibility and hyperactivity, and reinforces parent) and parent characteristics (depression, attachment, restrictions of role, sense of competence, social isolation, relationship with spouse, and parent health). It is primarily applicable to parents of children under the age of 3, but can be used up to age 10. Percentile scores can be obtained for each subscale, domain, and overall is based on age of child. Optional Life Stress Scale contains 19 items related to potentially stressful events outside the parent–child relationship. Norm group did not include a geographically or ethnically balanced sample (e.g., 92% white).

Title: Impact-on-Family Scale
Source: Stein, R. E. K., & Reissman, C. K. (1980). The development of an impact-on-family scale: Preliminary findings. *Medical Care, 18,* 465–472.
Description: Instrument is designed to be used to assess impact of a chronically ill child on family life (but can be used with handicapped children as well). It contains 24 items based on 5 factors (financial, familial, social, personal strain, and mastery) and can be used to determine effectiveness of interventions intended to reduce initial impact of a chronically ill child on the family.

Title: Impact-on-Family Scale Adapted for Families of Children with Handicaps (IFS)
Source: McLinden-Mott, S. E., & Braeger, T. (1988). The impact on family scale: An adaptation for families of children with handicaps. *Journal of the Division for Early Childhood, 12*(3), 217–223.
Description: Wording of the IFS was adapted to focus on handicapping conditions rather than chronic illness, and the format was changed from interview to paper-and-pencil testing. Parents were asked to rate items on a four-point scale (from strongly agree to strongly disagree). The first 27 items pertain to the family in general and the last 6 focus on the impact on siblings. Preliminary psychometric data support reliability and validity of the instrument, but article does not include the adapted version of the instrument.

Life Events

Title: Recent Life Changes Questionnaire
Source: Rahe, R. H. (1978). Life change measurement clarification. *Psychosomatic Medicine, 40,* 95–98.
Description: This is a revised version of instrument originally titled Schedule of Recent Events (Hawkins, Davies, & Holmes, 1957). It includes 55 items related to life changes in health, work, home and family, personal and social, and financial areas. Respondents indicate which events have occurred within the past two years and the length of time since the event occurred. Responses can then be compared to norms or evaluated individually as to the degree of adjustment each event required.

Title: Life Experiences Survey
Source: Sarason, I. G., Johnson, J. H., & Siegel, J. M. (1978). Assessing the impact of life changes: Development of the life experiences survey. *Journal of Consulting and Clinical Psychology, 46,* 932–946.
Description: Instrument has 57 items that represent potentially stressful frequent life events. Respondent marks those events that occurred within the past year, indicating which were within the last six months. She then uses a seven-point scale [−3 (extremely negative impact) to +3 (extremely positive impact)] to measure nature and extent of impact.

Title: Family Inventory of Life Events and Changes (FILE)
Source: McCubbin, H. I., & Patterson, J. M. (1987). *Family inventory of life events and changes.* In H. M. McCubbin & A. I. Thompson (Eds.), *Family assessment inventories for research and practice* (pp. 79–98). Madison: University of Wisconsin-Madison.
Description: Instrument measures the accumulation of life events by a family. It contains 71 items organized into nine scales (e.g., intrafamily strains, conflict, marital strains, pregnancy or childbearing strain, and illness and family care strains). A variety of scoring procedures can be used, resulting in a determination of the level of stress within the family (does not focus on individuals but on the family as a unit).

A.4. SOCIAL SUPPORT SCALES

Title: Psychosocial Kinship Inventory
Source: Pattison, E. M., DeFrancisco, D., Wood, P., Frazier, H., & Crowder, J. (1975). Psychosocial kinship model for family therapy. *American Journal of Psychiatry, 132,* 1246–1251.
Description: Instrument can be used to identify members of one's personal network and to assess 11 dimensions of support for each person in the network (e.g., kind of feelings and thoughts toward person, strength of feelings and thoughts, help provided by that person, degree of emotional support provided by that person, frequency of contact, degree of stability of relationship, physical proximity, kind of feelings and thought believed held by person toward them, strength of feelings believed held, help provided to person, and emotional support provided to person. Each dimension is rated on a five-point scale.

Title: Perceived Support Network Inventory
Source: Oritt, E. C., Paul, S. C., & Behrman, J. A. (1985). The perceived support network inventory. *American Journal of Community Psychology, 13,* 565–582.
Description: Instrument uses a three-step assessment process to identify members of a family's personal network and the quality of the relationships. Respondent first lists everyone he would routinely seek help from, then describes the type of support he would ask for, and finally rates a number of qualitative aspects of support exchanges.

Title: Family Support Scale
Source: Dunst, C. J., Trivette, C., & Deal, A. (1988). *Enabling and empowering families: Principles and guidelines for practice.* Cambridge, MA: Brookline Books.
Description: Respondent rates sources of support as to their helpfulness in raising a young child, including parent, spouse or partner, friends, neighbors, co-workers, church, professionals, and social groups or organizations, using a five-point scale ranging from "not at all helpful" to "extremely helpful."

Title: Inventory of Social Support
Source: Dunst, C. J., Trivette, C., & Deal, A. (1988). *Enabling and empowering families: Principles and guidelines for practice.* Cambridge, MA: Brookline Books.
Description: Matrix format intended to determine who provides help to a person, as well as the nature and quality of that help. First respondent indicates the frequency of contact (including face to face, group setting, and telephone contact) she has had with 18 possible support providers (with room available to add two additional persons or groups). Then the respondent indicates to whom she goes to receive help for 12 different needs.

Title: Personal Network Matrix
Source: Dunst, C. J., Trivette, C., & Deal, A. (1988). *Enabling and empowering families: Principles and guidelines for practice.* Cambridge, MA: Brookline Books.
Description: Instrument is divided into three parts designed to assess frequency of contacts and qualitative information about the support network available to a person.

Title: Exercise: Social Support
Source: In Johnson, B. H., McGonigel, M. J., & Kaufmann, R. K. (Eds.) (1989). *Guidelines and recommended practices for the individualized family service plan.* National Early Childhood Technical Assistance System and Association for the Care of Children's Health. (Authors of instrument are: Summers, J. A., Turnbull, A. P., & Brotherson, M. J.).

Description: Exercise in which respondent answers four questions aimed at identifying road-blocks toward obtaining social support and developing steps to overcome these road-blocks. All questions are open-ended. Both practical (e.g., lack of transportation) and value (e.g., believing that you should not burden others) roadblocks are to be identified as part of the exercise.

Analyzing Environments: The Home

CHAPTER OUTLINE

QUESTIONS ANSWERED IN CHAPTER 6

- What are the physical and nonphysical influences on child development found within the home?
- What are the effects of these influences on the growing child?
- What are the interactive effects of environmental influences and the presence of handicapping conditions?
- What data-gathering procedures and techniques can be used in the analysis of home environments?
- What instruments that help in the analysis of home environments are currently available?

CHAPTER OVERVIEW

While the previous chapter focused on the identification of family strengths and needs, this chapter is directed specifically toward analysis of the home environment. Early experiences and characteristics of the home environment unquestionably contribute substantially to a child's future functioning. What is the nature of the ideal home environment for a young child with special needs? Beyond the general features of a positive home environment for any child, such as adequate food and clothing, safety from harm, and sufficient nurturing and affection, the definition of an ideal home environment presents a challenging dilemma. It can vary according to the child's disability, his temperament, the community in which the family resides, and many other variables. The child who is deaf would profit little from an environment filled with sound-producing toys, while just such an environment would be recommended for the toddler with visual impairment. An infant with motor impairments who has difficulty moving or conveying his interest in a particular activity might do well in an environment responsive to his weak signals, whereas a less responsive environment might be more appropriate for the hyperactive child. The ecological congruity between a child's needs and the nature of the home environment can play a critical role in the developmental patterns the child exhibits. The purpose of this chapter is to cover techniques that can be used to gather data about the physical and nonphysical features of the home environment.

PARAMETERS OF THE HOME ENVIRONMENT

The home environment comprises both physical and nonphysical properties that interact to influence the behavior of everyone residing in the home. The interaction between and interdependence of the physical and nonphysical properties within the home jointly influence behavior (Simeonsson, 1988). For example, overcrowding in a home can increase aggression, leading to physical violence and possible abuse. With added physical space providing a place where an angry spouse, parent, or sibling can retreat, the anger might never lead to physical violence. However, a spouse, parent, or sibling with a less volatile temperament might never resort to physical violence despite the crowded conditions of the home. Although physical and nonphysical parameters are discussed as separate components of the home environment, the interactive relationship between them is critical to an accurate analysis of a home environment.

Physical Features

Physical features of the home environment that may be of interest to the early interventionist include basic architectural features, such as the presence of steps in the home, types and amount of furniture present, or size and configuration (e.g., number of rooms in the home). Available play materials and ease of access to and appropriateness of play materials for developmental levels of the children are also considered physical features. The number of persons living in the home and their relationships to one another constitute additional elements of the physical environment. The presence of adequate supplies of food, availability of sufficient heating and cooling to maintain body comfort, and adequate plumbing facilities are also included in physical features of the home environment.

Four variables in the home environment that have been positively linked to cognitive development in children are (1) availability of stimulus material; (2) short-term variety of stimulus material; (3) a "match" between organismic level and stimulus complexity; and (4) responsivity of the physical environment (Wachs, 1979). In contrast, negative influences on cognitive development result from: (1) the presence of noise-confusion in the home; (2) overcrowding; (3) irregularity in scheduling events in the home; and (4) physical restrictions on the child's exploration (Wachs, 1979). The interactive nature of many of the physical and nonphysical variables complicates attempts to determine the impact of specific aspects within the home. [See Laosa (1982) for further discussion of family influences on children's intellectual development.]

Research supporting the concept of *environmental specificity* in terms of racial or cultural environments suggests that no universal "best" home environment exists (Gottfried, 1984). The need for ecological congruence seems to be as applicable in the home environment as it is in a preschool setting.

To account for the environmental specifics, and yet acknowledge the global aspects of environmental influences, Wachs (1984, 1979; Wachs & Gruen, 1982) developed the *Bifactor Environmental Action Model* (BEAM). This model divides environmental parameters into two subsets. The first is "a *small subset of environmental parameters,* which influence *most areas of development* for most children in a given age span (Wachs, 1984, p. 275). The second group includes "the *majority of environmental parameters,* all of which are highly specific in their influence on development" (Wachs, 1984, p. 275). These parameters account for the discrepancies seen in cognitive development when "good" environments fail to enhance a child's development or when a child excels despite her "bad" environment. For the second group of parameters, the BEAM model is based on three hypotheses:

1. *The hypothesis of environmental specificity:* different aspects of the environment influence different aspects of cognitive development.
2. *The hypothesis of age specificity:* specific aspects of the environment will differ in the impact on development depending upon the age of the child experiencing them.
3. *The hypothesis of organismic specificity:* the individual characteristics of the child will affect the impact of the environment on development.

The global research that has resulted in high correlations between low socioeconomic status (SES) and low intelligence test scores and poor school achievement does not account for the child from a low SES background who excels, or why such wide variability in performance throughout all SES levels can be observed. Determining which elements of the environment contribute to healthy child development as contrasted to those which represent cultural nuances with no harmful effects to the developing child can be a challenging task. Regardless, professionals seeking to gain greater insight into the functioning of a particular child should be eager to obtain the maximum amount of information about that child's home environment.

Nonphysical Features

Nonphysical features of the home environment include both psychological and social elements of interactions. Interactions between others living in the home, both including and excluding the child with disabilities, can contribute to a child's developmental progression. For example, the relationship between the parents does not directly include the child, but does influence his development. In the case of Elizabeth Armstrong's parents, the father, who had mental health problems, was an additional drain on Mrs. Armstrong, rather than a source of support and comfort. When the responsibilities associated with Elizabeth's birth reduced Mrs. Armstrong's ability to support Donald emotionally, he was unable to adjust. In the case of Eduardo Manzolis, the spousal relationship was supportive and nurturing. Although Mr. and Mrs. Manzolis do not always agree on the best course of action for their son, they do provide support for each other so both are available competent parents.

The identification of nonphysical components of the home environment that might be targeted for analysis could become an endless task. This section is organized into six, somewhat arbitrary, broad features of the home environment: (1) family subsystems; (2) social climate and support systems; (3) the nature of interactions; and (4) stimulus deprivation and enrichment; (5) parents' beliefs and knowledge; and (3) child characteristics.

Family Subsystems.   According to Turnbull and Turnbull (1986), traditional nuclear families operate with four major subsystems. These subsystems are (1) the marital subsystem (husband and wife interactions); (2) the parental subsystem (parent and child interactions); (3) the sibling subsystem (child and child interactions); and (4) the extrafamilial subsystem (whole family or individual member interactions with extended family, neighbors, and professionals). Every family presents a unique combination of subsystems operating within the family. For example, if a child has no brothers or sisters there would be no sibling subsystem. However, she might have cousins who live in the same household with whom she interacts much in the fashion as siblings. Divorce and remarriage also create different subsystems, as do extended families residing within the same household or nontraditional household compositions (e.g., foster care and cohabitation).

Social Climate and Support Systems.   The social climate found within the home can have an impact on the development of young children. The availability of both formal and informal support systems, as well as parents' willingness and ability to use support systems, will influence their parental functioning, such as managing stress or obtaining needed counseling to increase acceptance of a child with disabilities. The home environment and the nature of parent–child interactions, in this context, cannot be separated from the larger exosystems and macrosystems within which they exist.

Dukes (1976) identified five ecological variables of socialization. Extending beyond the home environment, each contributes to the internal nature of the home environment and, thus, the quality of parenting and opportunities for positive child development. The variables are household composition, role status, community setting, climate and geographic location, and economic base of a given group.

Nature of Interactions.   Within the home the nature of interactions contributes to the social climate found there. The concepts of *cohesion* and *adaptability* are useful in describing how family members interact (Turnbull & Turnbull, 1986). Cohesion incorporates both the emotional bonding and the degree of independence for individual family members. It is best viewed as a continuum between high disengagement at one end and high enmeshment at the other. Families at the high enmeshment end of the continuum may be characterized as overinvolved and overprotective. All decisions and activities must be family-focused, with little or no tolerance for privacy. Such a family might be highly resistant to risk-taking, avoiding many opportunities for a young child with special needs to begin to develop—

striving to achieve independence. This family might need to be given small gradual opportunities for risk-taking rather than expecting immediate tolerance for normal risk-taking as a part of childrearing (Turnbull & Turnbull, 1986). At the other end of the continuum, highly disengaged families may be characterized as underinvolved, with rigid separate roles for each family member. When a child with a disability is born into such a family, the needed support and encouragement of a family system might not be available for the child or the caregiver for whom child care is a responsibility. A balance between enmeshment and disengagement is evidenced in well-functioning families.

Cultural patterns and value systems can also influence family cohesion. Rotunno and McGoldrick (1982) stipulate that Italian-American families value enmeshment to a greater extent than families from other ethnic backgrounds. Rural Appalachian families, while enmeshed within the family subsystem, highly value their independence from outsiders. Such values and attitudes must be considered if early childhood special educators hope to have young children with exceptionalities released into their care, even within the home setting. Theoretical assumptions consistent with the ecological perspective that are relevant to the understanding of parent–infant relationships are summarized in the following list, based on material from Parke and Tinsley (1987):

1. There is an interdependence among the roles and functions of all family members—families are social systems. To understand the behavior of one member of a family, the complementary behaviors of other members must also be recognized and assessed.
2. All family members directly and indirectly influence each other.
3. Different units of analysis are needed to understand families. Recognition of relationships among family members—mother–infant, father–infant, sibling–infant, or mother–father—require separate analysis. The family as a unit also requires separate analysis.
4. The embeddedness of the family within a variety of social systems must also be recognized.
5. The developmental perspective that one takes toward the consideration of family relationships will influence the interpretation of findings. A life-span perspective would address the age at which parenthood began, while the more common focus on perceptual-cognitive or social-emotional capacities of the child would not be concerned with parental age.
6. The level of development of the family as a unit can have mutual impact on relationships within the family. Changes in structure, norms, rules, and strategies can be observed as families grow.
7. Social changes within a culture have significant impact on families. Family size, timing of parenthood, and women in the work force are just three examples of the sociological shifts that are occurring in American families today.
8. A related assumption involves the appreciation of the historical time period in which family interactions are taking place (e.g., the Vietnam War era contrasted with Desert Storm).

9. Parental perception, organization, and understanding of infants and their roles as parents influence parent–infant interaction.

Stimulus Deprivation and Stimulus Enrichment.   Several classic studies of the effects of stimulus deprivation and stimulus enrichment have provided dramatic evidence of the role environmental influences play in the development of infants and young children. Extensive research documenting family experiences that foster reading in school-age children indicates the following factors are related to reading proficiency: (1) the promotion of verbal skills (through verbal interactions, encouragement of verbal expression, and time spent with the child); (2) modeling positive reading habits; (3) time spent reading to the child; (4) the availability of reading and writing materials in the home; (5) exposure to a variety of activities; (6) providing the child with help in reading; and (7) regulation and use of the television (Hess, Holloway, Price, & Dickson, 1982). Although this research is not targeted toward handicapped or at-risk populations per se, it does demonstrate strong evidence as to the powerful influence the home environment has on child functioning.

Parents' Beliefs and Knowledge.   Parental beliefs and knowledge exert powerful influences over the home environments of all children. This section includes a discussion of three related elements of beliefs and knowledge—knowledge of child development, parent teaching strategies, and mental health and substance abuse of parents. Embedded in parental beliefs and knowledge are cultural mores and religious beliefs. Interventionists attempting to study the home environments of young children must maintain respect of and value for the importance of individual beliefs. For example, if parents object to a needed surgical procedure because they believe God wants the child to remain as she was born, an appreciation of the individual's right to religious freedom must be balanced with the professional opinion that the child needs medical intervention. Working with the family to gain an understanding of its perspective might prove more effective than direct confrontation. As we maintain a focus on the goal of empowering families through effective intervention, valuing parental rights to beliefs other than our own is essential. Reduction of the physical disability at the cost of destruction of the child's family might not reflect the best interests of the child.

Knowledge of Child Development. What parents know and/or believe about child development directly influences interactions with their children. A father who expected his baby to be toilet trained by 6 months of age will not have the same attitude toward diapering a 15-month-old as one who knew toilet training would come later. The father who is unaware that, on the average, babies begin walking around 12 months of age might be unconcerned that his 20-month-old is not yet walking. The reciprocal nature of parent–child interactions further contributes to the importance of parental beliefs and knowledge in child development. The father who thought toilet training occurred at 6 months might assume that the child is misbehaving every time there is a toileting accident after 6 months of age. Research on adolescent parental knowledge of normal developmental norms does, in fact, reveal that teenage parents expected toilet training to be complete by 24 weeks of age. The teenage parents demonstrated a similar lack of familiarity with virtually all motor, language, and social developmental norms (Parke & Tinsley, 1987).

Parent-Teaching Strategies. The ways in which parents elect to instruct their children and help them learn to function in the world can influence their social and cognitive development. Style of communication can set the stage for the child's behavior. For example, the manner in which parents instruct children can foster independent free thinking or an insecure dependence on others. Sigel (1982) uses the concept of *distancing strategies* to study the mental operational demands parents place upon their children. Distancing denotes "the psychological separation of the person from the immediate, ongoing present" (p. 50). A parent's ability to separate herself from the child and the accomplishment of a task while providing the essential encouragement and support is at issue. Distancing is an essential element in the development of representational thinking in children.

Child Characteristics.   Child characteristics can affect the nature of parent–child interactions. In an extensive review of the literature on research related to interaction patterns of parent–infant pairs at risk, Hanson (1984) identified many child and mother characteristics that seem to be condition specific. For example, premature infants, who are biologically not ready to function in an extrauterine environment, demonstrate poor motoric processes and state modulation (Sostek, Quinn, & Davitt, 1979); show less frequent and acoustically different crying (Lester & Zeskind, 1979); require more stimulation to become attentive and socially responsive (Field, 1977a); and demonstrate a lower threshold for stimulation (Field, 1977a). Mothers of premature infants more actively stimulated infants during feeding, showing less sensitivity to the infant's rhythms and signals (Field, 1977b; Brown & Bakeman, 1979). The mothers of sick babies are more likely to hold the baby at arm's length and less likely to nestle the baby closely.

Research related to the interaction patterns of infants and young children with developmental delays or at-risk for delay provides evidence of the influence that handicapping conditions can have on these interactions as well (e.g., Thoman, Becker, & Freese, 1978; Kogan, Wimberger, & Bobbitt, 1969; Shere & Kastenbaum, 1966; Kogan, Tyler, & Turner, 1974; Fraiberg, 1975; Kekelis & Anderson, 1982).

Children who exhibit affective disorders raise the ultimate question, "Are disturbed interactional patterns caused by the infant's behavior, the parent's behavior, or both?" (Hanson, 1984, p. 196) Certain behavioral characteristics, which cut across disabilities, can have a direct impact on family functioning and, therefore, child development. Three domains in which infants and children exhibit differential patterns of behavior are *temperament, readability,* and *behavior* (Huntington, 1988). Each of these domains has a reciprocal influence on parent–child interactions and, therefore, an impact on the nature of the home environment. How the child behaves influences how the parent behaves, which influences how the child behaves. These characteristics are discussed in further detail in Chapter 12.

ALTERNATIVE CHILDREARING LOCATIONS

While most children are raised in home environments, many children, especially those with disabilities, have no traditional home. Institutions that provide these children with the basic necessities of life are unable to provide the stimulating and nurturing home environment children need to achieve their full potential. Provence and Lipton (1962) conducted a study of the development of institutionalized infants during the first year of life as compared with the development of infants in a family setting. At the end of the first year of life, the institutionalized infants showed a discrepancy between maturation of the motor system and their ability to use it in adapting to the environment. As early as the second month diminished output of vocalizations was noted, and by the end of the first year retardation of all forms of communication was clearly evident. The children had little interest in all aspects of the environment, even themselves. At the end of the first year of life, the basic processes of learning as well as the mastery of developmental tasks were seriously disturbed and distorted in the institutionalized infants. Previous studies by Spitz (1947) and Skeels and Dye (1939) also showed the dramatic contrast between a nurturing environment and an institutional placement devoid of such.

Infants with known disabilities are particularly at-risk to suffer detrimental effects of institutionalization, while at the same time being more likely to be so placed. Stedman and Eichorn (1964) analyzed the performance of Down's syndrome infants raised in an institution versus those raised at home. Those raised in the institution scored significantly lower on mental and social scales than the home-reared group. Jackson (1982) describes the danger of institutionalization on child development: "With the handicapped infant who may initially make minimal, or in some cases, no attempt to extract information from his or her environment, there is almost no potential for development in an institution" (p. 64).

Babies have taken up residence in hospital nurseries in states that prohibit release of newborns to known drug addicts. These infants have become known as boarder babies. Some children, whose home environments are not suitable, become the responsibility of the state in which they reside. An alternative for them is foster care. Another unacceptable but realistic alternative present today is homelessness. Such an option might make institutions appear more acceptable. However, a lack of stimulation and affection can be as devastating as physical discomfort. Further discussion of these issues is found in Chapter 14.

RATIONALE FOR ANALYSIS OF THE HOME ENVIRONMENT

Assessment models that fail to include an analysis of the home environment can miss critical information necessary for effective planning and intervention. Environmental influences from the home might be overlooked or misinterpreted if not directly assessed (Simeonsson, 1988). The 3-year-old who fails to notify the teacher when he has wet his pants might appear to be unconcerned with the discomfort of wet pants and therefore not developmentally ready to be toilet trained. On the other hand, an analysis of the home environment might reveal that the child is spanked if he comes home from preschool in the clean clothes kept at school for such accidents. The wet pants are uncomfortable, but not so much so as to be worth facing the certainty of a spanking that afternoon for having an accident at school.

Often simple modifications of the environment can provide the least intrusive most effective intervention strategy. For the mother who is having difficulty feeding her child with physical impairments, an environmental analysis might reveal the need to alter positioning for feeding, to change the sequencing of events to reduce activity level just prior to feeding, to adjust the number of people present in the room during feeding, or to turn the television off during feedings. Repeated training sessions on how to feed the child properly might never address the specific circumstances present in the home that are contributing to the difficulty and therefore might fail to lead to any improvement in functioning.

An awareness of the home environment can influence how the interventionist presents lessons in a center-based program. In planning for the child with feeding difficulties, it might be beneficial to create as similar as possible circumstances surrounding feeding times at the center and at home (e.g., use same seating, similar adapted utensils, plates and cups, and consistent verbal and nonverbal cues throughout the feeding period and maintain a stable routine and daily sequence related to feeding). Modifications in both the home routine and the center routine would be needed to achieve the most effective match. The center should adjust to those elements of the home environment that are primary to the home environment (e.g., two siblings present during a feeding session); the modifications at the home should be aimed toward maximizing the potential success (e.g., appropriate activity sequencing prior to feeding). Interventionists who plan lessons hoping the children will generalize the skills taught across environments must be cognizant of the nature of those environments.

DATA-GATHERING PROCEDURES AND TECHNIQUES

The systematic collection of data for the purpose of an analysis of the home environment is challenging. Scheduling interviews, honoring a family's right to privacy while fulfilling a professional responsibility to the child, and identifying relevant variables on which to gather data all require sensitivity and flexibility. If the collection of such data is viewed as part of an ongoing intervention program rather than an essential prerequisite to service delivery, relationships can be established over time, reducing initial hesitancy to share information. Once such barriers have been reduced or eliminated, a variety of procedures can be used. Wachs (1988) described three alternative methods of measuring a child's psychosocial environment: (1) *clinical interviews with parents,* (2) *questionnaires and attitude scales,* and (3) *direct observation of parent–child interactions.*

Clinical Interviews

Interviews can provide a relatively quick method of obtaining information about the past or the present and can cover incidents and settings for which other procedures cannot be used. They are most effective when combined with additional data-gathering procedures, since there are limitations to the interview process. Nonrepresentative reporting by the parents, lack of accurate recall of past events, and lack of adequate psychometric information reduce the confidence that can be placed in data obtained through the interview process. Reducing the effects of these limitations increases an interventionist's ability to obtain meaningful data. Nonrepresentative reporting by parents can be detected through the use of multiple sources of data if necessary. For example, siblings and extended family members can also be interviewed. Inaccurate recall of past events is eliminated as a concern when interviews focus entirely on current circumstances. The need for valid information may take precedence over the need for background information.

The lack of psychometric information can be reduced when semistructured interviews are used, with predetermined questions covering specific areas of concern (Wachs, 1988). Ragozin, Basham, Crnic, Greenberg, and Robinson (1982) developed such a technique for use with normal children in the *Satisfaction with Family Scale.* Another technique to increase psychometric information is a postinterview rating by the interviewer. Greenberg (1983) created such a scale for use with parents of young children with hearing impairments. It includes four components—parental overprotectiveness, quality of environment, child adaptation, and child attachment. A scale addressing five qualities of the environment of older retarded children is also available (Nihara, Mink, & Meyers, 1985). Appropriate use of the clinical interview procedure and circumspect interpretation of the information obtained through it can provide the early interventionist with new insights into a developing child.

Approaches to the Interview.   The diagrammatic assessment of family relationships through the development of an *eco-map* (Hartman, 1978) provides a visual image of the family operating within a multiplicity of systems. The eco-map is a visual representation of the major systems of which the family is part and the nature of the relationships within and among the various systems and family members. Figure 6.1 depicts a sample eco-map, which is most effectively completed through an interview process with members of the family. In the center, the members of the family should be represented in a traditional family tree, with squares representing males and circles representing females. The age of the individual should be placed in the center of the representative shape. Connections between the family and other systems within the environment, such as recreational programs, social welfare systems, health care providers, religious affiliations, employment, and extended family, are shown by connecting lines. The characteristic nature of the connection (strong, conflicted, or tenuous relationships) can be represented by the type of line drawn (see key in Figure 6.1) or through brief notes added to the drawing.

Hartman (1978) stresses the benefit such a visual image can have on family members, as "connections, the themes, and the quality of the family's life seem to

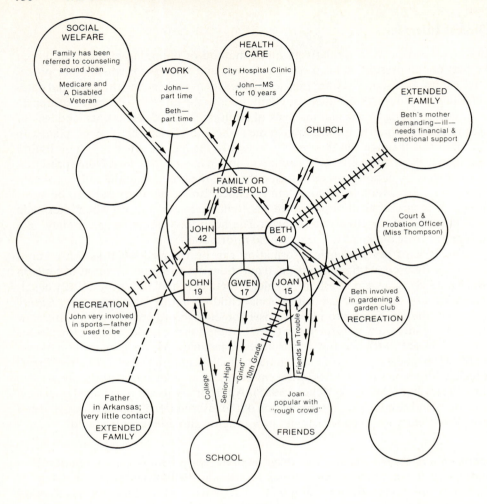

Fill in connections where they exist.

Indicate nature of connections with a descriptive word or by drawing different kinds of lines:
———— for strong, — — —for tenuous, ⊣⊦⊢ for stressful.

Draw arrows along lines to signify flow of energy, resources, etc. →-→-→

Identify significant people and fill in empty circles as needed.

Figure 6.1. Sample Eco-Map.
Source: A. Hartman (1978). "Diagrammatic Assessment of Family Relationships." *Social Casework,*
59, 465–476. Milwaukee: Family Service America. Reprinted by permission.

jump off the page and this leads to a more holistic and integrative perception" (p. 468). The eco-map has been used effectively with natural parents whose children were in temporary foster care as a result of abuse or neglect; it was beneficial in the development of task-oriented contracts, outlining the changes needed prior to a ·reunification of the family. The ecological view of the family as provided by the eco-map helps professionals identify essential systems of nurturance, stimulation, and support. The social and functional skills that family members must have to cope with the demands of their lives are also considered. As information is obtained to complete the eco-map, patterns of adaptive and maladaptive coping emerge. Programming can then become responsive to the concerns that result from this process.

The *Henderson Environmental Learning Process Scale* (Henderson, Bergan, & Hurt, 1972) is a structured interview designed to obtain information about such variables as aspirations of parents, environmental stimulation, parental guidance, models, and reinforcement. It covers five key factors: (1) extended interests and community involvement; (2) valuing language and school-related behavior; (3) intellectual guidance; (4) providing a supportive environment for school learning; and (5) attention. Questions such as, "How often do you read the newspaper?" "How often do you visit someone who is not related to you?" "When (child) goes someplace with you, how likely are you to try to point out things which he may not have noticed before?" and "Not counting what happens at school, how often does (child) go to the library, or a museum, or someplace like that?" The instrument has been correlated to child performance on the *Stanford Early Achievement Test* and the *Boehm Test of Basic Concepts*. Two factors, "valuing language and school-related behavior" and "providing a supportive environment for school learning," have the strongest predictive values. The only factor that was not significant was intellectual guidance. Interventionists can use results of the questionnaire to assist the parents in identifying ways to modify the home environment to enhance their child's development.

Parent Questionnaires

Information about parental attitudes toward their child and parental perceptions about the family environment and/or other nonfamily environmental factors, such as social support networks, can be obtained through the use of questionnaires. They are, however, subject to the same limitations as those related to the interview process. Although psychometric information is more available through some questionnaires than it is with interviews, the norming groups frequently represent a fairly narrow population (e.g., narrow age span of the children or parents of children with a specific disability). If questionnaires that were originally intended for one population are used with parents who were not represented by the norming group, either new reliability studies should be done or interpretations of results should be done with great caution. Additionally, parents may provide nonrepresentative information about the family environment. If older siblings are available, they can be used to provide a cross-check on the information provided by the parents (Daniels & Plomin, 1985).

Instruments.   Parental attitudes toward their developmentally disabled child can be assessed with the *Parent Attitude Research Instrument* (PARI) by Schaefer and Bell (1958). The PARI has 115 items representing 23 separate categories, such as autonomy of the child, strictness, encouraging verbalizations, fostering dependency, and suppression of aggression. The categories can be used to create two bipolar dimensions—warmth and authoritarianism. While the instrument has been challenged as being more a function of the level of education a parent has than of specific attitudes toward the child and her disability, some consistent attitudinal differences have been found (Cook, 1963).

A number of questionnaires have been developed to address parental perceptions of the family environments in which their handicapped children live. The *Questionnaire on Resources and Stress* (Holroyd, 1974, 1986), described in section A.3 of the appendix in Chapter 5, has been used with several handicapped groups, including the retarded (Holroyd & McArthur, 1976), the motorically impaired (Friedrich & Friedrich, 1981), the deaf (Greenberg, 1983), and the behaviorally disturbed (Holroyd & Guthrie, 1979). Another instrument designed to rate parental perceptions of the social climate of the family is the *Family Environment Scale* (FES) (Moos & Moos, 1981). The FES contains 90 true–false items that represent 10 dimensions of social climate, such as family conflict, family cohesion, and family achievement orientation. (Questionnaires addressing social support networks are included in Chapter 5.)

Direct Observation

Observation techniques can be used to gather data on both the physical and non-physical aspects of the home environment. Structured coding systems and/or predetermined categories can be used or running records can be kept to be analyzed for significant environmental factors affecting behaviors of people within the home environment. Specific concerns can also be targeted for observation. For example, a parent might request an observation that would focus on her response to her child's tantrums, or on her child's refusal to speak when her siblings are present, or how well her home is arranged to meet the needs of her blind toddler. Such a request would most often require the development of an individual observation plan that would employ personalized categories of behavior. On other occasions, a general analysis of the home environment might be more appropriate.

The *Purdue Home Stimulation Inventory* (PHSI) (Wachs, 1979; Wachs, Francis, & Mcquiston, 1978), which involves both interview and observation, can provide guidance for an overall analysis of the home environment. The most recent version includes both a physical and social scale. The complete scale contains four sections. Section I covers basics such as the number of siblings living at home, the frequency with which the child is taken out of the neighborhood, whether the child has a regular nap time, and the number of adults who actively take care of the child. Section II addresses specific characteristics of the physical environment, which can be easily noted during an observation. Items included in section II cover such features of the home environment as, home has a place where the child can be away from people and noise (stimulus shelter); free and easy access to appropriate toys, papers, books, and magazines; decorations of pictures and/or objects within the child's room and whether those are periodically changed; and the rate of maternal speech.

Section III of the PHSI is completed by the observer following a period of 15 minutes of direct observation. It covers a variety of physical features of the environment, such as the number of stimulus sources, sound and activity levels, and the total number of people in the house during the 15-minute observation. Section IV, the final section of the PHSI, addresses the social environment found within the home. It focuses on interactions between individuals within the home and is also completed based on 15-minute observation periods. Ratings include parental investment (e.g., ignoring the child, responsive to child-initiated acts, and parental-initiated acts), parental affect toward the child, spontaneous vocalizations made by adults to the child, and the number of times anyone names a definite object for the child.

The scales have been used extensively in research with the families of young children. Interobserver reliability checks that are satisfactory are reported for every item included on the scales. These data are based on 45-minute observations that were scheduled twice a month over a 1-year period of time.

The *Home Observation for Measurement of the Environment* (HOME) (Caldwell, 1972) is divided into two scales based on age of the child—one for families of infants and toddlers (birth to 3) and the other for families of preschool-age children. The HOME has undergone numerous revisions and is described now as the "current" version rather than the "final" one, because the developers believe that continual revision and improvement of the inventory are critical to its usefulness. The inventory should be administered by a person who goes into the home and observes the child's normal routine over approximately one hour. Some of the items require information that must be obtained through an interview with the parent. These deal with (1) trips out of the home and visits into the home; (2) toys available to the child; (3) ways the family arranges the daily routine; and (4) discipline. The current version of the HOME Inventory designed for use with families of infants and toddlers has 45 items divided into six subscales. These subscales and a brief description of each are presented in the following list:

I. Emotional and Verbal Responsivity of Mother
   Includes items that note the types of affection the mother displays and verbal interactions she initiates; scolding and other negative exchanges are not counted in this section

II. Avoidance of Restriction and Punishment
   Includes items that cover whether the mother interfered in the child's play or restricted his movements and the mother's negative verbal interactions with the child

III. Organization of Physical and Temporal Environment
   Covers the breadth of a child's environment (e.g., frequency of trips out of the home), the use of appropriate caregivers, and the safety of the child's play environment

IV. Provision of Appropriate Play Materials
   Addresses the types of toys available (e.g., muscle activity equipment) and the way the mother entertains the child during the interview (Are toys provided?)

V. Maternal Involvement with Child
   Covers mother's general supervision and awareness of the child (e.g., maintaining child within visual range and "talking" to the child while he is working)

   VI. Opportunities for Variety in Daily Stimulation
Includes variety available in the child's daily experiences (e.g., opportunities for interaction with the father and the frequency with which stories are read to the child)

The preschool version of the HOME has a total of 55 items divided into eight subscales. These subscales are shown in the list that follows:

    I. Stimulation through Toys, Games, and Reading Materials
Covers the breadth and depth of materials present in the home (e.g., Are puzzles or blocks with letters or numbers available? and Is newspaper read in the home on a daily basis?)

   II. Language Stimulation
Addresses the availability of toys and materials that encourage language development, parent requesting child to use appropriate speech (e.g., please and thank you), and permitting the child to make choices

  III. Physical Environment: Safe, Clean, and Conducive to Development
Reviews the characteristics of the environment (e.g., amount of living space per person, clutter, and safe outside play area)

  IV. Pride, Affection, and Warmth
Notes frequency of mother's positive interactions (both physical and verbal) with the child during the visit

   V. Stimulation of Academic Behavior
Notes the extent to which the mother encourages the child to learn (e.g., colors, letters, and simple reading words)

  VI. Modeling and Encouragement of Social Maturity
Covers range of characteristics (e.g., use of television and reactions to child's expression of negative feelings)

 VII. Variety of Stimulation
Addresses the child's exposure to variety in language, experience, and play (e.g., mother's use of complex sentence structure, trips of distances greater than 50 miles, and availability of musical instruments for play)

VIII. Physical Punishment
Notes the mother's avoidance of physical punishment (restraint, shaking, grabbing, and pinching) during the observation and over the past week as based on parent report)

Each item on both instruments is rated on a yes and no basis according to information gathered through the combination interview and observation. Reliability as measured by internal consistency estimates for the total scale and each subscale of both inventories were reported at acceptable levels. Stability of items has also been studied across extended time periods. While there appears to be some test–retest influence, scores are generally stable over time. If use of the instrument results in improved home environments, it could be viewed as an effective component of an intervention program. Construct validity is discussed at length in the HOME Manual.

The *Parent–Child and Family Interaction Observation Schedule* (Sigel & Flaugher, 1987) is designed to evaluate parent–child and family (i.e., mother, father, and child) interactions. Interactions are coded as to the level of mental operational demands (low-, medium-, or high-distancing demands), structuring, correction, and level of content of information. Additional characteristics of the interaction include verbal emotional support systems (e.g., approval, disapproval, and information giving), nonverbal behaviors (e.g., helping, taking over, modeling, and positive and negative affect), and behavioral responses (e.g., activity, initiative, resistance, parallel activity, and no time). The current version of this instrument has a range of interrater agreement between pairs of coders for mental operational demands of 72% to 99%, with a mean of 86.5% (based on a sample of 20% of 480 videotaped parent–child interactions).

Yarrow, Rubenstein, and Pedersen (1975) have also developed observational systems for use in research that cover several dimensions of home environments. One focuses on mother–infant interactions and includes the context in which the interaction takes place, the proximity of the caregiver, infant behavior, descriptions of sources of stimulation, social stimulation provided for the infant, changes in location of the infant, and inanimate stimulation. Specific definitions and instructions for observers are included. A second instrument provides a maternal rating on two dimensions—expression of positive affect and contingency of maternal responses to distress. Characteristics of the inanimate environment and infant problem-solving ability are addressed on two additional instruments. (Additional instruments useful for observing parent–child interactions were presented in section A.3 of the appendix in Chapter 5.)

SUMMARY

This chapter has addressed the need for early childhood special educators to be aware of and sensitive to home environments. An analysis of the home environment can be useful in functional program planning (i.e., teach the skills needed in the immediate environment); assisting the parents in management of the child (both physical and behavioral); altering the physical environment to improve child functioning (e.g., furniture arrangements that ease orientation and mobility training for a visually impaired child); and identifying negative factors within the home environment that could contribute to the child's developmental delays. A review of the literature on the effects of the home environment was covered, focusing on those contributing to an understanding of environmental specificity, including environmental factors, age, and characteristics of the child. Both physical and nonphysical features influence child development. Nonphysical features of the home environment include family subsystems, social climate and support systems, the nature of interactions, stimulus deprivation and enrichment, parents' beliefs and knowledge, and child characteristics.

With an emphasis on the importance of the home environment, an awareness that many children do not live in traditional homes or with intact families is important. The effects of alternative childrearing locations on child development has been the subject of several longitudinal research studies. As interventionists assess and work with children who live in alternative childrearing locations, they need to be sensitive to the impact made by the environment on the child's life.

The final section of the chapter covered data-gathering procedures and techniques that can be used in the analysis of home environments as related to effective early intervention. This section includes a review of the *Purdue Home Stimulation Inventory* and the *Home Observation for Measurement of the Environment*.

THE ECOLOGICAL PERSPECTIVE

- A child's development is influenced by her home environment, and therefore a child's assessment needs to acknowledge the nature of that child's home life.
- There is an interactive reciprocal relationship between physical and non-physical features of a home environment as related to influences on child development.
- Data gathering that emphasizes observations in the home can provide ecologically valid information about the child's home life.
- The process of data gathering about the home environment can be developed over an extended period of time, as relationships between parents and professionals become open and trusting.

Environmental Analysis: The Preschool Setting

Vey M. Nordquist
Sandra Twardosz

CHAPTER OUTLINE

QUESTIONS ANSWERED IN CHAPTER 7

- What is an activity-based model of a special preschool program, and what are its implications for environmental assessment?
- What does the term *environmental organization* mean, and what are the implications for assessing special preschool classrooms?
- What are some current methods of assessing preschool environments?
- Why is it important to assess the physical, social, and programmatic features of preschool environments?
- What are the steps involved in the process of assessing preschool environments for organizational problems?
- What are some possible benefits of organizational assessment?

CHAPTER OVERVIEW

During the past decade early interventionists have become increasingly interested in the organizational features of early childhood classrooms, as growing empirical evidence from a variety of sources documented how the classroom environment affects children's behavior (Bailey, 1989; Bailey & Wolery, 1984; Harms & Clifford, 1983; Rogers-Warren, 1984; Rogers-Warren & Wedel, 1980; Twardosz, 1984a). For example, organizational features such as predictable activity schedules (Fredericksen & Fredericksen, 1977), assignment of teachers to activity areas rather than groups of children (LeLaurin & Risley, 1972), and sequencing of activities (Krantz & Risley, 1977) have been shown to promote engagement and reduce behavior problems. Thus, the careful assessment of the organizational features of classroom environments would seem essential if children are to optimally benefit from participation in a classroom-based early intervention program (Dunst, McWilliam, & Holbert, 1986).

The task of describing, much less explaining, environment and development relationships is so complicated that only a small number of behavioral scientists have attempted to deal with both its breadth and its detail at the same time (Bricker, 1986). Most methods allow assessment of only selected aspects of the classroom such as the physical atmosphere (Stallings, 1977), arrangement of space (Moore, 1982), and availability of equipment (Frost & Klein, 1979). The comprehensive assessment of preschool environments is, therefore, in the infant stage of empirical development; only a handful of instruments are currently available for professional use.

Detailed descriptions of both comprehensive and limited assessment methods have appeared in the early childhood special education literature (e.g., Bailey, Clifford, & Harms, 1982; Dunst et al., 1986; Harms & Clifford, 1983; Moore, 1982; Risley & Cataldo, 1974) and are described in an excellent article on environmental assessment prepared by Bailey (1989). One purpose of this chapter, therefore, is not to reexamine this literature, but rather to draw on it as a means of illustrating how these methods have been used and to describe a different approach to environmental assessment, one that is useful as a first step in helping to solve problems posed by the environment.

In preparation for the discussion that follows, it is important to observe three caveats, two of which were noted by Bricker (1986). First, it is unlikely that the "goodness" or "badness" of classroom organization can be determined with an absolute scale. Rather, the appropriateness of a particular organization should be determined within the context of program goals that are established for individual children. Consequently, suggestions for organizational assessment that are offered in this chapter should be viewed as general guidelines that may require some modification before application to a particular classroom.

A second caveat is that the preschool environment should be seen as a dynamic relationship of its physical, social, and programmatic features. Nordquist and Twardosz (1990) recognized this relationship when they referred to the need for teachers to take an "integrative view" of environmental organization, one that appreciates how all aspects of the classroom environment work together to achieve optimal effects on children's development. For example, teachers may be able to overcome an inconvenient environment through thoughtful and creative activity scheduling and staffing assignments. However, even the most well-designed and equipped classroom may not be able to engage children's participation if scheduling problems result in a great deal of waiting. By remembering the dynamic nature of the preschool environment, teachers will better understand the need to assess all of its organizational features before drawing conclusions about the relationship between classroom organization and children's behavior.

Third, methods of environmental assessment that are described in this chapter are based upon empirical research. Most of the early studies were conducted in regular early education programs that served children without special needs. The principles and procedures that emerged from this literature were then applied and evaluated in special preschool programs. Most of this information is now available in early childhood special education textbooks (e.g., Bailey & Worley, 1984; Petersen, 1987) and needs to be thoroughly understood before it is possible to assess preschool environments effectively. However, the one method that is the primary subject of this chapter appears nowhere in the literature. It evolved from the authors' research experience and through repeated assessments of a variety of early childhood programs and other caregiving and educational settings. To date, the number of programs that have been assessed using this method is relatively small. Therefore, general guidelines are offered with the understanding that application of the method to some programs may not be fully possible. Hopefully, future advances in empirical knowledge and a greater diversity of educational applications will lead to the development of a more formal, generalizable, and comprehensive method of assessing preschool classrooms for organizational problems.

The chapter is organized into four sections. The first, *Current Trends and Conceptual Issues,* includes a discussion of philosophical developments and programmatic considerations that have evolved in the field of early childhood special education and have important implications for environmental assessment. The first section also includes a definition of environmental organization and an explanation of conceptual issues related to the organizational aspects of preschool classrooms.

The second section, *Current Methods of Assessing Preschool Environments,* includes descriptions of common instruments that have been used to assess preschool environments and present some of their advantages and disadvantages. In the third section, *Assessing Preschool Environments for Organizational Problems,* a method for identifying problems that are due to organizational features of environments is described. The fourth and final section of the chapter provides a summary.

CURRENT TRENDS AND CONCEPTUAL ISSUES

Early childhood special education classrooms vary in terms of program goals, staff composition, assessment and evaluation procedures, curriculum, and materials and activities (Petersen, 1987). However, within the past decade more of these programs have begun to share the common goal of promoting learning through activity-based instruction and experiences that encourage children to initiate their own activities, elaborate on the skills acquired during instruction, and generalize these skills to new situations (Beckman, Robinson, Jackson, & Rosenberg, 1986; Bricker, 1989). Furthermore, children with special needs are increasingly mainstreamed into regular early childhood programs where this type of approach to facilitating children's development and education is common. These trends have implications for the manner in which classroom environments are organized and assessed.

Activity-based instruction with opportunities for initiation, elaboration, and generalization contrasts sharply with the way in which special education programs have historically been provided. In the more traditional model, instruction is provided in specialized classrooms where each child's developmental needs are identified and then translated into learning goals through the Individual Education Plan (IEP). Teachers then select methods and activities directed toward achieving these individualized goals. Traditional classrooms typically incorporate schedules, materials, activities, and teaching methods that are "artificial" in the sense that they have little in common with those used in regular early childhood programs. For example, little time is devoted to free play, and most instruction is teacher-directed. Consequently, the developmental outcomes associated with these specialized classrooms often are quite different from those that characterize children's progress in normalized classrooms and probably account, in part, for the frequent difficulties that children with special needs have making transitions to more normalized classroom settings (Carta, Atwater, Schwartz & Miller, 1990).

With the passage of the Reauthorization of the Education for all Handicapped Children Act (PL 99–457), a large number of young children with special needs are bound to be enrolled in regular day care programs (McEvoy, 1990). Thus, teachers are increasingly expected to provide instruction and experiences that will help equip children with such skills as initiation, elaboration, and generalization, which are essential for successful placement in normalized classroom settings. Like their counterparts in regular education (e.g., Elkind, 1986; Bredekemp, 1987), special educators are beginning to shift from an emphasis on teacher-directed activities to more functional, play-oriented interventions that take advantage of children's natural curiosity and desire to explore and experiment through play. Of course, a shift from the traditional model of special education also necessitates a reconceptualization of what children should be doing in the classroom and how the classroom environment should be organized to promote individualized learning goals.

Children's Engagement with the Environment

Children's engagement or active involvement with their environment, including materials, equipment, activities, teachers, and peers, is a primary focus of the activity-based approach to early childhood special education, as it is in any environment that seeks to enhance development and learning (Twardosz & Risley, 1982). It is considered one of the best indicators of children's progress toward a variety of learning goals (McWilliam, Trivette, & Dunst, 1985). Its operational definition varies according to the type of ongoing activity and teachers' expectations for appropriate behavior during that activity (Bailey, Harms & Clifford, 1983). For example, during a teacher-directed story time engagement would include looking at the book or teacher, responding to or asking questions, listening to other children's comments, and requesting that the teacher read another book. Engagement would not include waiting for the teacher to locate a book, disturbing other children by poking them, or trying to leave the activity. Engagement during free play would include playing with materials alone or with others, becoming involved in a group game, reading a book, and watching a teacher demonstrate how a material should be used. It would not include wandering around the room, fighting, or waiting to use a toy or piece of play equipment.

As will be described in the next section of this chapter, children's engagement with their environment has been a primary focus of a number of the assessment methods that have been designed to describe and evaluate early childhood special education classrooms. And, as has been demonstrated in a variety of educational environments, children's engagement can be encouraged through specific arrangements of the environment.

Organizational Features of Preschool Environments

There are physical, social, and programmatic features of early childhood classrooms that can contribute to children's engagement with their environment. The physical features include the architectural layout, furnishings and equipment, play materials and activities, and food, including type and manner of serving. Social and programmatic aspects include the number and location of children and teachers, the division of responsibilities among teachers, activity schedules, and the way in which children move from one activity to another (Rogers-Warren & Wedel, 1980; Twardosz, 1984a).

Organizational features of preschool classrooms operate as setting events, that is, conditions that make it more likely that previously acquired behaviors will occur (Bijou & Baer, 1961; Twardosz, 1984a; Wahler & Fox, 1981). These may be of two types: immediate surrounding circumstances that make it more likely that children or teachers will behave in a particular way, or previous events that influence their future behavior. For example, a classroom that is organized into activity areas may "set the occasion" for more play and peer interaction than one where toys and materials are available but scattered around. Or, a child who has had a particularly stormy morning with parents before coming to school may react to the classroom routines differently than he will on more peaceful mornings.

Studies in a variety of caregiving and educational settings have demonstrated the results of arranging aspects of the environment to set the occasion for desired types of children's engagement. For example, family-style serving of meals, in which bowls of food are passed around by children, promotes more social interaction than the cafeteria-style method, in which food is placed on children's plates before they receive them (e.g., VanBiervliet, Spangler, & Marshall, 1981). If a brief rest period separates the end of outdoor play from the beginning of a quiet indoor activity, there are fewer disruptions during the quiet activity (Krantz & Risley, 1977). Consult Twardosz (1984a) for a review of the literature on the operation of environmental setting events and Nordquist and Twardosz (1990) for a discussion of their role in preventing behavior problems.

Aspects of the physical, social, and programmatic environment that operate as setting events are, therefore, key elements in increasing children's engagement and minimizing disruptions in early childhood education classrooms. In addition to affecting the children's behavior directly, these aspects of the environment also make it easier for teachers to implement other components of the curriculum. For example, if the majority of the children are profitably engaged with materials and each other during free play, it is more likely that a teacher will be able to spend some time encouraging a language-delayed child to speak more elaborately. Because of their widespread effects, these aspects have become the focus of a variety of assessment instruments.

CURRENT METHODS OF ASSESSING PRESCHOOL ENVIRONMENTS

A number of assessment instruments are available that quantify the environmental aspects of early childhood education settings that promote engagement. Dunst et al. (1986) described several of these instruments and noted that each one was designed somewhat differently, depending upon the manner in which the environment was defined, the expectations of how the environment affected children's development, and the purposes for which the instruments were intended. Some instruments reflect very broad definitions of the preschool environment, include measures of both the environment and child behavior, and are used to evaluate the total program or conduct comparative studies of different programs. Others are used to assess specific features of preschool classrooms such as the physical environment or certain aspects of children's behavior such as material use or peer interaction. These latter instruments were designed to assess only a limited range of environmental–behavioral possibilities, primarily because theoretical arguments or empirical evidence suggested that they could be used to formulate generalizations about the quality of the program as a whole. Instruments that only measure engagement, for example, do not provide direct information about environmental features such as open space, availability of materials, or assignment of teachers to areas, but they do suggest that these or other features of preschool environments may need to be reorganized if levels of engagement are low.

Most instruments for assessing preschool environments utilize rating scale or checklist methods. Rating scales are observational tools that indicate the degree to which a person or some aspect of the environment possess a certain feature or characteristic. The possibility of obtaining satisfactory agreement among observers is very good when characteristics are clearly defined and relevant behaviors or events occur often enough so that sufficient samples of the characteristics can be observed. Rating scales consist of a numerical or graphical continuum that is broken down into a sequential series of waypoints that usually reflect a range of the characteristic from very low to very high. Rating scales are easy to construct and apply, and they are very useful when it is important to know the degree to which a characteristic is present in the environment or manifested in behavior (Touliatos & Compton, 1983).

The Early Childhood Environment Rating Scale (ECERS; Harms & Clifford, 1980) and Preschool Assessment of the Classroom Environment (PACE; Dunst et al. 1986) are popular examples of rating scale instruments. They were designed to give an overall picture of preschool settings by assessing gradations of quality across a variety of environmental features. ECERS includes measurement categories such as the use of space, materials, and activities to enhance children's development, the daily schedule, and program supervision. The instrument consists of 37 items organized into seven subscales: personal care routines (1), furnishings and displays (2), language-reasoning experiences (3), fine and gross motor activities (4), creative activities (5), social development (6), and adult needs (7). Each of the 37 items is scored on a Likert-type scale from 1 (inadequate) to 7 (excellent) and every scale contains written descriptions of observable conditions that define ratings of 1, 3, 5, and 7.

Item scores reflect general qualities of the environment and do not pinpoint specific features that may need to be changed. If an ECERS rating for the item "room arrangement" is 1 (inadequate), for example, this could mean that any number of important features of the environment are missing or operating improperly. It might indicate, for example, that activity areas are not clearly defined, that the room is inconveniently arranged (e.g., traffic patterns interfere with activities), or that materials with similar uses are not placed together. It could also mean that quiet and noisy activity areas are near one another, water is not accessible when it is needed, or supervision of particular areas may be difficult. Thus, ECERS can be useful when there is a need to identify *general* areas or activities in a preschool environment that may need to be reorganized.

ECERS has been used primarily to compare environmental features of early education programs. In one study, for example, Bailey, Clifford, and Harms (1982) compared 25 classrooms that served children with handicaps with 56 classrooms that served children without handicaps. The classrooms for children with handicaps were rated significantly lower than those for children without handicaps on 12 of the 37 items; only one item ("provisions for exceptional children") was rated significantly higher for programs that served children with handicaps. The differences between programs were quite pronounced and suggested that preschool children with special needs attended programs that provided very different experiences and opportunities than those available to children without special needs. However, it is possible that some of the differences represented appropriate modifications for the children with special needs. This study demonstrated the usefulness of ECERS for revealing differences in the physical, social, and programmatic features of preschool environments, which raise legitimate questions about the relationship between environmental provision and the development of children. The study also suggested that after certain features of the environment are modified, ECERS could be used again to assess the nature and extent of change through pre–post comparisons of ratings. It could not be used, though, to assess changes in individual children's behavior once reorganization has occurred.

The Preschool Assessment of the Environment Scale (PACE; Dunst et al., 1986) is a 70-item rating scale that assesses four broad categories of the preschool environment: (1) program organization, which includes management of the classroom, parent involvement, and integration of children with and without special needs; (2) environmental organization, which contains measures of the physical environment, staffing patterns, daily schedule, and transitions; (3) methods of instruction, such as type of learning activities, plans for intervention, and behavior management; and (4) program outcomes, which includes assessments of the program evaluation plan and child engagement. Like ECERS, PACE items are scored using a Likert-type format. Ratings of individual items are made on five-point scales after the classroom is observed, teachers are interviewed, and records are reviewed. PACE has been used successfully to differentiate various aspects of preschool programs (e.g., program types, management, organization, and operation of preschool classrooms) and to relate environmental features to various child outcomes (e.g., engagement) as well as staff behavior (e.g., style of interaction).

Checklists are simliar in use and appearance to rating scales but require the observer to make an all-or-none judgment instead of representing the degree to which a characteristic of the environment is present or a behavior is manifested. They are useful when there is a need to know such things as the kinds of materials that are in the classroom, if there is adequate space per child in an activity area, whether a daily schedule is posted, or whether children are moved from one activity to another in groups or individually. In each of these instances the observer is required to check either yes or no.

Most of the checklists available for the assessment of preschool classrooms have been used to evaluate specific aspects of the environment rather than the overall program. The Physical Environment Information Checklist (PEIC) is a good example and was designed specifically to assess physical aspects of a classroom such as size, shape, lighting, ventilation, noise level, and seating arrangements, as well as the equipment and materials available for learning experience (Stallings, 1977). The implication is that engagement is more likley to occur when these conditions are present in the recommended proportion and in relation to one another.

Checklists and rating scales do not provide information about the specific behavior of teachers and children, such as the number of prompts teachers give to children or how often children interact with one another. Furthermore, they were not intended to preserve the temporal flow of events. They do provide, however, general impressions concerning the environmental features of preschool programs and/or behavior. In this respect they can help direct attention to aspects of the environment (e.g., number and variety of materials, availability of toys and equipment) or behavior (teacher roles and assignments) that may be causing organizational problems and impeding children's engagement. More detailed information, the type that captures both the content and flow of events, can be obtained by time-sampling methods.

Time-sampling methods preserve some of the flow of environmental events and behavioral units, but also place constraints on them by specifying what, when, and how recording is to take place. To use the method effectively, it is necessary to define events and units as precisely as possible and divide the observation period into intervals. Rows and columns on the recording form are used to designate behavior and event categories (rows) and observation intervals (columns). Events and behaviors are then coded for successive intervals by indicating whether the event or behavior is present or absent, thus providing some indication of the degree of temporal continuity among events and behaviors in addition to the number of percentage of intervals that include at least one incidence of the event or behavior (Irwin & Bushnell, 1980).

A time-sampling instrument for assessing early childhood education environments is the Ecobehavioral System for the Complex Assessment of Preschol Environments (ESCAPE; Carta, Greenwood, & Atwater, 1985). ESCAPE provides measures of classroom ecology as well as teacher and child behavior. It consists of 92 different measures arranged into 12 separate categories. The ecological categories include activities, activity initiator, materials, locations, groupings, and composition; teacher categories include teacher definition, teacher behavior, and teacher focus; and the child categories include target behaviors, competency behaviors, and talk. Detailed descriptions of the categories, code descriptions, and code examples can be found in Carta et al. (1985) and Carter, Atwater, Schwartz, and Miller (1990). The measures are recorded using a momentary time-sampling system made up of four 15-second intervals that are used to sample all 12 categories of measures one time per minute. The data are then analyzed at both molar and molecular levels (Carta, Greenwood, & Robinson, 1987). A molar analysis allows descriptions of a child's (or group of children's) typical day in the classroom or comparisons of typical days across programs. Carta, Sainato, and Greenwood (1988), for example, showed that the greatest portion of a child's day in special preschool programs is spent in transition activities.

A molecular analysis of ESCAPE data consists of a determination of the conditional probability of a specific measure given the occurrence of one or more other measures. Using this type of analysis, Carta, Greenwood, and Robinson (1987) assessed the probability of preschool children with special needs actively engaging certain types of activities and found that engagement was likely to be high during self-care, fine motor, and play activities, but lower during story and transition activities.

ESCAPE is more likely to reveal potential functional relationships between specific aspects of the environment and behavior than instruments such as rating scales and checklists; and it does so in a manner that assures a fairly close temporal linkage between environmental events and children's responses to them. It also allows a very wide range of events and behaviors to be recorded, making it possible to analyze samples for any number of effects that specific aspects of the preschool environment might have on the behavior of individual children or teachers. The main drawbacks of a time-sampling method such as ESCAPE for the purpose of assessing organizational problems are its dependence upon behavioral categories, which limit what is recorded, and utilization of a recording system that is complicated and requires a great deal of training.

A different type of time-sampling method, one that is not complicated or difficult to use, allows for the group assessment of children's engagement across time. Because engagement is a necessary precondition for most forms of developmental progress and is relatively easy for teachers to define (McWilliam, Trivette, & Dunst, 1985; Bailey et al., 1983), group measures of engagement can be used to assess the extent to which children are participating in an activity and, presumably, benefiting from it. The Planned Activity Check, or PLA-Check (Risley & Cataldo, 1974), provides assessments of engagement by comparing the number of children present in a given area or activity with the number who actually participate. If it is important to know, for example, whether materials in a block area are used frequently and appropriately by most children, PLA-Check will provide this information quite easily. It will not provide measures of individual children's engagement levels, however.

PLA-Check was designed to sample broad aspects of children's behavior in ways that allow inferences to be drawn about the impact of specific features of the environment. It is particularly useful for identifying problems that may be due to poor organization because it provides group percentages of children's participation. When features of the preschool environment are not organized properly, many children are likely to behave in ways that are incompatible with engagement (e.g., Nordquist & Twardosz, 1990; Twardosz & Risley, 1982). Under these circumstances, PLA-Check will reveal low percentages of engagement and thereby direct attention to specific times of the day that may need to be reorganized.

These assessment instruments are varied and reflect the growing appreciation for the role of the environmental context in preschool classrooms. Each has advantages and disadvantages as described earlier, and people who are interested in investigating a variety of issues in early childhood special education will perhaps be able to utilize one of these instruments rather than design another. Thus, the results of diverse studies may be able to be related to one another more easily. In the following section another method of assessing preschool environments is described, one that was developed in the context of helping to provide solutions to problems of environmental organization.

ASSESSING PRESCHOOL ENVIRONMENTS FOR ORGANIZATIONAL PROBLEMS

The method of assessment described in this section consists of four techniques: interviewing, drawing a map, PLA-Checks, and narrative recording. The assumptions that guide the application of the method are common to the methods described previously and include the beliefs that (1) child engagement is essential for achieving developmental and educational goals, (2) learning should be activity-based, and (3) the physical, social, and programmatic features of a preschool setting are constantly affecting children and teachers. The method draws upon techniques of naturalistic observation that are well known and often described in articles and textbooks that address issues and strategies of developmental and environmental assessment (e.g., Bailey, 1989; Petersen, 1987).

The method was not developed deliberately for assessing early education environments; rather, it evolved over a number of years as a useful procedure to follow when gathering information about the operation of programs prior to providing suggestions about how to reorganize them. These techniques have been used to assess day care centers, preschool and elementary classrooms for children with special needs, a residential setting for children with severe hearing impairments, and preschool programs that serve children both with and without special needs. Students analyze early education environments and make recommendations for solving organizational problems or explain why programs are functioning smoothly. The goals of such assessments and recommendations are to increase children's engagement, prevent behavior problems, and make the programs more pleasant for children and teachers.

Steps in the Assessment Process

Interviewing Preschool Personnel.   The first step in the assessment process is to interview the person primarily responsible for the overall program as well as key assistants, i.e., individuals who should be knowledgeable about all aspects of the preschool program and are in a position to bring about change, if necessary. The primary purpose of the interview is to gather information about program components and staff relationships that may have implications for the identification of organizational problems. This kind of information can usually be obtained by following a sequence of interview phases similar to the ones developed by Winton (1988) for interviewing families of children with special needs.

Winton's method includes five phases. In the *preliminary phase,* information about the program that can be gathered prior to the interview should be consolidated and summarized. Written statements about a program's philosophy, goals, and objectives should be read carefully because they may reveal quite a lot about staff knowledge, commitment to program quality, and willingness to consider recommendations based upon assessment results. For example, such materials may reveal a strong commitment to a traditional approach to special education. Written information about specific children might suggest questions that should be posed during the interview. For example, if several children are having similar behavior problems, this could mean that the environment is not organized effectively. Sometimes a teacher will refer to these problems in a telephone conversation, or anecdotal records kept by the staff may contain comments such as, "Children took a long time to go from lunch to nap area," or "Several scuffles occurred in the bathroom today." Comments such as these suggest that a particular routine (in this case a transition routine) may not be organized properly. If this kind of information is available before the interview takes place, it may be possible to expedite the interview process by pursuing focused lines of inquiry.

In the *introductory phase* of the interview, it is important to reduce any anxiety the lead teacher and key staff may have about the impending assessment. Even the most competent professionals may be a little nervous and somewhat skeptical about the usefulness of environmental assessment. Their responses are likely to be more intense in situations where they are having trouble managing children, where there are conflicts among them, when they have not requested the assessment but rather had it "imposed" upon them by someone else such as a system administrator, or when they have requested an assessment without the full support of an administrator.

An important goal of the introductory phase of the interview, therefore, is to create a climate of support for the assessment process. This is accomplished in part by explaining the purpose of the interview, confirming the time allotted and format that will be used, and clarifying issues such as confidentiality of information. Some of these issues should be discussed when the interview is arranged, for instance, establishing a mutually agreed on time for the interview when the lead teacher and other key personnel can be present. Scheduling a time for the interview can be a major undertaking depending on the number of people involved, but it should be done only when everyone can be there, preferably at a time convenient to all. Having everyone at the initial meeting is important because it may be the only time that signs of conflict or support among the staff will be revealed. The only reason to consider a different interview format is when the lead teacher requests meeting alone. If this happens, the request should be honored, but also considered a possible sign of staff conflict.

In the *inventory phase,* it is important initially to let the lead teacher and other key staff do most of the talking. The interviewer should listen and patiently validate and elaborate the assessment information previously gathered from the lead teacher and/or written records. It is also important to remain open to unanticipated issues, concerns, or problems that were not revealed during the preliminary phase of the interview process. Often discussion at this level will reveal strengths or weaknesses in the relationships among personnel. For example, staff may reveal warmth toward one another by smiling, complimenting one another's efforts, or teasing and joking. Dissatisfaction may be revealed by neutral or hostile facial expressions, silence, or even sarcastic remarks.

Once staff have aired their wishes and concerns, it is time to inquire further about program components and/or children in areas where clarification is needed. Usually questions will involve programmatic components such as supervision of activity areas, assignment of staff responsibilities, scheduling of activities, and movement of children from one activity to another, or social components that reflect difficulties that staff are having with individual children. Most teachers can describe the physical features of their program quite well but have difficulty specifying precisely how the programmatic features are organized. For example, teachers are not inclined to mention how daily activities and routines are scheduled unless they are asked. They are much more likely to list activities and describe how they are conducted, focusing on materials and/or learning goals first and methods of instruction second, often doing so in general rather than specific terms. This information may be useful from the point of view of curriculum issues, but it is not very useful from the point of view of identifying organizational problems, unless references are made specifically to the level and quality of engagement. If there are concerns about the behavior problems of individual children, staff may tend to conceptualize their origins in terms of family or personality factors and may need some guidance to see them, at least partially, as possible reactions to features of the environment, such as periods of waiting.

During the *summary, priority, and goal-setting phase,* it is important to summarize what has been discussed and formulate meaningful, practical agreements whose importance to all participants is clearly recognized. At the very least, it is important that (1) times be designated for conducting direct observation in the preschool program; (2) observational procedures be specified, including any restrictions on the times, activities, children, or staff that may be observed; (3) methods of informing other staff about the purpose and techniques of direct observation be clarified; and (4) ways be identified for informing people if any aspect of the assessment process must be changed.

During the *closing phase,* it is important to express appreciation and recognition of the participants' time and effort, make plans for future meetings, and give participants a final opportunity to reflect on feelings about the interview. Participants sometimes use this time to mention information that did not emerge during the formal phases of the interview. In addition, if participants shared personal or emotionally laden information or engaged in heated disagreements among themselves, they may have second thoughts about their candor. For these reasons, some time should be devoted to closure and an effort made to listen to and address the final thoughts, concerns, and questions of the participants. If the interview was particularly difficult, a follow-up phone call to the lead teacher often helps to reassure her.

Observing the Preschool Program.   Direct observation of a preschool program can be a confusing and unproductive experience without the benefit of some general guidelines. It is important to be unobtrusive and keep reactivity effects to a minimum. Therefore, it may be necessary to visit the program several times until teachers and children are accustomed to the presence of an observer. Teachers can help control reactivity effects by preparing the children for the visits. The observer can help too by following any suggestions that were made during the interview, making sure that a comfortable proximity is maintained between himself and the children and that he only briefly answer children's questions.

A useful way of thinking about the process of environmental assessment is to view it as a series of pictures that are taken of the same place and individuals, using a variety of different camera lenses and shooting angles. In some pictures the primary objects of interest may be various features of the physical environment; in others it may be aspects of the social and programmatic environment, including the behavior of the children and teachers. Once the pictures are made they need to be examined simultaneously by looking for prominent features and also identifying important components that are missing. Each picture will reveal something specific about the organization of the preschool program. Through the process of comparison, a pattern will eventually emerge that suggests possible ways that various aspects of the program function together. Instead of using pictures to obtain these views of the classroom, the three different but complementary methods of direct observation that were mentioned in the preceding section of this chapter are used: (1) drawing a map, (2) recording PLA-Checks, and (3) writing narrative records.

The first step in the direct observation process is to *draw a map* of the setting, emphasizing the (1) walls or partitions, (2) barriers or dividers that are movable, and (3) barriers or dividers that can and cannot be seen over by teachers. It should

be apparent in the map whether the classroom space is divided into specific activity areas. The map should also show the placement of large pieces of equipment and furniture, rocking chairs, and tables. Places where toys or instructional materials are stored should be labeled as well. At this point, it is good to note whether there seems to be a variety of materials and equipment by labeling areas, e.g., fine motor, music, reading, housekeeping, and water play.

Figure 7.1 is an illustration of how a map of a hypothetical preschool classroom for special needs children might look after it is completed. It is based on a map drawn by a colleague, Mary McEvoy, to illustrate a number of common problems that can be posed by features of the physical environment. For example, the map reveals that children's lockers are located far away from the classroom's entrance. Not only does the location require children to walk through the classroom before they can remove and store their clothing and other materials, it also appears to set the occasion for them to enter other areas in the classroom before they reach their lockers. Teachers will have to attend to children who stray, and in doing so they may have to temporarily ignore other children who are receiving instruction or assistance from them.

There are several other physical problems illustrated in Figure 7.1. Equipment that utilizes water (e.g., art easels and water table) is not located near a water source such as the bathroom. Unnecessary walking and spillage are therefore potential problems. The block area impedes the traffic lane between the classroom and the outdoor play area. Art and drawing materials are not located in the art area where they belong, but instead are located across the room in the fine motor area. The teacher's desk is situated in the center of the room and is impeding a primary traffic lane. Moreover, it is not located in a place that facilitates observation of the whole classroom. The high shelves that border two sides of the reading area also make it difficult for teachers to see children in this area. The large, circular carpet that is used for group activities is partially blocking a main traffic lane. It also may encourage children to crowd around each other because it does not have visual cues that tell children where they should sit.

The housekeeping area is located in front of a large storage room which is used to store play equipment and instructional materials. Teachers are likely to disrupt activities in the housekeeping area, therefore, by walking through it as they go to and from the storage room. Also, it does not appear that tables that could be used for instruction or play purposes are located near the storage room. As long as these kinds of materials are kept there, teachers will be required to walk to and from the room as they set up or prepare for instructional and play activities.

A detailed map can serve later as a reference for making decisions about areas and activities that may need to be examined more carefully for potential problems that are due to poor organization. To determine how social and programmatic features may be affecting the behavior of children and teachers, however, it is necessary to use other methods of direct observation. For example, it is important to *scan the room for a posted schedule* and note whether it is being followed. If activities are scheduled in a sequential rather than a concurrent manner, periods of low engagement may occur during transition periods (LeLaurin & Risley, 1972). Also, the schedule may reveal that some activities that occur earlier in the day are

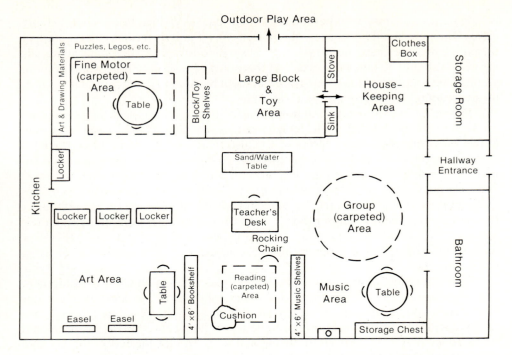

Figure 7.1. Map of a Hypothetical Preschool Classroom for Children with Special Needs

setting the occasion for problems during activities that occur later (Krantz & Risley, 1977). Finally, the activity schedule may reveal whether teachers have assigned themselves to areas with designated responsibilities.

If experience is a good predictor of the kind of information that is typically contained in a daily schedule, no mention will be made of concurrent scheduling or specific teacher assignments, even if they are operative in the classroom. Most schedules simply do not contain that level of detail. Consequently, this information will have to be obtained during the interview and cross-checked by means of direct observation. It is very important to obtain this information because both the type of schedule and ambiguity of teacher assignments can be significant sources of organizational problems (Nordquist & Twardosz, 1990).

Once the setting has been mapped and a copy of the daily schedule has been examined, it is time to *conduct a PLA-Check* to estimate the level of children's engagement. As we noted in the conceptual section of this chapter, definitions will vary depending on teacher expectations of appropriate behavior. However, waiting is never considered engagement, even though it is the teacher's wish that it occur, and should be noted separately in the narrative record. Sitting at a table, waiting for the teacher to bring materials, waiting for lunch to be served, waiting in line to go outside, or waiting for other children to return play materials to storage areas usually are not considered appropriate forms of engagement because the time spent waiting could be used for learning. Once definitions are clear, it is simply a matter of observing momentarily each child in the activity (beginning with the child who is farthest to the left and ending with the one who is farthest to the right) and deciding whether she is participating as defined. Engagement percentages are then computed by dividing the number of children participating by the number of children present. PLA-Checks should be repeated approximately every five minutes until the observation period is over.

After the first PLA-Check is done, a *narrative method of recording* should be used to obtain a detailed, sequential account of behavior and its immediate context (Touliatos & Compton, 1983). The narrative record provides information regarding each potential problem by describing how individuals in a given activity, area, or transition are behaving and to what extent environmental features may be facilitating or impeding the occurrence of desired behaviors. Descriptive statements can be further enhanced by periodically recording interpretive comments. Such spur-of-the-moment judgments are intended to focus attention on specific aspects of the situation that might otherwise be overlooked and are set apart from the descriptive accounts by using brackets. Finally, there may be places in the record where tentative generalizations or conclusions are made based upon the concepts and principles of environmental organization. These kinds of technical interpretations are usually made after the narrative record is completed and are, therefore, separated from the body of the record to make the distinction obvious.

A partial list of questions that an experienced observer will use to guide the observation process follows. It should be possible to answer most if not all of these questions after several observations are completed. As more information becomes available, answers to them will emerge from the narrative records that have specific implications for the identification of organizational problems.

Physical Environment

1. How "open" or "closed" is the space?
    a. Can children be easily supervised?
2. Are activity areas clearly defined?
    a. Do materials and equipment in the areas call attention to their purposes?
    b. Are materials and equipment accessible to all of the children?
    c. Are there a variety of and enough materials and equipment in each area?
    d. Are the materials and equipment safe?
    e. Are the materials and equipment developmentally appropriate?
    f. Are some of the materials and equipment responsive and provide opportunities for tactile and vestibular stimulation?
    g. Do the equipment and materials make it easier for the teachers to carry out their tasks?
    h. Are some of the materials and equipment periodically rotated?
3. Are traffic lanes blocked?
4. Are areas located such that their activities are compatible with one another?
5. What is the general appearance of the classroom?
    a. Does the classroom appear to be cluttered?
    b. Is the appearance of the classroom drab or is it warm, colorful, and inviting?

c. Are there places in the classroom for displaying the children's work?
d. Does there appear to be a lot of noise in the classroom?

Programmatic Environment

1. Are there an appropriate number of children and teachers in the available classroom space?
2. Is the daily schedule being followed?
    a. Is the amount of time allotted for each activity appropriate?
    b. Are activities scheduled sequentially, i.e., all children are engaged in the same activity and all must finish before another activity begins? or
    c. Are activities scheduled concurrently, i.e., at least two activities are occurring at the same time (or there is some overlap) so that children can move individually from one activity to another?
3. How much time do children spend waiting?
    a. When does waiting occur?
    b. Do behavior problems occur during periods of waiting?
4. If there is more than one teacher, how have they divided their responsibilities?
    a. Are teachers assigned to supervise areas or groups of children?
5. What happens when children must make a group transition from one activity to another?

Social Environment

1. What is the manner with which the children and teachers interact?
    a. Are interactions warm and friendly or distant and unpleasant?
2. When does disruptive and aggressive behavior occur?
    a. How do teachers respond when these behaviors occur?
3. What are the children and teachers doing? (The narrative should provide a description to complement the PLA-Check.)
4. How frequently do the teachers give instructions?
5. Are there children wandering in the classroom who appear disinterested or have nothing to do?

As narrative recording proceeds, interrupted every five minutes or so to record another PLA-Check, it also is important to *list the types of activities in which the children are involved.* For example, going to the bathroom, eating snacks or lunch, reading books, listening to a story, group instruction, and free play are activities that commonly occur in special preschool settings. A convenient time to record activities is immediately after PLA-Checks are completed.

Table 7.1 includes an abbreviated sample of a narrative record. It consists of two columns, one for recording the time of day and engagement percentages, and the other for recording written descriptions of events that occur in the classroom.

Several pieces of important information about the social and programmatic features of the preschool classroom, in addition to descriptions of physical features that could not be easily referenced on the map, are illustrated in this sample. It reveals, for example, that there are two teachers and 10 children in the classroom

TABLE 7.1 Abbreviated Sample of a Narrative Record

Time Engagement	Observations
10:05 A.M. E = 0/5	Five Cn seated at table in F-M area. Area well-stocked w/small manipulatives such as puzzles, legos, lincoln logs, bristle blocks, etc. All materials stored on shelves, accessible, not labeled. Blocks & legos in large cans. Cn waiting for T1. Some materials on table, but T1 looking for others at desk. T1 goes to storage room. Tells Cn to stay in chairs. Four Cn wait patiently. One C leaves table. Gets small cars off shelf, and begins to play on rug. T1 returns, tells C to put cars back on shelf, come to table. C protests, but complies. T1 praises, places materials on table, sits down, explains activity to Cn. T1 smiles, positive. **Too much waiting. Materials not ready before activity begins. Nearby materials may be distractors for some Cn.**
10:10 A.M. E = 3/5	Five other Cn w/T2 in MA. Area well-stocked w/interesting, responsive materials. Two Cn are listening to audio tape recorder. One C is playing xylophone, sitting on floor. Two Cn seated at table waiting for T2 who is talking to speech therapist near entrance. One C leaves table, takes xylophone from C. Victim protests. T2 hears. Come to area. Returns xylophone to victim and asks aggressor to sit at table. T2 asks C w/xylophone to come to table, takes xylophone, begins imitation training using xylophone. Cn take turns imitating T2. Very interested. Watch each other carefully as well as T2. Cn smile, laugh. T2 very warm, praises them. **T's seem to be assigned to groups. Cn may not be free to leave areas individually. May be problems of Cn waiting due to interruptions or need to locate materials.**

and that each teacher is working with five children in two different areas of the room. It also suggests that children are not participating in the activities as often as the teachers might want them to, and it pinpoints some possible reasons for low levels of engagement. In addition, it suggests that the children are, in general, well behaved despite unnecessary periods of waiting or other factors in the classroom (e.g., toys) that may be competing for their attention during instruction activities. Both teachers seem to interact with the children in positive ways, and there are several signs that the children enjoy activities and materials once they are engaged. Finally, there is an indication that teachers may be assigned to groups of children for at least part of the day. Additional observations would be needed, however, to assess how children move from one activity to another.

Unfortunately, it is not possible to record everything that might be important, as is true of any other method of assessment. One tactic that can be used when too much information is coming in at once is to jot down topics that can be developed in more detail when the pace of events slows. For example, if there is a great deal of hectic activity occurring during the transition to group activity, it might be possible to use the group time to go back and finish describing the transition routine, provided that less information pertinent to environmental organization occurs during group time.

When a narrative is being recorded, it is also important to be aware of and

record aspects of teacher and child behavior that appear to be linked to the organizational features of the setting. Table 7.2 contains examples of teacher–child interactions that might be recorded during a transition activity. It illustrates how children sometimes misbehave while standing in line, leading to teacher reprimands. It also shows how the affective tone of teacher–child interactions may be related to the way in which a setting is organized; negative tones are often the result of a poorly organized routine. In this example children have to wait because the sequential schedule and assignment of teachers to groups preclude an opportunity for children to move individually from one activity to another.

How long and how frequently should a setting be observed? There is no easy answer to this question. It depends on a lot of factors, but ultimately on how confident the observer is that what is seen constitutes a representative sample of the typical day. Teachers may provide some insight about this by noting whether the day was a particularly good or bad one. If there is continuity across days, it may be possible to obtain a representative sample of preschool organization after two or three observation sessions are completed. Regardless of the number of observations that are done, *each observation should last at least two to three hours*. Also, it is a good idea to have two people observe simultaneously, at least part of the time, to guard against the possibility of missing important information and to allow for some means of assessing interobserver agreement.

During the course of this discussion nothing has been said about the curricu-

TABLE 7.2. Abbreviated Sample of a Narrative Record

Time Engagement	Observations
11:45 A.M. E = 5/10	All 10 Cn and both T's are outside in OPA. T1 is asking Cn in her group to line up at entrance to classroom. Two Cn go immediately, stand at door, wait. T1 walks to other 3 Cn, two are playing in sandbox, one on swing. Asks Cn in sandbox to stop playing, go to door, wait. T1 goes to C on swing, repeats instruction. T2's group is playing, all 5 Cn engaged. T2 pushing one C on swing. Two Cn in sandbox walk toward door. One of the two runs to the slide. C on swing gets down, walks toward door, joins other three Cn there, waits. T1 looks for fifth C. Can't find him initially. Asks T2 if she sees C. T2 stops pushing C on swing. Both Ts look. Fifth C hiding behind slide, smiling, giggling.
	T's assigned to grps. Cn required to move in grps. Must wait in line for all Cn before grp can move.
11:50 A.M. E = 5/10	T1 sees C behind slide. Yells at C to go to door. C does not comply. Two Cn waiting at door start to scuffle, disagree about position in line. T1 does not see this. One C pushes the other C. Two Cn who went to door initially still waiting patiently. T1 at slide now, says, "_____, why can't you do what you are told!" Tone negative. Takes C by hand, leads to door. Sees two Cn scuffling, tells them "_____ stop that!" T1 makes Cn line up, ignores two Cn who waited patiently. Leads grp to lockers. T2 still pushing child on swing, says in loud voice to all Cn, "It's almost time to stop playing and line up!"
	Mild behavior problems probably due to extended waiting. T1 had to give a lot of instructions to Cn to line up. Frustrated, negative tone. T's definitely assigned to grps, not areas.

lum, that is, whether it is important to note what is being taught or whether teachers are using the proper instructional methods. These are aspects of the program that may need attention. If so, they are better addressed by other approaches to assessment. Most special education teachers know a great deal about curriculum matters such as the specification of learning goals, selection of appropriate materials, and instructional methods that are effective with children with special needs. Careful assessment of the environment allows teachers to do what they do best, namely teach (Hart, 1978).

Analysis of the Information.   Once the observations are completed, the records must be analyzed. The analytic process begins with an *examination of PLA-Check percentages,* which looks for patterns of high and low engagement across similar activities. Once it is clear that children consistently engage particular activities at low rates, the narrative records are reviewed for organizational factors that might explain the low rates of participation. To facilitate the review, it is helpful to *group incidents taken from the narrative records* and examine them for similarities that indicate if one or another type of organizational problem is evident. For example, if information on group instruction activities (such as the information contained in Table 7.1) was put together, it might reveal that teachers are taking a great deal of time locating and preparing instructional materials, thus causing children to wait, misbehave, or be off-task. *Reference to the map* may reveal physical aspects of the environment such as location and availability of materials or presence of competing materials that suggest why teachers and children are having problems.

Redrawing the map often helps to further highlight physical sources of organizational problems through visual comparisons with the original map. The map that is illustrated in Figure 7.2, for example, shows how the hypothetical classroom that is depicted in Figure 7.1 might look after the physical features of the classroom are reorganized.

Beginning with the entrance hallway, it can be seen that the lockers are now located so that children can store their belongings before they enter the classroom. The art area is now located near a water source and contains storage shelves for art and drawing materials. The sand and water table has been moved to the art area because it also needs to be near a water source. Consequently, a shelf has been placed near the table for storing sand and water toys.

The housekeeping area has been replaced by a gross motor area because children with special needs benefit in numerous ways from equipment that provides a variety of tactile and vestibular stimulation (Murphy, 1982). Also the storage room has been converted so that pieces of gross motor and other large play equipment that are not being used can be stored in a safe, convenient place until it is time to rotate that equipment back to the classroom.

The block area has been moved to a corner of the classroom and no longer impedes the passageway to the outdoor play area. The circular carpet that was used for group activities has been placed in this area to reduce noise. The fine motor area is now located where the block area used to be, but is situated in such a manner that traffic to and from the outdoor play area is not impeded. Low shelves that facilitate visual inspection are used to partially divide both of these areas. The shelves also encourage children to store materials properly when their activities are over.

The reading area is now located in a quiet corner of the room, and the teacher's desk has been placed very close to this area so that teachers might experience some amount of quiet too when they need time to plan activities. The desk placement also encourages teachers to visually inspect the room; every area can be seen easily from a chair that is situated behind the teacher's desk.

The music area has been moved to where the reading area used to be and is located between two areas that are more compatible with it from the standpoint of noise levels. The shelves that are used to store music materials allow teachers to see the children.

Finally, the group area has been moved to the center of the room away from the entrance and out of the way of the main traffic lanes. Carpet squares have replaced the circular rug and can be arranged in the group area in semicircle fashion, about the length of a child's arm apart, to facilitate attention and reduce the likelihood of disruptive behavior occurring during large group activities (Krantz & Risley, 1977). A storage box has been placed near the rug so that children can easily obtain and replace carpet squares before and after group activities, thus ensuring that the main traffic lane through the center of the classroom will not be impeded at other times of the day.

As is apparent from the preceding description of the redrawn map, this method

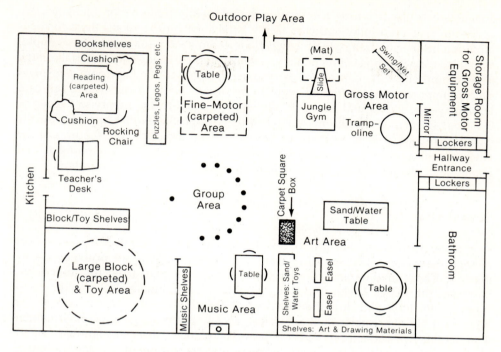

Figure 7.2. Redrawn Map of a Hypothetical Preschool Classroom for Children with Special Needs

of assessment merges easily into planning changes. Taking this example further, consideration should next be given to the information contained in the daily schedule and narrative record, which has implications for making changes in the social and programmatic aspects of the classroom. If the schedule does not contain information about the sequencing of activities and teacher assignments, then it is important to *design a master schedule;* this not only contains information about the types of activities and routines that are scheduled, but also designates which children and teachers will participate as well as teacher responsibilities during the activities and routines. Hart (1978) provides an excellent description of how to design a master schedule and notes how it helps teachers to recognize the advantages of concurrent schedules and assign themselves to areas.

Reference again to the narrative records will help to clarify problems that are due to ineffective scheduling and ambiguous teacher assignments. For example, the records may reveal periods or activities when children spend a lot of time waiting. This information can be shared with the staff and related to the master schedule. Staff can be shown, for example, how scheduling a free play activity to occur simultaneously with small group instruction allows children who meet instruction criteria to have immediate access to free play instead of being punished by having to wait until all of the children complete the activity successfully (Baer, Rowbury, & Baer, 1973); McEvoy & Brady, 1988). The staff can also be shown how their assignment to areas during a transition routine while two or more activities are occurring (e.g., free play, self-care in the bathroom, lunch) allows them to focus attention on the children in their assigned area who need it the most. For example, as children leave free play individually, perhaps after replacing play materials on the shelves, and enter the bathroom, the teacher assigned to the bathroom can spend time prompting and reinforcing them in accordance with their specific self-care learning goals. This would not be possible if the teacher had to supervise a group of children. By comparing the master schedule with problems that appeared in the narrative record, it is possible to see how social and programmatic features of the environment can be reorganized to complement the physical environment and eliminate or significantly reduce problems that are due to poor organization.

SUMMARY

As can be seen from the information presented in this section, the assessment method that is described lends itself easily to the next steps in the problem-solving process. These involve analyzing the information obtained from the interviews, mapping, the PLA-Checks, and narrative recording and imagining how the classroom would look and how the behavior of the children and teachers might be affected if various aspects of the physical, social, and programmatic environment were modified. The next phase, if the process continues, involves planning specific changes with the people who work in the setting and formulating a plan to implement and evaluate them. It is beyond the scope of this chapter to describe and discuss this process, but some idea of its possible complexity can be obtained by reading Twardosz (1984b).

There are various features of the assessment method that make it well suited for gathering the information necessary for problem solving. First, the techniques provide different types of information that can be integrated to more fully describe the operation of the classroom than any one of them alone. Second, the system is flexible because there are no previously defined category systems that would limit what can be seen and recorded. Thus, the observer is ready to record even the most unexpected methods of organizing the classroom. Third, information about the physical, social, and programmatic features of the environment can be recorded together as they are believed to contribute to problems or to the smooth functioning of the classroom. This is important because problem solving usually necessitates making judgments about how a change in one aspect of the environment will affect the operation of other aspects. Fourth, the temporal sequence of events is preserved in the narrative record, and this can be particularly useful when trying to determine if previous events might be affecting future behavior. Fifth, the individuality of each setting can be appreciated because the assessment method allows one to see that the same method of organizing an activity may mean different things in different settings depending upon how the rest of the day is organized and the teaching methods that are used. The attitude that no one method is always superior to another is very useful when entering the problem-solving process.

The advantages that this method has for analyzing the environment for problem solving make it less advantageous for other purposes, of course, such as comparing classrooms with one another or linking a particular behavior precisely with its environmental context. However, there are other systems, some of which have been described in this chapter, that are more suitable for those purposes. This particular method adds to the variety of assessment techniques already available in the field of early childhood special education and makes it possible for teachers and other professionals to address organizational problems in a fairly simple and useful way.

THE ECOLOGICAL PERSPECTIVE

- The preschool environment includes physical, social, and programmatic features—all of which influence a child's functioning.
- Child behavior is directly affected in a dynamic and reciprocal manner by the organizational elements of the classroom environment.
- Appropriateness of a classroom's environmental organization for the specific children and adults involved requires individualized application of general guidelines for preschool environmental organization.
- Linkages between program philosophy and goals and environmental organization can be used to facilitate achievement of program goals.
- Analysis of preschool environments to identify and reduce organizational problems requires the use of multiple data-gathering techniques, which involve direct and indirect assessments and naturalistic observations.
- Optimal environment arrangements can increase the opportunities that foster child development across cognitive, psychomotor, and social/emotional development and reduce maladaptive behaviors of children with developmental delays.

PART THREE

Child Assessment from an Ecological Perspective

The overriding theme of this text—an ecological perspective—is well illustrated in the following passage from Glick's (1975) review of research on cognitive development from a cross-cultural perspective.

> In the sorting task, twenty items representing five types of food, five types of clothing, and five types of cooking utensils were heaped on a table in front of a Kpelle subject. When the subject had finished sorting, what was present were ten categories composed of two items each—related to each other in a functional, not a categorical, manner. Thus, a knife might have been placed with an orange, a potato with a hoe, and so on. When asked, the subject would rationalize the choice with such comments as, "The knife goes with orange because it cuts it." When questioned further, the subject would often volunteer that a wise man would do things in this way. When an exasperated experimenter asked finally, "How would a fool do it," he was given back sorts of the type that were initially expected—four neat piles with foods in one, tools in another, and so on. (pp. 635–636)

The examiner, holding a different set of values, and having experienced a quite different ecological experience, held the "foolish" response in greater regard than the functional one chosen by the participant in the study. When the response is viewed from an ecological perspective, it looses the interpretation that this individual is less cognitively capable than one who sorts by category. Interpretation of child functioning across all developmental domains requires that examiners retain an understanding of the systems within which the child functions.

Additionally, the younger a child is, the more challenging it can be to obtain meaningful assessment results. Yang and Bell's (1975) comments about conducting research on infants applies equally well to assessment.

> The human infant has never been consistently cooperative. This well-established fact, when juxtaposed with the infant's ability to manipulate adult behavior with little more than a smile, has posed no small problem for researchers trying to develop objective scales of assessment. Trained as the researcher might be, he, or she remains responsive as a part of the measurement situation. (p. 137)

The emphasis in the assessment of infants, toddlers, and preschool children should be on obtaining a view of current functioning, rather than on predicting future performance. Such assessments should then be used to plan interventions, whether they be medical, behavioral, therapeutic, or educational. The use of standardized instruments that provide a label for the child and/or circular information is not always particularly helpful to the interventionist. Circular information is provided when the examiner gives back to the parents a clinical description of their child's behaviors that is the same information about the child that brought them to the specialist in the first place. They already knew what they have now spent significant time and money to be told again. The Ecologically Valid Assessment Model, presented in Chapter 8, is designed so the goals of assessment are matched to the eventual results and recommendations. Chapters 9 through 12 contain information pertinent to the definitions, theories, developmental sequence, assessment procedures, and instruments for cognitive, communicative, motor, and social and emotional domains of development.

CHAPTER 8

Child Assessment: Viewing the Whole Child

CHAPTER OUTLINE

QUESTIONS ANSWERED IN CHAPTER 8

- How can an assessment plan address a child's total surroundings?
- Can examiners weigh the impact of a child's cultural and linguistic heritage in the assessment process?
- What instruments are available for multidomain assessment?

CHAPTER OVERVIEW

The task of assessing the child without losing sight of the whole child is a significant challenge to anyone conducting child assessments. The child must be viewed within his context (that is, seen as a complex individual set within multiple systems and subsystems); this view, emphasized throughout this text, must be integrated with the analytical approach routinely used in child assessment. The amount of information that can be gathered about any one child necessitates that the task be broken down into manageable parts. Typically, this division is accomplished through the assessment of child functioning by developmental domains. Such divisions can provide teachers with a useful profile of a child's functioning across multiple domains. It also enables them to target specific areas of concern for in-depth study when a child's difficulties appear to be isolated in one domain. However, such division can interfere with the examiner's ability to maintain a view of the whole child. Impaired functioning often has an interactive effect on a child's ability to develop across domains, leading to inaccurate interpretations of child functioning by domain. For example, if a teacher tests a blind infant, who is experiencing motor delays typical of visually impaired children, by using a measure of cognitive functioning normed on sighted children, results may indicate that the child is cognitively delayed if the measure relies heavily on motor performance. Visually impaired chlidren are known to have delayed motor development, which is completely unrelated to their cognitive potential. Such interactive effects across developmental domains can be lost unless assessments include the reintegration of information about the child into a whole picture. A model of assessment designed to retain a focus on the whole child and his environments is presented in this chapter, along with a discussion of the impact of a child's cultural and linguistic heritage on performance. Also included in this chapter are descriptions of multidomain assessments, which are designed to be used in program planning and curriculum development.

THE ECOLOGICALLY VALID ASSESSMENT MODEL

The *Ecologically Valid Assessment Model* (EVAM) is comprised of five sequential phases that can be followed by an assessment team or individual examiner. Progression through each phase can reduce the production of unneeded and unwanted information as well as eliminate gaps in information. The EVAM facilitates the review of child functioning across settings while reducing erroneous interpretations of child performance. There are forms designed to accompany each phase of the process presented in Figures 8.1–8.5. Instructions for each of these forms are presented in the following subsections.

Phase One: Identification of the Purpose

Initiating Factors.   Describe the reason why the assessment has been initiated, including in what setting(s) behaviors were observed that triggered the current assessment.

Purpose of Assessment.   List people who need information from the assessment and their position (e.g., Melinda Craven/parent); identify their goals for the assessment.
     The first phase in the model is the identification of the purpose(s) of the assessment. While it may seem that once a child has been referred, the purpose of the assessment should be obvious, such is not the case. Goals for an assessment can vary greatly depending on who initiated the request. For example, a preschool teacher, frustrated with a child's acting out behavior, may need some very specific

suggestions on how to manage her in her class. She may even hope that if she is labeled as emotionally disturbed, she will not be allowed to remain in her class. If all that teacher receives as the result of extensive diagnostic testing is a report verifying that the child is exhibiting acting-out behaviors, her dissatisfaction with the assessment results is guaranteed. If the diagnostic information is accompanied by further clarification that the disruptive behaviors are due to unstable home conditions and by general suggestions for interventions in the preschool class, she at least knows how to begin addressing the situation. A final report with detailed intervention strategies based on direct observations in the setting as well as child assessments and study of the home environment would match the stated goal of the assessment.

During this phase, assessment teams should address the following three basic questions:

- Who is seeking information from the assessment (can be several individuals and/or agencies)?
- What were the initiating factors that led to the request for an assessment (include behavioral descriptions of child in several settings)?
- What are the goals of the assessment (include goals for each individual or agency who was identified as seeking information)?

Typical goals for assessment that would be appropriate to designate on the form include (1) developmental screening, with follow-up if needed; (2) diagnosis; (3) developmental assessment (present level of functioning as compared with a normal developmental sequence, e.g., receptive language age and adaptative behavior rating); (4) functional assessment in specific areas (how the child is coping in an area, e.g., functional vision and functional communication); (5) program planning and determination of intervention techniques; (6) identification of motivators; (7) program evaluation; and (8) transition to new settings. The record form used to compile information during this first phase of the model is presented in Figure 8.1.

Phase Two: Identification of Primary Behavior Settings

Current Primary Behavior Settings. Describe the primary behavior settings in which the child functions within the categories of home, school, and community; level of specificity needed will vary according to the level of functioning of the child; if initiating factors are clustered around one of these broad categories it might be desirable to emphasize that category during the assessment process; none of the categories should be omitted entirely unless the child is not in any home or center-based activity (including Mother's Day Out or group day care); settings in which the child is doing well should be included.

Percentage of Time. Include the time a child spends in a particular behavior setting in a 24-hour period. This time factor might vary depending on the specificity used in identifying behavior settings. Percentages can be calculated on waking hours rather

Figure 8.1. Ecologically Valid Assessment Model. Phase One: Identification of the Purpose

Child's Name _____ Phone No._____

Address _____

Parent(s)/Guardian(s) _____

Address _____

Assessment Team Members _____

_____

Initiating Factors:

Behavior Setting	Identified Behaviors	Attempted Interventions
1.		
2.		
3.		
4.		
5.		

Purposes for the Assessment:

Name and Position	Goals of Assessment
1. _____	_____
2. _____	_____
3. _____	_____
4. _____	_____

than on 24-hour periods; however, it is necessary to determine the number of waking hours specifically for each child due to variations in sleeping patterns. Time percentages based on a 24-hour period can be determined by dividing the number of hours spent in a behavior setting by 24 or by using the following chart:

**Time Percentages Based on
24 Hours**

10 hours	=	42% of the day
2 hours	=	8% of the day
1 hour	=	4% of the day
30 minutes	=	2% of the day
15 minutes	=	1% of the day

The next chart depicts time percentages for waking hours of a child who sleeps 10 hours per night and who is awake 14 hours.

Time Percentages Based on 14 Hours

10 hours	=	71% of the day
2 hours	=	14% of the day
1 hour	=	7% of the day
30 minutes	=	4% of the day
15 minutes	=	2% of the day

Each person or agency seeking information from the assessment should identify those settings in which the child spends a substantial portion of his time and/or has particularly troublesome behaviors. All *primary* behavior settings should be identified, not just ones in which the child exhibits problems. If only those behavior settings in which difficulties have been evidenced are listed, positive information about the child's functioning may be lost. It may be useful to categorize behavior settings according to home, school, and community. However, it is not necessary that every child have equal numbers of identified behavior settings across these three categories. An infant's primary behavior settings might only include home settings, whereas a preschool-age child is more likely to have a balance across all three categories. Figure 8.2 depicts the Identification of Behavior Settings form to use when the basic categories of home, school, and community are appropriate. Only current behavior settings should be identified during this planning phase. One possible expectation would occur when a change in placement is considered, and temporary placement of the child in possible future settings is possible. Examples of typical behavior settings in each of these three categories follow.

Home	**School**	**Community**
Mealtime	Circle time	Playing in neighborhood
Bathing	Snack time	Attending church
Bedtime	Free play	Visiting the zoo
Morning routine	Lining up	Doctor's office
Taking medicine	Bathroom	Community park
Being read to	Table activities	Friend's house
Watching television		

In some instances home, school, and community might not be the most appropriate categories by which to identify primary behavior settings. For example, a medically fragile child's primary behavior settings might be better classified according to hospital, home, and diagnostic center. A classification of bedroom, bathroom, and kitchen and dining area might be more functional for the very young infant. The form can easily be revised, so the broad categories are open rather than restricted to home, school, and community.

The approximate percentage of time a child spends in the setting in a 24-hour

Figure 8.2. Ecologically Valid Assessment Model. Phase Two: Identification of Behavior Settings

		Setting	Percent of Time in Setting
Home	1.	_____	_____
	2.	_____	_____
	3.	_____	_____
School	1.	_____	_____
	2.	_____	_____
	3.	_____	_____
Community	1.	_____	_____
	2.	_____	_____
	3.	_____	_____

Clusters within or across Settings (e.g., mealtime):   Percent of Time

_____   _____

_____   _____

_____   _____

period should be noted on the form. This time factor might vary depending on the specificity used in identifying behavior settings. For example, if breakfast, lunch, dinner, and snack times are all listed and described separately, each would represent a smaller percentage of time than if the behavior setting had simply been defined as mealtime. It is best to form clusters of behavior settings to indicate the total time spent in related or parallel activities. A child who has serious feeding difficulties might require a 1-hour time period for each meal, with a total feeding time of 3 hours (13% of a 24-hour period). The percentages can also be calculated based on waking hours of the individual child. Assuming the child just described sleeps for 10 hours each night and takes a 2-hour nap (for a total sleep time of 12 hours), she has available 12 waking hours. Three of those hours are spent eating, for a total of 25% time in feeding (nearly double the number when a 24-hour period was used). Since sleep patterns are individualized, the numbers used to calculate percentages based on waking hours must be determined on an individual basis. An autistic child may sleep as little as 3 hours a night, whereas a child with severe seizures who is heavily medicated may be hard to rouse for more than 3 hours in a 24-hour period. Waking hour percentages for the autistic child should be based on a 21-hour time period, but just 3 hours are available to the child with the seizure disorder.

Phase Three: Identification of Behavior-Setting Features

Specific features of each primary behavior setting need to be identified. These features include the following:

- Geographic location and physical features of the behavior setting
- Time of day and duration of the behavior setting
- Persons typically present in the behavior setting
- Role(s) of persons present
- Physical abilities required to fulfill role(s) in the behavior setting
- Affective features of the behavior setting

The Identification of Behavior-Setting Features form is presented in Figure 8.3.

Phase Four: Identification of Properties to Be Assessed

During the fourth phase, the assessment team identifies what properties need to be addressed in each of the primary behavior settings and selects appropriate procedures and/or instruments. Properties are clustered into four organizational components: *critical events, personal interactions, developmental functioning,* and *environmental analysis.* It is possible that some of these properties need to be assessed in only one behavior setting (e.g., reaction to emersion into water during bath time),

Figure 8.3. Ecologically Valid Assessment Model. Phase Three: Identification of Behavior-Setting Features

Settings	Features
A. Location: _____	
1. _____	_____
2. _____	_____
3. _____	_____
B. Location: _____	
1. _____	_____
2. _____	_____
3. _____	_____
C. Location: _____	
1. _____	_____
2. _____	_____
3. _____	

whereas other properties are relevant to all behavior settings (e.g., developmental level of communication and use of unstructured free time).

Critical events include such things as free play, meal time, departure time, nap and bed time, transitions, and so forth. A preschool teacher concerned about a child's aimless behavior during unstructured play periods would target free play as a critical event to be assessed through child observations. Critical events can also include categorical events, such as changes in the routine, visitors to the classroom, turn taking, and sharing.

Assessment of personal interactions can focus on specific interactions (e.g., parent–child interactions and interactions between two specific children) or be directed toward clusters of interactions (e.g., child-to-child interactions, child-to-adult interactions, and child-to-group interactions). When a child is acting out, observation of personal interactions is a critical element of the assessment. A child exhibiting scattered performance might also be better understood after assessing his personal interactions. For example, if one adult insists that the child can feed himself even though others have been unable to see this behavior in the child, analyses of the interaction patterns might reveal the cause for the discrepancy is low adult expectations.

The team can specify domains of child functioning that need to be assessed, then select appropriate techniques based on child characteristics (e.g., age and functioning level). The emphasis in planning this portion of the assessment must be on salient child characteristics that render certain instruments unsuitable. Psychometric soundness of the instruments and procedures considered must also be reviewed. Goals of the assessment provide another critical factor in the identification of useful procedures. Early childhood special educators and parents who are seeking specific suggestions for program planning are much better served through the use of criterion-referenced instruments designed to facilitate curriculum-building or informal play assessments than through the use of standardized instruments that generate developmental quotients.

Environmental features can be targeted for assessment independently as well as in interaction with child behaviors. The child with visual impairments would need her preschool environment assessed to determine its consistency with features conducive to the integration of children with visual impairments. She would also need assessments that focused on how she was coping within her environment (e.g., the tactile sign over her cubby is too high, and she is unable to reach it). The team should base their decisions about what to assess on the goals identified during the first phase. The team uses the form depicted in Figure 8.4 for each of the primary behavior settings identified in Phase Two. Properties that are to be assessed across multiple settings should be noted on the forms (e.g., communication skills and independence in dressing).

Phase Five: Analyzing and Interpreting Assessment Results

Once all of the assessments have been planned and conducted, the team analyzes and interprets the results based on the goals identified during Phase One (Figure 8.5). A return to the original goals of the assessment as a structuring focus of the final analysis helps assure the productivity of the results. When team members still have no answers for certain goals of the assessment, they must either acknowledge the limitations or return to a previous planning phase and continue data gathering. However, it may be desirable to initiate intervention while further assessments are planned.

MULTICULTURAL ISSUES IN ASSESSMENT

The impact of a child's cultural and linguistic heritage cannot be overlooked in the assessment process. Children raised within subcultures, which have values, religious beliefs, childrearing practices, and language structures that differ from those found in the dominant society, deserve to be assessed based on their own heritage. The number of limited English-proficient families with young children who need bilingual and/or English as a second language programs is rapidly increasing. These children need specialized assessment procedures that account for cultural as well as linguistic background. A climate that seeks to strengthen a child's understanding of his diverse cultural roots and skills in the language from these roots can ultimately lead to better assimilation into a dominant culture than one that tries to replace the primary culture with the dominant one.

The failure of professionals to acknowledge and value cultural and linguistic diversity has historically contributed to poor school performance of minority groups. For example, in the United States, Hispanic, black, and Native Americans

Figure 8.4. Ecologically Valid Assessment Model. Phase Four: Assessment Plan within Behavior Setting

Behavior Setting _____

Goals of Assessment _____

_____

_____

Assessment Plan:

      Properties to Be Assessed   Techniques for Assessment

___ Critical Events

___ Personal Interactions

___ Child Functioning

___ Environmental Features

tend to perform poorly in school; in Canada the Franco-Ontarians experience difficulty, as do the Finns in Sweden (Cummins, 1989). Devaluation of culture by a predominate group seems to have its greatest impact on children under the age of 10. Devaluations of minority language structures because they are perceived as innately inferior is just one example of the prejudices that can develop from cultural diversity. The social value of standard language systems is higher than nonstandard variations of a language, although they can be as highly structured and governed by rules. Bloom (1975) quotes from Baratz to convey the social and political meaning of such differentiated valuing of language systems.

Figure 8.5. Ecologically Valid Assessment Model. Phase Five: Analyzing Assessment Findings

Goals of Assessment	Assessment Findings
1. _____ _____	_____ _____ _____
2. _____ _____	_____ _____ _____
3. _____ _____	_____ _____ _____
4. _____ _____	_____ _____

> Linguists have also learned that within a large complex society where individuals from different social classes and different ethnicities live in close proximity, they often speak many varieties (dialects) of the same language. One of these dialects may be considered socially more prestigious than the others. It, thus, may be used as the standard for the nation. Although one dialect may be chosen as the standard language, it is important to realize that this is an arbitrary, or at most social decision which has nothing to do with that particular dialect's linguistic merits. That is to say, the dialect chose as standard is no more highly structured, well formed, or grammatical than any of the other dialects. The evolution of a particular dialect as the standard is due to sociopolitical considerations rather than to intrinsic linguistic superiority. (pp. 292, 293)

Early childhood special educators who must make decisions regarding the functioning level, linguistic competence, and cognitive potential of children with nonstandard dialects need to be aware of the linguistic environment in which the child is raised.

Assessment procedures used with minority populations that fail to reflect an ecological perspective inevitably lead to the identification of problems within the child which explain his poor performance. Research indicates that current practice in the assessment of school-aged minority students, in fact, fails to acknowledge and value cultural diversity. A summary of findings from two major research projects related to assessment procedures used with minority students revealed the following:

1. Language proficiency is not seriously taken into account in special education assessment.
2. Testing is done primarily in English, often increasing the likelihood of establishing an achievement or intelligence discrepancy.
3. English-language problems that are typically characteristic of second-language learners (poor comprehension, limited vocabulary, grammar, and syntax errors, and problems with English articulation) are misinterpreted as handicaps.
4. Learning disability and communication-handicapped placements have replaced the misplacement of students as educable mentally retarded of the 1960s and 1970s.
5. Psychometric test scores from Spanish or English tests are capricious in their outcomes, though, paradoxically, internally sound.
6. Special education placement leads to decreased test scores (IQ and achievement).
7. Home data are not used in assessment.
8. The same few tests are used with most children.
9. Having parents who were born outside the United States increases the likelihood of being found eligible for special education.
10. Reevaluations usually led to more special education. (Figueroa, Fradd, & Correa, 1989, p. 176)

The reader interested in further discussion of the inadequacy of current practices in psychoeducational assessment of linguistic minority students is referred to Figueroa (1989) and Duran (1989).

Test translations, use of interpreters, and use of bilingual examiners are of limited effectiveness in obtaining ecologically valid assessments. Even instruments available in the child's native language are not totally satisfactory options. While it is easy to describe what assessment practices should be discontinued, a wide array of acceptable alternative instruments are not available. The avoidance of inappropriate instruments can be coupled with increased reliance on dynamic assessment techniques and assisted performance in order to achieve a more accurate picture of the child's abilities (Duran, 1989). Use of the Ecologically Valid Assessment Model and reliance on concepts such as communication competence instead of language proficiency (Rivera, 1984) and dynamic assessment (Lidz, 1987) can direct the interventionist's attentions to the positive abilities of the multicultural child rather than her limitations.

The emphasis in early intervention on the empowerment of the family is particularly significant for culturally diverse families. The efforts made to communicate and collaborate with parents of children from cultural backgrounds that differ from the dominate culture directly influence the interventionist's effectiveness. For information on a parent training model that uses a training-of-trainers design, see Chan (1990). After parents have received training, they become trainers.

MULTIDOMAIN CRITERION-REFERENCED ASSESSMENTS

Although the goal of assessment is to achieve a better understanding of the whole child, it is necessary to break the task into manageable parts. Thus, child assessments are typically conducted by developmental domains. Instruments designed to be used in the development of an individual child's program offer various subtests that are defined by the domains each attempts to measure. For example, the *Memphis Comprehensive Developmental Test* includes five subtests: psychosocial, fine motor, gross motor, cognitive, and language. No composite score is derived. The *Learning Accomplishment Profile* includes fine and gross motor, language, self-help, and social and cognitive skills, whereas the *HICOMP Preschool Curriculum* covers communication, self-care, motor, and problem solving. Neither do all of the instruments include the same domains, nor do they necessarily define the domains consistently. For example, social scales on one instrument might refer to self-help types of behaviors, whereas another uses the same (or similar) title to mean the ability to play and get along with other children.

Multidomain instruments that are designed to be directly linked with inter-

ventions are summarized in the appendix to this chapter. Those selected for inclusion are primarily useful in the determination of present levels of child functioning, with a goal of facilitating intervention.

Multidomain Assessment of Special Populations

Some instruments have been developed for use with infants and young children who have specific disabilities. Although such assessment tools can be useful when assessing a child for whom instruments designed for the able-bodied or sensory-intact infant are inappropriate, they do not offer the psychometric soundness available in nationally normed instruments. The *Callier-Azusa Scale* (Stillman, 1978) is intended for use with deal-blind and multihandicapped infants. It covers assessments of motor functioning, perceptual skills, daily living skills, cognition, communication, language, and social development. There are 18 subscales: postural control, locomotion, fine motor, visual motor, vision, auditory, tactile, dressing, personal hygiene, feeding, toilet, cognition, receptive language, expressive language, speech, adults social, peers social, and environment. No normative data have been established for the Callier-Azusa; however, the instrument relies on items from other developmental assessments with normative data. The *Early Intervention Developmental Profile* (EIDP) (Schafer & Moersch, 1981) is a developmental checklist of milestones appropriately used with children whose developmental skills fall below 36 months. Subscales on the EIDP are perceptual and fine motor, cognition, language, social and emotional, self-care, and gross motor. The *Wisconsin Behavior Rating Scale* (Song, Jones, Lippert, Metzgen, Miller, & Borreca, 1980) is an instrument intended for use with individuals of any age who are functioning below a developmental age of approximately 3 years. Domains of the subscales are: gross motor, fine motor, expressive language, receptive language, play skills, socialization, domestic activity, eating, toileting, dressing, and grooming. Another version of this instrument, the *Wisconsin Behavior Rating Scale-Revised* expands up to a developmental level of 5 years.

The *Evaluation and Programming System: For Infants and Young Children* (Assessment Level I: Developmentally 1 Month to 3 Years [EPS-I]), an experimental instrument designed to assess children functioning between 1 and 36 months, was developed by Bricker and Gentry (1982). The EPS-I is intended to provide information: (1) to guide program planning for individual children, and (2) to assess program effectiveness. Although it is recommended that the assessment be conducted through observations of a child in his daily living environment, direct testing and parental report are accepted. The EPS-I is organized in six curricular domains: gross motor, fine motor, self-care, cognitive, social and communication, and social. Within each domain items are organized into strands of related behaviors (e.g., object permanence and imitation). Strands comprise long-range goals and training objectives, which are presented in a hierarchical training progression. During the assessment, a child's performance on each item is scored as pass or fail. Failed items become short-term objectives or long-term goals. Bailey and Bricker (1986) reported the results of reliability and validity studies on the EPS-I, in which 22 children with handicaps (chronological ages between 24 and 40 months) and 10 nonhandicapped children (chronological ages between 20 and 39 months) participated. Interobserver reliability for both groups combined ranged from a high of .95 on the gross motor subtest to a low of .23 on the cognitive subtest. Others ranged from .64 to .85. Test–retest reliability for the entire group ranged from .62 (fine motor) to .93 (gross motor). Reliability figures based on only the children with handicaps showed less consistency. They investigated concurrent validity by comparing child performance to developmental quotients and maturity ages derived from the Gesell Developmental Scales and through parent interviews. Correlations between all subtests and totals on both the EPS-I and Gesell for the whole group, nonhandicapped children, and children with handicaps were reported. Correlations on equivalent subtests (e.g., fine motor to fine motor) ranged from .57 (fine motor) to .83 (language and communication). Results from interviews suggested a strong relationship between EPS-I domain scores and parental report. The sample size used in this psychometric study restricts the generalizability of the findings; however, the study does offer initial support of the instrument.

A developmental profile of children with visual impairments from birth to 60 months can be obtained from the *Reynell-Zinkin Developmental Scales for Young Visually Handicapped Children* (Reynell & Zinkin, 1979). This norm-referenced scale is intended to measure current abilities; it does not serve as a predictor of future performance potential. It contains seven domains: social adaptation, sensorimotor understanding, exploration of environment, response to sound and verbal comprehension, vocalization and expressive language (structure), expressive language (vocabulary and content), and communication. Developmental age equivalents for blind, partially sighted, and sighted children can be derived from performance assessments, reports by caregivers and interventionists, and naturalistic observations. The norming sample included 109 children, some of whom were also cerebral palsied and/or hearing impaired. No additional psychometric data are available, nor are norming data available for normal children. The instrument offers a useful tool for identifying priority areas of intervention for children with visual impairments, but should not be used to evaluate their performance as compared with normal children.

The *Developmental Teaching Guide: Check List and Activity File* (Boston Center for Blind Children, 1988) offers a useful curriculum-based assessment and instructional planning guide for children who are visually impaired and multihandicapped. The developmental checklist can be used to (1) assess a child's present skills; (2) generate educational goals for an individual teaching plan; and (3) evaluate a child's progress. Domains included on the checklist are self-help, language, motor, social, and orientation and mobility skills. No developmental ages are provided with the checklist because it is designed as a criterion-referenced assessment tool.

An instrument specifically designed to measure small increments of change evidenced by young children with severely handicapping conditions is the *Uniform Performance Assessment System* (UPAS) (Haring, White, Edgar, Affleck, & Hayden, 1981). The UPAS is a criterion-referenced assessment of functional curriculum-based adaptive skills, covering the age range from birth to 72 months. The 250 items are organized in five domains: preacademic and fine motor, communication, social and self-help, gross motor, and behavior management. It also measures wheelchair needs, atypical behavior patterns, and developmental reinforcement levels. The UPAS can be directly linked to the development of goals and appropriate strategies for intervention. Reports of reliability and validity strongly support the psychometric soundness of the UPAS as a criterion-referenced measure. It can be used effectively as a measure of program efficacy for very young children with moderate to severe handicaps (Hanson, 1985).

The *Autism Screening Instrument for Educational Planning* (Krug, Arick, & Almond, 1980) is a norm-based battery that measures atypical behavior, language interaction skills, and learning rate of individuals from 18 months to 35 years of age. The complete battery comprises five separate instruments: Autism Behavior Checklist, Sample of Vocal Behaviors, Interaction Assessment, Educational Assessment of Functional Skills, and Prognosis of Learning Rate. Percentile ranks and cut-off scores are based on a norming sample of 1049, including 172 autistic, 423 severely mentally retarded, 254 emotionally disturbed, 100 deaf-blind, and 100 normal individuals. A full critique of the battery is available (Volkmar, Cicchetti, Dykens, Sparrow, Leckman, & Cohen, 1988).

SUMMARY

This chapter presents the Ecologically Valid Assessment Model as an organizational tool for assessment. The model comprises five phases: identification of the purpose; identification of the primary behavior settings; identification of behavior-setting features; identification of properties to be assessed; and analyzing and interpreting assessment results. Following a description of this comprehensive model of assessment, it was shown that a child's cultural and linguistic heritage can influence the assessment. In addition, inappropriate instruments should be avoided even if no other instruments are available. The final section of this chapter covered multidomain criterion-referenced instruments, including some developed specifically for a special needs population.

THE ECOLOGICAL PERSPECTIVE

- Assessments should be planned to occur across a variety of settings in which children spend a large percentage of their time.
- Assessments should be designed to provide the specific information needed by people requesting the assessment; they should not just cover a standard battery of tests for all children regardless of the interests of those involved with the child.
- Children whose cultural and/or linguistic heritage differs from the predominate culture must be assessed in a manner that accounts for and values their diversity.
- Use of multidomain criterion-referenced instruments can give an early child-

hood special educator concurrent information across all developmental domains, which is helpful in program planning.

APPENDIX

MULTIDOMAIN ASSESSMENT INSTRUMENTS

Title: Battelle Developmental Inventory (BDI)
Source: Newborg, J., Stock, J., Wnek, L., Guidubaldi, J., & Svinicki, J. (1984). DLM Teaching Resources, P. O. Box 4000, Allen, TX 75002.
Age Range: 0 through 8 years
Description: The BDI incorporates structured testing, interviews with parents, and observations of the child in natural settings. The manual includes specific modifications that can be made when assessing children with various handicapping conditions. According to the BDI Examiner's Manual, the developmental inventory serves four specific purposes: (1) assessment and identification of the handicapped child, (2) assessment of the nonhandicapped child, (3) planning and providing instruction, and (4) evaluation of groups of handicapped children. The full BDI battery consists of 341 test items grouped into five domains: personal and social, adaptive, motor, communication, and cognitive. Scoring system relies on a three-point scale, with partial credit given for emerging skills. A developmental quotient and percentile ranking for each domain and total performance can be calculated. There is also a comprehensive screening test available that includes 96 of the items.
Soundness:
   Standardization: Stratified quota sampling was used to select the 800 children in the norming sample, with a total of 42 test administrators giving the test in 24 states. Children from infancy through 8 years of age were selected to fill quotas that specified age, sex, race, and socioeconomic status (SES).
   Reliability and Validity: The interrater reliability, internal consistency, and concurrent validity of the Battelle for infants with handicapping conditions under 30 months of age were investigated and found to be at acceptable levels (McLean, McCormick, Bruder, & Burdg, 1987). The correlation with the Bayley MDI and the Battelle cognitive subtest was .92, and the Bayley PDI and the Battelle motor subtest correlated at the .92 level. Correlations with the Vineland Adaptive Behavior Scales—Survey Form ranged from a high of .95 (motor scales) to .73 (Battelle Personal social subtest and daily living from the Vineland). The Vineland did tend to produce higher scores than either the Battelle or the Bayley scales. The authors suggest that the Vineland's inability to produce scores low enough to reflect actual child functioning for delayed children in this chronological age range could explain why the discrepancy was found. Boyd, Welge, Sexton, and Miller (1989) in a comparison study with the Bayley scales found that the Battelle does appear to be an appropriate measure of development in infants with handicaps.
Comments: Boyd (1989) noted that children whose chronological ages are near cut-off points for scoring can have radically different scores from one day to the next with no changes in test performance. For example, a child with a chronological age of 5 months 27 days, who earned a deviation quotient of 102 and is ranked at the 56th percentile using the five-month scale, drops to a deviation quotient of 65 and a percentile rating of 1 on the six-month scale.

Title: Birth to Three Developmental Scale

Source: Bangs, T. E. & Dodson, S. (1979). DLM Teaching Resources, P. O. Box 4000, Allen, TX 75002.

Age Range: 0 through 36 months (chronological or developmental).

Description: The purpose is early identification of developmental delays. There are four behavioral categories: oral language (comprehension and expression), problem solving, social and personal, and motor. A three-point scale for scoring based on pass, fail, or emerging is used based on parent observations, passive observation, and active involvement by the examiner. A developmental age for each behavioral category can be plotted to form a graph comparing performance level and chronological age.

Soundness:

   Standardization: Sampling used 357 normal children from Utah, California, and Tennessee, equally representing age levels, gender, and urban and rural background.

   Reliability: Small samples produced high reliability for interrater agreement (range from .88 to .99).

   Validity: No validation studies reported in the manual; however, criteria for inclusion of an item at a specific age level were mastery by 80% of the standardization sample.

Title: Brigance Diagnostic Inventory of Early Development (Revised Edition)

Source: Brigance, A. (1991). Curriculum Associates, Inc., 5 Esquire Road, North Billerica, MA 01862.

Age Range: Birth up to age 7 (chronological ages)

Description: Instrument is based on a developmental task-analytic model, designed to integrate assessment with curriculum development. It uses comprehensive skill sequences to cover 12 developmental domains, including general social and emotional development, prespeech behaviors, fine motor skills, preambulatory motor skills, general knowledge and comprehension, written language, and math. Items are scored as satisfactory or needs improvement, which can be based on mutiple sources of data, including observation, performance, parent or teacher interview, and clinical teaching. It includes supplemental skill sequences useful in monitoring a child's developmental profile and instructional planning.

Soundness:

   Standardization: Separate norms not available, but items are placed according to traditional scales and developmental research into lists of milestone skills by developmental level.

Comments: The Brigance is most useful for individual program planning of children with mild to moderate handicaps. The first edition was limited in its usefulness with children exhibiting more severe impairments because of the size of the steps in each of the skill sequences. The revised version has more skills and includes a supplemental skill sequence as well. Computer-based programs can be generated, which translate assessment data into program plans. Additionally, the Brigance Prescriptive Readiness: Strategies and Practice offers a package of instructional activities that can be linked to the Brigance Diagnostic Inventory.

Title: Carolina Record of Individual Behavior (CRIB)

Source: Simeonsson, R. J. (1985). School of Education, CIREEH, Peabody Hall 037A, University of North Carolina, Chapel Hill, NC 27514.

Age Range: Birth through 48 months (developmental ages)

Description: The CRIB provides a framework to use during clinical observations in structured and naturalistic settings. It was developed to be used with severely handicapped preschool-age children who function below 3 years of age developmentally. The CRIB covers 22 developmental and behavioral domains, such as object orientation, receptive communication, reactivity, attention, motivation, endurance, body tone and tension, social orientation, and consolability. It also includes rhythmic habit patterns (e.g., head bang and hand flap) that children with severe handicaps often exhibit. The CRIB can be scored based on observations across situations and behavioral reports from parents and caregivers. It is based on the Bayley Infant Behavior Record and Brazelton scales. Scoring is based on three Likert scales: (1) from one (primitive) to nine (advanced), (2) normal is a rating of five and extremes are recorded as high as nine or low as one and, (3) a three-point scale (zero, one, two) to measure rhythmic behavior patterns.

Soundness:

    Standardization: Norms are based on a sample of approximately 600 severely handicapped preschool-age children.

Comments: Bagnato, Neisworth, and Munson (1989) pointed out that wording of some items is difficult and may limit the use of the instrument by parents and nonprofessional aides. However, they describe the CRIB as an instrument that can assist interventionists in tailoring "the level of intensity of stimulation and the organization of the environment to the child's capacity to adjust to and benefit from the program" (p. 78).

Title: Developmental Activities

Source: Fewell, R. R., Langley, M. B. (1984). Pro-Ed, 8700 Shoal Creek, Austin, TX 78758-6897.

Age Range: Birth through 60 months (functioning level)

Description: The DASI-II can be used for early detection of developmental delays and to provide information useful for instructional programming with children experiencing delays. It includes 67 items grouped across 11 developmental levels, tapping 15 skill areas: sensory intactness, sensorimotor organization, visual pursuit and object permanence, means—end relationships, causality, imitation, behaviors relating to objects, construction objects in space, memory, discrimination, association, quantitative reasoning, seriation, spatial relationships, and reasoning. Each item is rated as passed or failed, and raw scores are converted to a developmental age score, which can then be converted to a developmental quotient.

Soundness:

    Standardization: Over 200 children with multiple handicaps have been tested with the DASI.

    Reliability: No data are reported in the manual.

    Validity: Based on a sample of 45 children, a correlation of .91 was found with the *Merrill-Palmer Scale* and *Cattell Infant Intelligence Scale,* and a correlation based on 15 children with the DASH was .98. Additional correlational studies support the validity of the instrument.

Comments: No verbal skills are required and can be used with nonverbal children. Adaptive suggestions for administration to children with visual impairments are also provided.

Title: Developmental Assessment for the Severely Handicapped (DASH)

Source: Dykes, M. K. (1980). Exceptional Resources, Inc., 5341 Industrial Oaks Blvd., Austin, TX 78735-8897.

Age Range: 0 through 6 years (chronological or developmental age)

Description: The DASH provides a developmentally sequenced behaviorally defined measure of current and developing skills of children with severe handicaps. It can be used for screening, diagnosis, or identification of specific strengths and weaknesses for program planning criterion-referenced assessment of language, sensorimotor skills, social and emotional functioning, activities of daily living, and preacademic skills. The priority intervention worksheet is used to determine developmental task sequences for intervention.

Soundness:
  Reliability and Validity: A validity study reported in the manual produced an odd–even reliability of .99.
Comments: Although many children with severe handicaps have sensory and/or motoric impairments, no adaptive scoring instructions are provided for children with these conditions.

Title: Developmental Indicators for the Assessment of Learning—Revised (DIAL-R)
Source: Czudnowkski, C. M. & Goldenberg, D. (1990). American Guidance Service, Publishers' Building, P. O. Box 99, Circle Pines, MN 55014-9989.
Age Range: 2 through 6 years
Description: The DIAL-R is a screening tool to identify children who have potential learning problems and gifted children who may be in need of special services. A total of 155 behaviors are grouped into 24 subtests, which are organized into three broad categories: motor (i.e., catching a beanbag, jumping, hopping and skipping, building with blocks, touching fingers, cutting, matching, copying, and writing), concepts (i.e., identifying body parts, naming colors, counting, positioning, identifying concepts, naming letters, and sorting chips), and language (i.e., articulating, giving personal data, remembering, naming nouns, naming verbs, classifying foods, problem solving, and sentence length). Scoring (based on a five-point scale for each item) produces an age score for motor, concepts, and language and a total score that is interpreted with a range from "severe dysfunction" to "potentially advanced."
Soundness:
  Standardization: Sample included 2447 children representative of gender, geographic region, urban and rural setting, and ethnicity.
  Reliability: Test–retest on 65 children resulted in coefficients ranging from .76 to .90, and internal consistency was reported ranging from .86 to .96.
  Validity: Construct, description, and criterion-related validity has been investigated, and concurrent validity with the Stanford-Binet yielded a correlation of .40, with 10.4% identified as false positives for problems and 7% identified as potentially advanced who were not identified on the Stanford-Binet.

Title: Developmental Profile II (DPII)
Source: Alpern, G., Boll, T., & Shearer, M. (1980, 1986). Western Psychological Services, 12031 Wilshire Boulevard, Los Angeles, CA 90025.
Age Range: Birth through 12 years
Description: The DPII is a norm-referenced developmental screening instrument that uses a structured parental interview to determine the child's present level of functioning. It is particularly useful for children with severe handicaps. The structured interview contains 217 items, covering child functioning in five domains: physical, self-help, social, academic, and communication. Items are scored as failed or passed, then developmental age scores for each domain are calculated. These are compared to the child's chronological age to determine the extent of "developmental lag." Since these domains and the landmark skills used in the interview are comparable to those found in typical preschool curricula, Bagnato et al. (1989) consider the DPII a curriculum-compatible instrument.
Soundness:
  Standardization: The instrument has been standardized on a population of over 3000 children.
  Reliability: Adequate for general screening purposes.
  Validity: Concurrent validity with the Binet, LAP, and IPDS is adequate.
Comments: The DPII offers a standardized, psychometrically sound interview procedure that "establishes initial targets for curriculum prescriptions by highlighting perceived capabilities and deficits" (Bagnato et al., 1989).

Title: Diagnostic Inventory for Screening Children, second edition (DISC)

Source: Amdur, J. R., Mainland, M. K., & Parker, K. C. H. (1988). Kitchener Waterloo Hospital, 835 King Street West, Kitchener, Ontario N2G 1G3.

Age Range: Birth through 5 years

Description: The DISC is used to screen children for developmental delays, to provide useful programming information, and to identify children needing further assessment. It covers skills in these eight areas: fine motor, gross motor, receptive language, expressive language, auditory attention and memory, visual attention and memory, self-help, and social skills. Scoring is based on a pass and fail system, and raw scores are converted to percentiles.

Soundness:

Standardization: Four hundred children participated in the standardization study who were living at home, born no more than one month premature, had no apparent behavior or emotional problems, and the primary spoken language of the home was English. An additional 573 children participated with information regarding gender, age, occupation, and education of the male and female parent, job title of head of the household, geographic region, ethnic group (English, French, or other), marital status of guardian, and urban and rural residence compared to Canadian census.

Reliability: Correlation coefficients for observer reliability (.99), test–retest reliability (.94 to .98), and internal reliability (.98 to .99) are discussed in the manual.

Validity: No studies are reported in the manual, but item placement is based on performance by 75% of the standardization group.

Title: Project Memphis Comprehensive Developmental Scale

Source: Quick, A. D., & Campbell, A. A. (1987). Department of Special Education, Memphis State University, Memphis, TN 38152.

Age Range: Birth through 5 years (developmental age)

Description: The Comprehensive Developmental Scale is one part of the Project Memphis materials, which also include a Habilitation Program and Accountability Record and Lesson Plans. Developmental evaluation using the scale is the first in a three-step educational cycle. The other steps are program planning and program implementation. The scale provides a profile of development in five areas: gross motor, fine motor, personal and social, language, and perceptuocognitive. Scoring produces an average developmental age score for each domain, but the authors caution against interpreting it as an absolute score, recommending that it be used as an indication of where instruction should begin.

Soundness:

Standardization: No information is available.

Reliability and Validity: No information is available.

Comments: The most appropriate use of the scale is as a criterion-referenced guide for instructional planning, not as a diagnostic test that can yield a meaningful score. Additionally, the highest possible score is 60 months, so it cannot be used with children functioning at or near the 5-year-old level to have a complete view of a child's abilities.

Title: Rockford Infant Developmental Evaluation Scales (RIDES)

Source: Project RHISE (1979). Scholastic Testing Service, 480 Meyer Road, Bensenville, IL 60106.

Age Range: Birth through 4 years (developmental behaviors)

Description: RIDES is intended to give special educators a tool to guide and quantify their observations of infants and toddlers so as to provide "a skill-by-skill picture of the child's developmental and behavioral repertoire" (Project RHISE, p. 3). It can be used for initial informal assessment and ongoing assessment and is appropriate for assessments conducted in transdisciplinary settings. Reassessments are recommended no less than three and no more than nine months apart. There are 308 developmental behaviors classified into five skill areas: personal and social and self-help (awareness of self, others, and situation; social interaction and play skills; and responsibility in self-care); fine motor and adaptive (manipulative tasks, crayon-and-paper tasks, eye–hand coordination tasks, reach, grasp and release, imitative skills, and problem-solving skills); receptive language (ability to attend to and understand speech of others—auditory awareness and attention, verbal comprehension, and vocabulary development); expressive language (ability to communicate effectively with others—auditory memory and verbal imitation); and gross motor (development of postural system and mobility skills).

Soundness:

Standardization: Field testing through federally funded projects involved a total of 92 children ranging in age from under 12 months to over 3 years, but it has not been standardized.

Reliability and Validity: A group of 32 professionals from a variety of backgrounds critiqued the RIDES during the field testing. Revisions were made based on their comments, but no reliability or validity studies have been conducted.

Title: Kent Infant Development Scale (KIDS)

Source: Reuter, J., & Bickett, L. (1985). Developmental Metrics, 126 West College Avenue, P.O. Box 3178, Kent, OH 44240.

Age Range: 0 through 12 months (chronological or developmental ages)

Description: KIDS surveys an infant's behavioral repertoire to determine the child's developmental age. Emerging behaviors can be used to develop prescriptive objectives. It is scored primarily through parent–caregiver report and covers five domains: cognitive, motor, language, self-help, and social. KIDS includes items not routinely found on developmental scales (Bagnato et al., 1989), such as "gets startled by sudden voices or noises," "remembers where things are kept in the house," and "shows jealousy." The instrument contains 252 skills that are scored according to four categories (yes; did but outgrew; no longer able; and can't do yet). Developmental ages for each domain and for the total test are produced.

Soundness:

Standardization: Norms are based on 480 infants from northeast Ohio.

Reliability and Validity: Test–retest reliability is reported at .88 and higher and concurrent validity with the Bayley .70 and higher.

Comments: Bagnato et al. (1989) recommend using the KIDS in conjunction with other broad assessment instruments to provide a strong assessment and curriculum linkage, but not as the sole instrument for program development. The instrument has been field tested successfully with severely brain-damaged children who were functioning below the 1-year developmental level (Stancin, Reuter, & Bickett, 1984).

Title: Learning Accomplishment Profile—Diagnostic Edition (LAP-D)

Source: LeMay, D., Griffin, P. M., & Sanford, A. (1978). Kaplan School Supply Corporation, 1310 Lewisville-Clemmons Road, Lewisville, NC 27023.

Age Range: 0 through 6 years

Description: The LAP-D is a developmental task-analysis instrument that is designed to accompany the LAP curriculum materials. It contains developmental tasks in five domains: fine motor, gross motor, language, cognition, and self-help. Each of these is subdivided into subareas, such as manipulation, writing, matching, object movement, counting, comprehension, and grooming. The diagnostic profile that denotes the child's range of skills that are fully acquired, emerging, and absent is used for individualized goal planning. Scoring is based on direct performance, observation, and reporting by parents or caregivers.

Soundness:

Reliability and Validity: Initial reports of test–retest reliability, based on 35 children, are over .90 for all subtests, with a reliability of .98 for the total scale.

Comments: Although the title uses the word diagnostic, there are no norms currently available for the instrument, and therefore is more appropriately used in program planning than diagnosis. Further psychometric study of the instrument may increase its usefulness as a diagnostic instrument.

Title: Perceptions of Developmental Status (PODS)
Source: Bagnato, S. J., & Neisworth, J. T. (1989). American Guidance Service, Publisher's Building, P.O. Box 99, Circle Pines, MN 55014.
Age Range: 12 through 72 months
Description: The PODS is designed to facilitate team decision making based on multiple perceptions of child functioning. It is used to rate a child's abilities in six domains: communication, sensorimotor, physical, self-regulation, cognitive, and self-social. Children are rated on individual items using a Likert scale from one (severe impairment) to five (normal functioning) based on descriptions provided on the test protocol.
Soundness:

Reliability and Validity: Both reliability and validity studies support the psychometric soundness of the instrument (Bagnato, Neisworth, & Capone, 1987; Bagnato & Neisworth, 1981).

Comments: The instrument is one part of the System to Plan Early Childhood Services (SPECS) and is designed to be directly linked to service delivery and programming needs.

Title: Reynell-Zinkin Developmental Scales (RZS)
Source: Reynell, J., & Zinkin, K. (1979). Stoelting Company, 1350 South Kostner Avenue, Chicago, IL 60623.
Age Range: 0 through 60 months
Description: The RZS are designed to provide a functional assessment appropriate for and normed on a visually impaired population of children. It is not intended for prediction of future performance or classification purposes, but should be used for prescriptive program planning and program evaluation. The seven domains of functioning measured by the RZS are social adaptation, sensorimotor understanding, exploration of environment, response to sound and verbal comprehension, vocalization and expressive language (structure), expressive language (vocabulary and content), and communication. The emphasis of the instrument is on tactile and auditory tasks. Items are scored as pass and fail, and developmental age equivalents for blind, partially sighted, and sighted children can be generated. Bagnato et al. (1989) cite it as a curriculum-compatible scale because of its adaptive and instructional features.
Soundness:

Standardization: There were 109 children representing three diagnostic groups (blind—97; partial—86; borderline—20) who were scored a total of 203 times.
Reliability: No information is available.
Validity: No information is available.
Comments: The emphasis of the instrument is on functional assessment, and it is normed on the population for whom it is intended. Norms for normal children should also be developed and psychometric soundness needs to be established.

CHAPTER 9

Child Assessment: Cognitive Functioning

CHAPTER OUTLINE

QUESTIONS ANSWERED IN CHAPTER 9

- What are definitions of cognition, intelligence, and knowledge?
- What conditions are associated with cognitive dysfunction?
- How does cognition develop?
- What techniques and instruments for assessment of cognitive functioning can be used with neonates, infants and toddlers, or preschool-age children?
- What techniques are applicable to the cognitive assessment of infants, toddlers, and preschool-age children with motoric and sensory impairments?

CHAPTER OVERVIEW

The assessment of cognitive functioning requires an understanding of what is meant by cognition and how it manifests itself in infants, toddlers, and preschool-age children. The cognitive domain comprises a multitude of skills and abilities and is associated with intelligence and, therefore, intelligence tests. It is associated with skills related to attention, discrimination, imitation, spatial relationships, temporal relationships, causality, reasoning, classification, sorting, sequencing, and problem solving. As children reach school age, it becomes directly linked to performance in school. Views concerning what cognition is, how it develops, what causes impairments in it, and its relationship to the concept of intelligence all influence the assessment process.

Theories of cognitive development vary as to the signficance environmental influences hold over a child's cognitive abilities. It is a domain that is frequently assessed through a young child's observable functioning in motor and language domains. Tests for very young children, which purport to measure mental ability, intelligence, mental developmental age, and preacademic skills, are all considered measures of cognition. They are often based on the assumption that motor skills and/or language skills reflect cognitive ability. The inverse assumption, that children who lack certain motor or language skills are also lacking in cognitive ability, presents innumerable problems for the early childhood special educator. The motorically impaired child who is also nonverbal is in great danger of becoming a victim of this tenuous assumption. This chapter incorporates a review of traditional measures of cognitive assessment along with alternative approaches intended to avoid underestimates of the cognitive abilities of motorically or sensory-impaired children.

DEFINITIONS OF COGNITION

Cognition is an area of development that is particularly difficult to isolate from other domains in assessment. Although it can be conceptualized separate from other domains, such as motor or language functioning, the outward manifestation of cognition usually necessitates motor or language output (see Chapter 12 for further discussion of this point). Therefore, it is helpful to get as clear a picture as possible of what is meant by cognition. The separation of expressive actions and behaviors that provide evidence of cognitive understanding from cognitive understanding itself is critical to the assessment process.

Knowledge and Knowing

Cognitive development, intelligence, and the ability to learn are all related concepts. Three basic components that definitions of intelligence have in common are (1) the capacity to learn; (2) the sum total of knowledge an individual has acquired; and (3) the ability to adjust to various environments, particularly new situations (Robinson & Robinson, 1976). Some define intelligence as a global capacity (Wechsler, 1958), whereas others speak of multiple types of intelligence (Guilford,

1967). Still others theorize a general ability operating in conjunction with other more specialized skills (Vernon, 1950). Hunt (1975) speaks of intelligence as hierarchical learning sets, with multiple systems and skills, including information processing and motivation. Cattell (1963) and Horn (1985) developed the concepts of fluid (nonverbal mental efficiency) and crystallized ability (acquired skills and knowledge that are dependent on environmental influences). Watson (1976) speculated on three possible relationships between intelligence and learning: intelligence determines learning, learning determines intelligence, and learning exposes intelligence.

Cognitive development as defined by Meier (1976) includes the ability to think about past, present, and future events or thoughts in order to solve problems and to achieve a greater understanding about oneself and the world. A definition proposed by Glick (1975) has a similar theme of knowledge about the world: "The study of cognition is the study of the means by which an individual comes to have organized knowledge of the world, and of the way in which that knowledge is used to guide behavior" (p. 595). Understanding cognitive development as related to knowledge requires an understanding of knowledge and knowing. Glick includes four overlapping categories of skills in his definition of knowledge. While these categories are not mutually exclusive, each represents a critical component of knowledge, which is the basic element of cognition.

First is *the ability to detect environmental features*. The acuteness with which a human can gain and ascertain the significance of information in the environment is basic to her ability to develop cognitively. For example, learning to distinguish the significant features between a square and a circle is less challenging than a square and a triangle, which is easier than distinguishing between a square and a rectangle, and so forth.

The second category is *the ability to organize diversity into categories*. For example, a young child might begin playing with blocks by organizing all the blocks into similar sizes and shapes so he can find what he needs as construction begins.

The formation of plans of behavior and/or theories about the world is the third element within Glick's description of knowledge. How much planning and fore-thought go into an infant's actions as she moves about a room, stopping to put whatever she encounters into her mouth? Most often these behaviors appear to have very little, if any, advance planning. Gratch and Schatz (1987), in a discourse on Piagetian theory, describe the transition to planning as a progression toward symbolic play while flexibility and coherence of actions develop. As the child grows, behaviors clearly indicating advance planning begin to emerge. During imaginary play, children can be observed "setting the stage," assigning parts to themselves and others, and changing the script as needed to suit their purposes. Young children engaged in creative art activities will often stop to ponder before beginning to work.

The development of theories about the world may be less easily observed in young children, and yet the foundational thinking surely begins during this period. Some theories may be quite simple—temper tantrums are an effective method of obtaining my desires; death is only a temporary condition; playdough of two colors when mixed together can be separated; and so on. Experiences that contradict such theories will require the child to challenge their cognitive validity and replace them with ones more consistent with his experiences.

The fourth component of knowledge pertains to *the organization of thoughts,* as found in logic, mathematics, religion, and other advanced forms of thinking. These systems in which thoughts are organized are not necessarily based on the world of empirical knowledge. Such organized thought processes are used to come to an understanding of both real and theoretical aspects of the world.

Basic Psychological Processes

The attainment of cognitive skills requires that the child take advantage of basic sensory input as she explores her environment. In order for the child to do so, three basic psychological processes need to be operating—*attention, perception,* and *memory.* Before the infant can begin to detect salient features of the environment, she simply must attend to them, that is, become aware of them. (See Zeaman and House, 1963; Zeaman, 1973; and Atkinson and Shiffrin, 1968, for information about theories of attention.)

After becoming aware of features within the environment, the child must perceive those features, that is, translate them into meaningful information. Inter-preting the sensory information sent to the brain by the sense organs for vision, hearing, smelling, touching, tasting, and movement is perception. Perception dif-fers from acuity, although it is dependent on the accuracy of the information re-ceived in the brain to be processed. Damage to a sense organ or nerves connecting that organ to the brain affects acuity. Perception is a process that occurs within the brain, involving the recall of past experiences, comparing them to present ones, analyzing the information available, and finally interpreting present stimuli. (For information about perceptual theories see Neisser, 1976.)

If a child is to obtain any long-term knowledge about features of the environ-ment, he must store them in his memory to be available as needed. Memory is the

most complex psychological process involved in cognitive development. It includes the encoding, storage, and retrieval of information in the central nervous system. It has both short- and long-term components, which are related in a sometimes puzzling manner with the ability to retrieve needed information. Ellis's multiprocess memory model (1970), based on other theoretical models (e.g., Atkinson & Shiffrin, 1968; Bower, 1967; Hebb, 1949), includes three levels of memory. As input is attended to and rehearsed, it cycles through the primary memory into the secondary and tertiary memories. Material that is not attended to or rehearsed can be forgotten at any one of these memory levels.

THEORIES OF COGNITIVE DEVELOPMENT

Three basic perspectives regarding the cognitive development of young children were mentioned in Chapter 3—maturational theory, cognitive stages theory, and behavioral theory. *Maturational theory* is structured around the child's natural patterns of growth and development. A child develops cognitively as a result of her maturation. *Cognitive stages theory,* such as that developed by Piaget, focuses on a child's progression to higher cognitive functions in sequential stages. According to Piaget, movement from one stage to another results from environmental interactions characterized by *assimilation* and *accommodation* of the child's *schemes,* or understandings, of the world. A child assimilates information from the environment to fit her own schemes of the world. As she becomes aware that contradictions exist with her views of the world, *disequilibration* occurs, and the child accommodates her thinking to alleviate the contradiction. The *behaviorist theory* has as an underlying foundation that all behavior is learned. The behaviorist model incorporates both *classical conditioning,* in which the child has no control over her response, and *instrumental conditioning* where the child's response to stimuli determines consequences.

Cognitive development has been conceived in other frameworks as well. *Information-processing models* of cognitive development are grounded in the functioning of the psychological processes of attention, perception, and memory. The information-processing structure provides the basis for an alternative assessment procedure for infants with motoric impairments (Zelazo, 1982a, 1982b). These techniques of assessment are described later in this chapter. Other theories related to cognitive development include Hebb's theory of neurophysiological development (Hebb, 1949) and social learning theory (e.g., Bandura, 1978).

DEFICITS IN COGNITIVE DEVELOPMENT

Children who exhibit delays or deficits in cognitive functioning typically receive one of several diagnostic labels—mental retardation, developmental delay, learning disability, or attention deficit disorder (ADD). Although these labels do not always provide clarification as to the cause of the delay, they are often used to provide a diagnosis descriptive of the condition.

Mental Retardation and Developmental Delay

The most common definition of mental retardation in education is that used in PL 94–142 (see the definitions on pages 9–11). Infants, toddlers, and very young children with moderate-to-severe or profound retardation are routinely identified during the first 1 to 2 years of life. Often severe impairments can be detected within the first few weeks of life and are frequently associated with genetic disorders or brain damage. However, young children who are functioning within the range of mild retardation are not so readily identified. Additionally, professionals are hesitant to label preschool-age children functioning within the mild range as mentally retarded. The preferred label and one used frequently for children who are experiencing some mild cognitive delays is *developmental delay.* This term avoids the negative stigma associated with the mental retardation label, yet denotes an awareness that the child's development is not progressing normally. The instability of intelligent quotient (IQ) measures for children under 6 years lends further support to the professional preference for use of the less damaging label of developmental delay.

Learning Disabilities and Attention Deficit Disorder

The most widely used definition of learning disabilities, as used in PL 94–142 (*Federal Register,* December 29, 1977, Part 3), is included in the definitions on pages 9–11. Since 1977, numerous other definitions have been put forth. The basic tenet found in all the definitions is poor functioning in academic areas, such as reading, writing, mathematics, and/or spelling, when performance is compared to expected cognitive ability. The definitions separate the concept of cognitive potential and intelligence from academic ability. Although learning disabled children are not mentally retarded, they do exhibit disorders in the basic psychological processes, which can result in cognitive delays or impairment. The child who experiences difficulty in the classroom (e.g., reading failure, poor handwriting, and poor spelling) is the one most likely to be labeled as learning disabled. Others who might have processing deficits but manage to succeed in school rarely become so identified.

The related but not synonymous condition recently identified by the American Psychiatric Association, attention deficit hyperactivity disorder (ADHD), is defined primarily through behavioral descriptions, which are summarized in the following list (American Psychiatric Association, 1987):

A. A period of six months or more during which at least eight of the following behaviors are present:
   1. has difficulty remaining seated when required to
   2. often fidgets with hands or feet or squirms in seat
   3. has difficulty playing quietly
   4. often talks excessively
   5. often shifts from one uncompleted activity to another
   6. has difficulty sustaining attention to tasks and play activities
   7. has difficulty following through on instructions from others (not due to oppositional behavior or failure of comprehension), e.g., fails to finish chores
   8. is easily distracted by extraneous stimuli
   9. often interrupts or intrudes on others, e.g., butts into other children's games
   10. often blurts out answers to questions before they have been completed
   11. has difficulty waiting turn in games or group situations
   12. often engages in physically dangerous activities without considering possible consequences (not for the purpose of thrill-seeking), e.g., runs into street without looking
   13. often loses things necessary for tasks or activities at school or at home (e.g., toys, pencils, books, assignments)
   14. often doesn't seem to listen to what is being said to him or her
B. Onset before the age of seven years
C. Does not meet criteria for Pervasive Developmental Disorder

The case histories of many children with learning disabilities and attention disorders reveal that they displayed a consistent pattern of problems throughout their infancy and early childhood. For example, they are often described as irritable babies, with sleep disturbances and bed-wetting episodes beyond normal expectations (Wender, 1987). During the preschool years they exhibit difficulty with fine motor activities (e.g., cutting with scissors, coloring, buttoning, and tying shoes), as well as gross motor activities (e.g., running) (Wodrich & Joy, 1986). Poor balance and eye–hand coordination (e.g., throwing and catching a ball, tricycle or bicycle riding, or walking down stairs) is also frequently reported in the preschool history of school-aged children with these labels. These children have also been reported as experiencing social interaction problems, such as noncompliance to adults and resistance to social demands (Wender, 1987).

The identification of very young children as having either of these handicapping conditions can be tricky. Not every fussy baby, noncompliant toddler, or 6-year-old who cannot ride a bicycle needs to be referred or labeled. McCarthy (1989) matched child characteristics by age to a future diagnosis of learning disabled as shown in the following list:

0 to 3 months: Many begin their lives in the neonatal intensive care nursery as babies that are small for gestational age, premature, or suffering from birth trauma.

3 to 12 months: Delays in motor or physical development may emerge.

6 to 12 months: Babies with affective difficulties (e.g., lack of bonding and difficult to cuddle) are noticed during this age span.

18 to 36 months: Speech and language delays are evident at this point.

60 to 72 months: Entry into school leads to failures in the use of symbol systems (e.g., language and mathematics).

While the use of the label *learning disabled* for an infant or preschool-age child should be avoided, it is necessary to be familiar with the risk factors associated with specific learning disabilities.

STABILITY OF INTELLIGENCE QUOTIENTS

Interventionists need to interpret scores derived from instruments purported to measure a very young child's intelligence cautiously. The content of the instrument, psychometric qualities, and match between child and norm group are all important variables. The fluid nature of performance must also be taken into consideration for the very young child. The brief sampling of behavior that is witnessed during a clinical assessment may not be indicative of an infant's or young child's predominate capabilities. Additionally, cognitive tests cannot be used to predict the future mental ability of the child. Correlations between the scores on cognitive assessments during infancy and the preschool years and those at school age are not high. The correlations between scores on tests administered to infants between birth and 6 months of age and scores on assessments conducted on those same children during childhood (between ages 5 and 18) have been reported as low as .00 to .09 (McCall, 1982; McCall, Hogarty, & Hurlburt, 1972). Correlations do, however, gradually increase as children mature.

McCall reports that the best single predictor of IQ during childhood is the parent's level of education or IQ, with a correlation rate of approximately .50. The IQ is slightly more stable at extremes, so there is a greater likelihood that infants assessed as severely delayed will continue to function on the same level than infants closer to the mean of the group. Nevertheless, the use of infant assessments to predict any particular individual's future potential is questionable. As many as one out of four or five infants and toddlers (even up to ages 2 and 3) who are diagnosed as definitely mentally retarded lose this diagnosis during childhood (Holden, 1972; Koch, 1963).

A lack of predictive validity does not render the tests worthless. McCall (1982) illustrates their utility through a comparison with measurements of birth weights. "Birth weight does not predict adult weight, but it is a valid index of general health state at the moment. Apparently, the determinants of weight before birth are different from the determinants of weight after birth" (p. 178). The most appropriate use of instruments that assess cognitive functioning is in the determination of the child's *present level of functioning*. Examiners can use test results along with observations and parent interviews to make placement decisions or ascertain instructional levels. Such scores might also be useful in program evaluation to monitor child progress. Other uses, including diagnosis and labeling, are often of questionable validity.

TECHNIQUES FOR ASSESSMENT

The techniques used in the assessment of cognition change depending on the age of the child. Appropriate techniques for neonates differ from those used with a 1-year-old, and so on. Assessing the cognitive abilities of infants presents quite a different challenge than assessing preschool-age children who are engaged in many traditional cognitive activities and who have well-developed receptive and expressive language skills.

The age ranges for which instruments are intended vary widely. For example, the age range for the *Bayley Scales of Infant Development* are standardized on infants and toddlers from birth to 30 months, while the *Griffiths Mental Development Scales* cover birth to 8 years, and the *McCarthy Scales of Children's Abilities* can be used with children from ages 2 years 6 months to 8 years 6 months. Instruments with wide age ranges are appealing in that they can be used with many children. They offer consistency for longitudinal studies as well. However, instruments that attempt to cover wide age ranges tend to have less accuracy and adequate detail. The number of test items that can be included at each age level is often very limited on tests that cover a broad age span.

In addition to the variance in techniques according to age of the child, appropriate techniques vary according to certain child characteristics. Techniques appropriate for children with intact hearing and/or vision often are not suitable for the deaf or blind child. Children with motoric impairments, who may be nonoral as well, present some of the greatest challenges to persons interested in assessing their cognitive functioning. Standard testing procedures do not work, are very unfair, and should be replaced with adaptive approaches.

The determination as to which instruments and procedures to include and how to organize them in a text of this nature is a challenging task. Sheehan and Klein (1989) in addressing the proliferation of infant assessment instruments note that although approximately 300 infant assessment instruments have been developed, the number of uniquely designed tools is about 5. Some instruments are targeted exclusively toward the assessment of cognitive functioning, while others include multiple domains. Selected instruments that are primarily associated with cognitive assessment are included in this chapter and organized into three age categories: (1) neonates; (2) infants and toddlers; and (3) preschool and early childhood. Many of the instruments described overlap these age categories; however, they are presented in the section corresponding to their most frequent or appropriate usage. There is also a section on alternative assessment approaches for children whose handicapping conditions preclude traditional approaches.

Neonates

During the first 28 days of extrauterine life, infants are considered to be neonates. Infants born in hospitals typically receive their first assessment one minute after birth, and the second after five minutes. The tool used for these assessments is the Apgar scoring system (Apgar, 1953), which rates the infant on a scale of zero to two on five signs. The overall rating is derived from scores of heart rate, respiratory effort, reflex irritability, muscle tone, and color. A zero is given for no response (e.g., no heart rate and blue in color), and a two represents the best response (e.g., heart rate of 100 to 140 beats per minute and entirely pink in color). Infants who receive very low Apgar scores are considered to be at high risk for future complications. In summarizing the research on the predictive validity of the Apgar rating, Francis, Self, and Horowitz (1987) noted that the clearest findings are a strong relationship between low Apgar ratings and infant mortality. In regard to later developmental progress, the findings are inconsistent.

The *First-Week Evaluation Scale* (Cohen, Allen, Pollin, Inoff, Werner, & Dibble, 1972) provides a global rating of the newborn's constitution. Two raters review an infant's medical records and, using a scale from one to five, score the infant on the following measures: health, physiological adaptation, calmness, vigor, attention, and neurological status. Most other neonatal assessment devices require direct observation of the infant and provide opportunities for examiners to interact with the infant in an effort to elicit behaviors. Two such instruments that are frequently used are the *Graham/Rosenblith Scales* (Rosenblith, 1974a, 1975) and the *Brazelton Neonatal Behavioral Assessment Scale* (Brazelton, 1973, 1984).

The *Graham/Rosenblith Scales* contain a motor scale (e.g., head reaction in prone position), a tactile-adaptive scale (e.g., responses to cotton over the nose), visual responsiveness (e.g., fixation and degree of horizontal and vertical pursuit of object), auditory responsiveness (e.g., responses to rattle and bell), and muscle tone [e.g., nature (flexed or extended) of spontaneous lower limb position]. The examiner can also include an irritability rating, which she assigns to the infant based on the infant's behavior throughout the entire examination. Interscorer reliability coefficients have been reported in a number of studies and generally fall between .73 and 1.00 (Francis et al., 1987). Test–retest reliability on an earlier version of the instrument ranged from .62 to .73 (Rosenblith, 1961).

Follow-up studies have revealed some predictive relationships between the *Graham/Rosenblith Scales* and child functioning. For example, neonatal scores on the tactile-adaptive scale were predictive of the incidence of sudden infant death syndrome across ethnic subgroups in Hawaii (Rosenblith, 1974a, 1974b). Other significant correlations include the motor scale scores and IQ at age 7 (but not at age 4), and tactile-adaptive scores and whether or not the child had to repeat a grade in school (Rosenblith, 1979a, 1979b).

Since the number of neonatal behaviors that are measured on the *Graham/Rosenblith Scales* is limited, the *Brazelton Neonatal Behavioral Assessment Scale* receives wider usage. The Brazelton measures both reflexive/elicited and behavioral characteristics of the neonate. The reflexive/elicited behaviors that are observed include plantar grasp, standing, automatic walking, nystagmus, tonic neck reflex, and rooting and sucking. The 27 behavioral items on the scale include observation of infant behaviors, such as response decrement to light, rattle, bell, and pinprick, degree of alertness, cuddliness, consolability with intervention, amount of startle, and hand-to-mouth facility. Horowitz, Sullivan, and Linn (1978) developed a supplemented version (NBAS-K) in which five additional behavioral items are included. Interobserver reliability has been consistently reported as high, whereas test–retest reliability is poor (Francis et al., 1987). Research studies involving the Brazelton scale were reviewed by Francis et al. (1987) and demonstrate that it "might well be useful in predicting other infant behaviors, both in interaction with the caregiver and on standard infant assessments" (p. 752). The NBAS has been demonstrated to be an effective intervention device in the support of parenting with mothers of low socioeconomic status and adolescent mothers (Worobey & Brazelton, 1990).

Dubowitz (1985) identified the need for an additional instrument that , can be administered by staff untrained in neonatal neurology, can be used on preterm neonates, and requires no more than 10 to 15 minutes to complete and record. Dubowitz's instrument, designed to meet these criteria, covers habituation (state of the infant), movement and tone, reflexes, and neurobehavioral items (e.g., auditory orientation and alertness) and uses a five-point rating scale based on brief descriptions and/or illustrations of specific motoric responses. While she does briefly discuss data from some interobserver recordings, no psychometric properties of the instrument are reported. The instrument does, however, appear to be of potential use in the longitudinal study of at-risk neonates.

Infants and Toddlers

Approaches used in infant and toddler assessment include (1) traditional tests; (2) Piagetian-based criterion-referenced tests; (3) perceptual-cognitive processing tests; and (4) observation and analysis of behavior during perceptual-cognitive processing tasks.

Traditional Tests.   Traditional tests include norm-referenced tests and scales used to produce scores such as development quotient, developmental index, intelligence quotient, developmental age, and mental age. Criterion-referenced tests have also been developed that are similar in content to the norm-referenced developmental scales. Items on these traditional tests represent developmental landmarks in the child's maturation. The primary uses of traditional instruments that assess cognitive ability are screening or diagnosis.

Most traditional infant assessment instruments that are currently in wide use are derived from test items found on the *Gesell Developmental Schedules* (Gesell & Amatruda, 1947). The most recent revision of the Gesell scales was developed by Knobloch and Pasamanick (1974). The schedules contain items representing motor behaviors (gross and fine), language (verbal and nonverbal), personal and social behaviors (e.g., play behaviors and eating skills), and adaptive behaviors (e.g., finding objects and tower building). Gesell considered his developmental schedules as tools useful in determining the present condition of infants and toddlers, not in predicting future performance or establishing a child's IQ. However, the schedules have been used by many examiners as a measure of intelligence. In fact, developmental quotient has been treated as if it were an intelligence quotient (Kahn, 1988).

Although the schedules have questionable psychometric qualities and have consistently failed to demonstrate predictive validity (Yang, 1979), they do provide a useful description of a child's present condition. Bagnato, Neisworth, and Munson (1989) suggested that the schedules be used by early interventionists as a criterion-based measure in program planning and evaluation. Such a use is more consistent with the original intention of Gesell than is the generation of a score, which is treated as an IQ.

The *Griffiths Mental Developmental Scales* (Griffiths, 1954; 1979) are very similar in nature to the *Gesell Schedules*. These scales include *The Abilities of Babies,* which covers the first two years of life, and *The Abilities of Young Children,* which spans up to eight years of age. The Griffiths scales contain five separate scales of behaviors for the first 24-month period: locomotor, personal and social, hearing and speech, eye and hand coordination, and performance. They can be easily administered to infants and toddlers with deficits in communication, cognition, motor function, or vision or hearing. Each of the five scales produces a developmental age, and a general intelligence quotient can be obtained as well. The scales were developed in England and are based on a British standardization sample. Therefore, some items might reflect cultural influence, and norming data are not representative of children raised in the United States. Additional questions regarding the norms have been raised since Hanson and Aldridge-Smith (1987) reported that 1980 test administrations of certain items do not produce the same pattern of scores as those found in the original standardization sample. In one research study the scales were successfully modified for infants with severe malformations from thalidomide (Decarie, 1969).

The *Bayley Scales of Infant Development* (Bayley, 1984) include assessment of the mental, psychomotor, and social domains. The mental scale consists of 163 items intended to assess the following:

> Sensory-perceptual acuities, discriminations, and the ability to respond to these; the early acquisition of "object constancy" and memory learning, and problem-solving ability; vocalizations and the beginnings of verbal communication; and

early evidence of the ability to form generalizations and classifications, which is
the basis of abstract thinking. (Bayley, 1969, p.3)

Bayley engaged in extensive clinical study and research, using many of Gesell's
developmental landmark items in the production of these scales. She does not view
the scales as capable of producing predictive scores, rather stipulates that the
primary value of the scores is the determination of a child's current status. (The
motor scale is discussed in Chapter 11 and the Infant Behavior Record is reviewed
in Chapter 12.)

The standardization sample contained 1262 children (ages 2 to 30 months)
representative of selected strata of the United States population, according to the
1960 U.S. Census of Population. The controls in the sample were sex and color
within each age group, as well as controls related to residence (urban and rural) and
education of the head of the household. The sample only included "normal" children who lived at home. Premature children and children over 12 months of age
from bilingual homes were excluded as well. The mental scale is normed at half-
month intervals from 2 to 5 months and at 1-month intervals from 6 to 30 months.

Reliability coefficients (based on split-half procedures) for the mental scale
range from .81 to .93, with a median value of .88. Reliability was also established
using the percentage of tester-observer agreement (89.4% for the mental scale) and
test–retest (76.4% for the mental scale). The standard error of measurement ranges
from 4.2 to 6.9 on the mental scale.

The mental scale generates two different measures. The mental development
index (MDI) is a standard score similar to an IQ, based on a set of standard scores
with a mean of 100 and a standard deviation of 16. A mental age equivalent can also
be derived. It takes approximately 45 minutes to administer the mental and motor
scales, but individual variations must be expected. The Infant Behavior Record
requires no additional testing time. Testing takes place with the mother (or mother
substitute) present with the child. The order of item presentation is highly flexible
and can be adjusted as the properly trained examiner feels the need to do so. Items
on which the child is scored as a part of the mental scale include such things as
responding to sounds, visual recognition of mother, vocalizations, smiling in a
mirror, scribbling, and turning pages in a book.

A simplified questionnaire of Bayley items completed by mothers correlates
well with both the MDI ($r = .686$) and the mental age ($r = .845$); however, it does
yield significantly higher scores (Gradel, Thompson, & Sheehan, 1981). Therefore,
infants who receive a low score on the questionnaire are more likely to be candidates for early intervention.

The lowest possible MDI based on the normative sample is 50; therefore it is
necessary to use extrapolated MDIs for children falling below a score of 50. Since
extrapolated scores are derived from regression tables rather than norming samples, they must be viewed as estimates instead of actual scores. Many of the items
on the Bayley scales rely on psychomotor and sensory abilities. Children with
motor and/or sensory impairments cannot perform many of the tasks required in
these items and, therefore, are in danger of being misdiagnosed as cognitively
impaired if these scales are used.

Although the predictive ability of the mental scale is limited, when used in conjunction with other predictors it does appear capable of predicting mental retardation in infants and toddlers with low scores (Ramey & Brownlee, 1981; Ireton, Thwing, & Gravem, 1970; VanderVeer & Schweid, 1974). It has also been used to determine program effectiveness and can be used repeatedly without influencing test performance (Haskins, Ramey, Stedman, Blacher-Dixson, & Pierce, 1978; Ramey & Haskins, 1981; Ramey & Smith, 1976). The scales have been shown to be moderately stable for high-risk infants 6 and 12 months of age, with a correlation of .71 on the mental scale and .69 on the motor scale (Cook, Holder-Brown, Johnson, & Kilgo, 1989). Hoffman (1982) has developed modifications of the Bayley for the child with sensorimotor impairments known as "optimizing techniques." These techniques are consistent with Sattler's notion of testing the limits as discussed in Chapter 3.

The *Cattell Infant Intelligence Scale* (Cattell, 1969) was designed to be a downward extension of the *Stanford-Binet Intelligence Scale* and is predicated on the theory that a single (G-factor) intelligence exists and is measurable. It can be used with infants from 2 to 30 months and includes items from the Gesell schedules, which Cattell though were not extremely influenced by home training or gross muscular control.

There are norms every month from 2 to 12 months, every 2 months from 12 to 24 months, and every 3 months from 24 to 30 months. Correlations between Cattell scores and Stanford-Binet scores administered at 3 years of age gradually increase from .10 at 3 months, to .56 at 12 months, to .71 at 24 months. These weak correlations generally fail to support the stated purpose of the test, which is to serve as a downward extension of the Stanford-Binet. Task modification through increasing size and number of dimensions (from two- to three-dimensional) and changing the texture, brightness, or color of some items has been shown to improve scores of deaf-blind children (Kiernan & Dubose, 1974).

Piagetian-Based Criterion-Referenced Instruments.   The Piagetian-based criterion-referenced instrument that is used extensively in early childhood special education programs is the *Infant Psychological Development Scale* (IPDS) first developed by Uzgiris and Hunt (1975) for use with normal infants. Application of these scales for use with infants with handicaps has been expanded by the development of *A Clinical and Educational Manual for Use with Uzgiris and Hunt Scales of Infant Psychological Development* by Dunst (1980). The purpose of this instrument is to identify a child's level of functioning in sensorimotor development. Seven branches of sensorimotor development are measured through a variety of elicited situations. These branches are based on the domains of sensorimotor development identified by Piaget and emerge during the sensorimotor period. They are presented in the following list:

I. *Visual pursuit and permanence of objects* (designated as object permanence by Dunst): 15 steps sequentially representing the development of visual memory, including visually following an object, finding a partially covered object, finding a completely covered object, and other more complex or delayed patterns of pursuit.

II. *Means for obtaining desired environmental events* (designated as purposeful problem solving by Dunst): 12 sequential steps in the development of an understanding of means–ends relationships, such as hand watching, visually directed grasping, use of locomotion as a means, and the use of "tools."

IIIa. *Vocal imitation:* 6 sequential steps in the development of vocal imitations, including response to familiar vocalizations, imitation of familiar words, and imitation of new words.

IIIb. *Gestural imitation:* 4 sequential steps in the development of gestural imitation, including systematic imitation of familiar simple schemes and imitation of unfamiliar gestures visible to the infant.

IV. *Operational causality* (designated as causality by Dunst): 7 sequential steps measuring the infant's apparent understanding of the effects he can have on the environment, such as repetition of actions producing an interesting spectacle, behavior in a familiar game situation, and behavior to a spectacle created by a mechanical agent.

V. *Construction of object relations in space* (designated as spatial relationships by Dunst): 11 steps in the sequential development of an understanding of spatial relationships, including localizing an object by its sound, grasping a visually present object, placing objects in equilibrium one upon another, and making detours.

VI. *Schemes for relating to objects* (designated as play on the Dunst version): 21 steps in the sequential development of object manipulation and exploration, such as holding, dropping, throwing, showing, and naming.

The instrument includes no summary scores because the authors do not believe the multifaceted nature of a young child's functioning can be summarized in a single score. Additionally, they provide no norms, thus assuring that the focus is on the child's capabilities rather than on labeling the child as advanced or slow. Dunst (1980), however, developed *estimated developmental age (EDA)* placements for each of the scale steps to help examiners determine how a child is progressing. Dunst stresses that these EDAs have no normative value; however, he reports that their validity has been established through a correlational study with the *Griffiths Mental Development Scales,* which produced a correlation of .97. Further validation studies have been conducted that support the concurrent validity of the EDAs (Sexton, Miller, Scott, & Rogers, 1988). However, the EDAs as reported in the Sexton et al. study were an average of 2.1 months lower than Bayley MDI scores. These findings are consistent with those found by Dunst, Rheingrover, & Kistler (1986). Dunst points out that EDA scores have no predictive value but are of some limited use relative to achieving an understanding of an infant's current developmental status. The weakness of EDA scores is that all qualitative information about child performance and patterns of behavior is lost if examiners focus solely on the EDA.

While detailed instructions about each of the eliciting situations are provided, Uzgiris and Hunt encourage examiners to make adjustments as needed and appropriate, including specific materials used, position or location of the child, and the sequencing of situations. During the assessment, the examiner records all of the child's actions, which she analyzes to determine whether the child exhibited the *criteria actions* related to the sensorimotor scales. Criteria actions are those that demonstrate to the examiner that the infant has achieved a particular step on one of the scales. Behaviors relevant to all of the sensorimotor domains occur and should be recorded during each of the eliciting situations. Interventionists can plan programming based upon an infant's performance on the IPDS. Activities that are designed to develop these sensorimotor skills have been presented by Ulrey, Schnell, and Hosking (1978).

Two additional Piagetian-based instruments described by Uzgiris (1976) are the *Albert Einstein Scales of Sensorimotor Development* and the *Casati-Lezine Scale.* These scales have not been commercially published and are less widely used than the IPDS. The Albert Einstein Scales measure prehension, which covers the first three stages of sensorimotor development—object permanence, and space, both of which span stages III through VI. Research into infant performance on these scales indicates that completion of tasks at one stage prior to the development of skills related to the next stage was variable (Corman & Escalona, 1969). Uzgiris (1976) points out the flaws in a scoring system that does not reflect such discrepancies:

> If such variations are meaningful, then scoring infant development by stages glosses over important differences; however, until the meaning of these variations is understood, scoring in terms of number of items passed, which has been adopted by some investigators, does not seem to be justified. (p. 130)

Such findings are troublesome for a theory based on invariant sequential progression through stages or periods of development. Vygotsky's conceptualization of zones of proximal development could be useful in addressing this issue.

The *Casati-Lezine Scale,* which is composed of four tests, was developed and used in France. The four tests focus on object permanence, use of intermediaries to retrieve an object, exploration of objects, and the combination of objects. Scales of object concept and the development of causality have been developed and employed for research purposes by Decarie (Uzgiris, 1976). A Piagetian-based measure of a child's linguistic and nonverbal representational thinking has been proposed by Mehrabian and Williams (1971).

Neo-Piagetian Observational Assessment. Dunst and McWilliam (1988) created an observational system based on a neo-Piagetian developmental model of sensorimotor interactive competence particularly useful for young children with multiple handicaps. Interventionists can use the system, known as OBSERVE (Observation of Behavior in Socially and Ecologically Relevant and Valid Environments), to monitor the range of interactive competencies that is necessary for a child to "initiate, control, and master different aspects of the social and nonsocial environment" (Dunst, Holbert, & Wilson, 1990, p. 100). The system employs a simple running record procedure used in correlation with a five-level developmental model of sensorimotor interactive competence described in the following list.

Attentional Interactions: Ability to attend to and discriminate between stimuli; can be observed in infant's response to stimulus events through behaviors such as looking at object or person, orienting toward sounds, tracking moving object across visual field, smiling at familiar person, laughing upon seeing an interesting event, rooting toward nipple placed against cheek, grasping object placed in hand, cessation of body movement when familiar voice is heard, and crying after sudden loud noise

Contingency Interactions: Ability to initiate and maintain interactions with the environment in an efficient manner; can be observed when infant repeats actions to maintain interesting feedback such as batting at a mobile to hear sounds, touching adult's mouth for repetition of interesting sounds, banging rattle to hear sounds, vocalizing to keep someone's attention, smiling to encourage adult to repeat interesting behavior, and rolling over to return to a social interaction

Differentiated Interactions: Ability to coordinate and regulate behavior in a movement toward "conventionalized" behavior (i.e., socially and culturally defined and recognized behavior that leads to adaptive development across settings, such as cup drinking, walking, waving, or extending arms to be picked up); can be observed in behaviors that approximate social standards and expectations, including the using of intermediaries to secure objects, imitating novel sounds and gestures, socially recognized actions in object play, locomotion to obtain object, use of utensils in self-feeding, nonverbal gestures to communicate needs, and attempts at dressing and undressing

Encoded Interactions: Ability to follow rule-governed forms of behavior in the initiation or maintenance of interactions; can be observed in the child's use of verbal language, sign language, symbol systems, and pretend play

Symbolic Interactions: Ability to use words, images, figures, memory, drawings, numbers, and so forth as symbols in a rule-governed conventionalized manner in the absence of cues; characterized by decontextualization, distancing, and sign–signifier differentiation

The child's behaviors are individually recorded on the OBSERVE record sheet and rated according to which of the five levels of interaction they represent, resulting in a profile that depicts the child's range of interactive competencies during the observational period. Figure 9.1 depicts a sample OBSERVE record form. Examiners can use the Topography of Behavior Form to make across-setting comparisons of interactive competence. The mapping of an individual child's performance at each level of interactional development in several contexts enables the observer to note in which contexts the child is functioning at his highest level.

Perceptual–Cognitive Processing Tests. For many infants with disabilities, traditional measures and even Piagetian-based measures are unsatisfactory determinants of cognitive functioning. The prerequisite motor competence and dependence on cooperative behavior make these instruments inappropriate for infants with sensory or motor impairments. In an effort to develop alternative approaches to the assessment of motorically impaired infants, Zelazo (1979, 1982a, 1982b) explored infants' capacity to process information during sequential visual and auditory events.

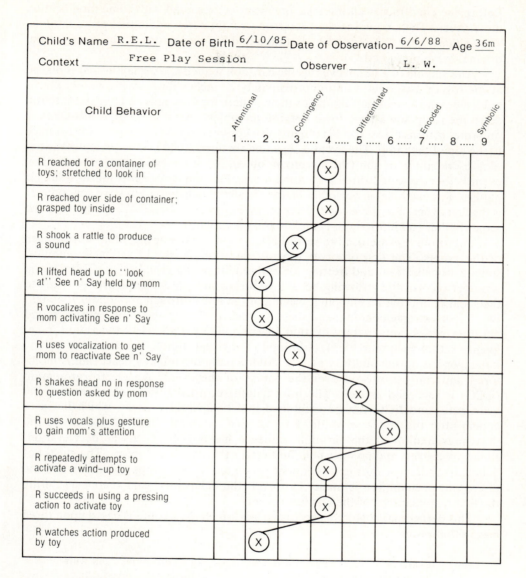

Figure 9.1. OBSERVE Record Form.
Source: C. J. Dunst, K. A. Holbert & L. L. Wilson (1990). "Strategies for Assessing Infant Sensorimotor Interactive Competencies." In E. D. Gibbs & D. M. Teti (Eds.), *Interdisciplinary Assessment of Infants: A Guide for Early Intervention Professionals.* Baltimore, MD: Brookes. Reprinted by permission.

The procedure he developed from clinical study includes five events (two visual and three auditory) and is appropriate for infants between the ages of 3½ and 36 months. The basic paradigm of the approach involves the presentation of an engaging visual or auditory event that is repeated until the child begins to expect it.

Before the child looses all interest, the event is presented with some modification three times. The original is then reintroduced for three additional presentations. The child's ability to create an expectation and her recognition of the return to the original event are noted.

An example of a visual event is the car–doll sequence. A small toy car is placed at the top of a wooden ramp approximately 22 inches long. A presenter, who is hidden behind a black curtain, holds the car there for 4 seconds and releases it to roll down the ramp and knock down a styrofoam object. After a wait of 4 seconds, the presenter returns the styrofoam object to an upright position and pushes the car back to the top of the ramp. The event is repeated six times, followed by three repetitions of a discrepant variation (the styrofoam object is not knocked over). The original event is then repeated three additional times. The auditory events follow a similar pattern. For example, in one of them, the phrase, "Hello baby. How are you today?" is the first event, and the second, "Are today. How baby you hello?" spoken with the same rhythm and intonation, is the discrepant variation.

Two observers are used to record selected behaviors of the infant during each of the events. The first observer records: duration of visual fixation to stimulus, smiling, vocalization, and fretting for both auditory and visual events. The second observer records the following behaviors during an auditory sequence: pointing to the speaker and baffle, clapping, waving of the arms through arc greater than 60°, twisting or extreme bending, and visual searching. During a visual event the second observer codes: anticipatory fixation (darting the eyes ahead of the action in sequence rather than searching), pointing to the visual stimuli, and the other behaviors recorded during auditory events. Additionally the infant's heart rate is monitored and can be tracked over the course of the event. An electrocardiogram (ECG) is recorded as well. The information recorded from both observers, the heart rate, and ECG can be combined into behavioral clusters, which begin to appear after the first year of life. For example, a typical 20-month-old during the third presentation of the car–doll sequence has a 12-beat cardiac deceleration, smiles, vocalizes, and points when the car taps the styrofoam object. The cluster of behaviors fades our during subsequent presentations and stops abruptly when the discrepant presentation is made. However, the behavior cluster reappears during the first reappearance of the standard event.

This perceptual-cognitive processing assessment procedure is based upon three basic assumptions.

1. Infants have the capacity to form a memory for a perceptual event without the necessity for gross motor involvement.
2. The capacity to form a memory for a perceptual experience begins almost from birth.
3. Infants form schemata for events in both visual and auditory modalities and presumably code information on a central level. (Zelazo, 1979, pp. 54, 55)

These assumptions offer new hope to examiners seeking to measure the cognitive functioning of severely motorically impaired infants. Alternative measures, such as those developed by Zelazo, can be critical in the accurate interpretation of child functioning during infancy. They continue to be refined and developed as early interventionists realize the need to use nonconventional means to assess many severely physically limited infants (Zelazo & Weiss, 1990).

Preschool and Early Childhood

As infants mature, develop language, and improve in gross and fine motor skills, examiners have more doors open to assess cognitive functioning. Standard approaches, including screening and readiness tests, traditional intelligence tests, behavioral checklists, and tests of basic concepts, are available for this age group. Alternative procedures, such as assessment of cognition through play, Piagetian-based tasks, and dynamic assessment paradigms, are particularly useful in the assessment of children with handicapping conditions.

Traditional Approaches to Preschool Assessment.   Traditional instruments used for cognitive assessment include screening instruments, diagnostic tests, and measures of concept attainment. This section includes descriptions of selected instruments from each of these categories.

Screening Instruments. Many screening and readiness tests designed to be administered in group form are available to persons seeking to determine large numbers of preschoolers' readiness for kindergarten or first grade. These are not included here. The two instruments that are reviewed are appropriate to administer to individual children who may already be exhibiting behaviors that raise concerns of physicians, parents, and/or early childhood educators. The *Denver Developmental Screening Test-Revised* is chosen because of its extensive use in the medical community, and the *Miller Assessment for Preschoolers* is reviewed because it has been developed recently and is specifically designed to screen for developmental delays.

The *Denver Developmental Screening Test-Revised* (DDST-R) (Frankenburg, Dodds, & Fandal, 1975) is designed as a screening instrument to identify children between 2 weeks and 6 years of age who need a complete assessment. It is not intended to diagnose mental retardation and should not be used to derive an IQ equivalent. It was developed by physicians for use in a medical setting. The original DDST was developed by Frankenburg and Dodds (1970) by using items from several infant and preschool instruments. Since then minor revisions in the interpretation of scores have been made. The 105 items, which represent four areas (gross motor, fine motor adaptive and imitation, language, and personal and social), are arranged according to chronological age associated with the task. Items were selected on the basis of ease of administration and scoring. There is not always a clear connection between the test items and the domains that they are intended to measure.

The child's performance on each item is scored as normal, questionable, or abnormal, based on a standardized sample. It is administered through observations and parent interview on an individual basis. A shorter version of the DDST, which speeds the screening process, is the *Revised Denver Prescreening Developmental Questionnaire* (Frankenburg, 1986).

A sample of 1036 healthy children ages 2 weeks to 6.4 years of age who reflect the occupational and ethnic characteristics of the Denver area (based on the 1960 census) comprised the norming group. Children who had serious impairments or who were adopted, premature, twins, or breech deliveries were excluded from the standardization sample. Since the standardization sample was exclusively from the Denver area, it has been seen as a major problem. The inappropriateness of using the DDST on minority children outside the Denver area has been noted (Moriarty, 1972). It was, however, standardized in 1984 with over 1000 children from Israel, Cuba, Philippines, Costa Rica, Chile, West Germany, Turkey, and the Netherlands.

Test–retest and interexaminer reliability, as reported by the authors, is satisfactory. The percentage of agreement across test administrations is reported at 95.8%, with an average of 90% across four examiners' administrations to four different children each. However, children are most often scored on the DDST with a reliance on parent reporting. As such, the issues using parents as informants must be considered when reliability of a specific score is considered. Validity was established through correlations of test scores with performance on the Revised Yale Development Schedule. The correlation when children were identified as falling within one of three categories was .97. Additional validity studies comparing the DDST with the Stanford-Binet and the Bayley scales have revealed weaknesses particularly for children under 30 months of age. Frankenburg, Camp, and van Natta (1971) report that screening children under 30 months with the DDST fails to detect approximately 13% who would obtain an abnormal rating on the Bayley scales. Diamond (1987) reported even higher rates of underreferral for 150 preschool children who ranged in age from 6 to 62 months (average of 40.8 months). A follow-up of children who had been tested 4 years earlier revealed that 17% had been correctly identified as having problems, and 83% had been missed. An additional 45% had been referred who were not experiencing difficulties in school. Overall, the instrument proved to be less effective as a predictor of school dysfunction than was parent report.

The *Miller Assessment for Preschoolers* (MAP) (Miller, 1988) was developed to achieve two goals: to identify developmentally delayed preschool-age children needing further evaluation with a statistically sound instrument and to provide a framework for the identification of a child's strengths and weaknesses, including recommendations for remediation. It is a screening device that should not be used for diagnostic purposes or for identifying children functioning above age level. The 27 test items are categorized into five performance indices (with some items in more than one). These indices are (1) the foundation index (e.g., walks line and supine flexion); (2) the coordination index (e.g., tongue movement, articulation, and building a tower); (3) the verbal index (e.g., follow directions and digit repetition); (4) the nonverbal index (e.g., sequencing, block tapping, and object memory); and (5) the complex tasks index (imitation of postures, maze, and block design). Sensory and motor abilities are measured by the foundation and coordination indices, cognitive abilities by the verbal and nonverbal indices, and combined abilities by complex tasks.

The child's performance on each test item is rated as red (stop), yellow (caution), or green (go). Red indicates that the child is functioning at or below the 5th percentile and needs further evaluation. A yellow rating means that the child is functioning in the 6th to 25th percentile and should be watched carefully. A child functioning at or above the 25th percentile receives a green rating, because he appears to be functioning at an average or above-average level. The total number of red scores and yellow scores are tallied and used to identify a total score (using tables in the manual), which is expressed as a percentile. Percentiles can also be obtained for each of the performance indices. The standard error of measurement is .59 for red scores and 1.4 for yellow scores. The test is individually administered in approximately 25 to 35 minutes. The MAP manual gives precise instructions on item administration, including materials needed from the kit, procedures to follow, scoring criteria, observations of behaviors that should be noted, and age-specific item administration. Test items include tasks such as building a tower using one-inch-square cubes, recall of hidden objects, and pointing to body parts. All items are presented in a gamelike manner.

The MAP was standardized in 1980 with a stratified sample across nine continental geographic regions of the United States. Stratification by age, sex, race, community size, and socioeconomic status was done with a total of 1200 children in the norm group. Populations excluded from the norm group included children for whom English was not the primary language and children with known physical, mental, or emotional dysfunction.

Interrater reliability based on an observation sample of 40 children ranged from .84 to .99, with only the coordination index falling below .97. Test–retest reliability was also calculated, based on the performance of 81 children. Stability ratios, which were based on the individual number of children who were classified in one of three groups, ranged from 72% to 94%. Split-half reliability was also calculated for some portions of the test and reported to be .82.

Concurrent validity was measured by comparisons to *Wechsler Preschool and Primary Scale of Intelligence* (WPPSI), the *Illinois Test of Psycholinguistic Abilities* (ITPA), and the DDST. Correlations to the WPPSI were very weak, with .37 correlation between complex tasks and the full scale IQ being the strongest. ITPA composite psycholinguistic age score correlations ranged from .05 (complex tasks) to .36 (coordination). When classifications of children based on the DDST were compared with results of the MAP, 72% were classified similarly. Twenty-four percent more children were identified in at-risk categories with the MAP. Extensive discussion of the test's predictive validity is included in the manual. Correlations between the MAP total score and *Wechsler Intelligence Scale for Children-Revised* administered four years later were between .45 and .50.

The MAP is primarily intended to identify children with mild and moderate handicaps and is not designed to detect severe developmental problems, such as cerebral palsy, mental retardation, or emotional disturbance. The manual contains no adaptations or accommodations for children with handicapping conditions. The scoring, which is expressed in percentiles, is more useful than a single score. Examiners can create a profile of test performance across indices to reveal scattered performance across the five areas. Percentiles of individual performance on specific items can be determined as well, which is useful in program planning.

Measures of Cognitive Ability. Other instruments that examiners use to measure abilities and diagnose impairments are available. The *Wechsler Preschool and Primary Scale of Intelligence-Revised* (WPPSI-R) (Wechsler, 1989) contains both performance and verbal scales, with six subtests in each. Content of each of the subtests is summarized in the following list.

Performance Scale

Object Assembly: Assesses eye–hand coordination, perceptual organization and synthesis, psychomotor speed, and the ability to extract a whole from a group of parts. Within a time limit the child must construct a puzzle (in full color).

Geometric Design: Part One assesses the ability to discriminate two figures that are alike when one of the figures is embedded in an array of dissimilar figures. Part Two measures the ability to visually perceive and then motorically copy a design.

Block Design: Assesses psychomotor speed and visual-spatial perception. Within a time limit the child reproduces patterns made with flat 2-colored blocks.

Mazes: Measures fine motor, planning, and visual-perceptual skills. Within time limits the child solves paper-and-pencil mazes of increasing difficulty.

Picture Completion: Assesses the child's ability to recognize what part is missing from pictures of common objects and activities.

Animal Pegs (optional): Measures psychomotor speed and working memory. The child places pegs of specific colors in holes below a series of pictured animals. Both accuracy and speed are used to calculate the score.

Verbal Scales

Information: Assesses knowledge of everyday objects and events. It begins with simple items that only require a pointing response. The remaining items are brief oral questions to which the child responds verbally.

Comprehension: Measures the child's ability to express in words her understanding of reasons for actions and the consequence of events.

Arithmetic: Requires the child to demonstrate an understanding of quantitative concepts. It begins with picture items, progresses through simple counting tasks, and ends with more difficult word problems.

Vocabulary: Assesses word knowledge in two domains: naming of pictured objects and defining orally presented words.

Similarities: Measures the child's grasp of the concept of sameness at increasing levels of abstraction. Initial items involve selecting similar pictured objects and require only a pointing response. The next items are orally presented analogies in which the child completes the sentence. Finally the child must explain how two verbally presented objects or events are alike.

Sentences (optional): Assesses short-term memory for meaningful verbal stimuli. The examiner reads a sentence aloud, and the child repeats it.

The age range for the WPPSI-R is from 3 years 0 months to 7 years 3 months (an expansion from the original version). A stratified random sample of 1700 children based on age, gender, and on 1986 U.S. Census demographics, including region, ethnicity, and parents' educational and occupational levels, was used in the standardization. An additional 400 minority children (black and Hispanic) were administered the test to investigate item bias. Items that were identified as biased were eliminated from the final version of the test. The verbal, performance, and full scale IQ scores have a mean of 100 and standard deviation of 15. Each of the subtest scores is expressed as a standard score with a mean of 10 and standard deviation of 3.

The internal reliability coefficients are generally above .80 for all subtests. Additional test–retest reliability studies are being conducted, as are extensive validation studies. Although psychometric information is not yet fully available, the WPPSI-R does incorporate changes in response to critiques of the WPPSI (e.g., extended age range, updated norming, increased number of items, and improved administration procedures).

Another individually administered measure of intelligence, which can be used with children as young as 2 years of age, is the *Stanford-Binet: Fourth Edition* (Thorndike, Hagen, & Sattler, 1986). The test is based on a three-level hierarchical model of intelligence. The highest level is a general intelligence factor, followed by crystallized, fluid, and short-term memory and, finally, specific abilities, such as verbal reasoning, quantitative reasoning, and abstract visual reasoning. It includes 15 subtests, which assess abilities in four broad areas of cognitive functioning: verbal reasoning, quantitative reasoning, abstract visual reasoning, and short-term memory. Three types of standard scores are produced: standard scores for the subtests ($M = 50$, $SD = 8$), area scores ($M = 100$, $SD = 16$), and a composite score ($M = 100$, $SD = 16$). The technical manual also provides a table to derive test age equivalents. Area scores can be further analyzed through factor scores, which is recommended by Sattler (1986). Although the standardization sample was supposed to be stratified according to 1980 U.S. Census variables of geographic region, community size, ethnic group, age, gender, and socioeconomic status, the final sample was overrepresentative of children with high socioeconomic status. A weighting procedure was used in the norming to offset this problem. Reliability for the composite score is excellent, with a range across all ages from .95 to .99. The median standard error of measurement for the composite score is 2.8. Variance of the standard error of measurement across age brackets, however, is a critical factor for preschool-age children (e.g., 68% confidence interval for 2-year-olds is ±4 points, but only ±2 points for 10-year-olds). Subtest reliabilities across all age groups range from .73 (memory for objects) to .94 (paper folding and cutting), with variable standard errors (the highest being 4.2). Validation studies support the fourth edition of the Stanford-Binet for children within the normal range of functioning, but indicate that it produces lower scores than does the criterion test with both the mentally retarded and gifted populations.

A number of other instruments are available that are intended to measure cognitive ability of preschool children. The appendix to this chapter contains descriptions of some of these other measures.

Concept Attainment. Instruments that can be used to determine what concepts a child understands are also useful in the assessment of cognition. The *Bracken Basic Concept Scale* (BBCS) (Bracken, 1984) can be used as a diagnostic instrument, measuring 258 concepts, or in a shortened version as a screening instrument. The screening tests (there are two alternate forms) include 30 items and are intended primarily for use with kindergarten and first-grade children. The age span for the screening tests is 5 years 0 months to 7 years 0 months, while the diagnostic scale can be used with children from 2½ through 7 years 11 months. The BBCS does permit flexibility on the response mode, so that a child with physical impairments might respond verbally, whereas a nonoral child could point. Other alternatives, such as directed eye gaze, are permissible as well.

Bracken (1984) defined a basic concept as a label for one of the basic colors, comparatives, directions, materials, positions, quantities, relationships, sequences, shapes, sizes, social or emotional states and characteristics, textures, and time. The 11 categories of basic concepts that are measured are: color, letter identification, numbers and counting (recognition and counting), comparisons, shapes, direction and position, social emotional, size, texture and material, quantity, and time and sequence. The standardization sample of 1109 children was stratified by age, sex, ethnic group, geographic region, community size, and socioeconomic status according to the 1980 U.S. Census.

During administration of the BBCS, the child is shown a set of four pictures and asked to identify the one that shows what the examiner says. For example, the child is presented with pictures of four different colors and the examiner says, "Show me which color is red." It should be noted that color blind children should not be administered the color subtest and are not penalized in their total score because of an inability to distinguish colors. Total test scores on both the screening tests and the diagnostic scale have a mean of 100 and a standard deviation of 15. The first five subtests of the diagnostic scale are combined to provide a school readiness composite (SRC), with a mean of 10 and standard deviation of 3. The six additional subtests also have means of 10 and standard deviations of 3. Normal curve equivalents (NCEs) and percentile ranks are produced for the subtests and for the total score as well. The standard error of measurement is reported for the SRC (subtests I - V), each subtest from VI to XI, and the total test. At the 68% confidence level, they range from .5 to 2.2 on the subtests and from 1.7 to 3.4 for the total test, with substantial variability across ages of children.

Alternative Approaches to Cognitive Assessment.   Assessment of cognitive functioning through observation of children at play offers an interesting alternative for children with multiple handicaps. Piagetian-based tasks appropriate for older children can provide freedom from the cultural bias apparent in so many instruments. The movement away from static assessments to dynamic assessments that focus on learning potential rather than current functioning can provide us with new insights into the capabilities of preschool-age children with impaired or delayed functioning.

Measuring Cognitive Functioning through Play. The manner in which children interact with objects is a reflection of their cognitive development. Three specific developmental transitions in a child's ability to play are: (1) decentration, (2) decontextualization, and (3) integration (Bond, Creasey, & Abrams, 1990). *Decentration* refers to the infant's transition to freedom from his own body to engage in symbolic actions. The child's ability to pretend in play beyond the immediate environment is *decontextualization,* and the transition to sequential organized play is *integration*. Play behaviors can be observed through naturalistic free play or structured elicitations. A variety of nonstandardized assessment procedures and guides for the observation of children's object play are available. The following list provides sources of play assessment procedures. Bond, Creasey, and Abrams provide an excellent review of these procedures as well as guidelines in selecting and using them.

Free-Play Assessments

Belsky, J., & Most, R. K. (1981). From exploration to play: A cross-sectional study of infant free play behavior. *Developmental Psychology, 17,* pp. 630–639.

Bromwich, R. M. (1981). *Play assessment checklist for infants.* (Available from author, Department of Educational Psychology, School of Education, California State University.)

Kearsley, R. B. (1984). *The systematic observation of children's play.* Unpublished scoring manual. (Available from author, Child Health Services, Manchester, NH)

Lowe, M., & Costello, A. J. (1976). *Manual for the Symbolic Play Test.* Windsor, England: NFR--Nelson.

McCune-Nicolich, L. (1983). *A manual for analyzing free play.* New Brunswick, NJ: Department of Educational Psychology, Rutgers University.

Rubenstein, J., & Howes, C. (1976). The effects of peers on toddler interaction with mothers and toys. *Child Development, 47,* pp. 597–605.

Elicited and Structured-Play

Belsky, J., Garduque, L, & Hrncir, E. (1984). Assessing performance, competence, and executive capacity in infant play: Relations to home environment and security of attachment. *Developmental Psychology, 20,* pp. 406–417.

Fewell, R. (1986). *Play assessment scale* (5th revision). Unpublished manuscript. University of Washington, Seattle. (includes both free play and structured play)

Watson, M. W., & Fischer, K. W. (1977). A developmental sequence of agent use in late infancy. *Child Development, 48,* pp. 828–836.

There are several advantages of the use of play assessment data over traditional testing (Fewell & Rich, 1987). First, the testing environment is nonthreatening and elicits better cooperation from the children. Procedures are flexible enough to allow for the exchange of toys a child might find unappealing (e.g., tactile sensitivity to certain features). Second, the procedures are easy to administer, with very few directions given and no mandatory order of item presentation. The examiner primarily observes and scores the actions of the child. Fewell and

Rich (1987) point out that freedom from time constraints permits the use of dynamic assessment techniques as well. Third, it is possible to observe a child's preferred learning strategies and toy preferences. Finally, both accomplished and emerging skills can be noted.

Dynamic Assessment. Minick (1987) described two somewhat divergent approaches to assessment of cognitive functioning that have developed from Vygotsky's (1978) zone of proximal development theory. Luria, followed by Brown, Campione, and others, chose to focus on learning efficiency and the ability of a child to transfer skills from one task to another. This focus is the basis for several dynamic assessment approaches that have been used with school-age populations, including moderately and severely retarded children (Budoff, 1987). Campione and Brown (1987) employed a test–train–retest model in which pre- and posttest comparisons and the number of hints required to accomplish the task during training provide quantitative measures.

Feuerstein and his colleagues (Feuerstein, 1979; Feuerstein, Miller, Rand, & Jensen, 1981), however, focused on learning potential and employed techniques that do not produce quantitative results. Feuerstein's model does not include the calculation of gain scores from pre- and posttest performance, but rather seeks to learn what the child can accomplish with help. Although Feuerstein's original work was targeted toward the assessment of adolescents, others have applied his concepts to young children. Mearig (1987) aptly described the goal of dynamic assessment

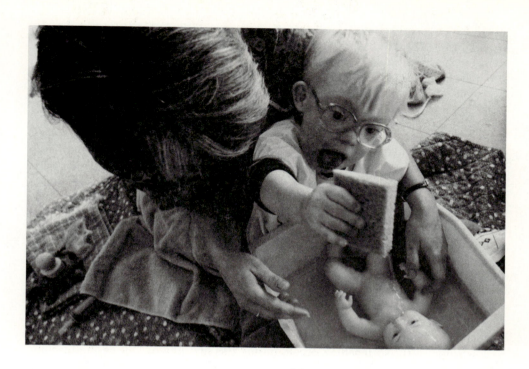

based on Feuerstein's model as to "discover *what can be learned with good teaching*" (p. 237). The emphasis in dynamic assessment is the identification and strengthening of *emerging* skills rather than on eliminating deficiencies.

One instrument based on the Feuerstein model that is designed for preschool-age children is the *Children's Analogical Thinking Modifiability* (CATM) developed by Tzuriel and Klein (1987). The CATM instrument uses 18 colored, flat blocks in three sets of analogical thinking problems, presented in four phases—preliminary, preteaching, teaching, and postteaching. Four levels of difficulty are involved in the instrument, which requires recognition and mastery of color (red, blue, yellow), shape (circle, square, triangle), and size (big, small). One dimension changes on level I items, while two dimensions change on level II and three dimensions on level III. On level IV, all three dimensions change, and two additional blocks are introduced. During the preliminary phase, the child is familiarized with the test materials and taught the basic rules for solving analogical problems. He is asked to construct a matrix using all of the blocks based on shape and color classifications. Clinical observations of the child's behaviors should be made during this phase (e.g., spontaneous comparative behavior, conservation of constancies, simultaneous consideration of two or three sources of information, and impulsive acting out behavior). During the preteaching phase, two blocks are presented, which represent an analogy. A third block is also presented, and the examiner asks the child to complete the analogy (e.g., small blue square: small blue circle, large yellow square: ?). No teaching occurs during this first phase. During the teaching phase that follows, the examiner teaches the child how to search for relevant dimensions, understand analogical principles, search systematically for correct blocks, and increase efficiency. This phase offers to the child *mediated learning experiences* (MLE). The postteaching phase involves a return back to preteaching phase conditions. Scoring can be done on an all-or-none basis or with partial credit given according to the number of dimensions correct in a response. Kindergarten children with low socioeconomic status and older mentally retarded children have demonstrated high cognitive modifiability (the ability to improve performance) on the CATM.

Another alternative appropriate for preschool-age children, *Preschool Learning Assessment Device* (PLAD), has been developed by Lidz and Thomas (1987). The PLAD involves the administration of the triangles, block-building design, and parquetry subtests from the *Kaufman Assessment Battery for Children* (see appendix for description) using a mediated learning approach. Initially the child is asked to perform the triangles task, and the examiner observes for problems with visual-motor coordination, color matching, spatial orientation, part–whole analysis, comprehension of nature of problem, perception of figure gestalt, trial-and-error and impulsive responding, and inflexibility of approach. During the mediated learning phase, following administration of the triangles subtest, the examiner asks the child to draw a picture of a child. Instructions for the examiner are based on areas where problems were noted during the triangles problem. For example, if the child exhibited trial-and-error and impulsive responding, the examiner is instructed to do the following:

Restrain child's excessive movements with verbal cues (e.g., "wait") or hand restraint. Ask child how he or she plan to proceed—what will he or she do first, next? Guide into a sequential plan, reinforcing concepts of first, next, last. If child is unable to verbalize, provide the language she needs. (Lidz & Thomas, 1987, p. 307)

The examiner then goes on to administer the block-building design, provide mediation and readminister block building, administer the parquetry subtest (figure of girl), mediate, and readminister. Finally, during the test phase the triangles subtest is readministered. The end result provides the examiner with an understanding of the child's ability to learn through targeted instruction.

Piagetian-Based Task Assessments. The Uzgiris–Hunt scales provided an alternative to traditional assessments for infants and toddlers. For elementary school-age minority and Mexican-American children, Piagetian-based measures that are intended to provide culture-fair assessments of cognitive functioning have been developed (de Avila & Havassy, 1974a, b). The system, know as the *Program Assessment Pupil Instruction* (PAPI), measures both achievement based on classroom activity and the child's current level of development. Four Piagetian-based tasks make up the battery of tests. The first, cartoon conservation scales (CCS), is intended to measure achievement while the other three are aimed at measuring level of development. The CCS involves the presentation of five series of cartoons, in which the child must select the correct panel from a choice of three to correctly complete the cartoon. Each of the five series focuses on conservation, but varies according to the dimension being conserved (e.g., number, length, and substance). The first frame is used to establish equality of two groups. In the second frame the materials are transformed (but retain equality), and in the third frame the question of equality is posed.

The second task, water-level task (WLT), measures the child's ability to break her perceptual set and realize that water levels always remain parallel to the horizon, regardless of angle of the container. The task is presented as a paper-and-pencil task in which the child is asked to draw lines where the top of the water would be in half-full bottles. Two- and three-dimensional bottles are presented in various angles. Figural intersections test (FIT), the third task, represents Piaget's work on the intersection of classes. The child is required to place a dot in the intersection space of various geometric figures. The fourth and final task, the serial task (ST), measures short-term memory and involves two phases. During the pretraining phase, the child is shown a series of 10 slides. As each slide is presented, the child is asked to state its name and color (e.g., a yellow hat). During the test phase, the examiner shows the child seven additional series of slides of varying lengths, asking the child to tell what she has seen.

Psychometric analysis of these four tasks indicates that the CCS and WLT are the most sound, with reliabilities over .80, and the ST was the least sound. Although these techniques have not received the wide use and therefore extensive critique many traditional instruments have been subjected to, they do offer special educators some intriguing options. In addition to their direct application for minority or ethnic populations not well represented by traditional norming groups, they could be of benefit to children with disabilities. For example, each of the tasks could easily be administered to nonverbal children. Such tasks used informally are more appropriate than the use of standardized tests that do not allow for adjustments based on disabilities and exclude children with disabilities from the norm group.

SUMMARY

The determination of what is meant by the terms *cognition, intelligence, learning,* and *knowledge* is prerequisite to the design of procedures to measure them. For infants, toddlers, and very young children, the issue as to how these concepts develop is as critical as what they are. Cognition and the related concept of knowledge were explored, as were definitions of intelligence. The basic psychological processes of attention, perception, and memory, which enable cognitive development to occur, were reviewed. The conditions of developmental delay, mental retardation, learning disabilities, and attention deficit hyperactivity disorder were defined and discussed. Theories of how cognition develops were covered as well.

The last portion of the chapter was devoted to techniques and instruments available for use in the assessment of cognition. Procedures for neonates, infants, toddlers, and preschool-age children were covered. Traditional approaches were presented along with procedures and instruments based on Piagetian concepts and information processing models. Dynamic assessment models, which are of particular use to populations at-risk or with known handicaps, were described.

THE ECOLOGICAL PERSPECTIVE

- Isolation of cognitive functioning from motor or linguistic performance during infancy and early childhood is very difficult.
- Labels are based on definitions that vary as societies change. Many children who met previous definitions of mental retardation do not meet the current one.
- The importance of environmental influence on cognitive development requires that a child's performance on cognitive assessments be interpreted in light of his own personal ecology.
- The origin of many instruments used today as predictors of the future performance of a child were designed as measures of current performance, with no predictive claims.
- Although a child might perform poorly on measures of cognition due to a lack of environmental stimulation in the home, the child, most likely, will have to compete in a school setting with age-appropriate expectations.

APPENDIX

PRESCHOOL COGNITIVE ASSESSMENT INSTRUMENTS

Title: Columbia Mental Maturity Scale, Third Edition (CMMS)
Source: Burgemeister, B. B., Blum, L. H., & Lorge, I. (1972). The Psychological Corporation, 555 Academic Court, P.O. Box 839954, San Antonio, TX 78283.
Age Range: 3 years 6 months to 9 years 11 months
Description: There are 92 cards (6 by 19 inches) presented to the child, and the child is asked to select the one drawing on each card that is different from the others. Discriminations of color, shape, size, use, number, missing parts, and symbolic material are required. Scoring produces age deviation scores with a mean of 100 and a standard deviation of 16 and range from 50 to 150. Maturity index can also be obtained (age equivalent).
Soundness:
 Standardization: There were 2600 children from 25 states, with representation based on geographic region, race, parental occupation, age, and sex, according to 1960 census data.
 Reliability: Test–retest and split-half reliabilities are reported in the high .80s. The standard error of measurement is 5 points for children from 3½ to 5½ years old.
 Validity: Concurrent validity is based on performance on the Stanford-Binet: Form L-M with below-average children reported at .74 (Ritter, Duffey, & Fischman, 1974). Other correlations are reported between .30 to .60 (Sattler, 1988).
Comments: CMMS offers an alternative assessment of concept development for children with handicapping conditions that restrict response modes. Norms are dated.

Title: Detroit Tests of Learning Aptitude-P
Source: Hammill, D. D. & Bryant, B. R. (1986). Pro-Ed, 8700 Shoal Creek Boulevard, Austin, TX 78758-6897.
Age Range: 3 through 9 years
Description: There are 130 items arranged from easiest to most difficult, comprising eight subtests (verbal aptitude, nonverbal aptitude, conceptual aptitude, structural aptitude, attention-enhanced aptitude, attention-reduced aptitude, motor-enhanced atptitude, and motor-reduced aptitude). Scoring produces standard scores for the eight subtests and one composite score—general overall aptitude (GIQ). All have a mean of 100 and standard deviation of 15.
Soundness:
 Standardization: There were 1676 children from 36 states, with representation from the U.S. population with respect to sex, residence, race, ethnicity, and geographic area.
 Reliability: Internal consistency reliability of GIQ is reported as .95, with a range from .89 to .92 for subtests. Test–retest correlations for the GIQ were reported as .85 and .89, and test–retest subtests fell between .63 and .89.
 Validity: Concurrent validity was satisfactory as measured between GIQ and WISC-R (full scale—.84; verbal scale—.84; performance scale—.80). Correlations of subtests to the GIQ also support construct validity.
Comments: The limited description of the standardization sample reduces an otherwise psychometrically sound instrument (Sattler, 1988).

Title: Extended Merrill-Palmer Scale
Source: Ball, R. S., Merrifield, P., & Stott, L. H. (1978). Stoelting Company, 620 Wheat Lane, Wood Dale, IL 60191.
Age Range: 3 years to 5 years 11 months

Description: The scale measures the content and process of thinking. It is based on Guilford's Structure of Intellect model and assesses along four dimenions of thinking: semantic production (use of language or other means of communication), semantic evaluation (judging actions, statements, or configurations according to a given criterion), figural production (production of responses through crayon, pencil, sticks, or description), and figural evaluation (matching configurations). Scoring produces weighted composite scores for each of four dimensions, which are converted to percentile ranges. No overall score is computed.

Soundness:

Standardization: There were 1124 white preschool-age children from Ohio and New York, stratified by mother's level of education.

Reliability: Range of part–whole coefficients for the four dimensions is .54 to .81; however, these figures do not represent accepted means of reliability measurement and, therefore, reliability is unknown (Sattler, 1988).

Validity: None reported in manual.

Comments: Standardization sample is not representative, and psychometric data are unavailable. Scoring as a range can be difficult to interpret because bands can cover as much as 20 percentage points. Scoring criteria are unclear, and no overall estimate of ability can be derived from the test.

Title: Hiskey-Nebraska Test of Learning Aptitude
Source: Hiskey, M. S. (1966). M. S. Hiskey, Lincoln, NE.
Age Range: 3 to 17 years
Description: The instrument contains 12 subtests: bead patterns, memory for color, picture identification, picture association, paper folding, visual attention span, block patterns, completion of drawings, memory for digits, puzzle blocks, picture analogies, and spatial reasoning. Skills required include verbal labeling, categorization, concept formation, and rehearsal. No verbal instructions or responses are required. Scoring produces deviation learning quotient with a mean of 100 and standard deviation of 16.

Soundness:

Standardization: There were 2153 children, including 1079 deaf and 1074 with normal hearing. Deaf children were primarily from schools for the deaf, but representativeness is unknown. Normal hearing children were selected to be representative of the 1960 census data according to occupational levels of parents. Deaf and normal hearing norms are provided.

Reliability: Split-half reliability for 3- to 10-year-old deaf children is reported as .92, and .93 for 3- to 10-year-old children with normal hearing.

Validity: Correlations with other intelligence tests range from .78 to .86, but correlations with achievement tests go from −.09 to .72 (Sattler, 1988).

Comments: Norm group dated, and representativeness is unknown for deaf population for whom the test is most needed. The WISC-R performance scale may be a preferred measure of the cognitive skills of hearing impaired children (Sattler, 1988).

Title: Kaufman Assessment Battery for Children (K-ABC)
Source: Kaufman, A. S. & Kaufman, N. L. (1983). American Guidance Service, P.O. Box 190, Circle Pines, MN 55014-1796.
Age Range: 2 years 6 months to 12 years 5 months
Description: The instrument contains four scales: sequential processing scale, simultaneous processing scale, achievement scale, and nonverbal scale. Sequential and simultaneous processing scales are designed to reduce effects of verbal processing, gender, and ethnic bias.

Sequential Processing Scale: Measures a child's ability to arrange stimuli in sequential or serial order. The subtests are hand movements, number recall, and word order.

Simultaneous Processing Scale: The scale measures a child's ability to solve spatial, analogical, and organizational problems while processing multiple stimuli concurrently. The subtests include magic window, face recognition, gestalt closure, triangles, matrix analogies, spatial memory, and photo series.

Achievement Scale: The scale measures a child's factual knowledge and skills. The subtests are expressive vocabulary, faces and places, arithmetic, riddles, reading and decoding, and reading and understanding.

Nonverbal Scale: This scale includes subtests from sequential and simultaneous processing scales that use gestures for instructions and require responses of movement. Subtests include face recognition, hand movements, triangles, matrix analogies, spatial memory, and photo series.

Scoring produces a mental processing composite (composed of scores from the sequential processing scale and simultaneous processing scale) with a mean of 100 and standard deviation of 15. All subtests are converted to scaled scores with a mean of 10 and standard deviation of 3.

Soundness:

Standardization: There were 2000 children with stratification variables of age, sex, geographic region, socioeconomic status (parental education), race or ethnicity, and community size based on 1980 census data; however, Hispanic-Americans and low-educational-level blacks were underrepresented by 24% and 10%, respectively.

Reliability: The average internal consistency reliability for preschool-age children for the mental processing composite was .91 and for the achievement scale it was .93. The standard error of measurement for preschool-age children on the mental processing composite is 4.6 points.

Validity: The construct validity is supported through factor analytical studies but is not supported by a study based on observed child performance on a sequential learning task (Ayres & Cooley, 1986). Concurrent validity has been established through comparisons to WISC-R, WPPSI, the Stanford-Binet: Form L-M, and a variety of achievement tests. Naglieri (1985) found the achievement scale a better predictor of later achievement than WISC-R or the mental processing composite for learning disabled and mentally retarded children. There is some evidence to support claims of it being a culture-fair test (Worthington & Berring, 1988).

Comments: Subtests on mental processing scale require a knowledge base, and achievement subtests require mental processing; therefore separation of these is inaccurate and can lead to inaccurate assumptions about child performance. The instrument is intended to measure intelligence but includes no measure of verbal ability in the mental processing component. There is heavy reliance on short-term memory, which overly penalizes children with attention problems or short-term recall disability. Between 2½ and 3 years the mental processing composite is based solely on five subtests. The lower age range of the test provides an inadequate differentiation of performance to classify children as mentally retarded (complete failure of all items on the sequential and simultaneous processing scales produces a mental processing composite of 79 for a 2½-year-old, 70 for a 3-year-old, and 60 for a 4-year-old). The low ceiling restricts use of the instrument in the classification of giftedness. The instrument can be of some use in the measurement of nonverbal cognitive abilities (Sattler, 1988).

Title: Leiter International Performance Scale

Source: Leiter, R. G. & Arthur, G. (1948, 1959). Stoelting Company, 620 Wheat Lane, Wood Dale, IL 60191.

Age Range: 2 years to 18 years; Arthur adaptation ranges from 3 to 8 years (Arthur, 1949)

Description: This is a nonverbal test of intelligence, including 54 tests arranged in age scales. On each test child is expected to arrange certain blocks and insert them into a frame so as to match appropriately to stimulus cues provided (ranging from pairing colors, shapes, or objects to challenging perceptual patterns and analogies). No verbal instructions may be given, but pantomime is appropriate. Scoring produces mental age (MA) (can be used to calculate a ratio IQ).

Soundness:

  Standardization: No adequate description of the standardization sample is provided in the manual.

  Reliability: No reliability data are contained in the manual. However, studies in which satisfactory test–retest reliabilities were reported with handicapped children are available (Sattler, 1988).

  Validity: Correlational studies between the Leiter and other intelligence tests range from .37 to .92 (reviewed in Sattler, 1988). Bonham (1974) reported that deaf children earned a mean IQ on the Leiter that was 14 points lower than the WISC performance scale.

Comments: Limitations of the Leiter include uneven item difficulty levels, outdated pictures, reliance on a ratio IQ, inadequate standardization, and lack of information about reliability. Leiter (1959) recommends that five points be added to the IQ obtained on the scale because the norms have been shown to underestimate children's intelligence. The Leiter may be of assistance in clinical diagnosis, but should not be used for placement or decision-making purposes (Sattler, 1988).

Title: McCarthy Scales of Children's Abilities

Source: McCarthy, D. (1972). The Psychological Corporation, 555 Academic Court, San Antonio, TX 78204.

Age Range: 2½ to 8½ years

Description: Contains six scales: verbal, perceptual-performance, quantitative, memory, motor, and general cognitive (some items are counted in more than one scale). The general cognitive index (GCI) is an estimate of the child's ability to integrate accumulated knowledge and adapt that knowledge into tasks. Scoring produces a GCI and profile measuring verbal ability, nonverbal reasoning ability, number aptitude, short-term memory, and coordination. Subtests have a mean of 50 and standard deviation of 10. GCI has a mean of 100 and standard deviation of 16.

Soundness:

  Standardization: There were 1032 children with stratification variables of age, sex, race, geographic region, father's occupation, and urban–rural residence based on 1970 census data.

  Reliability: Average split-half reliability of GCI is .93; other scales range from .79 to .88. Average standard error of measurement for GCI is 4 points.

  Validity: Correlations with Stanford-Binet: Form L-M, WISC, WISC-R, WPPSI, K-ABC, and Slosson Intelligence Test range from .45 to .91. Sattler (1988) comments that concurrent validity is acceptable, predictive validity is satisfactory, and that construct validity is questionable because the scales are not factorially independent.

Comments: GCI has a floor of 50, which renders the test inappropriate for assessment of severely mentally retarded children and developmentally delayed 2½-year-olds. Scales overlap in content, and construct validity is not supported for mentally retarded populations; therefore, GCI is more meaningful than profile scores, eliminating the ability to plan instruction based on profiles.

Title: Pictorial Test of Intelligence (PTI)

Source: French, J. L. (1964). Riverside Publishing Company, 8420 Bryn Mawr Avenue, Chicago, IL 60631.

Age Range: 3 through 8 years

Description: The test contains six subtests: picture vocabulary, form discrimination, information and comprehension, similarities, size and number, and immediate recall. Response requires selection from a multiple choice of items, but directed eye gaze can be used for children unable to point. Scoring produces a mental age that can be converted to the deviation IQ with a mean of 100 and standard deviation of 16.

Soundness:

Standardization: There were 1830 children with stratification variables of regional area, community size, and father's occupational level based on 1960 census data.

Reliability: The test–retest and internal consistency reliabilities were reported in the high .80s and low .90s. Sattler (1988) cites studies with lower reliabilties (.70s and .80s).

Validity: Correlations range from .42 to .75 between the PTI and other intelligence tests, and from .23 to .79 with achievement tests (Sattler, 1988).

Comments: The norms are dated, but the instrument does provide an option in evaluating motorically and speech-impaired children, although Sattler (1988) cautions against making decisions based on the PTI.

Title: Raven's Progressive Matrices: Coloured Progressive Matrices

Source: Raven, J. C., Court, J. H., and Raven J. (1986). Lewis, H. K., London.

Age Range: 5 to 11 years

Description: This is a nonverbal test of reasoning ability, measuring the ability to form comparisons, reason by analogy, and organize spatial perceptions. One section of a design is omitted, and the child must select one from a choice of patterns to complete the matrix. Scoring produces percentile ranks.

Soundness:

Standardization: The most recent normative study for North America (Raven & Summers, 1986) is based on separate samples of children throughout the United States, with no stratified random sampling; however, the large numbers of children sampled probably offset this deficiency (Sattler, 1988). Norms for Mexican-American and black children are also available.

Reliability: Split-half reliabilities range from .65 to .94.

Validity: Concurrent validity has been established through correlations with intelligence and achievement tests.

Comments: It is useful as a measure of nonverbal reasoning ability and provides an option for the assessment of nonoral children within a limited age range; however, it relies solely on figural reasoning and may underrepresent the ability of a child with deficits limited to this skill.

CHAPTER 10

Communication and Language Assessment

CHAPTER OUTLINE

QUESTIONS ANSWERED IN CHAPTER 10

- What are the definitions and components of language?
- What theories of communication and language development have been developed?
- How does early language develop?

- How can we conduct assessments using developmental milestones, functional communication skills, and standardized instruments?
- What assessment techniques are appropriate for preschool-age children?
- What is included in assessment for assisted augumentative communication?

CHAPTER OVERVIEW

The relationship among communication, language, and speech production is hierarchical in nature. *Communication* is the broadest term, including any interactions among living organisms. It is characterized by an exchange of information or ideas. Communication can occur with or without language, through gestures, touch, facial expressions, sounds, as well as through speech. Meaningful communication begins between infants and their caretakers long before children use formal language structures. *Language* involves the use of signs or symbols to which meaning is attributed. It includes much more than simply the use of written and spoken language. Body language sometimes coveys more information than verbal exchanges. Persons with hearing impairments communicate well using a number of different systems of sign language. *Speech* is simply one means of expressing language for the purpose of communication. Speech does require the precise coordination of the central nervous system and muscles used in the speech act. Other means of expression, using standard language systems (e.g., writing and typing) as well as alternative systems (e.g., American Sign Language, Bliss symbols), can also achieve the purpose of effective communication. This chapter addresses the assessment of communication and language functioning of infants, toddlers, and young children with special needs. A brief review of the definitions, theories, and developmental sequence provides a background for this area of assessment.

DEFINITIONS OF LANGUAGE AND LANGUAGE COMPONENTS

Language development is complex, requiring the interactive use of the basic psychological processes of attention, perception, and memory in both visual and auditory modalities. It is also dependent on cognitive conceptual development. Unless a child understands the conceptual meaning of "in" "out" "under" "over" big" and "little," it is very unlikely he can incorporate these words into his basic receptive or expressive language. Language has traditionally been conceived of as consisting of the five basic parameters: phonology, morphology, syntax, semantics, and pragmatics. *Phonology* is the sound system of a language. *Morphology* refers to the rules used to build words, including bound and free morphemes. Words such as hope, sad, and car are considered to be free morphemes. Bound morphemes are units that can be attached to free morphemes to alter meanings (e.g., hope*ful,* sad*dest,* car*s*). *Syntax* refers to the grammatical rules used in determining acceptable sequencing, combining, and functional use of words in a sentence. *Semantics* incorporates the meanings of words and word relations, and *pragmatics* pertains to the use of language in social contexts (i.e., communication).

Bloom and Lahey (1978) conceptualized language as composed of the three major components: form, content, and use. *Form* is the structure of language and consists of rules about phonology, morphology, and syntax. It comprises the system of symbols used in a language. Morphology and syntax combined form the grammatical rules of a language. The phonological and grammatical rules are guides in the pronunciation of words and the formation of sentences. Form includes the gestures and verbalizations characteristic of the preverbal child. As a child develops verbal skills, recognizable speech sounds are used as words and word combinations in an increasing compliance with grammatical rules.

Content, parallel to semantics, is defined as knowledge about objects and events in the environment. It is contingent upon cognitive development, achieved through sensorimotor means for infants and toddlers who are preverbal. Content increases in complexity and abstraction as the child develops cognitively and linguistically.

Use is similar to pragmatics, referring to the communicative or functional properties of language development. A newborn infant's behaviors, such as crying or smiling, which typically result in social interaction, do not represent intentional efforts to communicate with another person. However, they soon become intentional and are expanded to include gestures and specific vocalizations. Eventually the child uses words and word combinations to communicate. Use is viewed as the organizing principle in functionalist models of language development. This emphasis on pragmatics is based on the logic that a desire to communicate must precede the application of form and content to the communication process. Form, content, and use all involve both *production* (expression) and *comprehension* (reception).

THEORETICAL PERSPECTIVES TOWARD LANGUAGE DEVELOPMENT

The development of *linguistic competence,* as described by Chomsky (1965), involves the knowledge of linguistic rules, rules that come to be known without any study or conscious effort on the young child's part. This knowledge is separated from *linguistic performance,* which involves the application of linguistic competence in the production and comprehension of sentences. The manner in which linguistic competence and performance develop has been the focus of extensive research and theoretical development. Some theories hold to the view that language emerges in a sudden burst around 2 years of age. From this view, all speech and communication that an infant engages in prior to the onset of language is prelinguistic, having no direct relationship to the principles and mechanisms of language (Bickerton, 1984). This theoretical view supports the concept of *domain specificity,* that is, language develops isolated from other developmental domains, and the *discontinuity* of emergent language. When maturation of the neural mechanisms required for language and speech development occurs, phonological, semantic, and grammatical processing begins (Gardner, 1983).

An alternative view supports the *continuity* of language development and importance of *interaction* across domains in the developmental process. The relationship between language and other domains of development is a complex one. Although some early prespeech behaviors may be viewed as developing independently from cognitive structures (e.g., babbling), there comes a critical point beyond which further linguistic progress becomes contingent upon cognition. Vygotsky (1962) conceptualized the integration of linguistic and nonlinguistic processing skills as a prerequisite to the production or comprehension from the point of single words. Neither cognitive nor linguistic development alone could enable a child to advance in her linguistic skill. Rather the two domains must become integrated as one combined schema.

Perspectives of Language Development

Four broad perspectives that are used in the study of language development are (1) *behavioral theory,* (2) the *syntactic model of psycholinguistic theory,* (3) the *semantic and cognitive model of psycholinguistic theory,* and (4) *sociolinguistic theory* (Owens, 1989). These perspectives vary in the way language is seen as developing and in the importance given to the language components of syntax, semantics, and pragmatics. While none adequately explains all aspects of linguistic development, each offers an understanding of some parts of language development.

Behavioral theory is predicated on the understanding that language is a learned or conditioned behavior, developed through a stimulus–response association. This theoretical perspective emphasizes the importance of reinforcement (either positive or negative) toward skill development. Positively reinforced efforts of imitation of speech sounds are repeated and eventually are learned. However, the behavioral perspective fails to account for many aspects of language development (Chomsky, 1959) (e.g., production of immature word patterns never heard in adult speech).

The syntactic model of psycholinguistic theory emphasizes the mental processes involved in language form. Chomsky, the predominate syntactic psycholinguistic theorist, defined and described sentence structures across languages. He identified certain *phrase structural rules,* which are universal regardless of the language used, and *transformational rules,* which control such things as word order. Knowledge of these rules enables the production of a limitless number of grammatically correct sentences. This ability is acquired in a highly predictable sequential fashion, grounded upon an innate understanding of universal phrase structure rules. A child's language initially reflects the phrase structure rules, and only later do transformational rules emerge. This theory is limited by its focus on syntax and has no inclusion of phonetics or semantics in the language acquisition process. It has also been criticized as relying on adult language patterns to explain and understand the language used by children.

The semantic and cognitive model of psycholinguistic theory incorporates semantics, or meanings, into psycholinguistic theory. Bloom (1970, 1975) initiated and Schlesinger (1971, 1974) contributed to what became known as the semantic revolution, by emphasizing the importance of semantics in language development over syntactic structure. The language of children reflects an understanding of word meanings, so that words are combined in a sensible fashion, not just as strings of noun–verb combinations. This model refutes the innateness concept, by integrating language development with cognition in an inseparable relationship.

The sociolinguistic theory of language development focuses on the communication function of language rather than the structural emphasis evident in the previous theories. The pivotal concept of the model is that language has no meaning outside the context in which it is spoken. The quality of linguistic utterances cannot be judged based upon grammatical rules, but on the utterer's meaning (Bruner, 1975). The communicative context in which a person speaks includes such features as assumptions about the listener's knowledge and interest in the topic of discussion, previous history of listeners, and the roles and status of participants in the communicative act (Owens, 1989).

In sociolinguistic theory the *speech act* incorporates both grammatical and pragmatic rules as a speaker attempts to communicate his propositions and intentions and a listener interprets what was meant (Austin, 1962; Searle, 1965). Children can be viewed as using *primitive speech acts,* which occur before the child has the ability to speak in sentences (Dore, 1974). According to the sociolinguistic model, rules of dialogue and communication precede the development of syntax or semantics (Owens, 1989). This perspective is most compatible with the ecological precepts of this text.

EARLY LANGUAGE DEVELOPMENT

Early language development involves the development of many skills, including audition and auditory perception (both environmental and speech sounds), communication through sound and gesture, speech production, comprehension of meanings, understanding and application of grammatical and syntactical rules, and an early understanding of semantics and pragmatics. A summary of the developmental milestones of language acquisition is presented in Table 10.1.

The accurate articulation of specific phonemes follows a developmental sequence. Although there is some discrepancy in the literature as to the specific ages certain sounds are acquired, there is relative agreement as to the sequence in which sounds are produced accurately; by 8 years of age children should be correctly producing all sounds. Owens (1989) analyzed the findings of several studies on phoneme production and reached the following conclusions:

1. As a group, vowels are acquired before consonants. English vowels are acquired by age 3.
2. As a group, the nasals are acquired first, followed by the glides, plosives, liquids, fricatives, and affricatives.
3. As a group, the glottals are acquired first, followed by the labials, velars, alveolars, dentals, and palatals.
4. Sounds are first acquired in the initial position in words.
5. Consonant clusters and blends are not acquired until age 7 or 8, though some clusters appear as early as age 4. These early clusters include /s/ + nasal, /s/ + liquid, /s/ + stop, and stop + liquid in the initial position and nasal + stop in the final.
6. There are great individual differences, and the age of acquisition for some sounds may vary by as much as 3 years. (pp. 91, 92)

Progression of Language Skills

Language development proceeds through four levels: (1) prespeech; (2) first words; (3) first sentences; and (4) grammaticization (Bates, O'Connell, & Shore, 1987). These levels are based on the construct that there is continuity between and within levels of development. Bates, et al. also emphasize that language development is characterized by *individual differences*—individual variations in development at all levels, in contradiction with the view that language always develops in a universal sequential manner.

Prespeech

During the prespeech period, up to approximately 10 months of age, communication and language development is linked to development in three areas: the *development of sound,* both perception and production, the *development of gestures,* and *concomitant changes in nonlinguistic development.* The development of sound perception occurs rapidly, so that an infant who is a few weeks old can hear almost all the phonological contrasts used in human languages. Around 10 months of age, as speech is emerging, infants lose the ability to discriminate some sounds. Speech production is rooted in the 2- and 3-week-old's crying and vegetative noises. By 2 to 3 months the infant is laughing and cooing. After 3 months, the infant can be observed engaging in systematic play with speech sounds, including reciprocal imitation with others. By the 5- to 6-month period, an infant is producing consonant sounds in an effort to match the environmental input she has received. Between 6 and 10 months the infant enjoys canonical babbling, the systematic production of

TABLE 10.1. Milestones of Language Acquisition

Receptive	Expressive	
1 month — Reflex smile to Mother's voice		
2 months—Attends to speaking voice		Has a "hungry" cry; babbling begins
3 months—Localizes speakers with eyes and looks directly at speakers' faces	2 syllables (nonspeech)	Makes many vocal noises resembling speech sounds; vocalizes pleasure at social stimuli
4 months—Turns to noise and voice	Repeats 4 or 5 syllables in sound chain *ba-ba-ba*, etc.	Vocalizes by self-initiated sound play
5 months—Responds to angry tone by crying, to pleasant speech by smiling		Imitates his/her own noises; oohs, ahs, bas, das
6 months—Seems to understand meaning of voice tones of friendliness and anger; appears to understand a few words, like *Mama* and *Daddy*		"Lalling" begins; uses intonational pattern with jargon speech; directs sound and gestures to objects; tries to repeat sound sequences
7 months—Pays attention to speech of family; respondsappropriately to *bye-bye* and *up*		Vocalizes emotional satisfaction or dissatisfaction
8 months—Listens to greetings and other familiar phrases		Vocalizes syllable: da, ba, ka; vocalizes interjections and recognition
9 months—Action response to verbal request (open mouth when asked); understands *no-no, hot,* his/her name	3–4 syllables, but varies syllables in chain	Echolalia; tries variety of pitches; enjoys making lip noises; copies melody pattern of familiar phrases
10 months—Comprehends *bye-bye,* and waves; action response to verbal request: "Where's baby's shoe?"; shakes yes to some questions, no to other questions	Says wordlike syllable: *ma-ma-ma*	Tries to name familiar objects
11 months—Differentiates strangers from family; understands many action words	Median age of first word	Rudimentary language, proclaims biologic needs and psychological satisfactions; talks to self in mirror
12 months—Responds in action to commands; enjoys rhymes and	5–6 words: *mama, dada, baby, bye-bye, ball*	Communicative speech begins; copies melody patterns more accurately but in jargon speech

Receptive	Expressive	
simple songs; understands arrival and departure signals		
14 months—Seems to understand emotional tone when spoken to; interested in looking at pictures while they are named up to 2 minutes	1-word sentences	Uses some true words with jargon
16 months—Will bring object from other room; recognizes names of body parts		More true words occurring in communication
18 months—Carries out 2 consecutive commands; identifies correctly 2 out of 4 familiar objects; points to pictures of familiar objects		Repeats words spoken around him/her
20 months—Points to several body parts in pictures	10–20 words	imitates motor and animal sounds while playing; imitates 2- and 3-word sentences
22 months—Identifies 8–10 pictures of common objects; can follow 2 related directions		Begins combining words into 2-word combinations; uses jargon and real words when telling about events
24 months—Understands most linguistic units, but not separate word units; recognizes names of many familiar objects, persons, pets	50–75 words; nouns 75% of vocabulary; most words by phonetic reduplication; 1.5-word sentence length	Interjectional speech prevails; imitates speech segments, more bye-bye; uses prepositions and communicates by pulling person and showing
27 months—Can point to a few smaller body parts; identifies words like baby, mother		Uses some personal pronouns; usually uses 2- or 3-word sentences
30 months—Action response to verbal request (close door); distinguishes in from under; listens to simple stories	272 words; nouns 38.6%; verbs 21.0%; adverbs 7.1%; prounouns 14.6%; other 18.7%; 1.8-word sentences	Egocentric speech; asks simple questions; names 1 color; names or describes objects in environment; uses pronoun this; adjectives and adverbs increasing
33 months—Identifies common verbs in pictures; understands common adjectives		Will tell if a boy or girl; will tell about drawing (scribbling), at least by naming

(continued)

TABLE 10.1 (*continued*)

Receptive	Expressive	
By 36 months—Understands *yes–no, come–go, run–stop, give–take, grasp–release, push–pull;* identifies action in pictures; understands 3 prepositions; listens to longer and more varied stories; understands semantic difference in subject–object relations; comprehends time words	446 words; 3.1-word sentences	Continues egocentric speech; gives full name; recites 1–2 nursery rhymes; names 5 pictures; begins to use *me* and *I;* uses *this* and *that;* uses 2–3 prepositions; pronunciation
3.0 years—Fairly intelligible speech; final consonants appear more frequently	Generative grammar develops; 2-word phrases more frequent form; 3.4-word sentences; 896 words	Egocentric speech prevails; asks questions; names 2 colors; tells sex and full name; verbalizes toilet needs
3.6 years—All English vowels used; medial consonants often omitted; some blocks on initial syllables; rate of speech increased	Makes questions out of declarative statements; uses auxiliaries, adverbs, adjectives; 4.3-word sentences; 1200 words	Communicative speech developing; commands, requests, threats; asks "why"; relates experiences; says nursery rhymes; names primary colors; counts one by one
4.0 years—98% speech intelligible; omissions and substitutions reduced; vocal pitch controlled; adult rhythm patterns; repetitions reduced, but still some blocking	Beginning to use complex and compound sentences; 4.2-word sentences; 1500-word vocabulary; uses some slang	Whole sentences, not isolated words; perception still first person, and realistic; ideation becoming less concrete; refers to events and persons not in immediate environment; tells tales, talks a lot, threatens; counts 3 objects
4.6 years—Reverses order of sounds within words; intonational pattern of mother; begins sentences with /um//uh/	Increasing use of compound and complex sentences; reverses syllables, word order at times; spontaneously corrects grammar; uses conjunctions; 4.7-word sentences; 1800 words; uses colloquial expressions	More adaptive social communication appears; links past and present events; defines simple words; tries to use new words, not always correctly

Source: G. Ulrey (1982). "Assessment Considerations with Language Impaired Children." In G. Ulrey & S. J. Rogers, *Psychological Assessment of Handicapped Infants and Young Children.* New York: Thieme-Stratton. Reprinted by permission.

consonant–vowel sequences (also known as reduplicated babbling). Babbling has no symbolic content or any of the properties of language. After the onset of approximately the first 10 words in a child's spoken vocabulary, babbling becomes more wordlike, with intonation patterns also observable. As the infant develops sound perception and production, gestures also appear. The development of communication through sound and gesture combinations precedes word usage and includes intentionality, reference, and convention.

First Words: The Emergence of Naming

During the 10- to 13-month period four developmental components accompany the emergence of first words: single-word comprehension, single-word production, individual differences in single-word use, and gestures that function as words. Reliable responses to a child's name or other frequently heard words (e.g., car) appear around 9 to 10 months. Attention can be directed through the use of object names (e.g., "See the pony, Carl, pony"). By 13 months, middle-class children have a receptive vocabulary ranging from 17 to 97 words (Bates, 1985, as cited in Bates et al., 1987).

A review of research related to the initial production of single words has led to the identification of a series of three transitional stages starting around 9 or 10 months of age (Snyder, Bates, & Bretherton, 1981, as cited in Bates et al., 1987). The first stage involves the production of conventional sounds and comprehension of a few words and phrases. In the second stage the child produces sound sequences

that serve as names for people and/or objects. The third stage involves a burst of vocabulary and flexibility of word meanings. Some view this acceleration as the real beginning of word use, with previous object naming still a part of a prelexical stage (e.g., Nelson, 1985). As children are producing single words, they also begin to engage in the use of symbolic gestures. These gestures differ from previous showing, giving, and pointing behaviors that were seen earlier. As speech production increases in hearing children, the use of gestures does diminish.

Word Combinations

The period between 18 and 24 months, when the first multiword combinations typically appear, includes three features. First is the transitional link between the production of single words with complex meanings spoken during the one-word phase. The nature of word combinations and individual differences that are apparent is the second feature. The third pertains to the parallel developments occurring in other developmental domains.

Single words were used to refer to objects, people, or events, but word combinations initiate the shift into sentence use, involving more complex meanings (e.g., "out" means "take me out to play"). As the size of the spoken vocabulary is undergoing rapid acceleration, the types of words that the child uses are also increasing, with an expansion of verbs in particular. During the first-word stage of language development, two phenomena set the stage for multiword combinations— use of single words with complex meanings and the construction of sequences of single words with combined referencing (e.g., "water . . . pool . . . go"). Word combinations in both spoken and visual-manual language develop around 20 months of age. The content of first sentences also appears to be universal across spoken and signed languages (e.g., actions, possession and location of objects, and object qualities). However, individuality does influence the forms used to convey this content.

Bates and colleagues (1987) draw from the research many parallels in development that accompany the move from single-word to multiword speech. These parallel areas of development include gestural imitation, classification of objects, and multigesture strings in play. The implication of these parallels in development is that language development is contingent upon cognitive reorganizations. Without cognitive development, the child is limited in his potential to develop language.

Grammaticizations

Grammar, which embodies the principles or rules for speaking or writing according to form and use of a langugage, includes both morphology and syntax. The child acquires fundamentals of grammar on the average between 20 and 30 months of age. By 36 months of age, the average child has become a competent speaker, although not all syntactic forms are mastered, and morphological errors still occur (e.g., *mices, mans,* and *goed*).

Features relevant to the development of grammar are acquisition of rules of morphology and syntax, speed of morphemic acquisition, the nature and sequence of grammatical development, and the uniqueness of language development for this age range. Initially children use the same form of the word any time it is used, regardless of amounts or times (e.g., "baby go" might be used to mean that three babies went somewhere yesterday). Soon they learn frequently used irregular words (e.g., *go–went; come–came*). However, these correct forms are later replaced with incorrect overgeneralizations as rules are mastered (e.g., *goed* and *foots*). Eventually they master both irregular patterns and rules. The speed of skill acquisition during this period is dramatically faster than any previously observed development. Grammaticization appears to require a baseline of cognitive and language development, upon which it develops rapidly.

In the past, psycholinguistic theory has been predicated on the assumption that significant language development milestones follow a universal sequence such that language develops "in the same way, and in the same sequence in every natural language" (Bates et al., 1987, pp. 185, 186). Cross-cultural studies conducted in the late 1970s and throughout the 1980s provide evidence to contradict this assumption of universal sequence (e.g., Slobin, 1986). The syntactical and morphological features of the language being learned do seem to influence the patterns and age of skill acquisition. Contributing even further to a child's individuality in her language development is her own language-learning environment (e.g., ratio of adults to children in the home and grammatical patterns used by parents).

Developmental Sequences for Children with Hearing Impairments

For children with prelingual hearing impairments a system of total communication typically includes oral/aural and manual communication skills, which follows three basic stages of development (Schlesinger, 1978). First is the gestural stage, similar to the gesturing seen in hearing children. The second stage, baby signing, is characterized by the invention of signs and sign jabbering, which is parallel to the hearing child's babbling. The third stage, the true signing stage, incorporates phonology (handshapes), syntax (sign order), and semantics and pragmatics (sign meaning and function). Just as hearing infants produce sounds in a developmental progression, the following four handshape stages are evident (McIntrye, 1974):

Stage 1: 5, S, L, G, C and baby O
Stage 2: B, F, and adult O
Stage 3: I, Y, D, P, 3, V, H, W
Stage 4: 8, 7, X, R, T, M, N, E

A child who is developing signing as a means of communication makes errors equivalent to the hearing child's articulation errors. Substitution of signs formed in a similar manner, omission of parts of signs, and incorrect movements gradually decrease as skill increases.

Syntax or sign order progresses through five basic stages (Brown, 1970). In Stage 1 the child uses noun and verb phrases with an average of 1.75 words per sentence. In Stage 2, he develops a few inflections (i.e., ing, plurals, and irregular past tense), expressions such as "gonna," and uses 2.25 words per sentence. During

Stage 3 more inflections are present, questions are asked, and negatives are used, although incorrectly. Stage 4 involves the correct use of the negative and the use of all inflections, with an average sentence length of 3.5 words. Finally, at Stage 5, the child produces complex sentences and uses passive verbs.

The semantics and pragmatics of communication through signing are essentially parallel to that of speech. First utterances depict relationships among objects, people, and events. Other categories of meaning that the child develops include drawing attention to an object or person, expression of more or another of an object, descriptions of objects or persons, possession, and location of object or person (Brown, 1970). Typically, meanings develop in the following order: (1) agents (including proper names and common nouns); (2) actions; and (3) attributes (de Villiers & de Villiers, 1978).

The correct formation of true signs is generally seen in a developmental progression of: (1) location (putting the hand in the correct place); (2) movement (using correct motions); and (3) handshape (putting fingers in the correct positions) (Hoffmeister & Wilbur, 1980). Signs that look like an object (iconic signs) are produced before abstract signs (ones that do not look like their meanings). Wundt, as cited in Blanton and Brooks (1978), identified a developmental progression of signing based on four sign characteristics. The child first produces *directing signs,* which involve pointing to self or others or to body parts. *Copying signs,* which involve shaping the hands in an outline of the object, appear next. *Representative signs,* which incorporate some property or characteristic of the object, follow. Finally, *symbolic signs,* which have no relationship to the words they represent, develop.

TECHNIQUES IN LANGUAGE ASSESSMENT

Speech and language assessments involve the study of a child's developmental milestones, communicative patterns of interaction (including functional communication), and/or structured language. While there is considerable overlap of these three dimensions, each offers a somewhat different view of a child's communicative skills. Data need to be collected that produce meaningful results. As Roth (1990) emphasizes, "During the first years of life, the majority of pertinent diagnostic information is derived from documenting a child's routine auditory and visual behaviors" (p. 146). The primary advantage of language assessment through naturalistic observation is the ability to assess many components of the language system simultaneously,

> including the child's sound system, vocabulary, syntactic forms, and functional and communicative uses of language. Natural observation is also more likely to evoke the child's habitual, usual language skills, rather than an atypical performance that might result from standardized testing. (Olswang & Bain, 1988, p. 290)

However, reliance on naturalistic observations alone can be too limiting. Not all behaviors of interest will occur or occur with adequate frequencies so as to provide sufficient data on which to base recommendations. The most complete sampling of language behaviors is obtained through a combination of naturalistic observations and structured elicitations (Roth, 1990). Additionally, child functioning in the language domain needs to be understood within an integrated context across all domains. For example, the language-delayed 2-year-old who has been fed through a nasogastric tube since he was 6 weeks of age is not comparable to another 2-year-old who had no feeding difficulties, even if they have identical test scores. The tube-fed child may have intact cognitive functioning, but severe motor impairments have resulted in substantial language delay, whereas the other child may be severely mentally retarded. The interventions needed by these two children are quite different.

Patterns of performance need to be examined along with correct and incorrect responding. The manner in which the child approaches language-related tasks can be found in response patterns of both correct and incorrect answers noted during the assessment process. A thorough language or communication assessment should address comprehension as related to form and content, and production, including form, content, and use. Comparisons among cognitive functioning, comprehension skills, and production skills can provide useful information for both diagnostic and program planning purposes. Developmental checklists, language sampling, and the use of standardized instruments designed to measure linguistic structures all provide useful sources of data.

Developmental Milestones

A child's achievement of *developmental milestones* can serve as a determinate of language delay in young children. Developmental milestones form the basic framework for many assessment instruments. Some of these developmental scales are highly structured, whereas others serve as informal checklists for the interventionist. Many of the multidomain assessment instruments described in Chapter 8 contain subtests related to communication and language. Other selected instruments assess achievement of language milestones exclusively.

The *Preschool Language Scale-Revised* (PLS-R) (Zimmerman, Steiner, & Pond, 1979) is a highly structured scale, based on normative findings of hundreds of Head Start children. However, no formal standardization has been completed, which limits the usefulness of the age scores produced. The authors do recommend that examiners develop local norms for use in score interpretation. Such flexibility is responsive to the need to establish ecological validity. The PLS-R covers both comprehension and verbal ability of children from 1 year to 6 years 7 months. The scale includes form (i.e., syntax, phonology, and grammatical morphemes) and content (i.e., vocabulary). The child responds to and identifies pictures, manipulates objects, and follows directions. Scoring can produce a language quotient, auditory comprehension and verbal ability ages, and a profile of language use. Reliability coefficients of the 1969 version based on a split-half formula range from .75 to .92. The manual includes extensive coverage of the validity of the instrument, based on the 1969 version. A Spanish translation is available.

The *Environmental Language Intervention Program,* available from the Psychological Corporation, includes two highly structured developmental scales. The *Environmental Prelanguage Battery* (EPB) by Horstmeier and MacDonald (1978) is intended for prescriptive program planning with language-delayed children functioning at or below the single-word level and for program evaluation. Although it has received the widest use with children experiencing language delays and mental retardation, the instrument has been successfully adapted for use with children who have visual or hearing impairments and those who have multiple handicaps. Examiners can also use the EPB with children who require a nonvocal method of communication. It assesses prelanguage skills in a manner that permits training during the assessment, allows necessary adaptations, and focuses on the skills needed to express and receive meanings of communications. If a child is unable to be assessed formally, observations of spontaneous play can be used. The nonverbal section of the test contains two areas of functioning: foundations of communication (e.g., history of babbling; object permanence, gestural communication, and motor imitation) and early receptive language (e.g., identifying objects, understanding the meaning of action verbs, and following directions). The verbal section covers sounds, single words, and beginning social conversation. A differential scoring system permits a range of credit from correct when first administered, correct after training, incorrect, and no response. Nonverbal and verbal scores are expressed as percentages. It does not produce a language age score, a developmental quotient, or any other standard score, although the manual provides approximate age equivalents for each of the subtests. Unfortunately reliability and validity information is not available in the instrument manual.

The *Environmental Language Inventory* (ELI) (MacDonald, 1978a) is predicated on the semantic theories of Bloom (1970; 1975), Brown (1973), and Schlesinger (1974). It also is based on a training model of assessment, sampling three production modes—imitation, conversation, and free play—and follows many of the procedural guides found in the EPB (e.g., encouragement of adaptations as needed). It is intended to provide information about "what and how to teach a child whose communication is limited to primarily one- and two-word utterances with minimal social and spontaneous use" (MacDonald, 1978a, p. 15). The ELI is capable of producing scores related to semantic-grammatical rules, utterance length, and intelligibility for each of the three production modes assessed. Although validity of the test content cannot be established (because it is individualized), validity of the grammatical rules and testing procedures is covered in the manual. Reliability studies reported in the manual do indicate relatively reliable assessment of semantic rules and utterance length across imitation, conversation, and play. The *Environmental Language Intervention Program* also includes a communication inventory and prescriptive training programs used in conjunction with the assessments.

Communication Assessment

Initial assessments of infants under 6 months of age directed toward communication primarily involve the communicative behaviors of parents (Sheehan & Klein, 1989). The *Parent Behavior Progression* (Bromwich, 1981) can be used to assess reciprocal communication activities between the parent or child care provider and infant in routine situations. Although the psychometric soundness of the instrument is unknown, it was developed from the theoretical foundation that interactions between infants and caregivers provide the necessary stimulation for development to progress and that development occurs through a system of transactional communications, rather than through isolated attempts at communication (Sheehan & Klein, 1989). An example from the *Parent Behavior Progression* instrument, which is intended to facilitate program planning, is presented as follows:

> Sequences or chains of pleasurable interactions between parent and infant suggest mutuality in the relationship. Examples: Baby coos, mother nuzzles baby, baby coos back, etc. . . . , or mother moves her head side to side, baby follows visually and smiles, mother moves head to other side, etc. (Bromwich, 1981, p. 346)

As infants mature into toddlers, the assessment of communication incorporates *communicative intentions, presuppositions,* and *organization of conversational discourse* (Roth, 1990). Communicative intentions are concerned with the message a child is attempting to convey. At the preverbal level intentions are attention seeking (i.e., to self or to events, objects, or other people), requesting (i.e., objects, action, or information), greetings, transferring, protesting or rejecting, responding or acknowledging, and informing. Intentions at the single-word level are similar, but also include naming and commenting. Multiword-level intentions, which reflect a maturation and increased efficiency, are requesting information, requesting action, responding to requests, stating or commenting, regulating conversational behavior, and other performatives (e.g., teasing, warning, or conveying humor) (Roth, 1990).

Presupposition pertains to unspoken information critical to the effective communication of a message. The ability to draw inferences about communication partners and the contexts in which they are communicating is a key element. The information-processing assessment procedures of Zelazo, which are described in Chapter 9, relate to the child's ability to make presuppositions about events.

Communication also involves the organization of conversational discourse. The child must function as both a listener and a speaker. Components of conversational discourse include socialized versus nonsocialized speech, turn taking and talking time, conversational initiation, and conversational maintenance (Roth, 1990). Assessment of the components of communication can be accomplished through structured observations in naturalistic settings. Specific components can be targeted for the observation (e.g., percentage of socialized versus nonsocialized speech and attempts to initiate conversation) depending upon the individual needs of the child.

The communication index, *Gestural Approach to Thought and Expression* (GATE), designed for use with infants from birth to 36 months was developed by Langley and has been described by Fewell and Rich (1987). The GATE produces a single communication age score based on nonverbal communicative behaviors, including facial expressions, gestures, visual tracking, laughing, touching, imitation, and signing. The GATE has not been standardized, but items were selected and sequenced consistent with other standardized instruments and research on development. It is specifically intended for use with infants and toddlers who have sensory impairments.

Oliver: Parent-Administered Communication Inventory (MacDonald, 1978b) is a part of the *Environmental Language Intervention Program*. It is designed to gather information about the child's functional communication through a questionnaire that covers different ways the child communicates; hearing and listening; memory tasks; and child observations of attention, play, motor imitation, verbal imitation, receptive language, and expressive language. A system of comparison of vocal activity, smiling, and laughter between typical and atypical infants has been developed by Bridges and Cicchetti (1982).

The *Receptive Expressive Emergent Language Scale* (REEL) (Bzoch & League, 1971) uses an interview and observation format and taps both receptive and expressive language behaviors. It contains 132 items covering the period from birth to 36 months. Child performance is scored as typically exhibits, emerging, or not exhibited. The examiner records high frequency behaviors and arranges them into an ordinal sequence. Three scores are produced: receptive language age, expressive language age, and combined language age. The primary strength of the instrument is its breadth since it includes phonological, semantical, syntactical, and pragmatic skills (Roth, 1990). The instrument denotes speech and language acquisition in very small increments and reflects a framework in which the origins of language development appear in early infancy and are coupled with nonverbal social and communicative behavior. However, the instrument has been criticized for its lack of a clearly delineated theoretical basis, the inadequacy of administration and scoring directions, and the lack of psychometric information (Roth, 1990). The original standardization population was composed of only 50 children, none of whom had any handicapping conditions. Based on a study involving 60 infants and toddlers with mental retardation, Mahoney (1984) reported satisfactory construct validity, with greater validity for 2- and 3-year-olds than for 1-year-olds.

Assessment of communication skills of infants and toddlers from 4 months to 4 years is the purpose of the *Sequenced Inventory of Communication Development-Revised* (SICD-R) (Hedrick, Prather, & Tobin, 1984). Areas of communication assessed by the inventory are awareness of environmental sounds and speech sounds, discrimination of environmental sound and speech sounds, understanding, initiating of communication, imitating communication, and responding to communication. Items are assigned age levels based on the performance of normally developing children included in the standardization sample. The examiner collects a spontaneous speech sample and analyzes it for utterance length and structural complexity if the child is 3 or older. The SICD-R produces receptive and expressive communication ages, which can be compared to chronological and/or mental age of the child. Although the inventory is adequately reliable and valid, the standardization sample is restricted in race, social class, and geographic locations included. It has been recommended that an alternative set of norms for black children be developed (Roth, 1990). The restrictions of the standardization sample seriously limit the interpretation of scores for children other than those included. However, the inventory can provide a worthwhile profile of functioning that can be used for program planning.

A useful instrument for children with hearing impairments who are between the ages of 2 and 8 is the *Scales of Early Communication Skills for Hearing-Impaired Children* (Moog & Geers, 1975). The instrument contains four scales: receptive language skills, expressive language skills, nonverbal receptive skills, and nonverbal expressive skills. The scales were standardized with 372 children with hearing impairments who had no additional educationally significant handicaps. Scoring includes both a percentile rank and standard score with a mean of 50 and standard deviation of 10. Reliability coefficients based on a limited sample ranged from .76 to .91. No discussion of validity is included in the manual.

Structural Language Assessment with Standardized Instruments

When the purpose of a language assessment is to determine the linguistic competence of a child, examiners may prefer to use standardized instruments. Some instruments focus on specific components of language, such as articulation skills or receptive vocabulary, whereas others cover a broader range of skills. Some are designed to serve as screening instruments, and others are intended to provide comprehensive diagnostic information. The appendix to the chapter summarizes a sample of the standardized language assessment instruments available for very young children.

ASSESSMENT FOR AUGUMENTATIVE COMMUNICATION SYSTEMS

For a young child who is having extreme difficulty in the development of functional speech, it is essential to develop an alternative means of communication. Such a decision should be based on a comprehensive assessment using multiple procedures. Beckmann (1990) outlined a recommended sequence of a comprehensive assisted augumentative communication (AAC) evaluation. The first phase involves interviews of the parents and the primary interventionists working with the child. During this phase the following issues should be addressed:

1. Why should *this* student be considered for AAC?
2. What are the child's communication needs?
3. In what situations does the child need to communicate?
4. Does the child need more than one communication system across settings?
5. What is currently presenting communication frustration, and where is the child's frustration level?
6. What communication systems are in use now?
7. What percentage of the child's communication attempts (both verbal and nonverbal) is understood by *most* people?

The second phase of the AAC evaluation involves the formal assessment of child functioning. Throughout the assessment, the evaluator should look for sponta-

neous communication in the child's natural environments, all attempts at communication, and responses to communication (e.g., smiles and eye blinks). Assessment
instruments related to the speech, language, and cognitive level of the child can
provide helpful information. First, the examiner can use the *Nonspeech Test for
Receptive/Expressive Language* (Huer, 1983b) to assess the child's skill as a commu-
nicator. The test includes receptive and expressive communication skills ranging
from a functioning level of birth to approximately 48 months. The receptive portion
of the test contains 50 items, including responses observed when the child is approached and spoken to, makes eye contact and facial expressions, reacts to
changes in intonation patterns, and follows simple commands. The expressive portion has 50 items, including vocalizations of vowel-like sounds, vocal play, use of
gestures, use of meaningful signals, and spontaneous questioning. Receptive and
expressive age equivalency ranges can be calculated based on a multihandicapped
or a preschool-age norming group. The multihandicapped norms are based on a
standardization sample of 77 severely handicapped children ranging in age from 5
years 6 months to 21 years 4 months. The preschool-age group included 78 normally
functioning children from ages 1 to 63 months. Although the standardization samples are relatively small, Huer (1983a) presented reliability and validity data for the
instrument, which offers support for the test. The instrument does offer a critically
needed alternative for the assessment of multihandicapped children with severe
restrictions on their ability to speak. Test administration guidelines encourage flexibility and adaptation as needed, including breaks if the child becomes fatigued.

The *Comprehensive Screening Tool for Determining Optimal Communication
Mode* (CST) (House & Rogerson, 1984) offers another useful tool. The CST is
appropriate for children with a mental age of 6 months or higher and includes three
batteries: oral skills (vocal production); manual skills (gestural and motor production); and pictographic skills (response to symbols and pictorial content). The
scoring system is based on a five-point scale ranging from zero (failure to respond
or inaccurate response) to four (accurate, complete prompt response with no assistance). The instrument is a behavioral observation tool and can be adapted as
needed. The manual includes suggestions of specific adaptations for children with
mental retardation, cerebral palsy and other neurological impairments, visual impairments, and deafness or blindness. A total skill score for each of the three
batteries is produced. The skill area with the highest score should be considered for
training potential.

For cognitive assessment the Uzgiris and Hunt IPDS (described in Chapter 9)
is recommended. A child's ability to retain information in her short- and long-term
memory is directly related to her ability to use an AAC. Learning limitations (e.g.,
auditory discrimination deficits) and preferred learning styles (e.g., visual versus
auditory) can also influence the effectiveness of an AAC. If a spelling-based system
is considered, an assessment of the child's spelling level should also be included.
Related is the child's ability to use word prediction (e.g., can the letter *d* be used to
stand for *drink*).

The child's motor skills are also critical to the AAC process and must be
evaluated. First, the examiner should consider optimal seating and positioning
followed by the determination of the best method of control, including consider-

ation of the child's level of fatigue. If the child is worn out after three minutes of use with the control, it is not suitable, regardless of other positive features of the system. In order to determine the best method of control, all possible options should be considered and experimented with over several weeks. By the end of the fourth week, the examiner should be able to determine the best point of control. Once the anatomical site is determined, the child's ability to activate, release, and reactivate a control at a controlled pace should be investigated. Beckmann (1990) recommends use of the MSIP model developed by Watkins:

1. Movement (reliable function of muscle)
2. Site (anatomical site)
3. Interface (the type of switch)
4. Positioning (of the person and of the switch)

The child's functional vision is also a consideration. The size and distance of a display coupled with the range of vision required to see the entire display must be decided. The child's cognitive ability to use symbols in conjunction with his visual functioning can help determine how big the symbols need to be, how many can be put on one display, and how close together they can be positioned. The *Functional Vision Screening* developed by Langley (1980) offers a useful instrument for assessment of functional vision (see Chapter 12 for further description). The examiner may want to assess use of a keyboard with various pieces of adaptative equipment for children able to read and spell.

The third phase involves evaluation of switches. The examiner measures how much time it takes for a child to activate a switch five times in a row, placing the switch at various body parts (i.e., arms, shoulders, fingers, whole hand, head or neck, forehead, especially eyebrows, near mouth, legs, and feet). Avoid the mouth area if the switch is electronic and the child drools. At each body part consider the size of the switch needed, the force it takes to activate, the range of motion and vision required, the activation time, and the holding time. During this assessment time, tremors that cause the child to continually activate the switch involuntarily should be noted.

The fourth and final phase, which involves decision making, should become an ongoing process. Initially, the interventionists should place the child on a specific system and remain on that system consistently. However, if no progress is evident after three months, a temporary return to a simpler form of communication (e.g., directed eye gaze) to avoid frustration and anger should be considered. Whatever system is selected, it needs to be one that the child enjoys using or it will never take on an expressive communication function.

SUMMARY

This chapter covered the area of communication, which encompasses speech and language development. Definitions of language and the primary parameters of language (form—phonology, morphology, and syntax; content—semantics; and use—pragmatics) were presented. Communication involves both the production and comprehension of language. Differing theoretical perspectives attempt to explain how an infant matures into an adult with communication skills. The basic perspectives are those of behavioral theory, syntactic psycholinguistic theory, semantic and cognitive model of psycholinguistic theory, and sociolinguistic theory. Following the discussion of theoretical perspectives, the chapter included a section reviewing the developmental milestones and progression of communication skills.

The next section addressed techniques and instruments used in the assessment of communication skills. These were organized into instruments based on developmental milestones, those focused on communication skills, and those standardized instruments that provide structural language assessments. The final section presented procedures to be used when assisted augumentative communication is considered for a nonverbal child.

THE ECOLOGICAL PERSPECTIVE

- The development of communication skills is based upon the language and communication patterns with which the child is surrounded.
- Examiners should make comparisons of a child's communication patterns based on the language environment in which she lives.
- Reliance on instruments that lack information about their psychometric properties and observations necessitates that examiners use multiple sources of data.
- Since the early 1980s a wide array of criterion-referenced instruments have been developed that offer viable means of assessing the language and communication skills of children with multiple handicaps.
- An inability to speak no longer has to mean the inability to communicate, but the determination of what augumentative system is right for a particular child is a highly individualistic matter.

APPENDIX

STANDARDIZED LANGUAGE ASSESSMENT INSTRUMENTS

Screening Instruments

Title: Fluharty Preschool Speech and Language Screening Test
Source: Fluharty, B. (1978). DLM Teaching Resources, Allen, TX.
Age Range: 2 years to 6 years 0 months
Description: Instrument screens children in the areas of vocabulary, articulation, and receptive and expressive language. Permits favorable scoring of dialect-based responses.
Soundness:
    Standardization: There were 2147 children, ages 2 to 6, representing four racial or ethnic backgrounds, three socioeconomic classes, and a variety of geographical regions.
    Reliability: The interrater reliability coefficient was .96, and the intrarater reliability coefficient was .97 reported.

Validity: Validity reported as test performance related to the need for therapy for 211 children resulted in a correlation of .897.

Title: Northwestern Syntax Screening Test
Source: Lee, L. L. (1969, 1971). Northwestern University Press, Evanston, IL.
Age Range: 3 years to 7 years 11 months
Description: Instrument covers both comprehension and production, including syntax, personal pronouns, possessives, *wh*-questions, plurals, verb tenses, negation, yes–no questions, and passives.
Soundness:

> *Standardization:* There were 344 children between the ages of 3 years 0 months to 7 years 11 months with no apparent handicapping conditions, from middle-income and upper-middle-income homes in which standard American dialect was spoken.

Diagnostic Instruments

Title: Carrow Elicited Language Inventory
Source: Carrow, E. (1974). Learning Concepts, Austin, TX.
Age Range: 3 years 0 months to 7 years 11 months
Description: Instrument contains 1 phrase and 51 sentences designed to measure expressive syntax, sampling simple clause structure, negatives, questions, imperatives, pronouns, prepositions, verb inflections, and a variety of noun phrases.
Soundness:

> *Standardization:* There were 475 white children from middle socioeconomic status homes in Houston, Texas.
> *Reliability and Validity:* There were inadequate data (reported studies based on samples of 20 and 25 children).

Title: Expressive One Word Picture Vocabulary Test
Source: Gardner, M. F. (1979). Academic Therapy Publications, San Rafael, CA.
Age Range: 2 years to 11 years 11 months
Description: Instrument measures identification of single-word vocabulary, producing four scores—language age, language standard score, stanine, and percentile rank.
Soundness:

> *Standardization:* There were 1607 children residing in the San Francisco Bay area whose primary language was English, with stratification according to racial-cultural and sexual factors.
> *Reliability:* Split-half reliability ranges from .87 to .96 with a mean of .94.
> *Validity:* Content and item validity are discussed in the manual, and data related to criterion-related validity are reported with weak-to-moderate correlations with the PPVT, CMMS, WPPSI, and Comprehensive Testing Program.

Title: Peabody Picture Vocabulary Test-Revised
Source: Dunn, Lloyd M. & Dunn, Leota M. (1981). American Guidance Service, Circle Pines, MN.
Age Range: 2 years 6 months to 40 years
Description: Instrument measures receptive vocabulary through 175 items which require a pointing response. Each item contains four picture choices from which the correct response must be selected.
Soundness:

> *Standarization:* There were 4200 children stratified according to age, sex, geographic area, occupation of parents, and ethnic representation. Community size was based on 1970 U.S. census.

Reliability: Odd and even reliability coefficients range from .61 to .88. Alternate forms reliability is reported from .71 to .89.

Validity: Content, construct, and criterion-related validity have been established and meet the criteria to be acceptable in the revised version.

Title: The Rossetti Infant-Toddler Language Scale: A Measure of Communication Interaction

Source: Rossetti, L. (1990). LinguiSystems, Inc., 3100 4th Ave., P. O. Box 747, East Moline, IL 61244.

Age Range: Birth through 36 months of age

Description: This criterion-referenced scale is designed to produce a comprehensive assessment of preverbal and verbal aspects of communication and interaction. It covers the following six areas: interaction-attachment, pragmatics, gesture, play, language comprehension, and language expression. The scale relies on a parent questionnaire, direct observation of the mother and child in a play area, direct testing, observation of the child in free play, and reports from caregivers. Data are coded as observed, elicited or reported. The parent questionnaire, which is completed through an interview, involves 36 simple questions (e.g., did your child require frequent hospitalization, how does your child respond to simple questions, how does your child usually let you know what he/she wants) and a list of 127 words for the parent to indicate which the child is familiar with. Observations of the child at free play should include the gathering of a language sample of 50 spontaneous utterances.

Items were developed as a compilation of author observation, developmental hierarchies, and behaviors recognized and used by leading authorities in infant and toddler assessment. The scale has a weak predictive value and is designed for program planning.

Soundness: No norming group was used in test construction, and no studies related to reliability or validity have yet been conducted.

Title: Test for Auditory Comprehension of Language-Revised

Source: Carrow-Woolfolk, E. (1985). DLM Teaching Resources, 1 DLM Park, Allen, TX 75002.

Age Range: 3 years 0 months to 9 years 11 months

Description: Instrument contains three sections, each of which is scored separately. Section I is identified as word classes (e.g., nouns, verbs, and modifiers) and relations (e.g., word combinations). Section II covers comprehension of grammatical morphemes, pronouns, prepositions, and suffixes in simple sentences. Section III presents elaborated sentences, including question forms, negatives, passives, and clauses. Scoring produces percentiles based on chronological age or grade placement, and several additional standard scores.

Soundness:

Standardization: There were 1003 children stratified according to age, family occupation, ethnic origin, age, sex, community size, and geographic distribution.

Reliability and Validity: Split-half reliability is reported to range from .89 to .95. Manual offers extensive discussion of content, construct, and criterion-related validity.

Title: Test of Auditory-Perceptual Skills

Source: Gardner, M. F. (1985). Children's Hospital of San Francisco, Publication Department, OPR-110, P. O. Box 3805, San Francisco, CA 94119.

Age Range: 4 years to 12 years

Description: Instrument contains a battery of auditory-perceptual skills with six subtests: auditory discrimination, auditory sequential memory, auditory word memory, auditory interpreting directions, auditory processing, and hyperactivity. Scoring produces stanines, percentiles, auditory age equivalents, and auditory standard scores for each subtest.

Soundness:

> *Reliability:* Adequate reliability was reported by test author.
>
> *Validity:* Content, item, diagnostic, and criterion-related validity were reported by test author, with correlations to WPPSI, WISC-R, and EOWPVT ranging from .42 to .80.

Title: Test of Early Language Development

Source: Hresko, W. P., Reid, D. K., & Hammill, D. D. (1981). Sources Test Service, Monterey, CA.

Age Range: 3 years to 7 years 11 months

Description: Instrument assesses comprehension and production, including syntax and semantics. It produces language quotients, percentiles, and language ages.

Title: Test of Language Development-2 Primary

Source: Newcomer, P. L., & Hammill, D. D. (1988). PRO-ED, 5341 Industrial Oak Boulevard, Austin, TX 78735.

Age Range: 4 years to 8 years 11 months

Description: Instrument includes 170-item oral response test consisting of seven subtests—picture vocabulary, oral vocabulary, grammatic understanding, sentence imitation, grammatic completion, word articulation, and word discrimination.

Soundness:

> *Standardization:* It was standardized on over 2000 children from 28 states and 1 Canadian province.
>
> *Reliability and Validity:* Low reliabilities of some subtests on the original version necessitated a revision.

CHAPTER 11

Sensory and Motor Assessment

CHAPTER OUTLINE

QUESTIONS ANSWERED IN CHAPTER 11

- How is motor development defined?
- What concepts are involved in motor development?
- What are some theoretical perspectives toward motor development?

• What are normal and abnormal patterns of motor development?
• What assessment techniques can be used in the motor domain?
• What assessment techniques can be used to assess sensory functioning?

CHAPTER OVERVIEW

The difficulty in trying to separate child functioning into distinct domains is readily apparent when considering the motor domain. Controlled movements serve as the expression of brain functioning. Sperry (as quoted by Wolff, 1982) emphasizes the point:

> To the neurologist, regarding the brain from an objective, analytical standpoint, it is readily apparent that the sole product of brain function is motor coordination. To repeat: *the entire output of our thinking machine consists of nothing but patterns of motor coordination.* (p. 130)

Through controlled movements, such as the simple reaching movements of an infant, the utterance of first words, the achievement of bowel and bladder control, and coloring activities of the preschool-age child, young children demonstrate their overall development. The only concrete knowledge available about what children are doing, thinking, or feeling is based on our perceptions of their controlled movements (Wolff, 1982). Intact motor functioning affords the child the opportunity to explore and experiment with the environment, obtain an understanding of concepts such as cause and effect, and take full advantage of sensory stimulation.

DEFINITIONS OF MOTOR DEVELOPMENT

Development of motor skills involves changes in motor behavior and motor control as children grow from infancy into adulthood. Motor functioning is influenced by underlying biological and mechanical factors. Related terms and concepts include psychomotor, perceptual–motor, sensorimotor, and motor learning. *Motor development* and *psychomotor development,* used synonymously throughout the literature, refer to change and stabilization evident in a child's physical structure and neuromuscular function (Gallahue, 1982). *Perceptual–motor skill* is based upon the integration of perceived sensations in a decision-making process, resulting in observable movement. *Sensorimotor* is a term often associated with the developmental integration of the senses prevalent during the first 2 years of life. *Motor learning* involves a change in behavior linked primarily to body movement, which is a result of the interaction of experience and maturation.

Reflexive and Volitional Movement

Motor development involves the acquisition of volitional muscle control used to accomplish gross and fine motor tasks. *Reflexive movement,* predominant in a normally developing newborn child, is that which spontaneously occurs in response to stimuli. For example, if a person slips and falls, his arms automatically reach out into a protective extension as a reflexive motion. There are *primitive reflexes,* present in the normally developing infant, and *postural reactions,* which emerge as infants integrate primitive reflexes and develop motor skills. Children with motor impairments may exhibit *pathological reflexes,* never present in the normally developing infant, and/or abnormally persistent primitive reflexes. Table 11.1 describes some of the reflexes and postural reactions seen in infants and young children. *Volitional movements* differ from reflexive movements in that they are under a person's control and are consciously and intentionally made. People feed themselves, engage in sports activities, form letters and words through fine adjustments of their fingers while holding a pen, and speak through volitional muscle control.

Patterns of Development

Motor development progresses according to certain developmental patterns, which include *cephalocaudal, proximal–distal, gross to fine motor,* and *mass to specific.* The cephalocaudal pattern relates to development moving from head to toe, so that the first volitional muscle control involves the head and neck and progresses downward. Proximal–distal indicates a pattern of development from the trunk outward to the extremities, thus sitting precedes throwing a ball. Mass to specific refers to the gradually developing ability to isolate muscles for movement. Initially, when a child rolls over she does so as one unit, but soon gains adequate control over specific parts of her body so that the roll becomes more controlled and occurs in a smooth sequence of head and shoulders followed by trunk and hips and completed with the legs. Gross to fine motor is indicative of the pattern of large muscle control preceding small muscle control, so children can throw and catch a big ball before they can draw a picture.

Muscle Tone and Strength

Normal motor development requires adequate muscle strength and tone. *Strength* refers to the properties of the muscles, nerves that control muscle contraction, and motor control centers in the brain. Severed nerves, lack of exercise, or chemical changes (e.g., muscular dystrophy) can all adversely affect muscle strength. *Muscle tone* is the amount of tension present in the muscles, ranging from low tone (hypotonia) to high tone (hypertonia). An examiner can assess muscle tone using a range of passive movements, noting the amount of resistance the child shows. Observation of body parts at rest and in motion can also be helpful (Fetters, 1984). Abnormally high or low tone can be present in only those muscles used in flexion (flexors), those used in extension (extensors), or in both. Tone is influenced by enviromental factors such as fatigue, temperature, speed of movement, positioning, and task difficulty (Fetters, 1984). The infant placed in a prone position (lying on the stomach) assumes a predominantly flexed posture, whereas the supine position (lying on the back) increases extension. For a child whose flexor muscles are hypertonic, the prone position restricts the child's ability to move freely.

TABLE 11.1. Reflexes and Postural Reactions

Reflex	Description	Normal Age Span	Movement Limitations
Asymmetrical Tonic Neck Flex (ATNR)	When infant's head is turned to the side, arm (and sometimes leg) on face side extend, and arm (and sometimes leg) on skull side flex.	Birth to 4 months, then gradually fades, completely disappears by 6 months	Interferes with rolling over, bringing hands to midline and to mouth, grasping objects while visually exploring them, coordinating hands and eyes; causes hip dislocation and scoliosis if persists.
Symmetrical Tonic Neck Reflex (STNR)	When head is in extension, arms extend and hips and legs flex; when head is flexed, arms flex and hips and legs extend.	2 to 4 months, then gradually fades	Interferes with creeping and crawling and all functional ambulation; child cannot maintain a four-point kneel or normal sitting posture.
Tonic Labyrinthine Reflex (TLR)	Supine: predominant posture is extension—neck extends, shoulders retract, trunk and legs straighten. Prone: predominant posture is flexion—arms flex in under chest, hips and legs are tucked in under tummy.	Birth to 4 months	Interferes with all volitional movements, including raising head, extending limbs in prone position and flexing limbs from supine position, sitting, sidelying, and rolling over.
Moro Reflex	When there is a rapid change in head position or a sudden loud noise, the head falls back and arms and fingers extend and go out and up from the trunk.	Birth to 4 months, gradually diminishes, completely gone by 6 months	Interferes with sitting, equilibrium reactions and protection reaction (absence in the newborn denotes CNS dysfunction).
Palmar Grasp	Hand stays in fisted position, when hand is touched near the little finger (ulnar side) object is immediately grasped.	Birth to 4 months, still present in sleep at 6 months	Interferes with finger extension, volitional grasp and release, weight-bearing on palms, sitting, and pincer grasp.

Postural Reaction	Description	Age of Appearance
Neck-Righting Reaction	When head is turned to one side in supine position, the body turns as a whole toward the same side.	Birth to 4 months, then diminishes
Body-Righting Reaction: Acting on the Body	When head is turned to one side in supine position, the body turns in segments (shoulder girdle follows head, then pelvis) toward the same side.	Appears at 6 to 8 months and is inhibited by 3 years

(*continued*)

TABLE 11.1 *(continued)*

Postural Reaction	Description	Age of Appearance
Body-Righting Reaction: Acting on the Head	When feet are placed on the ground or child is lying down, the head comes into alignment with the trunk.	Appears at 4 to 6 months and is inhibited between 1 to 5 years
Equilibrium Reaction: Prone and Supine	When placed on a tilt board, head bends and body arches toward raised side with arms and legs extended, going out from midline.	Prone: 4 to 6 months and persists Supine: 7 to 10 months and persists
Quadrapedal	When positioned on hands and knees and gently tipped to one side, the arm and leg on raised side straighten and extend out from midline while the opposite arm reaches out in a protective extension.	10 to 12 months and persists
Equilibrium Reaction: Sitting	When in a sitting position and gently pushed to one side, head moves toward raised side, arm and leg of raised side straighten out from the midline and opposite arm and straighten in protection extension; when pushed forward, the legs flex, spine and neck extend, and arms move backward; when pushed backward, the head, shoulders, and arms move forward and the legs straighten.	12 to 14 months and persists
Standing	When in a standing position and one arm is pulled outward, the opposite arm and leg straighten outward and head is adjusted to maintain normal position.	12 to 18 months and persists
Landau Reaction	When child is suspended in prone position, head is raised up with symmetrical extension of spine and hips (shows integration of symmetrical tonic neck reflex and tonic labyrinthine reflex).	9 months

THEORIES OF MOTOR DEVELOPMENT

Some theories of motor development focus more on the influence of psychomotor factors on cognitive and emotional development than on how motor skills develop. The importance of the motor domain in the cognitive development of the child varies among the theories. Kephart (1971) views motor learning as the root of all higher forms of behavior, whereas Cratty (1979) considers movement as important in the opportunities it creates for learning, rather than the basis of the intellect. Theories vary as to factors such as the role primitive reflexes play in the development of volitional movement, how speed and accuracy are increased, the importance of the knowledge of results on performance, the role of practice and correction of errors, and how extraneous movements are inhibited (Wolff, 1982). Included in this section is a basic theoretical model of motor development, as well as neurodevelopmental and sensorimotor integration models linked to early intervention programming for young children with motor impairments.

Phases of Motor Development Model

The *Phases of Motor Development Model* (Gallahue, 1982) holds that a child's observable movement behavior is the window through which motor development can be viewed. Movement is classified in one of four categories: nonlocomotor (i.e., stabilizing or balancing movements), locomotor (e.g., creeping, crawling, and walking), manipulative (e.g., throwing, catching, cutting, and drawing), or combination movements. The Phases of Motor Development Model is based on an overlapping progression through four phases from birth through the early teen years. The *reflexive movement phase,* with an information encoding stage (birth to 4 months) and an information decoding stage (from 4 months to 1 year of age), is dominated by reflexive, involuntary, subcortically controlled movements. The *rudimentary movement phase* involves stability movements (e.g., head and neck control), manipulative movement (e.g., reach, grasp, and release), and locomotor movements (e.g., creeping, crawling, and walking). It contains a reflex inhibition stage (from birth to 1 year) followed by a precontrol stage (from 1 to 2 years) when the infant learns to gain and maintain equilibrium, manipulate objects, and move about in the environment. The *fundamental movement phase* ranges from age 2 to age 7. The 2- to 3-year-old is in the initial stage, the 4- to 5-year-old is in the elementary stage, and the 6- to 7-year-old is in the mature stage of this phase. The child in the fundamental movement phase is learning how to perform a variety of basic observable patterns of behavior, such as running, jumping, throwing, catching, and balance beam walking. As the skill develops, increased control by the child results in the increased fluidity of movement. The final stage, associated with children 7 years and older, is the *sport-related movement phase.*

Although Gallahue acknowledges the important influence cognitive and emotional development can have on motor development, psychomotor and mechanical factors affecting progression through the stages are emphasized in the model. *Physical fitness* (i.e., muscular strength, muscular endurance, circulatory-respiratory endurance, and muscular flexibility) and *motor fitness* (i.e., performance ability of a specific skill as influenced by movement, speed, agility, balance, coordination, and power) together make up the psychomotor factors. The mechanical factors influencing motor development are stability, giving force, and receiving force.

Neurodevelopmental Model

The most prevalent theoretical perspective influencing assessment and intervention of young children with motor impairments forms the basis of neurodevelopmental treatment (NDT) developed by Bobath and Bobath (1972, 1975) from their work with children with cerebral palsy. It is based upon two basic factors:

1. Damage to the central nervous system interferes with the normal maturation of the brain, leading to retardation or arrest of motor development; and

2. A release of abnormal postural reflex activity results in the presence of abnormal patterns of posture and movement. (Bobath, 1970)

The goal of neurodevelopmental treatment is to inhibit patterns of abnormal reflex activity and facilitate normal motor patterns. Specialized techniques of handling the child incorporate guiding the child's movements through normal developmental patterns. Such treatment might require the temporary loss of functioning, if a child has developed abnormal patterns of movement, which will eventually impede his functioning (e.g., abnormal sitting posture will encourage curvature of the spine and joint fixation). Abnormal movement patterns and excessive effort are replaced as the therapist controls the child, aiming to establish a normal postural tone and a normal pattern of movement.

Sensorimotor Integration Model

Another approach to the treatment of children with sensory or motor impairments is based on the sensory integration theory of Ayres (1973). The theory is based on the view that the functioning of the brainstem and early sensory integration processes are important influences on higher levels of the brain and, therefore, later cognitive development. From this theory sensorimotor integration therapy was developed for intervention with learning disabled children. It has come to be used in early intervention as well. Improving a child's functioning at the lower, less complex levels of sensorimotor skill development enables the child to become competent at higher, more complex levels (e.g., reading). The tactile, proprioceptive, and vestibular systems are viewed as important because of their contribution to generalized neurological integration and to enhanced perception in other sensory systems. Treatment based on sensory integration incorporates both perceptual motor theory and neurodevelopmental theory. The effectiveness of sensorimotor integration therapy in achieving improved functioning is subject to debate. Research clearly supporting its effectiveness is not readily available (see Jenkins, Fewell, & Harris, 1983).

EARLY SENSORY AND MOTOR DEVELOPMENT

As an infant matures physically and has opportunities to explore her environment, sensory and motor skills develop. As sensory skills develop, they become integrated and are coordinated with motor skills. An infant's initial attempt to reach for and secure an object 2 feet out of her reach will change in time to a successful pattern. First, the infant will move her body within reaching distance of the object. Then she will make contact with the object on the first attempt to secure it; this involves accurate eye–hand coordination. This section contains a brief review of sensory and motor development of the young child.

Sensory Development

Development of the senses enables the infant and young child to explore the environment, providing the opportunity for learning. When *tactile sensory develop-*

ment proceeds normally, the infant accepts touch. Normal caregiving routines (e.g., wrapping child in blanket, cuddling, patting, and stroking) help increase tolerance for tactile stimulation, leading the way to the development of tactile discrimination skills. The child can distinguish tactile stimuli by features such as temperature or texture. Tactile reflexes (e.g., rooting reflex, Babkin reflex—squeezing palm causes mouth to open without a cry) demonstrate the tactile sensitivity of newborns. The tactile sense is used extensively as the young child explores his environment. The child with neurological impairments may display an intolerance to tactile stimulation.

Visual sensory development follows a pattern of sensation to light, visual fixation (present in 2-week-old infants), visual tracking, convergence (i.e., using both eyes together), eye contact, reaching and grasping, and eye–hand and eye–foot coordination activities. At birth, an infant's eye differs from an adult's eye on several significant dimensions: the optic nerve is not fully myelinated, retinal cellular structures are undifferentiated, the diameter of the eye is smaller, the pupillary opening is smaller, pigmentation of the macular area is incomplete, and there is a tendency toward hyperopia (far-sightedness) (Hanson & Hanline, 1984). Cellular changes and maturation enable the infant by 4 months of age to approximate an adult's ability to focus. By 1 year of age "the infant displays a wide range of visual capabilities which allow for exploration of the environment" (Hanson & Hanline, 1984, p. 112).

The *auditory senses* also develop in a sequential pattern, beginning with auditory attention (i.e., attending to sounds in the environment) and localization (i.e., the ability to identify where the sound was coming from). Soon auditory discrimination and association also develop. The infant can first distinguish the sounds of mother's voice from the door bell or phone ringing and, shortly thereafter, from other voices. Human and environmental sounds become associated with certain events or conditions, so that parents resort to spelling certain words in the presence of even very young children. The anatomy of the auditory system is completely developed prior to birth. Myelinatization of the auditory nerve is complete at birth; however, the cortex is immature and may be limited in the ability to integrate sounds from both ears. Infants between the ages of 4 and 6 months can localize to environmental sounds, show differential smiling to mother's voice, are more soothed by a female voice than a male voice, and are able to discriminate many speech sounds (Hanson & Hanline, 1984).

The development of *gustatory and olfactory sensory systems* has received less attention than that of tactile, visual, and auditory development. It is known that the infant has a large number of taste buds and that newborns do show a preference for sugar over water solutions. It is also known that infants vary in their responses to differing odors. A preference for specific odors has been noted in infants as young as 72 hours (Hanson & Hanline, 1984). Although a clear pattern of development in gustation and olfaction development is not available, there is adequate evidence to suggest that even a newborn is able to use her senses of taste and smell to explore and learn about her world.

The *vestibular system* substantially influences sensory development and is sometimes considered a sixth sense. The vestibular receptors located in the inner ear detect the degree of balance, muscle tone, and eye movement. Alertness level is also influenced by the vestibular system. As primitive reflexes are inhibited and postural righting and equilibrium reactions emerge, the vestibular system enables the body to maintain an upright head position and keeps body parts in alignment for normal movement (Fetters, 1984).

Normal Motor Development

The normally developing child follows a sequence of motor development that serves to verify his physical and mental well-being. This sequence and the skills associated with chronological age of the child become the framework for assessment. Although a knowledge of motor development sequences and expected age of performance is critical to the early childhood special educator, the context of performance must never be forgotten. Progression through motor milestones is a continuous gradual development of skills—not a sudden burst of skill. The infant struggles to pull himself to standing only to find himself right where he started hundreds of times before, until finally he remains standing for a few seconds. The excitement of the event immediately causes him to fall again. The level of perseverance and determination that a young child displays in achieving "pulls to standing" cannot be justly represented in a checkmark on the assessment form. The developmental sequence described here is based upon material by Bobath (1970), Zelle (1983), Finnie (1975), and Bailey and Wolery (1984).

Birth through 4 Months.   The newborn in the prone position maintains a flexed posture, with her head turned to one side, pelvis tilted up high, and knees tucked up under the abdomen. She can raise her head to a 45° angle and hold it mostly in midline by 8 weeks. By 4 months, she can lift her head and chest up, with the plane of her face at 90° to the surface. Limbs can be stretched out into full extension. In the supine position, the tonic labyrinthine reflex reduces the flexor posture by stimulating the extensor muscles. Gravitational forces pull the head to one side asymmetrically and the flexed arms down to the surface. The infant at this age will display an asymmetrical tonic neck reflex, which gradually diminishes. By the end of 4 months the infant has a symmetrical posture, with the head in midline and hands capable of moving to the midline.

When the newborn is pulled to sitting, his head lags. When supported in a sitting position, the head falls forward and the back is completely rounded. The 4-month-old pulled to sitting displays only a slight head lag, and the back is not completely rounded. If the body is swayed during sitting, the head will wobble some. The arms remain flexed and forward and when extended can result in a fall backwards.

When held up with feet ligthly touching a surface, the newborn displays a primitive walking reflex, which disappears by 2 months. The 2-month-old will bear no weight, but the 3- and 4-month-old will bear a small amount of weight. The 4-month-old may rise up on her toes and claw with them. The newborn's hands are tightly fisted, with a strong resistance to being opened. By 2 months, however, the hands are often open. The grasp reflex present in the newborn fades by 4 months, and pulling at others' clothing and clutching emerge. The 4-month-old can oppose gravity and clasp objects between both hands at the point of midline.

5 through 8 Months.   The 5-month-old bears weight on his forearms and can move his legs flexed up under his trunk to move forward short distances. Soon he bears weight on his hands and begins reaching for toys while supporting himself on one forearm. The 5-month-old can roll from prone to supine. During this phase, the infant begins a modified combat (belly) crawl. When the infant spots something of interest to him, he waves his arms and rocks, providing vestibular stimulation. In a supine position the 5-month-old can lift his legs to his mouth and play with his toes. He will hold his arms out to be picked up. At 6 months, the infant can roll from supine to prone and can lift his head spontaneously. He begins reaching for toys from a sidelying position, bearing weight in a supine position. During this period the infant begins raising his hips off the surface, arching his back.

The 5-month-old shows no head lag when pulled to sitting, holding the back straight in a sitting position. The head does not wobble when the body is swayed. During this period the child develops the ability to sit on the floor unsupported with her hands stretched forward for support. When given the opportunity, the 5-month-old will bear almost all of her weight. By 6 months, the infant may begin bouncing while held in a standing position. Soon she can stand, holding on to furniture, and begins pulling herself up to stand. The 5-month-old enjoys putting objects in her mouth. She now has volitional grasp, can hold her own bottle, and grasp her own feet. During this period she begins transferring objects from hand to hand, feeding herself biscuits, banging objects on the table, and patting her image in the mirror.

9 through 12 Months.   Between 9 and 12 months, the infant is free to move from prone to a sitting position and back to prone. He can creep on the abdomen backwards and can soon creep forward with a pulling motion of the arms. Around 10 months, the infant begins rocking and creeping on his hands and knees. During this period he does not enjoy remaining in a supine position and most often rolls over or sits up. He can sit steadily with little overbalancing; has a protective extension forward, sideways, and finally backwards; and can pull himself to sitting. He pivots, rotating the head, shoulders, and trunk to pick up objects and crosses the midline in his reaching. Finger–thumb opposition develops during this period, and the infant is able to pick up very small objects using pincer grasp. The index finger is used to explore and poke at objects. Initially, during this period the infant holds objects to give to an adult, but does not release them. Soon, however, volitional release develops, and the infant can release a toy when giving it to an adult.

13 through 18 Months.   The infant begins the 13- through 18-month period by being able to pull to standing and cruise about the room holding on. She soon accomplishes the feat of taking her first independent steps and cannot be stopped. She develops the ability to rise to standing without pulling up on objects and sits in a chair on her own. Toward the end of this period, stiff running will begin. She can grasp very small items with a precise pincer movement, release objects one at a time, and move her hand to wave bye-bye. She will transfer even a speck of dust from one hand to the other and can clap hands and bang objects together. Crayons are grasped in a palmar orientation of the hand.

19 through 24 Months.   From 19 through 24 months, the child attempts to jump and kick a ball, increases walking ability and starts running, and rises to standing more efficiently. He can throw a ball in an overhand or underhand pattern. He catches a ball by trapping it against his chest with flexed elbows. Objects can be released onto another object (stacking). Crayons are grasped with a beginning radial-palmar orientation.

2 through 5 Years.   Between 2 and 3 years of age, a toddler spends a great deal of time running and jumping. She is able to turn the pages of books carefully. The 3-year-old rides a tricycle, climbs stairs in a reciprocal pattern, can stand on one foot for 2 seconds, and hops. She cuts with scissors, imitates circular and horizontal strokes, and copies a circle. By her fifth birthday, the preschool-age child can skip, march, and turn somersaults. She can walk backward heel-to-toe and can jump over objects as high as 10 inches. She starts holding a pencil in an adult manner, copies a cross, and laces shoes.

Abnormal Motor Development

Children deviate from normal motor development for a wide variety of reasons, such as muscular dystrophy, myelomeningocele, cerebral palsy, and pervasive developmental delay. The reasons for a motor impairment directly influence the nature of that impairment. Some children exhibit unusual, but normal, developmental variations in motor milestones (e.g., crawling with only hands and feet touching the ground) and should not be confused with those who have significant motor impairments. For some, the impairment will primarily be one of *delay,* where normal milestones will appear in the usual sequence at a delayed pace. Children with visual impairments often experience such delays in motor development. The determination of the need for intervention and the nature of the child's problem when a delay is present should be handled so as to avoid unnecessary delays in service as well as undue alarm to the parents.

For others, however, *abnormal patterns* or *pathological development* can be observed. Premature infants present abnormal patterns of early motor development, which do not always result in permanent impairments. They are frequently hypotonic and develop muscle tone from the legs progressing upward to the head, followed by the normal cephalocaudal pattern of postural control. The primitive reflexes may be weak when compared with those of full-term infants (Fetters, 1984). Infants with specific problems related to motor functioning, such as Down's syndrome or cerebral palsy, experience pathological motor development. The child with Down's syndrome frequently has low muscle tone and muscle weakness as well as developmental delays. Without intervention, joint instability and abnormal flexibility can develop with resulting complications in motor functioning. Cerebral palsy is used to describe a variety of syndromes caused by damage to the central nervous system; these are characterized by abnormal muscle tone and abnormal reflex patterns.

Effects of Sensory Impairments. The impact of sensory impairments can be observed even during the first 4 months of a child's life, influencing tolerance for weight-bearing in a prone position, recognition and response to caregivers, and integration of reflexive responses (Zelle, 1983). The infant with a visual impairment has no opportunity to participate in mutual gaze, gaze aversion, or eye brightening with his caregivers. He does not see the caregiver's smile, and therefore his own smile is not as distinct and is less frequent than the infant with intact vision. He has no visual lure to raise his head while in the prone position or to reach out toward objects and people and thus prefers to remain in a supine position. There may be a delay in the recognition and preference for caregivers. Even when provided with auditory stimulation, the infant with a visual impairment will not reach out because he does not associate the sound with objects available for exploration and play. The infant is not able to begin creeping about, distancing himself from a caregiver while keeping her in sight. However, once he has achieved the ability to reach toward sound cues, the sound of a caregiver's voice or desired objects can help stimulate self-initiated movements and position changes.

The infant with an auditory deficit does not hear the caregiver's voice and the cues available from voice and tone changes. Thus, she is deprived of information critical to both structural and emotional patterns with the language system. The opportunity to move in rhythm to sound is also impaired. When the infant is ready to move about, caregivers cannot restrict the child's movements or actions from a distance with a verbal warning. This inability to warn the child can result in greater than normal physical restrictions on the child, interfering with motor development as well as the separation and individualization process.

If the impairment involves the vestibular system, ocular control and visual and auditory processing can be affected. Severe impairment can result in the infant curling up in the corner of his crib, keeping his head down. Righting and equilibrium responses will be delayed because the child is afraid of gravitational shifts and rapid movements. Tactile impairments can make the infant stiffen and withdraw when caregivers attempt to cuddle, feed, or clothe him. The protective response against tactile stimulation interferes with his ability to tolerate weight-bearing in all positions. It is also possible for the infant to crave tactile stimulation to the point of banging his head, pinching, biting, and hitting himself.

TECHNIQUES OF ASSESSMENT

Several neurologically based assessment instruments for infants, which include motor behaviors, were described in Chapter 9. Developmental and neurodevelopmental assessment procedures are presented in this section along with an assessment procedure based on adaptive motor functioning. In addition, tests designed to measure visual–perceptual and perceptual–motor functioning are described.

The challenge of obtaining accurate information about the motor functioning of infants is reflected in the extent of false positives and false negatives associated with many of the instruments available in this area. In studies reported by Chandler (1990) this problem is substantial. Although the psychomotor index of the Bayley scales correctly identified normal infants 97% of the time, it correctly identified infants with a disorder only 17% of the time. A combined ultrasound and neurological examination correctly identified 100% of the infants with a disorder; however, only 57% of the normal infants were correctly identified. The high number of false positives and false negatives from these assessments can be attributed to four factors (Chandler, 1990). First, variability of infant performance is related to behavioral state, including time of feedings, wellness, fatigue, and temperament. The wide range of normal motor development is a second confounding factor. Standardized instruments are typically based on the performance of a norm group and a designated criteria for item difficulty. Some instruments require that 100% of the norming group perform a skill before the expected age is established, while others are based on lower percentages. Chandler (1990) noted that 17% of her norm group for The Movement Assessment of Infants moved about on all fours by 6 months of age; however, it took until 11 months of age for 100% of these normal infants to achieve the skill. This wide range of normal functioning can make age-equivalent scores hard to establish and even harder to interpret. A third factor relates to discrepancies that occur between instruments developed for research and those designed primarily for clinical use. Because they differ in norming procedures and intended purposes, they can produce scores with a wide variance. Finally, the weak psychometric properties of the instruments themselves can produce false positives and/or false negatives.

Developmental Assessment

Examiners can observe motor performance in conjunction with standardized instruments that produce age-equivalent scores (e.g., psychomotor scale of the *Bayley Scales of Infant Development* (BSID) or informal developmental checklists. Some developmental profiles do offer interventions based on child performance. Multidomain assessments that include a motor component are described in Chapter 8. Additional standardized instruments that can be used specifically to assess motor development are described later.

The Peabody Developmental Motor Scales (PDMS) (Folio & Fewell, 1983) assess both gross and fine motor development of children from birth to 6.9 years of age. The five gross motor skills assessed are reflexes, balance, nonlocomotor, locomotor, and receipt and propulsion. The four areas of fine motor development covered are grasping, hand use, eye–hand coordination, and manual dexterity. A strength of the PDMS is the large number of items within each age level (e.g., 10 gross motor items for the 0- to 1-month range). Since the scales are organized by age level rather than by category, the examiner must frequently switch back and forth between activities and materials. There is included in the assessment kit a set of cards that can be used for program planning following the assessment; however, Connolly (as cited in Chandler, 1990) questioned the appropriateness of these activity cards for severely impaired children. The instrument is both criterion- and norm-referenced and can produce age-equivalent scores, developmental quotients, percentiles, and Z scores. The norming group had 617 children, representing age groups, regions of the United States, sex, and racial and ethnic groups (i.e., white, black, and Hispanic—based on 1976 Census Bureau estimates). Reliability is reported based on interrater reliability of 36 children, with a mean coefficient of .97 on the gross motor scales and .94 on the fine motor scales. The mean reliability coefficient for test–rest reliability based on 38 children was .95 for gross motor and .80 for fine motor. The manual reported concurrent validity based on the BSID. The correlation between the fine motor scale and the mental developmental index (MDI) was strong ($r = .78$), but it was not when compared with the psychomotor developmental index (PDI) ($r = .36$). Correlations with the gross motor scale were .37 for the PDI and .03 for the MDI. The PDMS has been used in program efficacy studies with learning disabled 3- to 15-year-olds (Jenkins & Sells, 1984). It has also been used in other studies designed to measure the effectiveness of intervention (Haley, Stephens, & Larsen, 1988), to determine benefits of social integration programming (Jenkins, Odom, & Speltz, 1989), to compare effectiveness of sensory integrative theory with motor programming (Jenkins, Fewell, & Harris, 1983), and to evaluate the sustained benefits of intervention after intervention is stopped (Fewell, 1988).

The BSID (Bayley, 1984) contain three scales: the mental scale, the psychomotor scale, and the infant behavior record. The standardization sample and mental scale of the BSID are described in Chapter 9. The psychomotor scale, which produces the PDI, is described here. Because of the limited number of items on some levels of the scale, the psychomotor scale is best used as a screening tool (Chandler, 1990). It does provide a measure of the degree of control of the body, coordination of the large muscles, and finer manipulatory skills of the hands and fingers. The test comprises a total of 81 items, using direct assessment and incidental observation. Performance on the motor scale items is translated into a pass or fail score, which is converted to the PDI, with a mean of 100 and standard deviation of 16. The range of possible scores is limited to 50 to 150. Test–retest reliability, based on 28 infants, was 75.3%, and it was 93.4% for 90 infants, using a tester-observer reliability. Although the BSID has adequate psychometric properties, the motor scale has not proved adequate to correctly identify infants with neurological impairments (Chandler, 1990).

The *Bruininks–Oseretsky Test of Motor Proficiency* (Bruininks, 1978) assesses gross, fine, and general motor development and is available in both a long and short form. The long form is used to assist in decision making for appropriate educational and therapeutic placement, whereas the short form is a screening instrument. The skills measured include running speed and agility, balance, bilateral coordination, strength, upper-limb coordination, response speed, visual–motor control, and upper-limb speed and dexterity. Both direct assessment and observation of the child in a structured environment are used in the testing procedure. Standard scores for gross, fine, and general motor development can be obtained, as well as the age level of functioning for each area.

Doulah (1976) developed *A Motor Development Checklist* to assess motor development in terms of spontaneous action patterns that are most representative of a child's status up to the point of walking (approximately 15 months). A monthly observational record is maintained, with an emphasis on the sequence of motor development, and less attention is given to time and rate of development. The test can be scored on a pass or fail basis or using a scale that ranges from "does not perform task" to "performs task skillfully."

The *Test of Motor Impairment* (TOMI) (Stott, Moyes, & Henderson, 1984) is used to evaluate fine and gross motor performance to determine possible neural dysfunction. It is appropriate for individuals from 4 years of age to adulthood and covers four dimensions of motor performance: manual dexterity, ball skills, static balance, and dynamic balance. The score is a measure of impairment. Each item not demonstrated at or below age level is awarded 2 points. A well-coordinated child would score 0. A particular strength of the test is the play-type activities (e.g., jumping in squares and tossing a bean bag) that are used for the assessment. However, the test requires standardized equipment available only from the manufacturer.

Neurodevelopmental Assessment

The age range by which primitive reflexes are typically integrated and the age at which a child is expected to perform specific motor tasks (e.g., sitting unsupported) provide a benchmark for parents and early interventionists to monitor development. Observation and parent interview can provide information about a child's functioning. Fetters (1984) suggests the following general observations: independent control (i.e., ability of infant to control her body independently); movement patterns (i.e., presence of abnormal muscle tone as compared with age expectations); and primitive reflexes (i.e., integration of primitive reflexes and their influence on spontaneous movement). Additionally, parents can be observed handling their infants in order to elicit specific responses. First, examiners should observe for the effect of position on muscle tone and movement. As infants are moved through prone, supine, sitting, and standing positions, the effects are noted. Second, postural responses should be noted. The parents can attempt to elicit age-appropriate

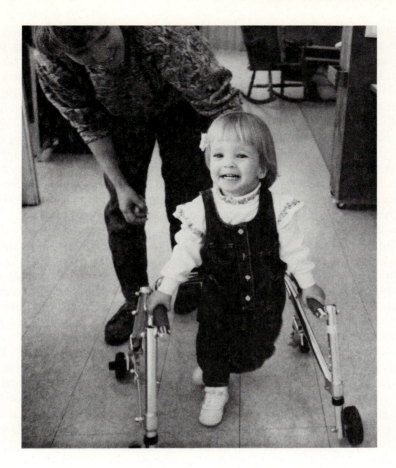

righting, equilibrium, and protective responses by changing the infant's position. Fetters recommends that the examiner handle the child to assess primitive reflexes, muscle tone, and muscle strength.

A guide to the neuromotor evaluation of infants under 6 months of age for the detection of cerebral palsy, based on the work of Illingworth, includes assessment of tone, primitive reflexes, and deep tendon reflexes (Taft, 1982). *Hypotonia* can be determined by examination for the anterior scarf sign (i.e., in supine position examiner can draw baby's hand circumferentially around face so that elbow is past chin while shoulder remains on surface), posterior scarf sign (i.e., in sitting position with head in midline, arm is pulled directly back by examiner and elbow passes the ear), and extreme hip abduction (i.e., turned outward). *Hypertonia* can be assessed through observation of the influence of primitive reflexes on the infant's posture when suspended in a prone position. Changes in infant position can also be used to detect hypertonic patterns.

There are several instruments available for neuromotor assessment. The *Milani-Comparetti Motor Development Screening Test* (MC) (Milani-Comparetti & Gidoni,

1967) is a neurological and developmental screening tool for newborns to toddlers 2.5 years of age. The MC covers basic components of movement, including postural control, active movement, primitive reflexes, automatic reactions, parachute reactions, and tilting reactions. These components are organized into two sections: (1) spontaneous behavior; and (2) evoked responses. The examiner can choose among four scoring systems (Trembath, 1977; Ellison, Browning, Larson, & Denny, 1983; VanderLinden, 1985). Each item on the test has a designated age equivalent. The simplest scoring procedure involves the notation of behaviors as normal or delayed according to age equivalents. Patterns in delays can then be interpreted by the examiner. The test is criterion-referenced and does not produce a summary score. No standardization sample was used in the development of age equivalents, and no reliability studies have been reported. Ellison et al. (1983) used it to identify children with persistent abnormal movements out of a total of 999 children.

A neurodevelopmental instrument useful in the identification of motor dysfunction in infants 1 year of age and younger is the *Movement Assessment of Infants* (MAI) (Chandler, Andrews, & Swanson, 1980). The instrument can be used with older children who are functioning developmentally below 1 year of age in their motor abilities. It assesses four components: tone, primitive reflexes, automatic reactions, and volitional movement. The instrument, which is criterion-referenced, contains a total of 65 items. Scoring involves a developmental rating of each item on a scale of one to four. Tone is based on a rating from 1 to five, with three being normal, one or two low tone, and four or five reflecting high tone. For infants at ages 4 and 8 months it is possible to calculate a total risk score and risk scores on each component. A interrater reliability coefficient of .72, based on 53 infants, has been reported, as well as a test–retest reliability coefficient of .76, based on 29 infants (Harris, Haley, Tada, & Swanson, 1984). A study of the accuracy of the MAI for the detection of neurodevelopmental delays indicates a high level of sensitivity (96.1%), with 64.5% of the normal infants correctly identified as not having motor delays (Swanson, as cited in Chandler, 1990). The *Chandler Movement Assessment of Infants—Screening Test* is an unpublished screening test that has been developed from the MAI (Chandler, 1990). It is also criterion-referenced and is being normed on a group of infants from Madigan Army Medical Center and a Tacoma public health facility. Preliminary psychometric reports, based on 10 children, show high test–retest reliabilities (87.2 to 97.4) and interrater reliabilities from 81.1 to 94.9 (Chandler, 1986).

Another battery, which is a screening tool for observing neurological signs, is the *Riley Motor Problems Inventory* (Riley, 1976). It measures oral, fine, and gross motor skills to determine the need for further clinical evaluation. Cutoff scores are provided, below which follow-up evaluations are recommended. It can be used with children between the ages of 4 and 9 years.

The *Erhardt Developmental Prehension Assessment* (EDPA) (Erhardt, 1982) measures three developmental prehension sequence clusters: primarily involuntary arm–hand patterns (i.e., positional-reflexive), primarily voluntary movements (i.e., cognitive emphasis), and prewriting skills. A total of 17 separate skill areas are assessed. The scoring system involves a three-point system for each test component: normal pattern, emerging pattern, or absent pattern. A pattern that has been replaced by a more mature pattern is also noted (++). Interobserver reliability is reported at 70.8% and 94.5% for two different groups of raters compared with the test author's scoring. No test–retest reliability studies have been done, and the manual does not include any validity information. The instrument is criterion-referenced and is intended to be used for remediation and intervention, not diagnosis.

The *Quick Neurological Screening Test* (Mutti, Sterling, & Spalding, 1978) assessed 15 components of neurological integration for children from 5 to 18 years of age. Components measured are maturity of motor development, large and small muscle skill and control, motor planning and sequencing, sense of rate and rhythm, spatial organization, visual and auditory perceptual abilities, balance and cerebellar–vestibular function, and attentional difficulties.

Motor Outcomes Assessment

An assessment approach focusing on a hierarchy of physical and motor outcome measures includes measures of self-initiated movements, prefunctional motor determinants, motor control and motor performance, motor skill, and adaptive motor function (Haley & Baryza, 1990). The lowest level of hierarchy, self-initiated movements, involves basics such as spontaneous movements, repeated practice of movements, and the motivation to move. Flexibility, strength, and postural responses are examples of the features of prefunctional motor determinants. Motor performance (e.g., speed, agility, and visual–motor processes) and motor control (e.g., timing of muscle movements) are both at the next level of the hierarchy. Walking, throwing, and prehension are examples of the motor skill level of the hierarchy. The highest level, adaptive motor function, involves basic skills such as dressing, eating, and mobility in the community. The *Pediatric Evaluation of Disability Inventory* (PEDI) (Haley, Faas, Coster, Webster, & Gans, 1989) provides a structure from which to conduct a motor outcomes evaluation. It is designed to measure child ability as well as the extent of caregiver assistance and environmental modification required for skill performance. The PEDI covers basic feeding, grooming and bathing, dressing, and toileting skills in the area of self-care. Mobility includes transfers and locomotion. The final section, social function, addresses communication, social interaction, and daily routines. Interventionists can use results of the evaluation to establish programming goals for the child.

Perceptual–Motor Tests

During the 1960s and 1970s a number of instruments based upon the theoretical perspective that a relationship exists between perceptual–motor ability and academic achievement were published. The relationship of perceptual–motor ability to academic achievement has not, however, been substantiated. These instruments can measure perceptual–motor ability, but should not be used to develop a remediation plan to improve academic achievement. The *Sensory Integration and Praxis Tests* (Ayres, 1987) are updated versions of a battery of tests based on Ayres's sensorimotor integration theory and are intended for children from 4 to 8 years of age. The battery includes 17 separate tests: space visualization, figure–ground perception, standing and walking balance, design copying, postural praxis, motor accuracy, kinesthesia, manual form perception, finger identification, graphesthesia, localization of tactile stimuli, sequencing praxis, oral praxis, praxis on verbal command, constructional praxis, postrotary nystagmus, and bilateral motor coordination. The *Developmental Test of Visual–Motor Integration* (Beery & Buktenica, 1982) has both a short form (for ages 2 to 8) and a longer form (for ages 2 to 18). The tests contain geometric figures that the examiner presents individually to the child to be copied. Each drawing is scored on a simple pass–fail basis.

Assessment of Auditory and Visual Abilities

The assessment of a child's hearing is usually conducted by an audiologist, and results are plotted on an audiogram. The audiogram is a graph depicting intensity of sound, or loudness (measured in decibels), and frequency of sound, or pitch (measured in hertz). A sample audiogram is presented in Figure 11.1. A child's hearing in each ear is plotted on the audiogram, and impairments can be noted by the audiologist. The most important sound range is between 500 and 2000 hertz. One system used in classifying the severity of a hearing loss is based on the loudness required for the child to hear. Losses in the 27 to 40 decibel range are considered mild, the 41 to 55 range is considered moderate, the 56 to 70 range is moderately severe, 71 to 90 is severe, and 91 and greater is a profound hearing loss. For a hard-to-test infant or young child, hearing acuity can be assessed using the *brainstem-evoked response,* which measures sensory functioning in the subcortical portions of the auditory pathway, providing an objective measure of peripheral and brainstem auditory acuity (Ensher & Clark, 1986).

Visual ability is measured by an ophthalmologist or optometrist. The *Snellen Chart* is frequently used to screen for visual acuity of distance vision. It has rows of letters or pictures (for young children) descending from very large to very small print. The classification of each row is a ratio (e.g., 20/20, 20/60). The first number depicts the distance a child stands from the chart and the second number is the distance from which a person with normal vision can read the letters or symbols. Vision of 20/20 is considered normal. A child who at a distance of 20 feet is only able to read the letters that can be read at 60 feet by a child with normal vision is considered to have 20/60 vision. Diagnosis of visual problems other than distance vision, such as near-point acuity, muscle imbalance, limited field of vision, color perception, and visual processing, requires specialized equipment.

The assessment of visual acuity of children with some disabilities may require alternatives, such as the *Washer Visual Acuity Screening Technique* (Washer, 1984), which examiners can use with children with a mental age of 2.5 and older. There is a preassessment training period during which the child becomes familiar with tasks he is asked to perform during the assessment (e.g., matching skills and eye occlusion). The test requires minimal motor or perceptual skills and no verbal skills.

The *Erhardt Developmental Visual Assessment* (Erhardt, 1986) assesses visual–motor functioning of children with multiple handicaps (with the exception of low vision or blindness). There are 424 items organized into two sections: involuntary visual patterns and voluntary eye movements. Performance on the test can deter-

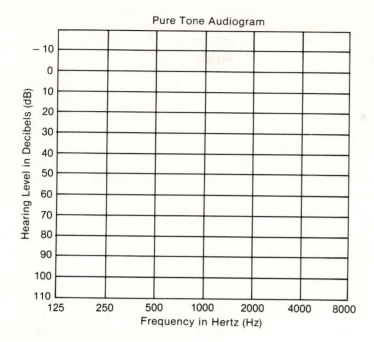

Figure 11.1. Sample Audiogram

mine developmental levels, important gaps, and present competencies. It is appropriate for children from birth to 5 years of age.

To plan intervention strategies for young children with visual impairments, interventionists assess their *functional vision* as well as the diagnostic information. Functional vision is the vision that a child is currently able to use in daily activities. The *Functional Vision Inventory for the Multiple and Severely Handicapped* (Langley, 1980) can be used for such an assessment. It covers seven basic areas of visual functioning: structural defects and behavioral abnormalities, reflexive reactions, eye movements, near vision, distance vision, visual field preference, and visual perception. An abbreviated version, which includes 12 items from the complete battery, can provide a quick look at a child's functional vision. It includes items such as blinks at shadow of hand, reaches for visual cue, and tracking—horizontally, vertically, and circularly.

SUMMARY

Included in this chapter was information covering both the motor domain and the senses. The information obtained from the senses is used to plan and direct motor movements. Movements are the primary conduit of cognitive activity. The motor domain encompasses a wide array of related terms, such as perceptual–motor functioning, sensorimotor integration, and psychomotor development. The chapter included definitions of these as well as primitive reflexes and patterns of motor development. Factors related to muscle tone and strength were also covered.

Theories of motor development address how motor skills progress as well as the relationship between motor development and development across other domains, particularly cognition. The Phases of Motor Development Model is a basic theoretical model focusing on the emergence of motor skills during early childhood. Neurodevelopmental theory, which forms the basis for neurodevelopmental treatment for infants and young children with motor impairments, is focused on the integration of primitive reflexes and the encouragement of normal voluntary movement patterns. A second theory, sensorimotor integration theory, was originally aimed at improved academic functioning of learning disabled children and has not been clearly established as an effective intervention technique.

The chapter contained a brief review of normal sensory development, including vision, audition, the gustatory and olfactory sensory systems, as well as the vestibular system—sometimes considered the sixth sense. Early motor development and abnormal motor development were reviewed, including a section on the effects of sensory impairments on motor development.

The final portion of the chapter focused on techniques of assessment. The procedures and instruments related to motor assessment were organized into four primary clusters: developmental assessments, neurodevelopmental assessments, motor outcomes assessment, and perceptual–motor tests. Assessment procedures available to assess auditory and visual abilities were also covered.

THE ECOLOGICAL PERSPECTIVE

- The senses provide a window to the world. People can interact only with those aspects of the environment that they can sense and perceive.
- People can communicate their cognitive knowledge only to the extent that they can employ purposeful movement in response to sensory input.
- Adaptation of the environment can increase the sensory stimulation that a child experiences.
- A child may have a secondary motor delay due to sensory impairment or deprivation. Such a delay is not indicative of motor impairment, but does suggest a need for intervention in motor development.
- Value placed on motor performance in a child's family or the surrounding community will influence the significance of motor delays or impairments, in turn influencing self-worth of the child.

CHAPTER 12

Social and Emotional Development and Adaptive Behavior

CHAPTER OUTLINE

QUESTIONS ANSWERED IN CHAPTER 12

- What is the significance of the development of attachment?
- How does the self develop?
- What patterns are seen in the development of emotions?
- How does development of play occur within a social context?
- How do adaptive and self-care behaviors develop?
- What are some theories of social and emotional development?
- What procedures for assessing social and emotional functioning can be used with young children?
- What procedures for assessing self-care skills are appropriate for young children?

- What research-based techniques can be applied to the assessment of mastery motivation for program planning?

CHAPTER OVERVIEW

The range of behaviors encompassed in the social and emotional domain of developmental is wide. A survey of multidomain assessment instruments that purport to measure social skills and/or emotional development provides evidence of this range. Some instruments focus on the child's interactions with other children and adults, some look at the child's ability to play, some look at self-esteem, and others contain items related to the child's skills in self-care. Broadly defined, the social and emotional domain involves the development of attachment, individuation (growth of self), emergence of emotions, and development of adaptive behaviors, including self-care skills.

SOCIAL AND EMOTIONAL DEVELOPMENT

Attachment and Emotional Development

Attachment, as defined by Sroufe (1979), is "an enduring affective tie between infant and caregiver" (p. 495). As a newborn, an infant displays indiscriminate attachment because she enjoys being handled by many people, although there is evidence that she can differentiate her primary caregiver as early as 5 weeks of age (Lewis, 1987). Around 5 months, however, an infant shows a strong preference for her primary caregiver and a rejection of others. The primary caregiver is visually tracked, receives more smiles, causes more distress when absent, and creates more pleasure when she picks up the child than others. Attachments then become established with other secondary caregivers and family members, followed by attachments to others with whom the child has contact. The failure of an infant to develop an attachment results in substantial affective impairments, as seen in the child with infantile autism. Variations in childrearing practices across differing cultures (e.g., communal care of all infants) do raise some questions as to the universality of this attachment sequence, but do not negate the need for enduring stable affective bonds as a precursor to healthy emotional development, as well as cognitive functioning (Lewis, 1987).

A child's future social and emotional development do not rest solely on his secure attachment to a single caregiver. A child raised in isolation who is securely attached to his mother will have difficulty in peer relations, whereas peer relations can be helpful in offsetting inadequate primary caregiver attachment relationships. However, maternal attachment problems may interfere with the development of compensating peer relationships for two reasons. First, mothers who fail to encourage secure infant attachments may also prevent the child from having peer experiences. Second, poor mothering, which results in poor attachment relationships, can produce a general fearfulness, in turn, affecting the child's ability to relate to his peers.

Child characteristics can influence relationships as well. Infants and children exhibit differential patterns of behavior in temperament, readability, and behavior (Huntington, 1988), which affect caregiver behavior. *Temperament* is the behavioral style of the individual child, focusing on how she behaves rather than what she is doing or why she is doing it. It refers to a cluster of characteristics including activity level, rhythmicity, approach and withdrawal, adaptability, intensity of reaction, quality of mood, distractibility, sensory threshold of responsiveness, attention span, and persistence (Thomas & Chess, 1977; Thomas, Chess, & Birch, 1968). Through a longitudinal study, Thomas and Chess identified three clusters of temperament characteristics related to the presence or absence of behavior disorders in later childhood. These clusters are as follows:

- *The difficult child:* arrhythmic, withdrawing, nonadaptable, intense, and negative (more likely to develop psychiatric problems)
- *The slow-to-warm-up child:* inactive, withdrawing, nonadaptable, mild, and negative (more likely to exhibit reactive disorders)
- *The easy child:* regular, approaching, adaptable, mild, and positive (not likely to develop behavioral problems)

A few studies have produced results that indicate that children with cognitive impairments combined with difficult temperaments are at particularly high risk of developing behavioral disturbances (Chess & Korn, 1970; Chess, Korn, & Fernandez, 1971). Other studies have correlated temperament with the type of disability a child has and the environmental context in which assessment of temperament characteristics was conducted (McDevitt, 1988). Infants with disabilities may be at a higher risk for demonstrating the characteristics of the "difficult" child. The child may have an impaired ability to respond to the environment and, therefore, characteristics such as activity level, distractibility, persistence, and sensory threshold are influenced by the disabling condition, not just natural temperament. While the child's temperament might not be that of a "difficult" child, he may function as one due to his physical limitations.

Readability is the second child characteristic influencing interactions. It relates to the child's ability to provide caregivers with distinct signals and cues through overt behaviors. The difficulty that parents of infants with disabilities experience in understanding and responding to unclear cues can result in parental feelings of incompetence (Bailey & Wolery, 1984; McCollum & Stayton, 1985; Yoder, 1987). However, lack of appropriate parental response can reduce the infant's understanding of cause and effect or her ability to interact with her environment effectively. Both parental feelings of incompetence and infant feelings of helplessness influence the others' behavior in a reciprocal relationship.

The third domain of child characteristics is *behavior*. While the elements of this domain overlap with temperament or readability and/or move into the realm of child functioning, it does include some child characteristics that might otherwise be overlooked. For example, certain characteristics such as unusual caregiving demands can increase parental stress and therefore affect the relationship. All new parents experience some stress as they begin feeding their infant solid foods—what to feed the child; how thick to mix the cereal; how much to give him; what to do if he spits it out; how to be certain he is getting enough to eat; and so forth. Add to this normal situation an abnormal gag reflex, an inability to control muscles in the oral cavity, and an asymmetrical tonic neck reflex, which makes feeding from the midline a greater challenge.

The *development of self* for an infant involves a knowledge of where she begins and ends. The first indication of the development of a self-concept is the social smile, which appears by 2 months of age. The awareness of self as a separate being is an essential prerequisite to social development and the establishment of relationships. There are two components in the process of individuation (Lewis, 1987). First, the infant becomes aware of her existential self, which involves an understanding of self-permanence similar to the conceptual development of object permanence. Second, the infant establishes a categorical self, that is, the way she understands herself (e.g., gender, age, competence, and value).

Between birth and 3 years of age there are five periods in the growth of the self. The period between 0 to 3 months is one primarily controlled by biological needs and reflexes. The infant's responses and reflexive actions stimulate interactions with his caregivers. Through the infant's social and object interactions self-differentiation may begin toward the end of the period. Between 3 and 8 months active learning replaces reflex patterns as cause–effect relationships are developing. Reflected images of the infant are interesting to himself because of the mirrored actions when he moves. During the 8- to 12-month period the infant can stop and think before acting on a stimulus (i.e., response inhibition). Self-other differentiation is established, resulting in the understanding of self across different situations (i.e., conservation of self). The infant's ability to maintain his identity independent of the setting, persons, or interactions occurring emerges between 8 and 9 months of age. The awareness of the permanence of self leads the way to object permanence and more complex means–end relationships. Between 12 and 18 months the child becomes self-conscious, showing embarrassment in front of a mirror if self-recognition is shown. Fear of loss of the mother intensifies as self-other differentiation increases. The child points himself out in a picture or in a mirror, using feature analysis rather than mirrored actions as the cue. Language reveals that during the 18- to 30-month period the infant has self-knowledge, such as his gender, age, and goodness or badness. He responds to his own name and can use his own name to refer to himself.

The *development of emotions* must be inferred from an infant's behavioral responses to social and object interactions. However, there is a basic assumption that no true emotions exist until self-differentiation has begun. Based on Bridges's (1932) classic work on the infant's differentiation of emotions and other more recent research, Sroufe (1979) developed a theoretical view of affect development, involving an eight-stage sequence. These stages are similar to but more specific than a five-stage social development model described by Sander (1969) and are intentionally parallel to the cognitive stages of development defined by Piaget. The stages associated with specific emotional reactions represent an approximate age at which the emotion is a common behavior, not necessarily when it first appears, nor when it is at its peak occurrence.

> *Stage One: 0 to 1 month.* There is an *absolute stimulus barrier* during the first month that provides built-in protection for the newborn. Infants are generally safe from external stimulation.
>
> *Stage Two: 1 to 3 months.* The infant becomes vulnerable as she begins *turning toward* stimulation and becomes oriented to the outside world. It is during this stage that the exogenous (social) smile appears.
>
> *Stage Three: 3 to 6 months. Positive affect* becomes possible since the infant now has the capacity for awareness and anticipation. This ability can also cause frustration and negative emotions, such as rage and wariness. The infant can actively attempt to avoid noxious stimulation and can laugh when vigorously stimulated.
>
> *Stage Four: 6 to 9 months.* This stage involves *active participation,* engagement, and mastery by the infant. He is aware of his emotions, including joy, fear, anger, and surprise. He will initiate interactions with his caregiver and intentionally act on objects in the environment to create his own pleasure.
>
> *Stage Five: 9 to 12 months. Attachment* to the primary caregiver is the preoccupation of the infant during this stage, as she is the predominate source of security. Emotional reactions are further differentiated and refined, and some coping functions emerge.
>
> *Stage Six: 12 to 18 months.* During this *practicing phase* the infant establishes a balance between attachment and exploration. The child is busy actively exploring and mastering his environment, which creates a sense of confidence and well-being. However, it is accompanied by an awareness of separateness from the caregiver.
>
> *Stage Seven: 18 to 36 months. Formation of self-concept* is the task of the infant during this stage. Balancing a sense of self-awareness with the anxiety felt toward separation and the increasing awareness of limited power is the task of 2-year-olds.
>
> *Stage Eight: Preschool years.* The resolution of self-identity is achieved through *play and fantasy.*

The emotional reactions associated with each stage are presented in Table 12.1.

Play and Social Interactions

The social or emotional status of a child is often determined by observing that child at play. The interaction of the child's growing self-awareness, cognitive understanding of objects in the environment, and attachment to and investment in caregivers enables the child to begin playing. Parten's (1932) classification system for play has become the foundation for understanding a child's social participation with her peers. She identified the following developmental sequence of social play: unoccupied behavior, onlooker behavior, solitary play, parallel play, associative play, and organized supplementary play (commonly referred to as cooperative play). Since

TABLE 12.1. Development of Emotions

Emotional Reactions	Stage of Affective Development							
	One	Two	Three	Four	Five	Six	Seven	Eight
Pleasure–Joy								
Endogenous smile	X							
Turning toward		X						
Pleasure			X					
Delight			X					
Active laughter			X					
Joy				X				
Elation						X		
Positive valuation of self-affection							X	
Pride, love								X
Wariness–Fear								
Startle, pain	X							
Obligatory attention		X						
Wariness			X					
Fear (stranger aversion)					X			
Anxiety						X		
Immediate fear						X		
Shame							X	
Rage–Anger								
Distress (due to covering the face, physical restraint, extreme discomfort)	X							
Rage (disappointment)			X					
Anger				X				
Angry mood, petulance						X		
Defiance							X	
Intentional hurting							X	
Guilt								X

her classifications are dated and based on a small number of children, these descriptions may not accurately represent the characteristics of social play of preschool-age children today. Solitary play is often a constructive, self-directed form of play seen simultaneously with other more advanced stages of social play and should not be automatically interpreted as a lack of social maturity. Researchers have also noted that the parallel play of preschool-age children does not diminish as they mature, casting additional doubt over the sequential nature of Parten's classifications (Rogers, 1982). The classification system is more useful when considered as a description of various types of social participation in young children, rather than as a developmental continuum.

Other classifications of play include a categorical system (Smilansky, 1968) and the identification of modes of play (Sutton-Smith, 1970). Using these and other resources on play, Bailey and Wolery (1984) described a sequence of play development across four types of play for children between the ages of 12 and 60 months. *Exploration/manipulation* begins with sensorimotor/perceptual exploration through touching, looking, banging, tasting, putting in and taking out. As the toddler matures, wider exploration, such as field trips, becomes meaningful. Initial *construction play* involves simple towers made with blocks and expands to include making simple puzzles, working with clay, block building, and so forth. Later construction play is more complex and includes an element of self-criticism not seen in the younger child. *Dramatics,* the third type of play, begins with imitation of adult routines and soon includes doll play. As children mature, they enjoy imitating more complex adult roles and incorporate props and costumes into their play. Play with puppets is another dramatic activity children will begin to engage in between 36 and 48 months. Dramatics eventually becomes a social activity, involving cooperative play as children negotiate parts and scripts. *Games* begin simply, such as peek-a-boo, and gradually expand to include storytelling and rhyming games. By age 5, the child can participate in simple board games, hunts for missing objects, hide-and-seek, and other simple games.

Wehman (1977) identified hierarchies of exploratory and toy play appropriate for assessment of and intervention with severely or profoundly retarded young children. The four levels of exploratory play are (1) orientational responses, (2) locomotor exploration, (3) perceptual investigation and manipulation (i.e., examination of an object), and (4) searching (i.e., seeking new stimuli for exploration). Bailey and Wolery (1984) have organized Wehman's nine levels of toy play into the following six levels: (1) repetitive manual manipulations and oral contacts; (2) pounding, throwing, pushing, or pulling; (3) personalized toy use; (4) manipulation of movable parts of toys; (5) separation of parts of toys; and (6) combinational use of toys.

Adaptive Behavior and Self-Care Skills

Adaptive behavior is required in the physical, social, and emotional adjustment of a child to the environment. Physically, it involves such basic functions as eating, keeping warm, and avoiding danger. Socially related adaptive behaviors include communicating basic needs, cooperative play skills, and appropriate use of toys. Emotional adaptive behaviors involve the formation of relationships in a manner designed to preserve self-esteem and self-identity. Adaptive behaviors range from the primitive sucking reflex of the newborn to the complex skills involved in maintaining a home, having a job, paying bills, raising a family, and other behavioral expectations of adults.

Coping is the process of learning to use adaptive behaviors to function in the world. For the young child, coping behaviors center on nutrition, security, and a combination of activity and rest, coupled with an opportunity to pursue individual interests, motivations, and satisfy the drive to achieve mastery (Zeitlin, Williamson, & Szczepanski, 1988). Children can develop *maladaptive* or *adaptive coping styles,* which influence their effectiveness in meeting their physical, social, and emotional needs. For example, a child when initially placed in a car seat begins to cry. The caregiver soothes the child and offers him a few toys, and the child is soon distracted from crying. After a few trips in the car seat, the child no longer cries but does reach out and gesture to indicate his desire for the usual car seat toys. This

child has adjusted to the expectation that he remain in the car seat and is using an adaptive coping style. Another child who screams upon being placed in the car seat, refusing all efforts to be comforted and throwing away all of the toys that are offered, is demonstrating a maladaptive coping style. His maladaptive behavior could result in his being removed from the car seat, thus increasing his risk of injury during an accident and breaking the law in many states. If allowed to remain in the car seat, he will, at the least, increase the stress of the driver and all others present in the car. Eventually this maladaptive behavior could result in his never being taken on any unnecessary trips in the car, thus reducing his opportunities to learn about and explore the environment.

A significant component of adaptive behavior is the development of *self-care skills*. For the young child, these involve the basic skills involved in eating, dressing, toileting, and basic grooming skills (e.g., handwashing, face washing, toothbrushing, and nasal hygiene). The general developmental sequence of eating, toileting, and dressing skills for the normal child can be used in developmental assessments.

Mastery Motivation

The motivation that a young child exhibits as she attempts to learn new skills will directly influence her opportunity for development. For the child who lacks the motivation to engage in an activity, there will be few chances for her to gain new skills. Therefore, knowledge about a child's motivation to master tasks is a critical component of assessment for planning intervention. Motivation may be influenced by physical factors, such as motor impairments that increase the difficulty of even simple tasks, social factors, such as peer accomplishments, and emotional factors, including the interactive patterns of primary caregivers with the child. Gaensbauer, Mrazek, and Harmon (1981) described a study in which the free play of abused, neglected, and normal infants was compared. The normal infants displayed more persistence in play than either the abused or neglected infants. The neglected children demonstrated disinterest in the toys, while the abused infants explored the room and the toys in a disorganized and destructive manner.

Research that compared the mastery motivation of preschool-age children with physical disabilities (e.g., cerebral palsy and spina bifida) to that of nondisabled children incorporated structured tasks, free play, and mothers' perceptions (Jennings, Connors, Stegman, Sankaranarayan, & Mendelsohn, 1985). Structured tasks were used to assess persistence at difficult tasks and curiosity. Free play was observed to assess attention span, complexity of play, the degree of involvement, and the level of social participation. Mothers' perceptions included measurement of (1) general mastery motivation, (2) preference for easy and familiar tasks, (3) need for adult help or approval, (4) need for adult structure, and (5) resistance to adult direction. Differences in the development of mastery motivation were found between the two groups. The children with physical disabilities demonstrated less motivation, particularly in the free play time when the children were expected to structure their own activities. Even during the adult-structured activities, they showed less persistence on difficult tasks. Likewise, the mothers of the children with physical disabilities reported that their children were more dependent, frequently seeking adult help and approval. However, the presence of a handicapping condition did not alter curiosity. These findings are consistent with the theoretical assumption that children with orthopedic impairments are faced with more failure in their attempts to perform tasks independently and must rely on adults to direct their play.

Implications for interventionists and parents center on the need to facilitate child-initiated free play activities, rather than to always present adult-structured play opportunities. Environmental needs and proper programming techniques can be better anticipated after observing a child's task-directed behavior during free play situations. [For further reading on mastery motivation and its integration into early intervention programming see the July 1990 issue of *Early Education and Development* (vol. 1, no. 5).]

PROCEDURES FOR ASSESSMENT

Attachment and Emotional Development

The observation of frequencies and/or duration of specific behaviors within a timed sampling has proved unsuccessful as a reliable measure of the amount or strength of attachment. However, the quality of attachment from assessment of the attachment–exploration balance and the child's ability to seek and obtain comfort when distressed can be noted (Sroufe, 1979). For example, the securely attached 12-month-old, accompanied by her caregiver, in an unfamiliar location will become interested in available toys and objects. After the child leaves the caregiver's side to go exploring, he will occasionally reestablish contact, by briefly moving back for physical contact, returning to give the caregiver a toy, visually noting the caregiver's continued presence. How the child behaves in the presence of a stranger or when left by the caregiver with a stranger can also indicate secure and insecure attachment patterns. While specific adaptive behaviors are somewhat individualistic and fall in a wide range of signs of distress, timidity and wariness, resistance to contact, and contact seeking, the securely attached infant is capable of seeking comfort when distressed and maintaining contact until comforted. Infants who show resistance to contact with the caregiver following distress are demonstrating one of the maladaptive patterns of attachment. Other maladaptive patterns involve ambivalence (i.e., contact seeking coupled with resistance to contact—squirming to get down and pushing away), passivity (i.e., crying unaccompanied by actively seeking contact), and avoidance of the caregiver, which may be accompanied by ambivalent proximity-seeking behavior.

The *Ainsworth Strange Situation Procedure* (Ainsworth, Blehar, Waters, & Wall, 1978; Teti & Nakagawa, 1990) is useful in the assessment of attachment relationships of children between the ages of 10 and 24 months. The procedure involves eight episodes over a 22- to 24-minute period, during which time the infant, the primary caregiver (or other attached adult), and an unfamiliar person proceed through structured episodes in a laboratory setting (with age-appropriate toys). Each episode lasts 3 minutes (or less if the child is in extreme distress and cannot be comforted) and involves participants as indicated in the following chart:

Participant	Episode							
	1	2	3	4	5	6	7	8
Infant	X	X	X	X	X	X	X	X
Caregiver	X	X	X		X			X
Observer	X							
Stranger			X	X			X	

Infant behavior during episodes 2 through 8 is rated on six dimensions, using a seven-point scale: (1) proximity- and contact-seeking behavior, (2) contact-maintaining behavior, (3) resistant behavior, (4) avoidant behavior, (5) distance interaction, and (6) search behavior during separations. The observer can then analyze infant behaviors as to the patterns of attachment that the child displayed. Extensive research validating the Ainsworth Strange Situation Procedure as useful in the assessment of attachment has been summarized by Teti and Nakagawa (1990). Since the procedure is based on the assumption that the child has established person-permanence, it is not appropriate for cognitively delayed children who have not obtained that concept. Otherwise it can be adapted for children with disabilities, although no validation studies using children with disabilities have been reported in the literature (Teti & Nakagawa, 1990).

This procedure should not be used in isolation as a single measure of an individual child's emotional functioning, but rather can be useful as one part of an assessment plan. First, many factors within the child (e.g., hunger and illness) and the setting (e.g., time of day and physical appearance of the stranger) can affect an individual child's response patterns. Second, dysfunctional attachments of younger children are not always apparent using this procedure, because the influence of poor caregiving increases as the child matures.

The Ainsworth Strange Situation Procedure has been extended in a clinical assessment system developed by Lieberman and Pawl (1988). This system includes a measure of how attachment develops, as well as present attachment behaviors, and can be used with children up to 4 years of age. It is based on the following three identified categories of attachment disorders with associated characteristic behaviors.

Category of Disorder	Characteristic Behaviors
• Nonattachment (no consistent caregiver was available for attachment)	Cognitive and language delays Low frustration tolerance Inability to regulate aggressive impulses Unable to form emotionally satisfying relationships when older
• Anxious, ambivalent attachment	Recklessness and accident proneness Inhibition of exploration Precocious competence in self-protection
• Disrupted attachment	Extreme separation anxiety Inability to form trusting relationships

Reliability of this classification system remains to be verified, but the instrument does offer information about a child's attachment not available through the strange situation procedure.

The *Attachment Q-Set* (Waters & Deane, 1985), a research instrument designed to measure secure base behaviors in the home, contains 90 behavioral descriptors that are sorted into nine groups with 10 descriptors in each. The groups represent a range from "very much like the child" to "very much unlike the child." The results of the sorting are compared with average sorting scores, which are based on opinions of attachment experts as to how a hypothetical "most secure child" behaves. A correlation coefficient can be used to compare a child's score with the hypothetical secure child. A high correlation would be indicative of a similarity in secure base behavior between the real and hypothetical children. The correlation can be transformed into a z score, yielding a security score. Since validity studies support the use of the Q-Set as a measure of attachment and it is relatively easy to administer, it has potential to become a useful clinical instrument.

The *Greenspan-Lieberman Observation System for Assessment of Caregiver–Infant Interaction during Semi-Structured Play* (GLOS) (Greenspan, Lieberman, & Poisson, 1981; Greenspan & Lieberman, 1988) might also be useful in clinical assessments. It provides a structured coding system of infant and caregiver behaviors, which is intended for use with videotapes. Further description of the Attachment Q-Set and GLOS is provided by Teti and Nakagawa (1990).

Play and Social Interactions

Social interactions and play skills can be assessed through naturalistic observations, rating scales, sociometric nominations or ratings by peers, criterion-referenced assessments, and norm-referenced tests. The *Systematic Anecdotal Assessment of Social Interaction* (SAASI) system, developed by Odom, McConnell, Kohler, and Strain (1987), can be used to provide structure to anecdotal reporting. In this system, the teacher identifies one child to observe in interactions with her peers. A simple form that has rows of boxes can be used to record each social interaction in which the targeted child participates. The form can then be analyzed in terms of behaviors of interest (e.g., frequency of initiations of social interactions and aggressive behaviors toward peers). The *Observational Assessment of Reciprocal Social Interaction,* developed by McConnell, Sisson, and Sandler (1984), is a direct observation instrument based on an interval sampling system, which can measure initiation behaviors, response behaviors, summative behaviors, and teacher behaviors. Both of these instruments are described further by Odom and McConnell (1989).

The *Behavior Deviancy Profile* (Ball & Winberg, 1982) provides a structure for recording subjective impressions of individuals with social and emotional problems ages 3 to 21 to determine the degree of deviancy or disturbance. The child is rated on 236 behaviors organized into 18 categories of behavior, including physical growth, sensory perception, motor activity, intelligence, language, relationship with mother, and "ego-self" behavior. Based on his own expectations, the observer rates the child's behavior according to a scale from -3 to $+3$, with 0 indicating no deviancy. A lack of clear definitions and subjectivity of the instrument does require that results be interpreted with caution.

The *Scales of Socio-Emotional Development* (Lewis & Michalson, 1983) is an appropriate observational procedure for children from birth to 3 years of age. Emotional functioning of the child is assessed in various areas, including competence, happiness, affiliation, and fear. The *Direct Observation Form—Revised Edition* (Achenbach, 1986b) is another instrument that can provide structure to the observation of children between ages 4 to 16. After observing for 10-minute intervals, the observer records a narrative description of the child's behavior and rates the behaviors that occurred.

Rating scales have been developed that are designed to document behavioral characteristics of infants and young children with handicaps. Wing and Gould (1978) developed the *Children's Handicaps Behavior and Skills Schedule,* which includes assessment of both developmental skills and abnormalities of behavior. The *Carolina Record of Individual Behavior* (CRIB) (Simeonsson, Huntington, Short, & Ware, 1982) is designed to assess the child's level of arousal or state as well as eight developmntal behaviors, including social orientation, participation, motivation, endurance, receptive communication, expressive communication, object orientation, and consolability. The *Social Interaction Rating Scale* (Hops, Guild, Fleishman, Paine, Street, Walker, & Greenwood, 1979) includes eight behavioral descriptions (e.g., engages in long conversations) on which the child is rated on a seven-point scale from "not descriptive or true" to "very descriptive or true." It can be used with children in preschool and elementary school.

The *Behavioral Characteristics Progression* (BCP) developed by the Office of the Santa Cruz County Superintendent of Schools (1973) is a comprehensive criterion-referenced checklist with 2400 observable traits organized into 59 behavioral strands. These strands, which contain a hierarchy of approximately 50 items each, include a wide range of categories, such as attendance and promptness, feeding and eating, toileting, nasal hygiene, self-indentification, sensory perception, listening, adaptive behaviors, responsible behaviors, honesty, social eating, reasoning, homemaking skills, wheelchair use, and swimming. The instrument is designed so as to be useful in assessment for instructional planning and record keeping. Since the instrument is strictly criterion-referenced, it can be used with children of any age.

A brief checklist designed to determine a child's ability to function in an integrated setting (with nonhandicapped peers) based on social skills has been developed by Johnson and Mandell (1988). The *Social Observation for Mainstreamed Environments* (SOME) contains 15 items on which a child's performance and setting expectations are compared. Discrepancies are noted and resolutions developed. Samples of items included on the SOME are "plays well with others," "attends to tasks for short periods of time," and "practices turn taking." Guidelines for the instrument require that the child be observed across multiple settings (e.g., classroom, bus, and playground) during a variety of different types of activities (e.g., free play and teacher-directed activities) for a minimum of 10 minutes per observation, with a total observation time of approximately 50 minutes. The SOME can be useful in developing goals and objectives related to social development and in program planning for anticipated transitions.

The *Meadow–Kendall Social-Emotional Assessment Inventory for Deaf and Hearing Impaired Students* (Meadow, Getson, Lee, & Stamper, 1983) can be used to assess the social and emotional development of preschool-age children who are deaf and hearing impaired. The inventory produces scores related to sociable and communicative behaviors, impulsive dominating behaviors, developmental lags, anxious and compulsive behaviors, and special areas. Although the instrument needs further standardization and reliability and validity studies, it is a particularly needed instrument since it compares both hearing and hearing-impaired children.

Sociometric assessment procedures can be used to determine the social acceptance and social preference of children functioning within a group setting. *Peer nominations* for preferred and disliked playmates can be obtained from preschool-age children using pictures of children in the group. These nominations can be used to create four sociometric groups: (1) those with many positive and few negative nominations, (2) those who received very few nominations at all, (3) those who received primarily negative nominations, and (4) those with high numbers of both positive and negative nominations (Odom & McConnell, 1989). However, they caution that the use of negative nominations is controversial and could potentially have harmful effects on the children involved in the assessment. *Peer ratings* involve the qualitative rating of each child by each child with a Likert-type scale on various criteria of interest such as, "how much do you like to talk with _____?" A sum or average of all ratings can be used to obtain a sociometric rating score. For preschool-age children, the procedure can be modified so that pictures are sorted

into boxes that represent points on the Likert scale. Odom and McConnell offer a note of caution regarding the reliability of sociometric measures, particularly when used with preschool-age and younger children.

Another measure designed to be useful in the analysis of behavioral characteristics is the infant behavior record (IBR), which is the third part of the *Bayley Scales of Infant Development* (BSID) (Bayley, 1984). The IBR contains a series of descriptive behavioral rating scales for children up to 30 months of age. Areas covered on these scales include interpersonal and affective domains (i.e., social orientation, general emotional tone, and fearfulness), motivational variables (i.e., goal directedness, attention span, and endurance), and the child's interest in specific modes of sensory experience. The IBR standardization sample matched that for the MDI and PDI for children over 15 months of age. About one half of the children 15 months and younger were drawn from a different sample. The IBR is completed immediately following administration of the mental and motor scales, as the examiner rates the behavior exhibited during those tests. No additional items are administered. The child's ratings can be compared to characteristic behavioral descriptions by age provided in the manual. A table in the manual shows the range and mode of ratings for the standardization sample.

When assessing hyperaggressive preschool-age children, Landy and Peters (1990) recommend the inclusion of four components. First, the child should be assessed in regard to attachment disorders, neurologic and physiologic problems, difficulties with symbolization (e.g., use of language), and/or difficulties with impulse control and frustration tolerance. Second is the area of parent–child interactions, including aspects of the relationship such as parental use of positive reinforcement, parental response to negative behaviors, and sensitivity of the parent to child cues. The third area for assessment involves the parents and family. The personality structure of the parents and family dynamics within the home are considered. The final area covers social and environmental factors, such as socioeconomic level, housing, social supports, and educational level.

Adaptive Behavior and Self-Care Skills

The *Early Coping Inventory* (ECI) (Zeitlin, Williamson, & Szczepanski, 1988) measures the coping and adaptive behavior of children whose developmental functioning level falls within the range of 4 to 36 months. The inventory contains 48 items divided into three categories: sensorimotor organization (i.e., behaviors used to regulate psychophysiological functions and to integrate sensory and motor processes), reactive behavior (i.e., actions used to respond to the demands of physical and social environments), and self-initiated behavior (i.e., self-directed actions intended to meet personal needs and to interact with objects and people). Based on observations of the child, the examiner rates the child on a five-point scale according to the level of effectiveness, ranging from one (the behavior is not effective) to five (the behavior is consistently effective across situations). The manual provides numerous examples to clarify the rating scale, which is based on subjective judgment of the rater. There is also a caution in the manual about motor disability interfering with a child's ability to cope that should not be interpreted incorrectly. Raw scores on each of the scales are converted to effectiveness scores, which are used to compute the adaptive behavior index. Examiners can also create a coping profile for the child. Validity studies based on expert opinion, field-testing, and factor analysis are reported in the manual. Reliability studies using a test–retest procedure yielded interrater reliability coefficients ranging from .80 to .94. The manual also provides extensive review of procedures used to establish item reliability. The *Coping Inventory* (Zeitlin, 1985) has 48 items and can be used with children 3 through 16 years of age. The organization and administration is similar to that used in the ECI.

The *AAMD Adaptive Behavior Scale—School Edition* (Lambert, Windmiller, Tharinger, & Cole, 1981) is designed to measure an individual's personal independence and social responsibility. The instrument includes 21 domains and can be used with children from ages 3 to 16. The first 9 domains, which use a rating scale of dependence to independence, include independent functioning (i.e., eating, toileting, cleanliness, appearance, care of clothing, dressing and undressing, and travel), physical development (i.e., sensory and motor development), language development (i.e., expression, comprehension, and social language development), responsibility, and socialization. Domains 10 through 21, which comprise the second part of the scale, are rated according to the frequency with which a behavior occurs. This part covers behaviors such as aggressiveness, rebelliousness, trustworthiness, mannerisms, and interpersonal manners. Percentile ranks for each domain can be derived, and five clusters of functioning (i.e., personal self-sufficiency, community self-sufficiency, personal–social responsibility, social adjustment, and personal adjustment) can be used to analyze the child's functioning. The standardization group had a total of 6500 normal, mildly retarded, and moderately retarded children aged 3 to 16. Variables controlled for in the norming process were age, sex, classification of retardation, ethnic status, population density of residence, and socioeconomic status. Validity and reliability studies support the use of the instrument.

The *Vineland Adaptive Behavior Scales* (Sparrow, Balla, & Cicchetti, 1984) can be used with children from birth to 18 years 11 months. The classroom scale is specifically designed for children ages 3 to 12 years 11 months. Two other interview editions cover the other age ranges. All of the scales cover four adaptive behavior domains: communication (i.e., receptive, expressive, and written); daily living skills (i.e., personal, domestic, and community); socialization (i.e., interpersonal relationships, play and leisure time, and coping skills); and motor skills (i.e., gross and fine). Scoring produces standard scores for each domain and a composite score. The interview editions also include an optional maladaptive domain. Additional adaptive behavior instruments are summarized in the appendix to this chapter.

Mastery Motivation

There is a growing body of literature on the techniques used in research concerning the assessment of children's mastery motivation. While these techniques have been used predominantly in clinical research studies, they can be used to provide important information about specific children for interventionists as well.

> An assessment of mastery motivation delineates the developmental domains on which the child is focusing his energies as well as the persistence and effectiveness with which the child is working on each domain. (Brockman, Morgan, & Harmon, 1988, p. 270)

The four forms of mastery motivation assessment in use today are (1) the structured mastery-task situation, (2) parental reports of observed mastery behavior, (3) global ratings of goal directedness, and (4) the free play situation (Brockman, Morgan, & Harmon, 1988).

The objective in creating a *structured mastery-task situation* "is to elicit and to observe systematically the child's attempts to master challenging tasks" (Brockman, Morgan, & Harmon, 1988, p. 271). The role of the examiner is to observe carefully how much of the child's behavior is task-directed. *Task-directed behavior* is behavior related to trying to complete part of the task with no assistance. Whether or not the task is completed successfully is not particularly relevant. The structured mastery-task situation involves the use of mastery motivation tasks to determine an individual child's desire to master a given task. A developmental hierarchy of these tasks is presented in the following list (Brockman, Morgan, & Harmon, 1988).

I.   Exploration and Curiosity (5 months and older)
     Is the child motivated to explore all parts of the object, and will she maintain interest until exploration is completed?
     Measures of both the duration of persistence and the variety of behaviors should be recorded.
     Object should be complex enough to promote sustained exploration.
II. Persistence Tasks
     A.   Practicing an emerging skill—9 months
          (three overlapping categories)
          1.   Effect production tasks
               (e.g., cause–effect toys—busy box)
          2.   Combinatorial tasks
               (e.g., putting pegs in holes)
          3.   Means–ends tasks
               (e.g., getting toy from behind barrier)
     B.   Completing multipart task—15 months
          (two overlapping categories)
          1.   Combinatorial tasks
               (e.g., shape sorter and formboard)
          2.   Means–ends task
               (e.g., appropriate use of all parts of cash register)
III. Preference for Challenging Tasks—3 years
     Child is presented with a choice between a relatively hard and easy task (e.g., build a six-block tower or a two-block tower) and is asked which she wants to work on.

During the structured mastery-task situation, an examiner should observe two types of behavior: mastery pleasure and persistence. *Mastery pleasure* is related to the amount of positive affect the child displays while engaged in task-directed behavior or upon completion of the task. *Persistence* is an indicator of the amount of time the child is working toward task solution.

An ecologically valid assessment of a child's motivation to master a task should include data gathering in regard to the *parent's perceptions* of the child's mastery motivation. The *Dimensions of Mastery Questionnaire* (DMQ) (Morgan, Maslin, Jennings, & Busch-Rossnagel, 1988) is intended to be used to gather such data. It can be used to assess parents' perceptions of the mastery behaviors a child displays including (1) general persistence, (2) mastery pleasure, (3) independent mastery during challenging play, and (4) competence. The DMQ also elicits ratings of a child's persistence at five specific types of play: (1) gross motor, (2) combinatorial (3) means–ends, (4) symbolic, and (5) social.

For a *global rating of goal directedness,* Maslin and Morgan (1984) developed a scale that can be used in conjunction with BSID. It offers a guide to assessing purposeful activity exhibited by the child while he is being tested. The emphasis is on the child's persistence in seeking to perform the task successfully independent of adult encouragement or coaxing. The rating scale is presented in the following list.

1. No evidence of directed effort or purposeful activity
2. Makes an occasional attempt at goal-directed action but does not repeat attempts
3. Makes some attempts to attain a goal with some repetition but does not show interest in carrying attempts to completion
4. Attempts at goals are more frequent but generally lack sustained persistence; does not continue if initial attempt fails
5. Usually makes an initial attempt to attain a goal and shows some repetition of efforts; however, quits fairly soon if not successful
6. Makes initial attempts to attain goals with moderate persistence; however, gives up if task requires repeated efforts; usually does not repeat solution of tasks
7. Initial attempts are followed by moderate-to-high persistence, even if task is somewhat difficult; repeats solutions of some tasks
8. Persistence in attaining goals is high, even when task is challenging, but without the marked absorption that characterizes a score of 9; often repeats solutions of tasks
9. Very high absorption in task; willingly repeats solutions of tasks, stays with tasks until they are solved even if they are very difficult; practices tasks until they are thoroughly mastered

The determination of a child's *task-directed behavior during free play* can assist early interventionists in identifying children who may lack mastery motivation. Scoring systems that can be used during nonstructured free play times are being used for research purposes (Glicken, Couchman, & Harmon, 1981; Harmon, Glicken, & Couchman, 1981; Morgan, Harmon, & Bennett, 1976). These scoring systems can also be used by an interventionist who is attempting to design appropriately interesting activities for children.

SUMMARY

This chapter covered the areas of social and emotional development and adaptive behavior. The development of attachment is the initial task in the course of social and emotional development. Attachment can be influenced by parental and environmental characteristics. Child characteristics that can influence attachments are temperament, readability, and behavior. The difficult child or child whose disability results in the caregiver being unable to interpret her signals may face a greater challenge in establishing normal attachment patterns. Concurrently emerging with the development of attachment is the development of the self. The child moves from the newborn state to a gradual understanding of her separateness from her mother to a full realization of her own identity. The infant is also expanding her range of emotional experiences, so that by the time the child reaches preschool age she has a wide range of affective responses. The infant grows in her ability to play and engage in social interactions. She expands the types of play and broadens the nature of her social interactions as she matures. Adaptive behavior and the development of self-care skills accompany social and emotional development. The child grows in her ability to cope with tasks confronting her. She adapts and develops skills as she strives for independence and freedom within a secure environment. The child's motivation to master tasks is a reflection of the interactive effects of social and emotional, physical, and cognitive development that the child has experienced.

Techniques that can be used in the assessment of social and emotional development reflect the goals of the assessment. Investigation of an infant's attachment to a primary caregiver is accomplished through structured observations of infant–caregiver interactions. Assessment of a child's play and social interactions can involve observations, rating scales, sociometric procedures, criterion-referenced assessments, and norm-referenced tests. Adaptive behavior is measured through naturalistic and structured observations, parent report, and criterion-referenced and norm-referenced instruments. Mastery motivation can be measured through observation of structured situations, parental report, global ratings during assessment, and observation during free play.

THE ECOLOGICAL PERSPECTIVE

- Social and emotional development occurs within the environment of the child.
- Social and emotional development is grounded in the attachment pattern of the infant and caregiver(s).
- A cycle of effects are reflected in the child's mastery motivation, which can foster or limit future achievement.
- Adaptive behavior and self-care are related to the encouragement and freedom provided in the environment as influenced by and influencing the child's cognitive and motor abilities.
- The reasons for poor performance in any domain may reside in issues associated with the social and emotional domain.

APPENDIX

INSTRUMENTS TO ASSESS ADAPTIVE BEHAVIOR

Title: Adaptive Behavior Inventory for Children (ABIC)
Source: Mercer, J. R., & Lewis, J. F. (1978). The Psychological Corporation, 55 Academic Court, P.O. Box 839954, San Antonio, TX 78283.
Age Range: 5 years through 11 years
Description: The ABIC was originally developed as a part of the System of Multicultural Pluralistic Assessment (SOMPA). It uses the role expectations of the family, peer group, school, and community as a basis from which to measure a child's functioning. The parent or most knowledgeable adult responsible for the child is asked questions about how the child functions in six areas: family, community, peer relations, nonacademic school rules,

earner and consumer, and self-maintenance. Scaled scores for each of these areas and an overall average scaled score can be obtained. If the child falls below the third percentile, he is considered to be at-risk.

Soundness:
> *Standardization:* Norms are based on interviews with 1259 parents.
> *Reliability and Validity:* Reliability of the average scaled score is reported at .95 using split-half procedures.

Title: Adaptive Behavior Scale for Infants and Early Childhood
Source: Leland, H., Shoace, M., McElwain, D., & Christie, R. (1980). Ohio State University, Nisonger Center.
Age Range: Birth to 6 years
Description: The scale measures the child's ability to cope with environmental demands.

Title: Behavior Evaluation Scale-2
Source: McCarney, S. B., Leigh, J. E., & Cornbleet, J. (1990). Pro-Ed, 8700 Shoal Creek Boulevard, Austin, TX 78758.
Age Range: Grades K through 12
Description: The scale is used to screen for behavior problems, assist in the diagnosis of behavior disorders or emotional disturbance, and aid in program planning and program evaluation. Five subscales measure learning problems, interpersonal difficulties, inappropriate behavior, unhappiness and depression, and physical symptoms and fears. Frequency of occurrence of behaviors is rated by the child's teacher. These ratings are converted to percentile ranks, standard scores, *T*-scores, and stanine scores.

Soundness:
> *Standardization:* The norm group contained over 2200 students from more than 25 states. The demographic characteristics of the population approximated the population in terms of sex, residence, race, and occupational status of parents.
> *Reliability and Validity:* Both reliability and validity of the instrument are reported in the manual and appear to be acceptable, with test–retest coefficients generally exceeding .90.

Title: Behavior Problem Checklist—Modified Version for Preschoolers (BPC)
Source: Quay, H., & Peterson, D. R. (1983). original version published in *Journal of Abnormal Child Psychology,* 5(3), 277–287; revised version available from Herbert C. Quay.
Age Range: Grades 1 through 12
Description: The BPC can be used to identify the deviant behaviors of children through 56 items (modified version). Six factors can be identified: conduct (i.e., negativism, disruptiveness, destructiveness, impertinence, and fighting); personality (i.e., feelings of inferiority, shyness, lack of self-confidence, and anxiety); social withdrawal (i.e., social withdrawal, sluggishness, preoccupation, doesn't have fun, and aloofness); attention seeking (i.e., attention seeking, jealousy, and wanting help on things that should be done alone); hyperactivity (i.e., restlessness, hyperactivity, easily startled, tension, and rowdiness); and distractibility (i.e., distractibility, short attention span, and clumsiness).

Title: Child Behavior Checklist for Ages 4–16 (CBC)
Source: Child Behavior Checklist for Ages 4–16. Achenbach, T. M. (1981, 1986b). Burlington: University of Vermont.
Age Range: 4 through 16 years
Description: The CBC measures a child's competencies and problem areas, including assessments of domains such as depression, aggression, somatic complaints, and hyperactivity. The checklist, which has separate forms for each gender and is divided into three age brackets (i.e., 4 to 5, 6 to 11, 12 to 16), is completed by the parents (or self-administered

for older children). Another version of the CBC for children ages 2 to 3, which has 99 items, is also available (Achenbach, 1986a).

Title: Children's Adaptive Behavior Scale
Source: Children's Adaptive Behavior Scale. Richmond, B. O., & Kicklighter, R. H. (1980). Atlanta, GA: Humanics.
Age Range: 5 through 10 years
Description: This is a direct assessment instrument that covers five domains: language development, independent functioning, family role performance, economic–vocational activity, and socialization. Through questioning and observation of skill performance, the examiner can measure the adaptive behavior and skill development of mentally retarded children.

Title: Comprehensive Behavior Rating Scale for Children
Source: Neeper, R., & Lahey, B. B. (1988). The Psychological Corporation, 555 Academic Court, P.O. Box 839954, San Antonio, TX 78283.
Age Range: 6 through 14 years
Description: The five-point scale contains 81 descriptive statements on which a teacher can rate a child. These statements are organized into seven separate scales: inattention and disorganization, linguistic and information processing, conduct disorder, motor hyperactivity, anxiety and depression, sluggish tempo, and social competence.

Title: Assessment of Child Behavior Problems: The Validation of a New Inventory.
Source: Ross, A. W. (1978). *Journal of Clinical Child Psychology, 7,* 113–116; Robinson, E. A., Eyberg, S. M., & Ross, A. W. (1980). Inventory of child problem behaviors: The standardization of an inventory of child conduct problem behaviors, *Journal of Clinical Child Psychology, 9,* 23–29.
Age Range: 2 through 18 years
Description: Parents rate their child according to 36 behaviors on two scales: frequency (from never to always) and whether or not the behavior is currently a problem (yes or no). Examples of behaviors on the inventory are "dawdles in getting dressed," "refuses to go to bed on time," "hits parents," and "teases or provokes other children."

Title: Kohn Social Competence Scale—Research Edition
Source: Kohn, M. (1986). The Psychological Corporation, 555 Academic Court, P.O. Box 839954, San Antonio, TX 78283.
Age Range: Preschool and kindergarten age
Description: The scale measures social and emotional functioning. Teachers rate child functioning on 73 items for the child in a full-day program or 64 items for the child in a half-day program. The dimensions included are cooperative–compliant versus angry–defiant behavior and interest–participation versus apathetic–withdrawn behavior.

Title: Social-Emotional Dimension Scale
Source: Hutton, J. B., & Roberts, T. G. (1986). Pro-Ed, 8700 Shoal Creek Boulevard, Austin, TX 78758-6897.
Age Range: 5.5 through 18.5 years
Description: The scale contains 32 items, which identify inappropriate behaviors according to six areas: physical and fear reaction, depressive reaction, avoidance of peer interaction, avoidance of teacher interaction, aggressive interaction, and inappropriate behaviors.

PART FOUR

Accountability and Emerging Populations

Early childhood special educators are accountable to the populations they serve. This accountability necessitates that they evaluate the effectiveness of service delivery programs and that they have a clear understanding of the characteristics and needs of the population being served. To offer a traditional day care program to children who have been abused would lead to chaos. The children would likely be very aggressive toward one another, be unable to sustain play activities, and be destructive to toys and physical surroundings. A simple "time-out" approach for this misbehavior will not work. The children need a program designed to address their needs, not one that pretends the problems do not exist. A school-based preschool teacher cannot put a homeless child or child whose mother is a drug addict into her class and assume that the child can simply divorce herself from reality for the brief times she spends in her class.

Chapter 13 presents models of program evaluation and describes child assessment procedures useful in evaluation designs. Chapter 14 addresses some of the current issues and trends that have an impact on early intervention, such as drug-exposed babies, homelessness, and advancing technology.

Determining Program Effectiveness

CHAPTER OUTLINE

QUESTIONS ANSWERED IN CHAPTER 13

- What does program evaluation include?
- What models of evaluation are appropriate for early intervention?
- How can child assessment in program evaluation be used?
- How can progress for developmentally delayed children be evaluated?

CHAPTER OVERVIEW

Evaluation is the process through which the quality of a program is assessed. Accountability and the determination of efficacy of programming are essential elements in the evaluation process. Many variables need to be considered in a comprehensive program evaluation, such as child progress, achievement of stated outcomes for the child and the family, needs of the community, structural features of the program, parent satisfaction with the program, attitudes of the program staff toward the program, curricular components of the program, reputation of the program within the community, number of program graduates who remain in special education, and receipt of competitive funding. The focus of this chapter is limited to techniques of child assessment that are useful components of program evaluation. A brief review of models of evaluation useful in early intervention is followed by a discussion of procedures that can be used to determine a child's progress.

Program evaluation should be done not only for the entire program, but also for each individual child within the program. If half of the children in a program show dramatic gains while the other half fail to progress, the program could appear as a moderately effective one overall. This interpretation of the program's effectiveness is inaccurate, misleading, and would probably result in inappropriate recommendations and continued ineffective programming for half of the children while possibly reducing its effectiveness for the others.

ELEMENTS OF PROGRAM EVALUATION

The selection of an evaluation model is dependent on multiple factors, such as goals of the evaluation, program philosophy, and requirements of funding agencies. Wolery and Bailey (1984) identified the following seven questions as those that should be addressed as a part of a comprehensive evaluation.

1. Can the program demonstrate that the methods, materials, and overall service delivery represent the *best educational practice?*
2. Can the program demonstrate that the methods espoused in the overall philosophy are implemented accurately and consistently?
3. Can the program demonstrate that it attempts to verify empirically the effectiveness of interventions or other individual program components for which the best educational practice has yet to be verified?
4. Can the program demonstrate that it carefully monitors client progress and is sensitive to points at which changes in service need to be made?
5. Can the program demonstrate that a system is in place for determining the relative adequacy of client progress and service delivery?
6. Can the program demonstrate that it is moving toward the accomplishment of program goals/objectives?
7. Can the program demonstrate that the goals, methods and materials, and overall service delivery system are in accordance with the needs and values of the community and clients it serves? (pp. 28, 29)

Answers to these questions require multiple component evaluation designs, ranging from a review of the stated program philosophy to implementation of "best practices" in program design.

Child progress has been monitored in efficacy research to determine what programmatic features are the most effective. Programs vary greatly in terms of theoretical and philosophical perspectives, target populations, levels of comprehensiveness, funding, and resources. These variances impede the ability of researchers to draw all-encompassing conclusions about the characteristics of effective programs. Nevertheless, intervention program administrators must evaluate their effectiveness as accurately as possible, as well as review results of ongoing efficacy research. Program factors that have received the most attention in efficacy research are the following:

- Length of intervention
- Content of intervention (e.g., speech and language therapy as contrasted to programming designed for behavioral improvements)
- Home-based programs as compared with center-based programs
- Provision of support services
- Differing diagnoses and levels of severity
- Variance between biologically at-risk and environmentally at-risk children
- Functioning level upon program entry
- Child characteristics (e.g., motivation and temperament)
- Parent and family characteristics. (Dunst, Snyder, & Mankinen, 1989)

Persons engaged in program evaluation need to be cognizant of these factors so as to avoid narrowly based conclusions. For example, a program might be appropriate for a child, but because his attendance is so poor or because he is scheduled to come so infrequently it has little or no impact on his functioning. The program itself is not inappropriate, but structural features of the program prevent its effectiveness.

MODELS OF EVALUATION

A variety of educational evaluation models can be useful in the evaluation of early intervention. These models vary as to the emphasis placed on the stated goals of the program, the importance of planning and needs assessment, the role of the evaluator, the intended use of the data obtained, and procedures used in data gathering. Five types of evaluation models are (1) goal-attainment, (2) judgmental with emphasis on inputs, (3) judgmental with emphasis on outputs, (4) decision-facilitation, and (5) naturalistic (Popham, 1988).

Goal-Attainment Evaluation

Goal-attainment models focus on the accomplishment of stated goals and objectives of the program. Tyler's goal-attainment model is predicated on the identification of objectives and the measurement of child progress on those objectives. The success of a program rests on child and/or family performance according to the stated program objectives or outcome statements. Such an evaluation model is simple to implement and interpret since it relies on measurable objectives. However, dimensions of the program, which are not easily expressed as behavioral objectives, may be overlooked, despite their significance to program efficacy. Additionally, there is no evaluation of the appropriateness of the objectives, simply whether or not they were reached.

Input-Based Judgmental Evaluation

The judgmental models have as a foundation the expert opinions of best practices. In the *input model,* the emphasis is on elements of planning and needs assessment and program structure (e.g., ratio of adults to children and qualifications of personnel). Programs can be examined as to the extent they are designed according to "best practices," as documented in the literature (e.g., McDonnell & Hardman, 1988).

Output-Based Judgmental Evaluation

With the output model, both the appropriateness of goals and objectives and the attainment of them are evaluated. Scriven's (1973) goal-free model of evaluation, which is a judgment based on the output model, eliminates some of the limitations found in Tyler's (1971) objective-based model. An outside evaluator, who has little knowledge of the program, is used to determine the actual impact of the program, regardless of stated objectives. Scriven's premise is that preknowledge of program goals interferes with the evaluator's unbiased identification of program effects.

Decision-Facilitation Evaluation

The decision-facilitation model is designed to reduce or eliminate personal judgments. The evaluator gathers data, which are then presented to the program's decision makers for action. It is then the responsibility of the decision makers to act on the options available to them. Stufflebeam's (1971) decision-making model involves a three-step process: (1) identifying information that is sought, (2) collecting the information, and (3) giving the information to the decision makers. This process involves four cyclical components: (1) planning and needs assessment (context evaluation); (2) program structure, including management, budget, and staffing (input evaluation); (3) program implementation (process evaluation); and (4) program continuation, termination, or modification (product evaluation). In this model, evaluation is a continual element of the program, incorporating all aspects within it. In reality, very few programs would have the time or financial resources to fully implement such a comprehensive model.

The *triphase evaluation process* (Johnson, 1988) is built on the evaluation models of Tyler (1971, 1974), Scriven (1973, 1974), and Stufflebeam (1971, 1974). The triphase evaluation integrates three phases (i.e., input, process, and outcome) into a single process. The input phase involves the identification of child, family, and community needs and the development of a program designed to address those needs. During the process phase, progress toward meeting those needs is monitored. The input and process phase together provide formative evaluation information (i.e., information used to guide and influence program development). Summative or final evaluation data gathering occurs during the outcome phase, with the impact of the program as the focus.

Naturalistic Evaluation

The naturalistic models, which are based on an ethnographic approach to data gathering, emphasize the importance of why and how data are collected. Techniques of data gathering include case studies, observations, interviews, and participant surveys. Scott (1980) described such a naturalistic method, which involves the collection of data through a chronology. The chronology contains a running record of an individual child's behavior, including everything that she says and does and everything that is said and done to her. It is accompanied by a description of the context in which the behaviors are occurring. The chronology method does not require that verbatim remarks be recorded when a general summary can convey the general intent (e.g., "David ran up and asked Beth if he could use the bathroom"). Scott suggests that three to five observational sessions be conducted prior to actual data taking in order to acclimate program participants to the observation. Chronologies are analyzed according to a two-step process. The first step, utilization, involves the division of the running record into its own naturally occurring structural units, which can overlap. These activity units are marked as to their beginning and ending points on the running record. Each activity unit is labeled with a simple descriptive title (e.g., trying to get teacher's attention, talking to boy, and listening to story). The second step in the analytical process is categorization and involves the identification, definition, and study of the activity units. Analyses can focus on specific aspects of the activity units, such as goals of the units and mechanisms used to achieve the goals, participation of others in the units, and initiation–termination behaviors within the units. Through the analysis, patterns of individual behaviors and interactions can be discovered.

CHILD ASSESSMENT IN PROGRAM EVALUATION

The use of child assessment data is a crucial part of the evaluation of early intervention programs. Program administrators cannot rely solely on parent satisfaction or employee morale to determine their program's effectiveness. However, it is critical that the data gathered are appropriate for use in program evaluation. First, there must be a distinction made between program efficacy for each individual child in the program and that for the entire group of children. Much of the efficacy research has focused on group performance, whereas a child's parents may only be concerned about their own child. Both individual and group performance should be monitored as a part of program evaluation. Some procedures offer reliable group data but are of uncertain value for the individual child, whereas other procedures are more appropriate for the individual child.

Procedures can involve the calculation of gain scores, comparison of a child's progress with the rate of progress expected for a normal child of the same age, comparison of the child's rate of progress with his previous rate of development, and mastery of objectives. Each of these methods has limitations and flaws that restrict its usefulness. Therefore, a well-designed program evaluation relies on multiple sources of data and is not restricted to a single source.

Gain Scores

Gain scores reflect the difference between a child's performance before and after intervention. Gain scores can be differences in age-equivalency scores, increases in the intelligent quotient (IQ) or other developmental quotients, tallies from the observation of specific behaviors in pre- and postassessments (e.g., on-task behavior and number of initiated social interactions), or improved performance on criterion-based instruments. The use of gain scores in program evaluation is simple, but subject to serious restrictions when used with special needs children. They depict the amount of progress the child has made according to the instrument used for the assessment. For example, a child who has been in a preschool program for a total of nine months during the school year could be tested in September and again in May. The difference between these two scores is the gain score. For tests that report scores in age equivalents, the gain score is readily compared with the amount of time the child was in the program. A gain score of four months over a nine-month period does not appear to be very good, and yet for a child with severe delays it might be excellent. Use of the gain score in isolation from other procedures leaves the interventionist and parent guessing as to how to evaluate the rate of progress of the special needs child. Reliance on an increase in IQ can also lead to inaccurate conclusions about program effectiveness. If the program is aimed at improving socialization skills of the young child, IQ would certainly not be an appropriate measure of program effectiveness. Even when cognitive development is the target of the intervention, traditional assessments of mental ability may not be appropriate. For example, increases in a child's understanding of operational causality could best be evaluated using Uzgiris's and Hunt's *Infant Psychological Development Scale* rather than using a more traditional intelligence test. An additional restriction in the use of increases in IQ is lack of stability of IQ in very young children (discussed in Chapter 9). Other gain scores, such as increases in the amount of engaged time a child exhibits, must be evaluated in a subjective manner. How much increase was expected and was that expectation exceeded or not reached are all a matter of professional or parental judgment and subject to dispute. Nevertheless, such counts are based on directly observable behavior and are critical in the use of assessment for ongoing program planning and formative evaluations.

Rate of Development Compared with Normal Rates

Gain scores can be compared with the length of time a child receives intervention to calculate the intervention efficiency index (Bagnato & Neisworth, 1980). The formula used to calculate the index is as follows:

$$\frac{\text{Developmental Gain (months)}}{\text{Time in Intervention (months)}} = \begin{matrix}\text{Intervention}\\\text{Efficiency}\\\text{Rate}\end{matrix}$$

An intervention efficiency rate of 1.00 indicates that the child's developmental gain is equivalent to the number of months in intervention. Rates below 1.00 show a slower rate of progress than the amount of time in intervention, while rates above 1.00 indicate that developmental gains exceed the length of time in the program. The intervention efficiency index can be calculated for an entire group of children and for individuals. For programs that rely on multiple instruments to monitor child progress, it can be interesting to compare derived intervention efficiency rates across tests.

Comparison with Ideal Rates of Development

An alternative procedure, which includes a weighing of the child's developmental status, is the efficiency index (Simeonsson & Wiegerink, 1975; Simeonsson, 1982). The efficiency index formula is as follows:

$$\frac{\text{Actual Gain}}{\text{Ideal Gain}} \div \begin{matrix}\text{Developmental}\\\text{Status}\end{matrix} = \begin{matrix}\text{Efficiency}\\\text{Index}\end{matrix}$$

Actual gain is the child's gain score as based upon pre- and posttesting, whereas the ideal gain is based on the length of time in intervention. If age-equivalent scores are used to determine actual gain, months in intervention is used for ideal gain. Developmental status can be determined efficiently using a developmental quotient divided by 100. For example, a child with a mental developmental index of 75 on the

Bayley scales would have a developmental status of 75/100. If she participated in an intervention program for 12 months, with an actual gain of 9 months, her efficiency index would be 1.0 (9/12 − 75/100 = 1.0). Had her actual gain been only 6 months, the efficiency index would have been .66. A gain of 12 months over a 12-month period would yield an index of 1.33 for a child with a developmental status of 75/100.

Comparisons with Previous Rates of Development

A child's progress during intervention can also be compared with his rate of development prior to intervention. Such a comparison is particularly useful for young children with developmental delays. If a child who made five months' progress during a nine-month period is 6 years old and began the intervention functioning at a 2-year-old level, her rate of development actually increased during intervention. Although her gain score is only five months for a nine-month period, it is a substantial increase over her previous rate of development. However, if the child had already been functioning at a four-year-old level, the rate of development would not have been equivalent to previous progress. The proportional change index (PCI) (Wolery, 1983) can be used in the calculation of a child's rate of development compared with her rate of development prior to intervention. The following formula is used in calculating the PCI:

$$\frac{\text{Developmental Gain}}{\text{Time in Intervention}} \div \frac{\text{Pretest Developmental Age}}{\text{Pretest Chronological Age}} = \text{PCI}$$

Progress equivalent to the developmental rate prior to intervention will produce a PCI of 1.00. Lower rates during intervention result in PCIs below 1.00, while increased rates of development are evident when the PCIs are over 1.00. The PCI Calculation Worksheet, a form which can be used to calculate the PCI, is presented in Figure 13.1. The Group PCI Record Form, which is displayed in Figure 13.2, can be used to monitor the rate of progress for several children over multiple testing periods. Individual progress can be monitored across multiple domains with the Individual PCI Record Form, shown in Figure 13.3. The Cumulative Multidomain PCI Record Form (Figure 13.4) summarizes the PCIs for many children across multiple domains and multiple testing periods.

Various other formulas are available for use in comparison of previous rates of development with those seen during intervention (Rosenberg, Robinson, Finkler, & Rose, 1987). The primary differentiation in them is not the elements put forth in the formula, but the interpretation of the final calculation. One is formulated so that a score of 0.0 is indicative of expected progress, whereas others use 1.0 as the indicator of expected progress. Users of these formulas need to understand the appropriate interpretation of final results.

Uses of Rate of Development Indices.   The PCI and other similar rate of developmental change indices have multiple uses (Benner & Beckmann, 1990). First, comparisons across developmental domains can be used to identify intraindividual devel-

NAME	1. Pre Rate of Development $\frac{\text{Pre DA}}{\text{Pre CA}} = \text{Pre RD}$	2. Months in Program $\frac{\text{Post} - \text{Pre}}{\text{CA} \quad \text{CA}} = \text{MP}$	3. Gain Score $\frac{\text{Post} - \text{Pre}}{\text{DA} \quad \text{DA}} = \text{GS}$	4. Post Rate of Development $\frac{\text{GS}}{\text{MP}} = \frac{\text{Post}}{\text{RD}}$	5. PCI $\frac{\text{Post RD}}{\text{Pre RD}} = \text{PCI}$
1. ____	___ + ___ = ___	___ − ___ = ___	___ − ___ = ___	___ + ___ = ___	___ + ___ = ___
2. ____	___ + ___ = ___	___ − ___ = ___	___ − ___ = ___	___ + ___ = ___	___ + ___ = ___
3. ____	___ + ___ = ___	___ − ___ = ___	___ − ___ = ___	___ + ___ = ___	___ + ___ = ___
4. ____	___ + ___ = ___	___ − ___ = ___	___ − ___ = ___	___ + ___ = ___	___ + ___ = ___
5. ____	___ + ___ = ___	___ − ___ = ___	___ − ___ = ___	___ + ___ = ___	___ + ___ = ___
6. ____	___ + ___ = ___	___ − ___ = ___	___ − ___ = ___	___ + ___ = ___	___ + ___ = ___

Pre DA = developmental age before treatment

Pre CA = chronological age before treatment

Pre RD = rate of development before treatment

MP = months in program

Post DA = developmental age after treatment

Post CA = chronological age after treatment

GS = gain score

Post RD = rate of development during treatment

PCI = proportional change index

Figure 13.1. PCI Calculation Worksheet

Figure 13.2. Group PCI Record Form

Domain: _____
Test Used: _____

	Date: _____			Date: _____			Date: _____		
Child's Name	Pre RD	Post RD	PCI	Pre RD	Post RD	PCI	Pre RD	Post RD	PCI

opmental progress. This information is particularly helpful to a comprehensive program designed to enhance a child's development across all domains. Scattered rates of change might indicate variable effectiveness of programming. Second, a rate of change index can help in communicating program effectiveness to parents of children with developmental delays. The rate of change index provides a benchmark to determine reasonable expectations of progress. Third, program administrators who are faced with decisions about 12-month versus 9-month program delivery can find the indices helpful in regression and recoupment assessments. Fourth, interindividual developmental progress for groups of children can offer an interventionist insight into program strengths and areas needing improvement. For example, the calculation of PCIs for a group of 20 children might reveal that 15 exceeded expected development in speech and language and cognition, but 12 failed to achieve expected progress in social and emotional development or self-care skills. A curricular review might be needed to address this imbalance in progress if the program was designed to enhance development across all domains.

Cautions in Interpreting Developmental Rate Changes.   Indices based on changes in rate of development are subject to several limitations that restrict complete reliance on them in program evaluation (Rosenberg, Robinson, Finkler, & Rose, 1987).

Figure 13.3. Individual PCI Record Form

Domain	Date: _____			Date: _____			Date: _____		
	Pre RD	Post RD	PCI	Pre RD	Post RD	PCI	Pre RD	Post RD	PCI

Child's Name: _____

Test Used: _____

First, they are based on an assumption of the linearity of development (i.e., a child makes one month's developmental progress evenly across all developmental domains in a one-month period). The reality is that children display developmental spurts and plateaus across domains in individual patterns. If a child has experienced a developmental spurt just prior to entry into a program, a plateau may occur during intervention. Failure to progress might not mean inappropriate or ineffective programming, but could easily be interpreted as such. A second limitation is based upon the statistical properties of the instruments used to assess the child. Tests may have limited ranges that restrict calculation of gain scores (e.g., highest possible score is 60 months, but child may actually be at 5-year 6-month level). Standard error of measurement can also reduce the significance of differences between pre- and posttest scores. Additionally, instruments that do not reflect the content of programming are not indicative of program effectiveness and should not be used for evaluation purposes. Finally, an increase or decrease in a child's rate of development during intervention cannot be arbitrarily attributed to the intervention program. Other changes in the child's life might also be contributing to the change. For example, a child is removed from an abusive home, placed in a stable foster home, has her nutritional needs adequately met for the first time, and is placed in an early intervention program. During the first six months in intervention,

Figure 13.4. Cumulative Multidomain PCI Record Form

Child's Name	Domain: ____			Domain: ____			Domain: ____			Domain: ____			Domain: ____		
	PCI 1	PCI 2	PCI 3	PCI 1	PCI 2	PCI 3	PCI 1	PCI 2	PCI 3	PCI 1	PCI 2	PCI 3	PCI 1	PCI 2	PCI 3

Test Used: _____

the child makes dramatic progress. Would that progress have been evident had none of the other changes occurred in the child's life? Would the progress have occurred with all of the other changes except the intervention program? Program evaluators must remember that cause and effect is not an issue that can be isolated from other elements in the child's life. Variance of program effectiveness among children who received similar programs, started at the same age, began with similar functioning levels, remained in the program an equivalent length of time, and so forth can occur. The program evaluator is faced with the challenge of investigating why one child seemed to thrive while another failed to make satisfactory progress, perhaps even regressed.

Mastery of Objectives

The determination of child progress in special education programs is often based on the achievement of specific objectives stipulated at the outset of the program. This procedure eliminates the problem of matching the assessment instrument with the actual content of the program. For example, if the stated objective for a child is to eat independently within a 30-minute period, program effectiveness would be based on the progress made toward this specific goal, not a standardized test score. The number of objectives reached and progress toward the achievement of others is the indicator of child progress. The limitation of this approach is in the evaluation of the objectives themselves. Even if a child achieved 100% of his stated objectives, the program might have not been effective for him if he were capable of achieving far greater objectives. However, the child who failed to achieve any of his stated objectives might have inappropriate objectives rather than poor programming. While the results of the program evaluation are highly individualized according to curricular content, no evaluation of the curriculum and its appropriateness for specific children is included.

A strategy that can be used to reduce these limitations is *goal attainment scaling* (GAS) designed for use in early intervention programs (Simeonsson, Huntington, & Short, 1982; Shuster, Fitzgerald, Shelton, Barber, & Desch, 1984). At the initiation of programming, the interventionist develops a goal attainment scale for each child for a designated time period. Each child should have approximately five objectives that will be monitored. The relative importance of each objective is reflected in a designated weight value. For example, the most important objective for Elizabeth Armstrong initially was improved feeding, so it would be given the highest value (e.g., $w = 5$). Communication and motor skills would have lower weights (e.g., $w = 3$), and play behavior would be lowest (e.g., $w = 1$). A five-point range of possible outcomes for each objective is then developed, with the worst possible outcome reflecting current functioning. The range should be based on the following scale:

Attainment Level	Score
Most unfavorable treatment outcome thought likely (should represent current functioning)	-2
Less than expected success with treatment	-1
Expected level of treatment success	0
More than expected success with treatment	$+1$
Best anticipated success with treatment	$+2$

Progress over the course of treatment can be plotted on a graph that depicts the level a child has achieved (Shuster, Fitzgerald, Shelton, Barber, & Desch, 1984). Objectives that remain unachieved for an extended period of time and those that are achieved can easily be monitored, and programming adjustments made accordingly. The data can also be converted into a standardized *t* score, which accounts for the weighted value of each objective, of overall gain scores, and percentages of improvement (Simeonsson, Huntington, & Short, 1982).

Single Subject Research Design.   Techniques used in single subject research design (Alberto & Troutman, 1986) can also be effectively applied in formative evaluation and program monitoring. The first phase in single subject designs is the collection of baseline data, which provide descriptive information about the existing level of student functioning and can be used as the basis for predicting the future level of

performance if no intervention is provided. At least five baseline data points should be collected and analyzed prior to intervention. The stability of these data can be determined by analysis of the variability and trends of the data points. Variability of baseline data for classroom intervention purposes should not exceed 50%. This criterion can be checked by calculating the mean of all the data points and multiplying by .50. This number is then added to and subtracted from the mean to determine the acceptable range of data points. If no points exceed the range, the baseline is considered stable. Baseline data should show no trend, an increasing trend, or a decreasing trend in the anticipated direction of intervention effects. Ascending baselines, which reflect naturally increasing behaviors, are of particular interest when the goal of intervention is to decrease the behavior being charted. Intervention effectiveness must be weighed against naturally occurring increases or decreases obtained through the baseline data.

Following baseline data collection, intervention is begun using a series of repeated measures of a child's behavior. Changes in the child's performance are indicative of program effectiveness. Alberto and Troutman (1986) described both teaching and research designs that are used in single subject research. The simplest design, which can be easily applied to early intervention programs, is the *AB* design. The first phase of the design, represented by *A*, is the baseline period. Once a stable baseline is achieved, *B*, the intervention phase, begins. The teacher makes decisions regarding program continuation and changes in programming based on trends observed during the intervention as compared with those seen during baseline. An example of data collected based on a single subject teaching design is presented in Figure 13.5.

Objective: Todd will eat a snack of two crackers and three ounces of juice within a 15–minute period.

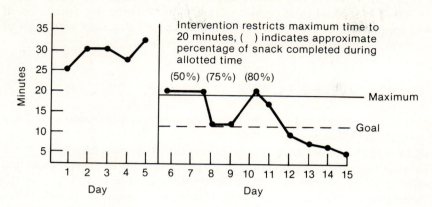

Baseline Stability

Day 1   25

   2   30

   3   30

   4   27

   5   34

         146

$146 \div 5 = 29.2$

$29.2 \times .50 = 14.6$

Acceptable range 29.2 ± 14.6
Baseline is stable with no trends

Intervention Plan

Remove remaining snack after 20–minute time period and rearrange schedule so Todd's favorite activity (sand and water play) begins immediately when he finishes his snack.

Figure 13.5. Single Subject Design for Formative Evaluation

SUMMARY

The focus of this chapter is child assessment as related to program evaluation. There are many factors that must be addressed in a comprehensive evaluation. Wolery and Bailey (1984) recommend that evaluation designs address certain questions regarding early intervention services. Efficacy research, which has covered such issues as length of intervention, service delivery models, and use of parents as trainers, can also help direct program evaluation design.

There are five basic models of evaluation that can be applied to early intervention programs. These are goal-attainment, input-based judgmental, output-based judgmental, decision-facilitation, and naturalistic. Child assessment data can be used in a variety of ways in program evaluation, both in terms of overall program effectiveness and individual child progress. Techniques include the calculation of gain scores; comparison of ideal and previous rates of development with rates of development during intervention; and mastery of objectives.

THE ECOLOGICAL PERSPECTIVE

- Program evaluation takes into consideration the desired outcomes as defined by parents as well as program staff.
- Emphasis in child assessment for program evaluation must be placed on the context of the child's performance (e.g., previous rates of development and desired levels of attainment as contrasted with current levels).
- A variety of evaluation models, which emphasize various program components and can be used collectively to detect program weaknesses, are available.
- Acceptable child progress does not necessarily indicate an effective program, nor does lack of progress by a child automatically imply poor programming.

CHAPTER 14

Emerging Issues in Early Childhood

CHAPTER OUTLINE

QUESTIONS RAISED IN CHAPTER 14

- What impact does drug and alcohol abuse have on infants and young children?
- What is the future for a baby born of an AIDS-infected, crack-cocaine-dependent, single, teenage mother with no resources?
- What becomes of the children of the thousands of homeless adults?
- What impact can early intervention have on medically fragile infants whose lives are sustained through expensive medical technology?

CHAPTER OVERVIEW

At any given time in history there are critical issues influencing the needs of a society. The children and families who are in need of early intervention are representative of the society in which they exist and, therefore, also have these needs. Many of the serious concerns of the past (e.g., polio and scarlet fever) are no longer such grave threats to children. New issues emerge as solutions to existing problems are found. The issues challenging present and future early childhood interventionists are complex, ranging from the detrimental effects of cocaine use by pregnant women to the technological advances resulting in the miraculous survival of extremely premature, low-birth-weight babies. As a conclusion to this text some of the most salient issues confronting early childhood professionals and families are offered for discussion.

HEALTH ISSUES

Fetal Alcohol Syndrome

The dangers associated with alcohol consumption during pregnancy have been a point of discussion for many centuries (Rosman & Oppenheimer, 1985). The term *fetal alcohol syndrome* relates to the characteristics of a child exposed to the injurious effects of alcohol during fetal development (Jones & Smith, 1973). In order for a child to receive this diagnosis he must show signs in each of three categories: 1) pre- and/or postnatal growth retardation, (2) central nervous system involvement, and (3) characteristic facial disfigurement (microcephaly, microphthalmia, flat or absent philtrum, thin upper lip, and/or flattening of maxillary area) (Rossetti, 1980). Reports indicate that approximately 1 out of every 750 babies born has fetal alcohol syndrome (Centers for Disease Control, 1984). Some children may exhibit partial features of the syndrome and are more accurately diagnosed with "suspected fetal alcohol effects" (Clarren & Smith, 1978).

Confounding the impact of alcohol use on a developing fetus is the fact that heavy drinkers have a higher frequency of tobacco, marijuana, and drug usage (Rosman & Oppenheimer, 1985). Each factor alone has been associated with specific neonatal outcomes. For example, marijuana use has been linked to offspring with birth weights 300 grams lower than those seen in offspring of nonusers (Hingson, Alpert, Day, Dooling, Kayne, Morelock, Oppenheimer, & Zuckerman, 1982). For a child whose mother used multiple substances during pregnancy, the impact is even greater. Additionally, poor nutritional habits often accompany maternal alcoholism, and the fetus is totally dependent on nutrients provided by the mother. Alcohol consumption by the mother is toxic to the fetus and appears to result in a reduction of nutrient absorption independent of maternal eating habits. A poor nutritional environment combined with decreased nutrient absorption compound fetal risk for growth retardation (Phillips, Henderson, & Schenker, 1989).

Babies Prenatally Exposed to Drugs

The February 1990 issue of *Exceptional Children* begins with a commentary on "drug babies" in which Jeptha Greer discusses the newly emerging "bio-underclass"; that is, a group of children who have entered the world as drug addicts, afflicted with numerous problems that remain with them long after the addiction has been eliminated. He makes reference to reports that indicate that drug usage among pregnant women varies from a low estimate of 15% to between 20 and 30% at Washington D.C. General Hospital. The number of newborns exposed to prenatal drug abuse is estimated at 375,000 per year (Schneider, Griffith, & Chasnoff, 1989). The damage caused by cocaine and crack-cocaine, which have grown in popularity, far exceeds previous withdrawal symptoms seen in the newborn nursery.

The characteristics of babies born exposed to cocaine include poor body-state regulation, poor feeding, tremors and trembling, stiffness and rigidity, chronic irritability, difficulty sleeping, and poor visual orientation. Since these conditions last well beyond the first few weeks of life, they are more indicative of lasting changes in the central nervous system than of withdrawal symptoms (Schneider, Griffith, & Chasnoff, 1989). Strokes and seizures, small head size, missing bowels, and malformed genitals in babies have all been related to crack-cocaine-addicted mothers. These children continue to exhibit multiple problems as they enter school, such as poor abstract reasoning and memory, poor judgment, inability to concentrate, inability to deal with stress, frequent tantrums, and violent acting out.

> These children will be prominent among the next generation of special ed students and each of them may be a neurochemical time-bomb, likely to experience the same dysphoria and thought and mood disorders as a recovering addict, which is what the child is. . . . And do not forget, many of these children—perhaps the majority—will be caught in the same socio-economic bind of disadvantage and abuse that contributed to their mothers' drug abuse in the first place. (Greer, 1990, p. 383).

Cocaine easily passes into the fetal circulatory system and remains there longer than in the maternal system. Chemical properties of the drug have led to speculation that the fetus is continually exposed through the amniotic fluid, following a single use of the drug by the mother. Screening tests are available to determine exposure of a newborn to cocaine as well as other drugs (e.g., opiates, amphetamines, barbiturates, phencyclidine, and marijuana). The urine screening test is relatively low cost (between $18 and $25 for cocaine), but may require confirmatory testing since both false positives and false negatives are possible. False positives will occur if a test reacts positively to substances other than the drug; however, no such cross-reactants with cocaine are known other than derivatives of the drug (Brayden, 1990). Laboratory technician error might also cause false positives or false negatives. False negatives could also result from "doctored" urine samples, or the amount of time elapsed since drug usage. The screening test is also limited in that it cannot reveal how much of the drug is present in the infant's system.

Decisions that follow a positive screening have serious long-term implications for the newborn child. Some of these children become "boarder babies," residing for extended periods in the hospital setting. Some make their way into foster care, and others are simply released into the care of their drug-addicted mothers.

Schneider, Griffith, and Chasnoff (1989) note four common behavioral patterns that may appear in the cocaine-exposed newborn. First, they may move into a deep sleep in response to any stimulation. Although this behavior protects their delicate nervous systems, all infant–caregiver interactions are eliminated. The second pattern is an agitated sleep state. They startle, change coloring, whimper, but do not awaken in reaction to external stimulation. Third, they vacillate between extreme states (e.g., sleeping to hard crying) during handling. The final pattern is characterized by a panicked awake state. The infant remains alert, but appears to be experiencing extreme stress. These patterns interfere with the child's opportunities to interact with her environment as well as with her caregivers. The implications for future relationships and learning cannot be ignored. Intervention plans that help the baby remain calm while alert emphasize swaddling and rocking, appropriate handling techniques, gentle tactile oral stimulation, and facilitation of normal muscle tone and movement patterns. For any intervention program to be effective, it must be a family-centered approach that provides parents with assistance in becoming and remaining drug-free coupled with training in the care and management of their child. (For a review of interventions for specific child behaviors, see Lewis, Bennett, and Schmeder, 1989.)

Assessment of these babies as they grow into toddlers can produce misleading results. The structure of standardized assessments enables children to score in a normal range when actual functioning is poor (Howard, Beckwith, Rodning, & Kropenske, 1989). Observations of the child during unstructured free play, which requires self-organization, self-initiation, and follow-through without assistance, reveal a lack of representational play, characterized by scattering, batting, and picking up and putting down toys available for play. Discrepancies between "scores" and observable behaviors were also noted with the strange situation paradigm (see Chapter 12 for discussion of this paradigm).

Acquired Immunodeficiency Syndrome and Human Immunodeficiency Virus

Acquired immunodeficiency syndrome (AIDS) is a disease caused by a virus that can damage the brain and destroy the body's ability to fight off illness. The virus causing AIDS and related disorders has several names: HTLV-III (Human T-Lymphotropic Virus Type III), LAV (Lymphadenopathy-Associated Virus), ARC (AIDS-related Complex), and HIV (Human Immunodeficiency Virus). It is possible for an individual to be infected and transmit the related virus without displaying any symptoms. Although AIDS cannot be spread by casual contact in schools or other public places, it is a concern to all professionals working with children. AIDS is primarily spread in three ways: (1) having sex with an infected person; (2) sharing needles and syringes with an infected person and other users of heroin, cocaine, and other drugs; or (3) infecting infants in utero, perinatally or postnatally. On rare occasions, AIDS has been transmitted through blood transfusions. According to cumulative figures based on all known AIDS cases published in 1987, 2% of AIDS cases were the result of blood transfusions and 1% occurred in persons with hemophilia who received blood-clotting factors. Since March 1985, all blood donations are screened for the AIDS virus and no donations are accepted from high-risk individuals, thus it is less likely to be spread through transfusions in the future. However, today 1 out of every 37 individuals with hemophilia has AIDS (Hutchings, 1988).

For early childhood special educators, the greatest concern is transmittal of the disease during pregnancy and the newborn period. According to the Surgeon General's report on AIDS (Koop, 1986), the fetus and newborn baby are at-risk from several sources.

> If a woman is infected with the AIDS virus and becomes pregnant, she is more likely to develop ARC or classic AIDS, and she can pass the AIDS virus to her unborn child. Approximately one third of the babies born to AIDS-infected mothers will also be infected with the AIDS virus. Most of the infected babies will eventually develop the disease and die. Several of these babies have been born to wives of hemophiliac men infected with the AIDS virus by way of contaminated blood products. Some babies have also been born to women who became infected with the AIDS virus by bisexual partners who had the virus. Almost all babies with AIDS have been born to women who were intravenous drug users or the sexual partners of intravenous drug users who were infected with the AIDS virus. More such babies can be expected. (pp. 20–21)

Transmittal from an infected mother can occur in utero through transplacental passage of the virus during labor and delivery when the infant may be exposed to maternal blood and vaginal secretions, or postnatally through breastfeeding (Hutchings, 1988). It is estimated that the biological parents of 25 to 33% of infants born with AIDS will not care for them (Tourse & Gundersen, 1988).

The Centers for Disease Control reported 53,814 cases of AIDS through February 1988, including 839 children between the ages of 0 and 12. Over one half of these children have already died. Estimates of pediatric AIDS infection by 1991 is 3000, and predictions of HIV infection range from 10,000 to 20,000 (Hutchings, 1988). A disproportionately high number of pediatric AIDS occurs in minority populations. Although 15% of the total U.S. child population is black, 35% of all childhood cases involve black children, and while 10% of the total population is Hispanic, 23% of all cases involve Hispanic children. Figures from 1988 indicate that 1 out of every 61 infants born in New York City was delivered by an HIV-infected mother. Recent research on the incidence of AIDS indicates dramatic increases in populations of teenagers, women, crack smokers, and heavy drinkers (Associated Press, June 21, 1990). The risk to infants is increasing because the proportion of AIDS cases in women increased from 6 to 10% between 1982 and 1989.

The early symptoms of HIV infection in infants and children include failure to thrive or weight loss, chronic or recurring diarrhea, persistent or recurring fever, and persistent and severe oral fungus infection. Additional conditions that also appear include recurring bacterial infections, encephalopathy (developmental delay), lymphoid interstitial pneumonitis, and heart, liver, kidney, and skin involvement (Hutchings, 1988). Neurologic impairments may also appear, including ataxia, spasticity, paralysis, cortical atrophy, calcifications of basal ganglia, dementia, and slowing of brain electrical activity (Bale, 1990).

Since the majority of AIDS-infected children come from families with multiple problems, including drug abuse and poverty, effective intervention to meet their medical needs must take on a family-focused approach. Project WIN offers such a model, using a transagency approach to service delivery (Woodruff & Sterzin, 1988). A transagency board, which includes representatives of 31 agencies, has the responsibility of coordinating the project. Activities of the project staff, including case-finding, intake and assessment, individualized family service plan development, program implementation, and family and program evaluation, are reviewed and monitored by the board.

The nature of the disease dictates that it be viewed from an ecological perspective. Dokecki, Baumeister, and Kupstas (1989) emphasize the social and political aspects and identify eight options that reflect a philosophy of community- and family-based care.

1. Mandatory antibody screening and testing of any kind should be avoided at this time.
2. The availability of voluntary antibody screening and testing programs should be expanded, with significant attention paid to the issue of confidentiality.
3. The availability of interdisciplinary developmental screening, assessment, reassessment, and early intervention programs should be expanded for young children who have or are at risk of having HIV infection.
4. The individualized family service plan (IFSP) can be a useful tool in planning and providing early intervention services.
5. Case management can be a powerful mechanism for providing a coordinated continuum of early intervention services.
6. Early intervention agents can work actively with children with pediatric AIDS without undue concern about being infected with HIV.
7. Early intervention programs should look to a wide variety of funding sources for serving children with pediatric AIDS and their families.
8. Early interventionists should develop and support efforts to prevent AIDS. (pp. 109, 110)

SOCIOPOLITICAL AND ECONOMIC ISSUES

Poverty

Child- and family-related issues are favorite topics of politicians, ranging from presidents (and presidential candidates) to local city and county officials. Most recently, programs such as Head Start and Medicaid and increased federal support to ensure adequate day care for the children of working women have been highlighted. The special education legislation described in Chapter 1 reflects a politically favorable stance on issues pertinent to children with disabilities. However, political rhetoric and actual legislation intended to support family structure and protect children have not always achieved their goals. Dukes (1976) points out the negative impact studies related to effective childrearing practices have had on attitudes toward the black population by creating a myth regarding the inadequacy of childrearing practices among poor and minority groups. The impact of this myth has resulted in three negative outcomes for these families. First, it has misplaced the focus on the child and family as elements that foster pathogenic retardation. Second, families with low socioeconomic status are viewed and treated as an inferior element of American society. Third, the dynamics of the American social stratification system work to keep an inordinate number of these families at the bottom of the economic ladder, thus limiting their chances for a better life.

> Of the 35 million poor people in this country, over 13 million are children, which amounts to one in every five children. Added to this is the growing Dickensian nightmare of homelessness. Forty percent of the homeless nationwide are children. Of the 11,000 homeless children in New York, 5000 are under five. And yet only 10 percent of all homeless families in emergency housing participate in formal child-care arrangements. (Ayers, 1989, p. 97)

The ramifications of being poor in America today are overwhelming. Housing, adequate nutrition, transportation, and employment all become unobtainable when an individual or family faces extreme poverty. Public policy has attempted to respond to the needs of poor children through income support programs (e.g., Aid to Families with Dependent Children), health care (e.g., Medicaid), protection from abuse (e.g., Child Abuse Prevention and Treatment Act and the Adoption Assistance and Child Welfare Act of 1980), nutritional assistance (e.g., Special Supplemental Food Program for Women, Infants and Children—WIC), and child care (e.g., Head Start). However, the number of children and families who qualify for many of these programs far exceeds the number who actually receive benefits (Washington, 1985). Only 15% of eligible children participate in Head Start programs. Approximately 6 million women, infants, and children are eligible, but do not receive WIC program benefits. If these programs were to serve a higher percentage of the eligible population, budget constraints would have to result in adjusted eligibility standards or significant budgetary reallocations.

Homelessness

The impact of extreme poverty is particularly evident in the homeless population in America today. Although determining the actual number of homeless individuals is impossible, several attempts to gather such data have been undertaken. Rossi (1989) presents a comprehensive picture of homelessness and reviews much of the data available to date. First, the challenge of defining what constitutes homelessness must be faced. Does a single-parent family with three children living in a shelter for the homeless count as homeless? Or should just those out on the streets be counted? Or those often sleeping night by night in mission shelters? The definition used influences the estimate of homeless individuals and can explain some of the widely varying numbers (e.g., an estimate of 350,000 from the Department of

Housing and Urban Development versus 1.5 million estimated by advocates for the homeless). Regardless of the actual numbers, homelessness and extreme poverty are significant social problems that inflict lifelong impairments on many young children in America today.

> A majority (54%) of the homeless have had children, despite the low proportion who have ever been married. A fair proportion (one in nine) have had four or more children, and one homeless man claimed to have fathered seventeen! Taking into account the marital status of the homeless, this pattern also means that few of the homeless have taken any responsibility for the children they brought into the world.
>   . . . Homeless women were significantly more likely to have been parents; almost four in five have had at least one child. Males have apparently fathered children but never formed legal marriages and most likely never have formed households with their children and the women involved. (Rossi, 1989, pp. 131, 132)

A program in New York City designed to assist homeless families regain their ability to function in society and maintain housing offers a preschool program for young children (Ayers, 1989). The impact of homelessness can be felt in this quote from a 12-year-old brother of one of the children participating in the preschool:

> As I lay in bed crying myself to sleep in the Prince George Hotel, the largest hotel used to house homeless families in NYC, I could not bring myself to overcome the fear of what was happening to me. Over and over again I keep telling myself that I don't deserve this. I'm only 12 years old. I feel so alone. People in school call me a hotel kid. . . . It seems like people are so afraid of ending up where I'm at that they want to punish me for reminding them that being homeless is possible. They have no right to punish me for something I have no control over. I'm just a little boy living in a hotel, petrified, wanting to know what's going to happen to me. (p. 103)

Substandard housing is a crisis affecting more than one out of every eight children, but has its most significant impact on minority children. The ratio jumps to about one in four for black and Hispanic children. Compounding the problem is the increasing number of births to unmarried women, about 44% of whom are adolescents (Washington, 1985).

A description of a walk to a nearby "playground" for the preschoolers participating in the program for homeless families depicts a harsh reality (Ayers, 1989).

> There is a vacant lot cluttered with wrecked automobiles and broken glass. In an alley with a chain-link fence is a battered, broken-down delivery truck, a pile of old tires, and, incongruously, a huge white yacht on cinder blocks with an American flag flapping at the stern. Maurice says, "Don't step on that man," as the little line of walkers snakes past someone passed out on the sidewalk. The street is littered with garbage, and a block away two hookers lean in a doorway smoking. The walkers pass by a group of men playing cards on the sidewalk, using a little box for a table, and everyone calls out friendly greetings. They pass a fried-chicken restaurant and a

little bodega, then two deserted buildings whose broken doors and gaping windows stare back at the children. It is a whole landscape of abandonedness.

The playground is under an enormous bridge and is littered with broken fences and scattered glass. There is a lot of traffic noise and no sunlight. Somehow the children see beyond it and fashion the games all children play: tag, chase, and their favorite, hide-and-seek. (p. 104)

Changing Family Structures

Significant structural changes in American family life have a substantial impact on children. Frost (1986) identified descriptors of the lives of American children of the 1990s, based on statistical trends. Several of these descriptors are critical for educators to be aware of as they strive to understand the ecological conditions in which children exist.

The child will experience the divorce of his parents and live with a single parent. The estimated number of children under 18 years of age involved in divorces was 1,181,000 in 1979, a rate of 18.9 children per 1000. One out of every two marriages ends in divorce. Figures from 1980 indicate that 14.6 percent of the 8,530,000 families in the United States have a female as the head of the household. Twenty-five percent of all children under 18 years of age live with only one parent. Some time before they reach the age of 18, 60% of all children will reside with one parent.

The child's mother will work outside the home. Maternal employment patterns projected for the year 1990 yield estimates that 80% of all women with preschool-age children are in the work force. Over 10,000,000 children need child care. Frost (1986) recounts a 1985 NBC "White Paper" documenting the impact maternal entry into the work force has had on female roles.

> As women enter the work force, men are not assuming their share of home chores. The working mother performs two major roles, professional woman and homemaker—either of which could be considered full-time roles. The addition of a baby adds complexity as the mother assumes a third major role—infant care. Since it appears clear that few indeed can effectively manage all three roles, something must break. All too frequently it is the marriage. Many mothers are now putting in 16-hour days, competing with men at work—men who don't have dual and triple roles. Family relationships become strained as one or both parents become exhausted. . . . The typical American work place does not accommodate dual roles. Pregnancy can damage chances of promotion and job security. (p. 244)

The child's major activity will be watching television. The average amount of time children spend watching television is between 30 to 31 hours per week, with exposure to 350,000 commercials and 18,000 murders. Watching television consumes more time than any other waking activity. The effects of watching television range from increased aggression and violent behavior to poorer performance in school, weight gain, and a decrease in physical endurance (Frost, 1986).

The female will become pregnant during the teen years or before. The current pregnancy rate for teenagers between the ages of 15 and 19 is 96 out of 1000. In fact,

5 out of 1000 14-year-olds will become pregnant. In 1982, the birth rate for illegitimate children reached 20% of all births in the United States. The New York City illegitimacy rate for 1984 was 37%, with an 80% rate in central Harlem. These figures combined with the known risks of teen pregnancy and the impact poverty has on children and their families create a crisis that early childhood special educators must acknowledge.

TECHNOLOGICAL ADVANCES

Any infant born weighing less than 2500 grams (approximately 5.5 pounds) is defined as low birth weight. Those below 1500 grams (about 3.3 pounds) are considered very low birth weight. The survival of low- and very-low-birth-weight infants has been steadily increasing since the development of neonatal intensive care units (Rossetti, 1990). For example, during the period between 1965 and 1969, 35 infants weighing between 1251 and 1500 grams were born in the San Francisco metropolitan area. Twenty-one of these children survived (60.0%). Between 1976 and 1981, 104 infants were born in this weight range, and 97, or 93.3%, survived. Survival percentages for children with even lower birth weights rose as well. The incidence of infants below normal weight is higher for nonwhite infants than for whites. The 1983 percentage of very-low-birth-weight infants ($<$ 1500 grams) was 0.9 for whites, while it rose to 2.54 for nonwhites.

Survival rates have not improved without significant costs. Of those infants surviving, those who weighed less than 1000 grams spent an average of 89 days in a neonatal intensive care unit. The average stay for those below 1500 grams is 57 days. For those between 1501 and 2000 grams, the average stay is 24 days (Rossetti, 1990). Financial resources and insurance policies are quickly exhausted for a family confronted with the expenditures of a low- or very-low-birth-weight infant. Many are dependent on technology for their continued survival (e.g., respirators, intravenous nutrition, and kidney dialysis). These children become "million dollar" babies (Fackelmann, 1988). Many parents are unable or unwilling to make renovations to their homes and/or assume 24 hour a day nursing of their child. Many teenagers, who are at high risk to deliver low-birth-weight infants, make the choice to abandon their infants. These children become stranded in the hospitals. Even if Medicaid picks up a portion of the costs, the hospitals are running up enormous bills for these children. For example, one abandoned 5-year-old cost Cardinal Glennon Hospital in St. Louis $2 million (Fackelmann, 1988). Although home-based care would often be much cheaper than hospital-based care, Medicaid and/or insurance requirements have forced the parents to keep the child in the hospital.

> Whatever the cost, a society that has decided to support advances in medical technology must foot the bill for the needy children that result. Kids forced to grow up in the impersonal halls of a hospital often fail to thrive. No one likes to think about such abandoned children, but until we take responsibility for them, youngsters . . . will wait in their hospital beds. (Fackelmann, 1988, p. 27)

Additionally, these children are at high risk of developing handicapping conditions that will require further expense beyond early childhood.

IMPLICATIONS FROM AN ECOLOGICAL PERSPECTIVE

These issues and concerns facing American society today emphasize the need to view children from the contexts in which they exist. The reality of providing pre-school services to homeless children demands acknowledgment of their condition. To run such a preschool "just like any other preschool" would clearly fail to meet the needs of these children and their families. The preschool teacher in the program for homeless families describes her intake procedure: "I try to build up a sense of trust first. They're supposed to fill out a lot of forms, but I try not to start with that. I try to start with a kind word or just talk about the kids" (Ayers, 1989, p. 101). The temptation to look at the child in isolation, apart from her home environment, is no longer an effective option for early intervention programs. The number of children needing such services is increasing, while the nature of their needs is expanding.

In 1988, Odom and Warren made eight predictions regarding early childhood special education in the year 2000. One of those predictions was, "There will be far more children to include in intervention" (p. 267). This prediction is based on the long-term effects of poverty and social–cultural disadvantage, demographic trends indicating an increase in handicapping conditions (e.g., mental retardation and mental health disorders in children), and increased survival of infants born with disabilities. The far-reaching needs of these children and their families require that professionals across multiple disciplines learn to work together in a coordinated fashion, as intended in PL 99-457.

APPENDIX

Case Studies

ELIZABETH ARMSTRONG*

On August 7, 1983, Suzanne Armstrong went into labor with her third child. She and her husband, Don, quickly made arrangements for a babysitter for Joshua, age 4, and Steven, 18 months old. Shortly after Suzanne arrived at the hospital, she suffered a prolapsed umbilical cord and was given an emergency cesarean section. When she awoke two hours later in the recovery room, she was told that she had a little girl upstairs in the nursery. When she asked about her, the nurse replied that the doctors would speak with her. When the doctor came in, he explained that the child had been born dead. He explained, however, that she had been revived and was now looking good, with a nice pink color. On the way from the recovery room to Suzanne's hospital room, she and Don stopped by the nursery to look at Elizabeth. She noticed the baby was experiencing an unusual twitching and insisted on seeing the pediatrician immediately. The pediatrician assured her that he had seen Elizabeth when she was 5 minutes old and she looked fine at the time, but since the twitching had begun he would check for a calcium imbalance. Within two hours, Elizabeth was suffering prolonged seizures and was given phenobarbital. Elizabeth was repeatedly "bagged" (resuscitated) and had erratic glucose levels (possibly related to the seizures, the asphyxia accompanying the seizures, or her mother's borderline diabetes). The hospital staff decided Elizabeth needed to be transported to a neonatal intensive care unit in one of two hospitals approximately 30 miles away and asked Suzanne to select one. This first major decision had to be made quickly with no substantive information upon which to make it. Suzanne had not been permitted to touch her child. She refused to let Elizabeth be moved to the other hospital until she had done so. She was allowed to reach in and touch her as

---

*All names in this appendix are fictitious.

326

Elizabeth lay in her Isolette. Suzanne was stricken by the child's swollen appearance and the continued squinting of her eyes.

At the second hospital, Don had the opportunity to talk with a social worker, who provided some information about follow-up medical clinics that were available for his daughter. Later that day, Don visited Suzanne who remained in the hospital where Elizabeth had been born. As he sat at her bedside discussing their baby, the other mothers were given their babies. When a nurse started reprimanding Don for not being properly scrubbed and dressed for the visit, Suzanne lost her temper for the first time. The nursing care she received during this stressful time varied from insensitivity to empathy. On the third day following Elizabeth's birth, Suzanne was released from the hospital after receiving two units of blood. On the fourth day of Elizabeth's life, Suzanne began the daily phone calls and visits to the neonatal intensive care unit 30 miles from her home. During the first week of life, Elizabeth continuously seizured. She was receiving phenobarbital, dilantin, and peraldyhide enemas, as well as oxygen. Suzanne was told that an electroencephalogram (EEG) showed nothing and that the computed tomography (CT) scan had a "spot" on it, but it did not cause the seizures. Later, Suzanne learned from her pediatrician that this "spot" was an interventricular hemorrhage. After the first week, Elizabeth's seizures diminished and finally stopped.

During the second week Elizabeth began receiving feedings by nasogastric tube, accompanied by some attempts at nipple feeding. However, she continued to have serious medical needs and was bagged twice during that week. Elizabeth did not seem to be visually focusing, nor did she cry aloud during her first week of life. Even during the second and third weeks, she had a very weak "funny cry," symptomatic of infants with neurological damage, and had started projectile vomiting. After three weeks, Suzanne was given permission to take her baby girl home. She continued feedings by nasogastric tube, accompanied by attempts at nipple feeding, and gave Elizabeth phenobarbital. Suzanne was told that her baby was "within normal limits," but could possibly have cerebral palsy or a learning disability later. She was instructed to return for an EEG in three weeks and a CT scan in six months and to see a pediatrician within one week. It was predicted that the tube feeding would be necessary for about two more weeks.

During the first visit to the pediatrician's office, he noted the interventricular hemorrhage as well as other abnormal motoric behaviors and recommended that Suzanne contact a nearby infant stimulation program. He also attempted to connect her with another parent whose child had experienced similar difficulties. Suzanne did not contact the program. However, problems feeding Elizabeth increased, and she was unable to gain weight. Nipple feeding became impossible, and tube feeding resulted in persistent projectile vomiting. After Elizabeth's second visit to the pediatrician, Suzanne finally agreed to contact the infant stimulation program. She desperately needed help feeding her child. The only goal she had in mind for Elizabeth when she made this contact was improved feeding. Even as the difficulties in caring for Elizabeth occurred, other more hopeful signs also emerged. She was a happy child, who had begun smiling at 5 months of age. She smacked her lips when pleasant cooking odors were in the house—she was developing a personality and knew how to torment her mother just like any other baby. Around one year of age, she could direct her eye gaze in the appropriate direction when asked where specific things in her immediate environment were. These encouraging behaviors helped Suzanne persevere despite the many discouraging ones she faced.

Prior to Elizabeth's birth, Suzanne had been working as a nursing assistant in a community health center. Don was receiving social security disability payments as a result of prolonged mental health problems and was unemployed. He did serve as the primary caregiver to their two boys. In November 1983, three months after Elizabeth's birth, Suzanne returned to work. Her oldest son, Joshua, needed double hernia surgery in January, and Steven, the youngest, was battling frequent ear infections, resulting in the insertion of tubes in his ears. On February 18, 1984, Don killed himself. While the death was shocking to Suzanne, Don had not been a source of emotional support to her. However, his death eliminated her partner in child care, so she was on her own with the tube feedings and projectile vomiting, as well as the day-to-day care of three young children.

During an examination at a clinic for children with disabilities, a nutritionist recommended that Elizabeth be seen by a speech therapist who specialized in feeding problems. Suzanne decided to stop the phenobarbital because the nutritionist mentioned its interference with protein absorption, and Elizabeth had not seizured since she had been released from the hospital. Two months later, Elizabeth experienced a serious febrile seizure and stopped breathing for several minutes. Elizabeth was given a shot of valium and put back on phenobarbital. A neurological examination was then arranged. The evaluation by the speech therapist with expertise in feeding helped Suzanne understand the physiological reasons why her child had so much difficulty eating and retaining food. She arranged to have Elizabeth receive services from this therapist and, therefore, removed her from the infant stimulation program. There were new recommendations—consideration of a gastrointestinal tube to avoid possible damage from prolonged use of the nasogastric tube and other medical specialists to be seen. The pediatric gastroenterologist noted the absence of motion in the esophagus (needed to properly swallow food) and the lack of strength in the esophageal muscle. Suzanne's impression of his advice to her was—put in a stomach tube and wait for her to die.

Instead, Suzanne began experimenting with new flavors and textures in feeding Elizabeth. Her reasoning was, how could she have these muscle reactions when she had experienced so little opportunity to eat. As a result of her mother's persistence and help from a speech therapist, by age 2½, Elizabeth was free from tube feeding on a routine basis. As a 6-year-old Elizabeth has a typical 6-year-old diet, including pizza. She still needs substantial assistance in bringing small bites of food to her mouth, but is able to adequately chew and swallow solid foods under careful supervision.

When Elizabeth turned 4, she entered a preschool special education class located in a regular school building in her rural community. The following year, she participated full time in a regular kindergarten class. An aide was provided to assist

Elizabeth in her self-care and to ensure maximum participation in the kindergarten program. The plans for first grade are full-time placement in a first-grade class, with aides available to assist Elizabeth. After one month in the first-grade classroom, a review of her functioning is scheduled, so additional academic support from the resource teacher can be arranged if needed.

Summary of Test Results

A partial accumulation of Elizabeth's files is approximately 4 inches thick. Much of this information is redundant, with the case history reported over and over again by each professional who has written a report on the child. The amount of new information available to the parent or professional working with Elizabeth is, in fact, very limited. A chronological sampling of the information in her records is presented here.

At 3 months of age Elizabeth was admitted into an early intervention program with the following stated goals:

> *Psychosocial:* Provide stimulation in all developmental areas and provide parent training
> *Physical therapy:* Neurodevelopmental stimulation and parent training
> *Occupational therapy:* Improve suck-swallow and parent training
> *Sensory-integration:* Improve tone and vestibular and sensory integration.

Excerpts from occupational therapy evaluation conducted at 4 months follow.

> *Oral:*
> A gag reflex was present while "walking" the tongue with a tongue depressor and her tongue retracted. . . . Infantile tongue thrust was not present. She appears tactually defensive.

> *Vestibular System:*
> Children who are developmentally delayed frequently have vestibular systems that are not completely integrated. It is known that the vestibular system is fully formed at birth. Scores are expressed in standard deviations with -1 to $+1.5$ *SD* falling in the normal range. Any score above or below that range is considered indicative of problems. She was spun 10 times in 20 seconds first to the left then the right with her head positioned to stimulate the horizontal semicircular canal. Spinning to the left, Elizabeth has a 7-second, intermittent nystagmus, barely perceptible in excursion with a score of -0.7 *SD*. To the right, she had a 12-second, barely perceptible, vertical rolling nystagmus, with a score of $+1.1$ *SD*. A normal nystagmus for this test is horizontal with a smooth, continuous excursion. Elizabeth could track a light smoothly from left to right, but moving from right to left, the movement is jerky, indicating some difficulties in moving from one hemisphere to the other. This is probably due to the influence of her vestibular system on ocular motor control. Although her scores fall within normal limits, the typical nystagmus response coupled with her inability to swallow would indicate a need for a vestibular stimulation program.

Tactile System:
Elizabeth was found to be tactually defensive in that she hyperresponds to a light-moving touch on the face and trunk. This hypersensitivity on the face could possibly be one of the reasons her suck-swallow was poorly developed.

Excerpts from a physical therapy evaluation also completed at 4 months follow.

Reflexes:
Elizabeth shows a good suck, but very poor swallow. Mother feeds by nasogastric tube. The following reflexes were negative: rooting, suck-swallow, gallant spontaneous stepping, labyrinthine head righting, and questionable optical righting. Positive reflexes and reactions were as follows: suck; Moro; traction; neonatal neck and body righting; asymmetrical tonic neck; palmar grasp; tonic labyrinthine; associated movements, especially in lower extremities; avoidance; and body righting acting on the head.

Range of Motion:
Passive range of motion in all extremities is within normal limits. No obvious spasticity noted, although there is more extensor tone than flexor tone at this time.

Developmental Skills:
Elizabeth can roll prone to supine. Hands have not yet come to mouth, but are coming up toward face, not yet to midline. There is visual tracking horizontally to light. There is little vertical tracking. Elizabeth seems to follow a light or visual stimulation toward the right better than toward the left. Eye movements are not symmetrical. Elizabeth does regard a person's face momentarily. Elizabeth can lift head from a prone position approximately 45°.

A developmental specialist assessed Elizabeth using the *Memphis Comprehensive Development Scale.* The following are subtest scores for administrations at 3 months and 16 months of age:

Domain	3 Months	16 Months
Personal social	2 months	3 months
Gross motor	1 month	3 months
Fine motor	3 months	3 months
Language skills	3 months	7 months
Perceptual–cognitive skills	1 month	5 months

The following excerpts are from the written report accompanying the 16-month assessment.

Language:
Receptive language skills appear to be much higher than standardized testing indicates. Elizabeth is beginning to use her eyes to point to named people and objects. The motoric involvement limited the examiner's ability to fully assess receptive language

skills. A speech-language therapy evaluation may be wanted to further assess receptive language skills and possible need for augmentative communication systems.

Motor:

Muscle tone today was judged to be closer to normal tone than the previous evaluations. She does continue to exhibit spasticity in all four extremities. She appears to be able to use her left hand better than her right. The asymmetrical tonic neck reflex was present throughout the evaluation. However, she easily moved in and out of it.

Hearing:

Behavioral hearing assessments revealed adequate auditory acuity at this time. However, this is a subjective measure and should not be substituted for pure tone audiometry. Elizabeth responded to her name whispered and spoken in a normal tone of voice. She also responded to dropping wooden blocks, squeaky toys, and whistles. Responses were noted as localization to the right and the left.

Vision:

The Functional Vision Screening Test revealed adequate visual mobility and acuity at this time. The only item on the test that she did not pass was reaching on visual cue. However, this was failed because of the motoric involvement, not because of a visual problem.

Excerpts from a speech pathologist's report of a feeding evaluation done at 16 months follow.

Background:

Elizabeth reportedly had a functional although somewhat lethargic suck as an infant. Suzanne noted that Elizabeth has always had problems with swallowing. When she left the hospital at 3 weeks of age, she was tube fed and somewhat nipple fed, however, she could not maintain her weight without the tube feeding. Suzanne reported that Elizabeth does not like to have the tube inserted, and this insertion seems to trigger undesirable motor responses and behavioral responses.

Subjective Observations:

Elizabeth is a pleasant and responsive child. She was very interested in her environment although her physical condition limits her capacity to interact in her environment. She did not cry when held by the clinician. She exhibited appropriate social smiling and eye contact during play interaction. Elizabeth was responsive to both auditory and visual stimulation. When placed in a corner chair that had appropriate strapping with positional stability, Elizabeth maintained head control very efficiently. Suzanne is a very interested and concerned parent.

Feeding Evaluation:

Elizabeth's feeding was observed from another room via audiovisual equipment. Suzanne was asked to feed Elizabeth just as she does in the home environment. Elizabeth was positioned in supine position across from mother's lap with her head slightly elevated. Here food was of a strained consistency and at room temperature. Some gagging and coughing were triggered initially by the introduction of the food, but this was not excessive and improved as the feeding progressed. Slight tongue protrusion was observed intermittently. Lip closure was lacking, and the swallowing response appeared to be somewhat hypoactive. An active munching pattern was observed. Elizabeth was capable of an efficient suck although she did not maintain the suck consistently. Downward extension of the jaw was triggered intermittently. Suzanne interacted well with Elizabeth during the feeding. She seemed to be aware of the nonverbal cues that Elizabeth used to regulate intake of food.

Recommendations:

While Elizabeth displays a number of difficulties in feeding, she appears to have the basic skills necessary for functional oral feeding. It is the examiner's impression that her feeding skills are adequate to warrant taking the nasogastric tube away. It is probable that complete removal of the tube would be preferable to slowly reducing the food intake by tube and increasing the oral food intake because of behavioral considerations; however, either procedure could be considered. Also we should consider the possibility of using the tube only for giving water. Based on parental information and subjective observation, the following recommendations are made:

1. During oral feeding, position Elizabeth upright as much as her stability allows. Upright positioning will allow Elizabeth more time to manipulate the food in her mouth before it flows down. This will help her to be a more active participant in feeding.
2. Obtain an appropriate corner chair for feeding and use developmental stimulation activities. With this type of seating, the feet, pelvic girdle, and shoulder girdle are in vertical alignment with appropriate positional stability. Strapping in the formation of an "x" across Elizabeth's chest may also be advantageous.
3. Provide jaw control as needed to inhibit inappropriate extension of the jaw.
4. Use firm pressure patting, deep pressure stimulation, and vibration around the lips to stimulate lip closure for more efficient sucking and removal of food from the spoon.
5. Stimulate for central grooving of the tongue for more efficient sucking and swallowing by providing pressure in a downward and outward motion using, for example, a tongue depressor or rubber toy.
6. Stimulate for active but controlled movement of the oral structures in mouthing play as Elizabeth mouths a variety of small toys and common objects. Combine this activity in sound play and music activities.
7. Stimulate Elizabeth to actively use her lips to remove food from a spoon by presenting the spoon in front of her, applying light pressure downward on the tongue, and removing the spoon slowly and without angling upward.
8. Gradually thicken the consistency of Elizabeth's food and observe the changes this creates in her oral motor skills. Thickening her food may improve oral skills as thicker foods do not flow as quickly and allow more time to gain control of oral movement.
9. Begin working on drinking from a cup. Use this as an activity for stimulation of jaw control.
10. In all oral motor activities, particularly those in any way invasive, it is important

that Elizabeth enjoy the experience. Care should be taken that no negative associations between tactile stimulation to the oral region and feeding are developed.

Excerpts taken from an initial motor development evaluation by the physical therapist when Elizabeth changed programs at 16 months of age follow.

Background:

Elizabeth is an 18-month-old child who has athetoid-like movement patterns and postures. Concerning speech and language activities, Elizabeth appears to understand most of what is said to her, however, she is not able to express herself. She has no speech at present and uses crying to make her needs known. She does socially smile. She is fed by a nasogastric tube with augmented oral feeding programs. In the prone position, she will not bear weight on her upper extremities or elbows and she does not exhibit head control. In the supine position she is unable to participate in midline activities or to maintain a controlled posture. In the propped sitting position, she will momentarily maintain her head in alignment. Her mother reports that she reaches for objects and is able to maintain a grasp if the object is placed in her hand. This was not noted during the evaluation.

Assessment:

Range of motion is within functional limits, however motor control is severely impaired. Elizabeth lacks graduation of movement, appropriate stabilization for functional movement, and appropriate integration of tonic reflexes. Prognosis for improvement is fair.

Recommendations:

1. Elizabeth will be scheduled to receive individual motor developmental therapy two times per week.
2. We need to assess a functional seating arrangement for Elizabeth.
3. The mother should be given a verbal home program.

Excerpts from an occupational therapist's report at 2 years of age follow.

Background:

Elizabeth is a 2-year-old who has athetoid-like movement patterns and postures. She appears to understand much of what is said to her and responds appropriately to many one- and two-stage commands requiring simple hand movements. Speech therapy is currently working on consistent eye gaze as a means of indicating her wants and a consistent yes and no response. Feedings by nasogastric tube continue with an augmented oral feeding program. Active range of motion is extremely limited due to increases in both flexor and extensor tone. Passive range of motion is within normal limits to both upper extremities. Tightness in hamstrings and hip flexors is seen at the end range bilaterally in the lower extremities. Elizabeth is now able, when placed, to bear weight in a prone position momentarily and can roll prone to supine and vice versa. She will push up onto extended arms when placed in a half-kneeling position at the bench or table. When placed in supine, Elizabeth displays bilateral asymmetrical tonic neck reflex, but with minimal effort is able to move through these to participate in midline activities in sitting, side-lying, and supine. In propped sitting, she can maintain head control for up to 30 seconds at a time. Fine motor coordination and grasp are difficult for Elizabeth but continue to improve.

Assessment:

Elizabeth is functioning at a 4-month fine and gross motor level because of severely impaired motor control. Problem areas continue to be graduation of movement, appropriate stabilization of movement, and complete integration of tonic reflexes.

Equipment:

Elizabeth now has a corner chair and standing frame in daily use at home. She has a feeder seat and pogon chair used for both feeding and transportation.

Recommendations:

1. Continue to see Elizabeth twice weekly for motor development therapy.
2. Consider Elizabeth for enrollment twice a week for fine motor coordination and control therapy.
3. Investigate a sidelier as a means of facilitating more use of hands at midline.

Excerpts from a reevaluation by a speech pathologist when Elizabeth was just over 2 years old follow.

Elizabeth at 2 years 1 month continues to attend therapy regularly on a one-hour-per-session, two-session-per-week basis. Elizabeth's mother is very supportive and involved in her treatment program. During the previous reporting period, she showed progress. In fine motor activities, Elizabeth improved in her ability to bring her hands together at midline, pull string toys, pick up and release her grasp of small objects, and bring her hands to her mouth. In receptive language skills she identifies common objects at the object level, identifies body parts (e.g., eyes, nose, and mouth), and demonstrates verbal directions within her physical capability. In expressive language skills Elizabeth developed a reasonable functional yes and no head-nod response. She imitates the animal sounds for dog and cat and a car sound inconsistently. Concerning oral motor skills, Elizabeth is receptive to mouthing objects and often independently brings objects to her mouth. She continues to take most of her nourishment through a nasogastric tube but the amount of food she is able to take by mouth has increased. Elizabeth continues to experience what could be described as a tightening of the pharyngeal muscles upon presentation or even anticipation of food. This is accompanied by watering eyes and breakdown of the rhythm of her respiration. She does much better when she is relaxed and when the interaction allows her to be in control of what is coming into her mouth. No objective test measures were used to evaluate Elizabeth's progress during this reporting period. The value of such measures in adequately describing the language function of children as physically impaired as Elizabeth is very limited.

Recommendations: Based on interaction with Elizabeth and her mother, the following recommendations are made:

1. Continue individual therapy on a two-session-per-week, one-hour-per-session basis, focusing on language skills, oral motor development, and fine motor development.

2. Participate in the Mother's Day Out Program regularly to provide opportunity for stimulation of language skills and socialization skills in group context and a break from the responsibilities of child care for Suzanne.

3. Consult a nutritionist and other medical specialists concerning the appropriateness of her diet and of long-range use of nasogastric tube feedings.

EDUARDO MANZOLIS

After 27 weeks of gestation, Eduardo Manzolis was born weighing in at 1 pound, 11 ounces. He was unable to breathe and was immediately taken from St. Theresa's Hospital to Metropolitan Children's Hospital to be admitted to the neonatal intensive care unit (NICU). During transit, the hospital staff began efforts to start him breathing. He was 11 minutes old before they could finally get a tube down his throat to assist his breathing. He remained on a respirator and lived on a warming table in the level I unit of the NICU for the next six weeks. During this time, an electrical storm left the hospital without electricity for a brief period, and the backup generator malfunctioned. For Eduardo, this power failure gave him the opportunity to take his first independent breath. He was able to sustain his own breathing. He then moved up to level II of the NICU where he was placed in an incubator. His last three weeks in the NICU were spent in a level II unit in a bassinet. Eduardo never experienced seizures or cerebral hemorrhaging. His family was able to have immediate direct contact throughout his stay in the NICU. After three months in the hospital, parent training in CPR and in the use of a heart monitor, and accumulated bills of $200,000, the Manzolis's brought their 4 pound 14 ounce son home. The parents' scrap book of memories from their child's birth and first few months of life is filled with all the wonderful pictures of their newborn, alongside daily reports of the oxygen levels used in his ventilator, concern for formula in his lungs, brain scan results, and so forth. Reports of 2-ounce weight gains were the cause for much celebration and joy. Family members provided a source of support for Eduardo's parents throughout the long stay in the NICU.

Eduardo's mother, Rachel, is a native of Abington, Virginia, and his father, Roberto, is from El Salvador, Central America. Late in her pregnancy Rachel was fired from her job with a retail store. As it was apparent that the firing was due to her complicated pregnancy, she pursued legal action against the company. Three months after Eduardo was born and two weeks before he was dismissed from the hospital, she regained her job. Although she had no desire to return to work at that time, she really could not abandon her efforts to protect her legal rights. There was a large hospital bill at issue as well. At the time of Eduardo's birth, Roberto was a student and held several part-time jobs, none of which offered insurance. Rachel remained on the job for three months, but finally quit because working conditions were unpleasant and Eduardo continued to have medical needs.

At the end of Eduardo's first year of life, he could hold his head up and had some grasping ability, but he could not sit up, did not crawl, and had weak muscle tone (hypotonic). He laughed out loud for the first time at about 8 months and started babbling after 10 months. The pediatrician never commented on these delayed motor and language milestones until Eduardo was 1 year old, when he referred him to Lakemont Children's Rehabilitation Center.

After being evaluated by a physical therapist, Eduardo began receiving physical therapy once a week. Although he received no diagnosis other than being very floppy (low muscle tone), Rachel read that cerebral palsy was a possibility in one of his records. He began receiving physical therapy once a week for 50 minutes. Initially, therapy was very traumatic for Eduardo. The first six to eight months he screamed for the entire 50-minute period. The therapist explained to Rachel that the crying was not an unusual transition into therapy, and Eduardo eventually adjusted. Shortly after he began enjoying physical therapy, scheduling changes were made and Eduardo was faced with therapy from a different therapist. After a few weeks of displeasure, he was able to adjust to his second therapist with whom he remained for the next two years.

Eduardo still had very little expressive language. Although he was babbling, Eduardo was not using any words. Magnetic resonance imaging revealed no signs of neurological damage. Since the rehabilitation center where Eduardo received physical therapy also had speech therapy, it was arranged for him to be evaluated and treated there. Scheduling constraints made it necessary for Rachel to bring Eduardo to the center twice a week. Since the center was on the far side of town from Rachel's home, she waited at the center during the therapy sessions. The one-on-one clinical approach to speech therapy did not prove effective for Eduardo. He spent much of his time refusing to cooperate and therefore was isolated. When Rachel learned from a friend about an alternative language intervention program, she immediately investigated. As a result, she enrolled Eduardo twice a week in a group preschool language intervention program designed around developmental play activities. He adjusted well in this setting, and Rachel felt that here his speech needs were addressed. However, the weekly schedule now included one trip to the rehabilitation center for physical therapy and two trips to the group language intervention program. Fortunately, the language intervention program was in the vicinity of Roberto's part-time job, so he was able to assist with drop-off and pickup. Eduardo spoke his first words between 2 and 2½ years of age.

At this point, Rachel began working as a teacher's aide in an elementary school, where she remained for two and one-half years. The parents of another child enrolled in this program asked her if she would like to leave her aide position and become their babysitter, which she did. Rachel then decided to return to school full time to earn her degree in early childhood education. Eduardo's father recently graduated with degrees in industrial engineering and computer science and now has a permanent full-time job as a systems analyst.

When Eduardo first began the therapy programs, both Rachel and Roberto were concerned about their son's development. They were anxious to have him receive any intervention that would help him improve in his motor skills and language development. After almost three years of intervention, Eduardo's father, although pleased with his son's progress, does not see that it accomplished much more than would have occurred through his natural maturation. His view is that Eduardo will progress at his own speed, regardless of attempts to speed up his development. Rachel, however, is still very committed to the need for intervention. She feels that Eduardo has made significant improvement in his social skills through group intervention in addition to the progress evident in his motor and language skills. Rachel has expressed some concern that professionals seem to report to her in terms of what Eduardo cannot do, rather than in reflecting on the progress he is making. Eduardo is now speaking without hesitation. He uses words and sentences in combination with gestures to communicate effectively, although articulation is still not always distinct.

As Eduardo's fourth birthday approaches, Rachel and Roberto have been concerned with what, if any, intervention he should receive over the next year. Recent scheduling conflicts at the center have forced the temporary cancellation of physical therapy, and the group language intervention program does not serve 4-year-olds. Rachel learned from staff at the language intervention program that the local education agency provides free preschool intervention for 4-year-olds with special needs five days a week from 8:00 to 2:30. These classes are housed within regular school buildings. Assessments were conducted, and a multidisciplinary team (M-team) meeting was scheduled to discuss Eduardo's possible placement in one of these classes for the next school year. Initially, Rachel was strongly opposed to such a placement. On the morning of the M-team meeting, she decided that it might not be so bad. She had anticipated negative comments about Eduardo. Instead she found that the meeting had a very positive tone. Several possible placements were discussed, with two different preschool teachers in attendance to assist in the decision making. Discussions centered around the best match between Eduardo's needs and the programs available. Rachel feels comfortable with the decision to enroll Eduardo in one of the preschools. Her attitude is basically that it can do no harm and might have some benefit.

Today Rachel is not nearly as anxious about Eduardo as she was when his survival was so uncertain. During the neonatal period, he became the main focus of her life. Today she is able to lead a more balanced life, pursuing her own educational interests and outside activities. As his fourth birthday approaches, she no longer views her son as a fragile premature infant who must be treated delicately.

Summary of Test Results

Test results for a variety of instruments given to Eduardo while he participated in the group language intervention program follow. Age at the time of administration is reported in months.

Carolina Curriculum for Handicapped Infants and Infants At Risk

	(CA 28 months)	(CA 40 months)
Cognition	9–18	21–24
Receptive language	18	22
Expressive language	9	15

Self-help	12	21–24
Social skills	15–18	21
Gross motor	6	15
Fine motor	9–15	15–18

Sequenced Inventory of Communication Development (CA 40 months)

| Receptive language | 28 |
| Expressive language | 12 (with scatter at 16–20 level) |

Preschool Language Scale (CA 46 months)

| Receptive | 37.5 |
| Expressive | 24 |

Brigance Inventory of Early Development (CA 46 months)

Gross motor	16–20
Fine motor	24–28
Cognition	32–36
Receptive speech	40
Expressive speech	24–28

Birth to Three Checklist of Learning & Language Behavior (CA 28 months)

Motor behaviors	14.25
Social and personal	23.25
Avenues to learning	21.75
Language comprehension	25.50
Language expression	12

References

Achenbach, T. M. (1981). *Child Behavior Checklist for Ages 4–16.* Burlington: University of Vermont.

Achenbach, T. M. (1986a). *Child Behavior Checklist for Ages 2–3.* Burlington: University of Vermont.

Achenbach, T. M. (1986b). *Direct Observation Form—Revised Edition.* Burlington: University of Vermont.

Ainsworth, M. D. S., Blehar, M. C., Waters, E., & Wall, S. (1978). *Patterns of attachment: A psychological study of the strange situation.* Hillsdale, NJ: Erlbaum.

Alberto, P. A., & Troutman, A. (1986). *Applied behavior analysis for teachers.* Columbus, OH: Merrill.

Amdur, J. R., Mainland, M. K., & Parker, K. C. H. (1988). *Diagnostic Inventory for Screening Children* (2nd ed.). Kitchener, Ontario: Kitchener Waterloo Hospital.

American Psychiatric Association (1987). *Diagnostic and Statistical Manual of Disorders* (3rd ed., revised). Washington, D.C.: American Psychiatric Association.

Anastasi, A. (1982). *Psychological testing* (5th ed.). New York: Macmillan.

Anastasiow, N. J., & Mansergh, G. P. (1975). Teaching skills in early childhood programs. *Exceptional Children 41*(4), 309–317.

Apgar, V. (1953). A proposal for a new method of evaluation of the newborn infant. *Current Researches in Anesthesia and Analgesia, 32,* 260–267.

Arthur, G. (1949). The Arthur Adaptation of the Leiter International Performance Scale. *Journal of Clinical Psychology, 5,* 345–349.

Associated Press. (1990). Heavy drinking, crack cocaine linked to AIDS spread. *The Knoxville News-Sentinel.* June 21, A13.

Atkinson, R. C., & Shiffrin, R. M., (1968). Human memory: A proposed system and its control processes. In K. W. Spence and J. T. Spence (Eds.), *The psychology of learning and motivation: Advances in research and theory* (Vol. 2). New York: Academic Press.

Austin, J. (1962). *How to do things with words.* London: Oxford University Press.

Ayres, A. J. (1973). *Sensory integration and learning disorders.* Los Angeles: Western Psychological Services.

Ayres, A. J. (1987). *Sensory Integration and Praxis Tests.* Los Angeles: Western Psychological Services.

Ayers, W. (1989). *The good preschool teacher: Six teachers reflect on their lives.* New York: Teachers College Press.

Ayres, R. R., & Cooley, E. J. (1986). Sequential versus simultaneous processing on the K-ABC: Validity in predicting learning success. *Journal of Psychoeducational Assessment, 4,* 211–220.

Baer, A. M., Rowbury, T., & Baer, D. M. (1973). The development of instructional control over classroom activities of deviant preschool children. *Journal of Applied Behavior Analysis, 6,* 209–298.

Bagnato, S. J., & Neisworth, J. T. (1980). The intervention efficiency index: An approach to preschool program accountability. *Exceptional Children, 46*(4), 264–269.

Bagnato, S. J., & Neisworth, J. T. (1981). *Linking developmental assessment and curricula.* Rockville, MD: Aspen Systems Corporation.

Bagnato, S. J., Neisworth, J. T., & Capone, A. (1987). Curriculum-based assessment for the young exceptional child: Rationale and review. *Topics in Early Childhood Special Education, 6*(2), 97–110.

Bagnato, S. J., Neisworth, J. T., & Munson, S. M. (1989). *Linking developmental assessment and early intervention: Curriculum-based prescriptions* (2nd ed.). Rockville, MD: Aspen Systems Corporation.

Bailey, D. B. (1988). Rationale and model for family assessment in early intervention. In D. B. Bailey & R. J. Simeonsson (Eds.), *Family assessment in early intervention.* Columbus, OH: Merrill.

Bailey, D. B. (1989). Assessing environments. In D. B. Bailey & M. Wolery (Eds.), *Assessing infants and preschoolers with handicaps* (pp. 97–188). Columbus, OH: Merrill.

Bailey, D. B., Clifford, R. M., & Harms, T. (1982). Comparison of preschool environments for handicapped and nonhandicapped children. *Topics in Early Childhood Special Education, 2*(1), 9–20.

Bailey, D. B., Harms, T., & Clifford, R. M. (1983). Matching changes in preschool environments to desired changes in child behavior. *Journal of the Division of Early Childhood, 7,* 61–68.

Bailey, D. B., & Rouse, T. L. (1989). Procedural considerations in assessing infants and preschoolers with handicaps. In D. B. Bailey & M. Wolery (Eds.), *Assessing infants and preschoolers with handicaps.* Columbus, OH: Merrill.

Bailey, D. B., & Simeonsson, R. J. (1988). *Family assessment in early intervention.* Columbus, OH: Merrill.

Bailey, D. B., & Wolery, M. (1984). *Assessing infants and preschoolers with handicaps.* Columbus, OH: Merrill.

Bailey, E. J., & Bricker, D. (1986). A psychometric study of a criterion-referenced assessment instrument designed for infants and young children. *Journal of the Division for Early Childhood, 10,* 124–134.

Bailey, D. B., Simeonsson, R. J., Winton, P. J., Huntington, G. S., Comfort, M., Isbell, P., O'Donnell, K. J., & Helm, J. M. (1986). Family-focused intervention: A functional model for planning, implementing and evaluating individualized family services in early intervention. *Journal of the Division for Early Childhood, 10,* 156–171.

Bailey, D. B., & Wolery, M. (1984). *Teaching infants and preschoolers with handicaps.* Columbus, OH: Merrill.

Bale, J. F. (1990). The neurologic complications of AIDS in infants and young children. *Infants and Young Children, 3*(2), 15–23.

Ball, R., & Winberg, R. (1982). *Behavior deviancy profile.* Chicago: Stoelting.

Ball, R. S., Merrifield, P., & Stott, L. H. (1978). *Extended Merrill-Palmer Scale.* Chicago: Stoelting.

Bandura, A. (1978). The self system in reciprocal determinism. *American Psychologist, 33,* 344–358.

Bangs, T. E., & Dodson, S. (1979). *Birth to Three Developmental Scale.* Allen, TX: DLM Teaching Resources.

Barker, R. G. (1968). *Ecological Psychology.* Stanford, CA: Stanford University Press.

Bates, E., O'Connell, B., & Shore, C. (1987). Language and communication in infancy. In J. D. Osofsky (Ed.), *Handbook of Infant Development.* New York: Wiley.

Bayley, N. (1984). *Bayley Scales of Infant Development.* New York: Psychological Corporation.

Beckman, P. J., Robinson, C. C., Jackson, B., & Rosenberg, S. A. (1986). Translating developmental findings into teaching strategies for young handicapped children. *Journal of the Division for Early Childhood, 10,* 99–122.

Beckmann, B. W. (1990). Personal communication. Knoxville, TN.

Beckwith, L. (1990). Adaptive and maladaptive parenting—Implications for intervention. In S. J. Meisels & J. P. Shonkoff (Eds.), *Handbook of early childhood intervention.* New York: Cambridge University Press.

Beery, K., & Buktenica, N. (1982). *Developmental test of visual–motor integration.* Chicago: Follett.

Benner, S. M., & Beckmann, B. W. (1990). Is the child making expected progress? Measuring change in rate of development with young children. *Early Education and Development, 1*(6), 424–437.

Bennett, F. C. (1982). The pediatrician and the interdisciplinary process. *Exceptional Children, 48*(4), 306–314.

Bickerton, D. (1984). The language bioprogram hypothesis. *The Behavioral and Brain Sciences, 7,* 173–187.

Bijou, S. W., & Baer, D. M. (1961). *Child development I: A systematic and empirical theory.* New York: Prentice-Hall.

Blanton, R., & Brooks, P. (1978). Psycholinguistic affects of sign language. In I. M. Schlesinger & L. Namir (Eds.), *Sign language of the deaf.* New York: Academic Press.

Bloom, L. (1970). *Language development: Form and function of emerging grammars.* Cambridge, MA: MIT Press.

Bloom, L. (1975). Language development review. In F. D. Horowitz (Ed.), *Review of child development research* (Vol. 4). Chicago: University of Chicago Press.

Bloom, L., & Lahey, M. (1978). *Language development and language disorders.* New York: Wiley.

Bobath, B. (1970). *The concept of "neurodevelopmental treatment."* London, England: Western Cerebral Palsy Centre.

Bobath, B., & Bobath, K. (1975). Motor development in the different types of cerebral palsy. London: Heinemann Medical Books.

Bobath, K., & Bobath, B. (1972). *Cerebral palsy.* In P. H. Pearson and C. E. Williams (Eds.), *Physical therapy services in the developmental disabilities.* Springfield, IL: Thomas.

Bond, L. A., Creasey, G. L., & Abrams, C. L. (1990). Play assessment: Reflecting and promoting cognitive competence. In E. D. Gibbs & D. M. Teti (Eds.), *Interdisciplinary assessment of infants: A guide for early intervention professionals.* Baltimore, MD: Brookes.

Bonham, S. J. (1974). Predicting achievement for deaf children. *Psychological Service Center Journal, 14,* 35–44.

Boston Center for Blind Children (1988). *Developmental teaching guide: Check list and activity file.* Boston: Boston Center for Blind Children.

Bower, G. A. (1967). A multicomponent theory of memory trace. In K. W. Spence & J. T. Spence (Eds.), *The psychology of learning and motivation: Advances in research and theory.* New York: Academic Press.

Boyd, R. D. (1989). What a difference a day makes: Age-related discontinuities and the Battelle Developmental Inventory. *Journal of Early Intervention, 13*(2), 114–119.

Boyd, R. D., Welge, P., Sexton, D., & Miller, J. H. (1989). Concurrent validity of the Battelle Developmental Inventory: Relationship with the Bayley scales in young children with known or suspected disabilities. *Journal of Early Intervention, 13*(1), 14–23.

Bracken, B. A. (1984). *Examiner's manual: Bracken Basic Concept Scale.* New York: Psychological Corporation.

Brandt, R. M. (1975). An historical overview of systematic approaches to observation in school settings. In R. A. Weinberg & F. H. Wood (Eds.), *Observation of pupils and teachers in mainstream and special education settings: Alternative strategies.* Minneapolis: University of Minnesota.

Brayden, R. (1990). Medical, neurodevelopmental, and behavioral influence of cocaine on the fetus and infant. Cocaine use during pregnancy: Consequences for fetus, infant, and family conference. Sponsored by Tennessee Department of Human Services, John F. Kennedy Center, Peabody Vanderbilt University, Our Kids, Nashville Child Abuse Program, Johnson City, TN, September.

Brazelton, T. B. (1973). Neonatal Behavioral Assessment Scale. *National spastics society monograph.* Philadelphia: Lippincott.

Brazelton, T. B. (1984). *Neonatal Behavioral Assessment Scale.* Philadelphia: Lippincott.

Bredekemp, S. (1987). *Developmentally Appropriate Practice in Early Childhood Programs Serving Children from Birth Through Age 9* (expanded ed.). Washington, D.C.: NAEYC.

Bricker, D. & Gentry, D. (1982). Evaluation and programming system: For infants and young children. Assessment level I: Developmentally 1 month to 3 years (EPS-I). Unpublished manuscript, Center on Human Development, University of Oregon.

Bricker, D., & Squires, J. (1989). A low-cost system using parents to monitor the development of at-risk infants. *Journal of Early Intervention, 13*(1), 50–60.

Bricker, D., Squires, J., Kaminski, R., & Mounts, L. (1988). The validity, reliability, and cost of a parent-completed questionnaire system to evaluate at-risk infants. *Journal of Pediatric Psychology, 13*(1), 5–68.

Bricker, D. B. (1986). *Early education of at-risk and handicapped infants, toddlers, and preschool children.* Greenville, IL: Scott, Foresman.

Bricker, D. B. (1989). An activity-based approach to early intervention. Paper presented at the annual meeting of the Division of Early Childhood, Council for Exceptional Children, Minneapolis, MN, October.

Bridges, F., & Cicchetti, D. (1982). Mother ratings of temperament characteristics of Down syndrome infants. *Developmental Psychology, 18,* 238–244.

Bridges, K. (1932). Emotional development in early infancy. *Child Development, 3,* 324–341.

Brockman, L. M., Morgan, G. A., & Harmon, R. J. (1988). Mastery motivation and developmental delay. In T. D. Wachs & R. Sheehan (Eds.), *Assessment of young developmentally disabled children.* New York: Plenum.

Bromwich, R. (1981). *Working with parents and infants: An interactional approach.* Baltimore, MD: University Park Press.

Bronfenbrenner, U. (1976). The experimental ecology of education. *Educational Research, 5*(9), 5–15.

Bronfenbrenner, U. (1986). Ecology of the family as a context for human development research perspectives. *Developmental Psychology, 22,* 723–742.

Bronfenbrenner, U., & Crouter, A. (1982). Work and family through time and space. In S. N. Kammerman & C. D. Hayes (Eds.), *Families that work: Children in a changing environment of work, family and community.* Washington, D.C.: National Academy of Sciences.

Bronfenbrenner, U., Moen, P., & Garbarino, J. (1984). Families and communities. In H. R. Parke (Ed.), *Review of child development research.* Chicago: University of Chicago Press.

Browder, D. M. (1987). *Assessment of individuals with severe handicaps.* Baltimore, MD: Brookes.

Brown, R. (1970). Derivational complexities and order of acquisition in child speech. In R. Brown (Ed.), *Psycholinguistics.* New York: Free Press.

Brown, R. (1973). *A first language: The early stages.* Cambridge: Harvard University Press.

Brown, J. V., & Bakeman, R. (1979). Relationships of human mothers with their infants during the first year of life. In R. W. Bell & W. P. Smotherman (Eds.), *Maternal influences and early behavior.* New York: Spectrum.

Bruininks, R. H. (1978). *Bruininks-Oseretsky Test of Motor Proficiency.* Circle Pines, MN: American Guidance Service.

Bruner, J. (1975). The ontogenesis of speech acts. *Journal of Child Language, 2,* 1–19.

Budoff, M. (1987). Measures for assessing learning potential. In C. S. Lidz (Ed.), *Dynamic assessment: An interactional approach to evaluating learning potential.* New York: Guilford.

Bzoch, K., & League, R. (1971). *Assessing language skills in infancy: A handbook for the multidimensional analysis of emergent language.* Baltimore, MD: University Park Press.

Caldwell, B. (1972). *HOME Inventory.* Little Rock, AK: University of Arkansas.

Campione, J. C., & Brown, A. L. (1987). Linking dynamic assessment with school achievement. In C. S. Lidz (Ed.), *Dynamic assessment: An interactional approach to evaluating learning potential.* New York: Guilford.

Carta, J. J., Atwater, J. B., Schwartz, I. S., & Miller, P. A. (1990). Applications of ecobehavioral analysis to the study of transitions across early education settings. *Education and Treatment of Children, 13,* 298–315.

Carta, J. J., Greenwood, C. R., & Atwater, J. B. (1985). Ecobehavioral system for the complex assessment of preschool environments: ESCAPE, Kansas City, KS: ERIC (ED 288 268) (EC 200 587).

Carta, J. J., Greenwood, C. R., & Robinson, S. L. (1987). Application of an ecobehavioral approach to the evaluation of early intervention programs. In R. Prinz (Ed.), *Advances in behavioral assessment of children and families* (Vol. 3, pp. 123–156). Greenwich, CT: JAI Press.

Carta, J. J., Sainato, D. M., & Greenwood, C. R. (1988). Advances in the ecological assessment of classroom instruction for young children with handicaps. In. S. L. Odom & M. B. Karnes (Eds.), *Early intervention for infants and young children with handicaps: An empirical base* (pp. 217–239). Baltimore, MD: Brookes.

Cattell, P. (1960). *Cattell Infant Intelligence Scale.* New York: Psychological Corporation.

Cattell, R. B. (1963). Theory of fluid and crystallized intelligence: A critical experiment. *Journal of Educational Psychology, 54,* 1–22.

Centers for Disease Control. (1984). *Morbidity and Mortality Weekly Report.* Atlanta, GA: U. S. Department of Health and Human Service.

Chan, S. (1990). Early intervention with culturally diverse families of infants and toddlers with disabilities. *Infants and Young Children, 3*(2), 78–87.

Chandler, L. (1986). Screening for movement dysfunction. In J. K. Sweeney (Ed.), *The high-risk neonate: Developmental therapy perspective.* New York: Haworth.

Chandler, L. (1990). Neuromotor assessment. In E. D. Gibbs & D. T. Teti (Eds.), *Interdisciplinary assessment of infants: A guide for early intervention professionals.* Baltimore, MD: Brookes.

Chandler, L., Andrews, M., & Swanson, M. (1980). *The Movement Assessment of Infants: A manual.* Rolling Bay, WA: Infant Movement Research.

Chess, S., & Korn, S. (1970). Temperament and behavior disorders in mentally retarded children. *Archives of General Psychiatry, 23,* 122.

Chess, S., Korn, S., & Fernandez, P. (1971). *Psychiatric disorders of children with congenital rubella.* New York: Brunner/Mazel.

Chomsky, N. (1959). A review of Skinner's *Verbal Behavior. Language, 35,* 26–58.

Chomsky, N. (1965). *Aspects of the theory of syntax.* Cambridge, MA: MIT Press.

Clarren, S. K., & Smith, D. W. (1978). The fetal alcohol syndrome. *The New England Journal of Medicine, 298*(19), 1063–1067.

Cohen, J. (1960). A coefficient of agreement for nominal scales. *Educational and Psychological Measurement, 20,* 37–47.

Cohen, D. J., Allen, M. G., Pollin, N. W., Inoff, G., Werner, M., & Dibble, E. (1972). Personality development in twins. *Journal of the American Academy of Child Psychiatry, 11,* 625–644.

Comfort, M. (1988). Assessing parent–child interaction. In D.B. Bailey & R. J. Simeonsson (Eds.), *Family assessment in early intervention.* Columbus, OH: Merrill.

Cone, J. D. (1982). Validity of direct observation assessments. In D. P. Hartmann (Ed.), *Using observers to study behavior.* San Francisco: Jossey-Bass.

Cook, J. (1963). Dimension analysis of child rearing attitudes of parents of handicapped children. *American Journal of Mental Deficiency, 68,* 354–361.

Cook, M. J., Holder-Brown, L., Johnson, L., & Kilgo, J. L. (1989). An examination of the stability of the Bayley Scales of Infant Development with high-risk infants. *Journal of Early Intervention, 13,* 45–49.

Corman, H., & Escalona, S. (1969). Stages of sensorimotor development: A replication study. *Merrill-Palmer Quarterly, 15,* 351.

Cratty, B. J. (1979). *Perceptual and motor development in infants and children.* Englewood Cliffs, NJ: Prentice-Hall.

Cross, L. (1977). Diagnosis. In L. Cross & K. Goin (Eds.), *Identifying handicapped children: A guide to casefinding, screening, diagnosis, assessment, and evaluation.* New York: Walker,

Cummins, J. (1989). A theoretical framework for bilingual special education. *Exceptional Children, 56*(2), 111–120.

Czudnowski, C. M., & Goldenberg, D. (1990). *Developmental Indicators for the Assessment of Learning—Revised* (DIAL-R). Circle Pines, MN: American Guidance Service.

Dale, P. S., Bates, E., Reznick, J. S., & Morisset, C. (1989). The validity of a parent report instrument of a child language at twenty months. *Journal of Child Language, 16,* 239–249.

Daniels, D., & Plomin, R. (1985). Differential experience of siblings in the same family. *Developmental Psychology, 21,* 747–760.

Deal, A. G., Dunst, C. J., & Trivette, C. M. (1989). A flexible and functional approach to developing individualized family support plans. *Infants and Young Children, 1*(4), 32–43.

de Avila, E. A., & Havassy, B. (1974a). *Intelligence of Mexican-American children: A field study comparing Neo-Piagetian and traditional capacity and achievement measures.* Austin, TX: Dissemination Center for Bilingual Bicultural Education.

de Avila, E. A., & Havassy, B. (1974b). *I.Q. tests and minority children.* Austin, TX: Dissemination Center for Bilingual Bicultural Education.

Decarie, T. G. (1969). A study of the mental and emotional development of the thalidomide child. In B. M. Foss (Ed.), *Determinants of infant behavior* (Vol. 4). London: Methuen.

de Villiers, J. G., & de Villiers, D. A. (1978). *Language acquisition.* Cambridge, MA: Harvard University Press.

Diamond, K. (1987). Predicting school problems from preschool developmental screening: A four-year follow-up of the Revised Denver Developmental Screening Test and the role of parent report. *Journal of the Division for Early Childhood, 11,* 247–253.

Dokecki, P. R., Baumeister, A. A., & Kupstas, F. D. (1989). Biomedical and social aspects of pediatric AIDS. *Journal of Early Intervention, 13*(2), 99–113.

Dore, J. (1974). A pragmatic description of early language development. *Journal of Psycholinguistic Research, 3,* 343–350.

Doulah, A. M. (1976). *A motor development checklist.* Madison, WI: Central Wisconsin Center for the Developmentally Disabled.

Dubowitz, L. M. S. (1985). Neurological assessment of the full-term and preterm newborn infant. In S. Harel & N. J. Anastasiow (Eds.), *The at-risk infant.* Baltimore, MD: Brookes.

Dukes, P. J. (1976). The effects of early childrearing practices on the cognitive development of infants. In R. C. Granger & J. C. Young (Eds.), *Demythologizing the inner-city child.* Washington, D.C.: The National Association for the Education of Young Children.

Dunst, C. J. (1980). *A clinical and educational manual for use with the Uzgiris and Hunt Scales of Infant Psychological Development.* Austin, TX: Pro-Ed.

Dunst, C. J., Holbert, K. A., & Wilson, L. L. (1990). Strategies for assessing infant sensorimotor interactive competencies. In E. D. Gibbs & D. M. Teti (Eds.), *Interdisciplinary assessment of infants: A guide for early intervention professionals.* Baltimore, MD: Brookes.

Dunst, C. J., & McWilliam, R. A. (1988). Cognitive assessment of multiply handicapped young children. In T. Wachs & R. Sheehan (Eds.), *Assessment of developmentally disabled children.* New York: Plenum.

Dunst, C. J., McWilliam, R. A., & Holbert, K. (1986). Assessment of preschool classroom environments. *Diagnostique, 11*(3–4), 212–231.

Dunst, C. J., Rheingrover, R. M., & Kistler, E. D. (1986). Concurrent validity of the Uzgiris–Hunt Scales: Relationship to Bayley scale mental age. *Behavioral Science Documents, 16,* 65.

Dunst, C. J., Snyder, S. W., & Mankinen, M. (1989). Efficacy of early intervention. In M. C. Wang, M. C. Reynolds, & H. J. Walberg (Eds.), *Handbook of special education: Research and practice* (Vol. 3, low incidence conditions). New York: Pergamon.

Dunst, C. J., Trivette, C., & Deal, A. (1988). *Enabling and empowering families: Principles and guidelines for practice.* Cambridge, MA: Brookline.

Duran, R. P. (1989). Assessment and instruction of at-risk Hispanic students. *Exceptional Children, 56*(2), 111–120.

Dykes, M. K. (1980). *Developmental Assessment for the Severely Handicapped.* Austin, TX: Exceptional Resources.

Elkind, D. (1986). Formal education and early childhood education: An essential difference. *Phi Delta Kappan,* 631–636.

Ellis, N. R. (1970). Memory processes in retardates and normals. In N. R. Ellis (Ed.), *International review of research in mental retardation* (Vol. 4). New York: Academic Press.

Ellison, P., Browning, C., Larson, B., & Denny, J. (1983). Development of a scoring system for the Milani–Comparetti and Gidoni method of assessing neurologic abnormality in infancy. *Physical Therapy, 63*(9), 1414–1423.

Ensher, G. L., & Clark, D. A. (1986). *Newborns at risk: Medical care and psychoeducational intervention.* Rockville, MD: Aspen.

Erhardt, R. P. (1982). *Developmental hand dysfunction.* Laurel, MD: Ramsco.

Erhardt, R. P. (1986). *Erhardt Developmental Visual Assessment.* Fargo, ND: Erhardt.

Escalona, S. K., & Corman, H. H. (1966). *Albert Einstein scales of sensorimotor development.* Unpublished manuscript. New York: Albert Einstein College of Medicine.

Eyberg, S. M., & Ross, A. W. (1978). Assessment of child behavior problems: The validation of a new inventory. *Journal of Clinical Child Psychology, 7,* 113–116.

Fackelmann, K. (1988). Children who need technology—and parents. *Technology review, 91*(1), 26–27.

Federal Register (1977, August), *42* [163]. 20 U.S.C. 1401 [1], [15].

Federal Register (1977, December), Part 3.

Feldt, L. S., & Brennan, R. L. (1989). Reliability. In R. L. Linn (Ed.), *Educational measurement* (3rd ed., pp. 105–146). New York: Macmillan.

Fetters, L. (1984). Motor development. In M. J. Hanson (Ed.), *Atypical infant development.* Baltimore, MD: University Park Press.

Feuerstein, R. (1979). *The dynamic assessment of retarded performers: The learning potential assessment device, theory, instruments, and techniques.* Baltimore, MD: University Park Press.

Feuerstein, R., Miller, R., Rand, Y., & Jensen, M. R. (1981). Can evolving techniques better measure cognitive change? *The Journal of Special Education, 15,* 201–219.

Fewell, R. (1988). Follow-up findings of a program for motor skill achievement. *Topics in Early Childhood Special Education, 7*(4), 67–70.

Fewell, R. R. (1983). Assessing handicapped infants. In S. G. Garwood & R. R. Fewell (Eds.), *Educating handicapped infants: Issues in development and intervention.* Rockville, MD: Aspen Systems Corporation.

Fewell, R. R., & Langley, M. B. (1984). *Developmental Activities Screening Inventory-II.* Austin, TX: Pro-Ed.

Fewell, R. R., & Rich, J. S. (1987). Play assessment as a procedure for examining cognitive, communication, and social skills in multihandicapped children. *Journal of Psychoeducational Assessment, 2,* 107–118.

Field, T. M., (1977a). Effects of early separation, interactive deficits, and experimental manipulations on infant–mother face-to-face interaction. *Child Development, 48,* 763–771.

Field, T. M., (1977b). Maternal stimulation during infant feeding. *Developmental Psychology, 13,* 539–540.

Figueroa, R. A. (1989). Psychological testing of linguistic-minority students: Knowledge gaps and regulations. *Exceptional Children, 56,* 145–153.

Figueroa, R. A., Fradd, S. H., & Correa, V. I. (1989). Bilingual special education and this special issue. *Exceptional Children, 56*(2), 111–120.

Finnie, N. (1975). *Handling the young cerebral palsied child at home.* New York: Dutton.

Folio, M. R., & Fewell, R. R. (1983). *Peabody Developmental Motor Scale and Activity Cards.* Allen, TX: Teaching Resources.

Fraiberg, S. (1975). Intervention in infancy: A program for blind infants. In B. Z. Friedlander, G. M. Sterritt, & G. E. Kirk (Eds.), *Exceptional Infant* (Vol. 3): *Assessment and intervention.* New York: Brunner/Mazel.

Francis, P. L., Self, P. A., & Horowitz, F. D. (1987). The behavioral assessment of the neonate: An overview. In J. D. Osofsky (Ed.), *Handbook of Infant Development.* New York: Wiley.

Frankenburg, W.K. (1986). *Revised Denver Prescreening Developmental Questionnaire.* Denver: Denver Developmental Materials.

Frankenburg, W. K., & Camp, B. W. (Eds.) (1975). *Pediatric screening tests.* Springfield, IL: Charles C Thomas.

Frankenburg, W. K., Camp, B. W., & van Natta, P. A. (1971). Validity of the Denver Developmental Screening Test. *Child Development, 42,* 475–485.

Frankenburg, W. K., & Dodd, J. B. (1970). *Denver Developmental Screening Test.* Denver, CO: LADOCA Project and Publishing Foundation.

Frankenburg, W. K., Dodd, J. B., & Fandal, A. W. (1975). *Denver Developmental Screening Test.* Denver, CO: LADOCA Project and Publishing Foundation.

Frankenburg, W. K., Fandal, A., & Thorton, S. (1987). Revision of the Denver Prescreening Developmental Questionnaire. *Journal of Pediatrics, 110,* 653–657.

Fredericksen, L. W., & Fredericksen, C. B. (1977). Experimental evaluation of classroom environments: Scheduling planned activities. *American Journal of Mental Deficiency, 81,* 421–427.

Friedrich, W. N., & Friedrich, W. L. (1981). Psychosocial assets of parents of handicapped and non-handicapped children. *American Journal of Mental Deficiency, 85,* 551–552.

Frost, J., & Klein, B. (1979). *Children's play and playgrounds.* Boston: Allyn and Bacon.

Frost, J. L. (1986). Children in a changing society: Frontiers of challenge. *Childhood Education, 62*(4), 242–250.

Fuchs, D., Fuchs, L. S., Benowitz, S., & Barringer, K. (1987). Norm-referenced tests: Are they valid for use with handicapped students? *Exceptional Children, 54*(3), 263–271.

Gaensbauer, T. J., Mrazek, D., & Harmon, R. J. (1981). Behavioral observations of abused and/or neglected infants. In N. Frude (Ed.), *Psychological approaches to the understanding and prevention of child abuse.* London: Batsford.

Gallahue, D. L. (1982). *Understanding motor development in children.* New York: Wiley.

Garbarino, J. (1990). The human ecology of early risk. In S. J. Meisels & J. P. Shonkoff (Eds.), *Handbook of early childhood intervention.* New York: Cambridge University Press.

Gardner, H. (1983). *Frames of Mind.* New York: Basic.

Garland, C. (Ed.). (nd). Transdisciplinary approach to early intervention child development resources. Unpublished manuscript. Lightfoot, VA.

Gearhart, B. R., & Litton, F. W. (1975). *The trainable retarded.* St. Louis, MO: Mosby.

Gesell, A. (1925). *The mental growth of the preschool child.* New York: Macmillan.

Gesell, A., & Amatruda, C. S. (1947). *Developmental diagnosis.* New York: Hoeber.

Glick, J. (1975). Cognitive development in cross-cultural perspective. In F. D. Horowitz (Ed.), *Review of child development research* (Vol. 4). Chicago: University of Chicago Press.

Glicken, A. D., Couchman, G., & Harmon, R. J. (1981). *Free Play Social Scale.* Denver: University of Colorado School of Medicine, Infant Development Laboratory.

Gottfried, A. W. (1984). Issues concerning the relationship between home environment and early cognitive development. In A. W. Gottfried (Ed.), *Home environment and early cognitive development.* Orlando, FL: Academic Press.

Gradel, K., Thompson, M. S., & Sheehan, R. (1981). Parental and professional agreement in early childhood assessment. *Topics in Early Childhood Special Education, 1,* 31–39.

Gratch, G., & Schatz, J. A. (1987). Cognitive development: The relevance to Piaget's infancy books. In J. D. Osofsky (Ed.), *Handbook of infant development.* New York: Wiley.

Greenberg, M. (1983). Family stress and child competence: The effects of early intervention for families with deaf infants. *American Annals of the Deaf, 128,* 407–417.

Greenspan, S. I., & Lieberman, A. F. (1988). A clinical approach to attachment. In J. Belsky & T. Nezworski (Eds.), *Clinical implications of attachment.* Hillsdale, NJ: Erlbaum.

Greenspan, S. I., Lieberman, A. F., & Poisson, S. S. (1981). *Greenspan–Lieberman Observation System for Assessment of Caregiver–Infant Interaction during Semi-Structured Play (GLOS).* Bethesda, MD: Mental Health Study Center, National Institute of Mental Health.

Greer, J. V. (1990). The drug babies. *Exceptional Children, 56*(5), 382–384.

Griffiths, R. (1954). *The abilities of babies.* London: University of London Press.

Griffiths, R. (1979). *The abilities of young children.* London: Child Development Research Center.

Guilford, J. P. (1967). *The nature of human intelligence.* New York: McGraw-Hill.

Haley, S. M., & Baryza, M. J. (1990). A hierachy of motor outcome assessment: Self-initiated movements through adaptive motor function. *Infants and Young Children, 3*(2), 1–14.

Haley, S. M., Faas, R. M., Coster, W. J., Webster, H., & Gans, B. M. (1989). *Pediatric Evaluation of Disability Inventory: Examiner's manual.* Boston: New England Medical Center.

Haley, S. M., Stephens, T. E., & Larsen, A. M. (1988). Patterns of physical and occupational therapy implementation in early motor intervention. *Topics in Early Childhood Special Education, 7*(4), 46–63.

Hammill, D. D. (1985). *Detroit Tests of Learning Aptitude-P.* Austin, TX: Pro-Ed.

Hanson, M. J. (1984). Parent–infant interaction. In M. J. Hanson (Ed.), *Atypical infant development.* Baltimore, MD: University Park Press.

Hanson, M. J. (1985). Analysis of the effects of early intervention services for infants and toddlers with moderate to severe handicaps. *Topics in Early Childhood Special Education, 5*(2), 36–51.

Hanson, R., & Aldridge-Smith, J. (1987). Achievements of young children on items of the Griffiths' scales: 1980 compared with 1960. *Child: Care, Health, and Development, 13,* 181–195.

Hanson, M. J., & Hanline, M. F. (1984). Behavioral competencies and outcomes: The effects of disorders. In M. J. Hanson (Ed.), *Atypical infant development.* Baltimore, MD: University Park Press.

Hargis, C. H. (1987). *Curriculum based assessment.* Springfield, IL: Charles C Thomas.

Haring, N. G., White, O. R., Edgar, E. B., Affleck, J. Q., & Hayden, A. H. (1981). *Uniform Performance Assessment System.* New York: Psychological Corporation.

Harmon, R. J., Glicken, A. D., & Couchman, G. M. (1981). *Free play scoring manual.* Denver: University of Colorado School of Medicine, Infant Development Laboratory.

Harms, T., & Clifford, R. M. (1980). *Early Childhood Environment Rating Scale.* New York: Teachers College Press.

Harms, T., & Clifford, R. M. (1983). Assessing preschool environments with the Early Childhood Environment Rating Scale. *Studies in Educational Evaluation, 8,* 261–269.

Harris, S., Haley, S., Tada, W., & Swanson, M. (1984). Reliability of observational measures of the movement assessment of infants. *Physical Therapy, 64,* 471–475.

Hart, B. (1978). Organizing program implementation. In K. E. Allen, V. A. Holm, & R. L. Schiefelbusch (Eds.), *Early intervention—A team approach* (pp. 309–330). Baltimore, MD: University Park Press.

Hart, V. (1977). The use of many disciplines with severely and profoundly handicapped. In E. Sontag, J. Smith, & N. Certo (Eds.), *Educational programming for the severely and profoundly handicapped.* Reston, VA: Council for Exceptional Children, Division of Mental Retardation.

Hartman, A. (1978). Diagrammatic assessment of family relationships. *Social Casework, 59,* 465–476.

Hartmann, D. P. (1982). Assessing the dependability of observational data. In D. P. Hartmann (Ed.), *Using observers to study behavior.* San Francisco: Jossey-Bass.

Haskins, R., Ramey, C. T., Stedman, D. J., Blacher-Dixon, J., & Pierce, J. E. (1978). Effects of repeated assessment on standardized test performance by infants. *American Journal of Mental Deficiency, 83,* 233–239.

Hebb, D. O. (1949). *The organization of behavior.* New York: Wiley.

Hedrick, D., Prather, E., & Tobin, A. (1984). *Sequenced Inventory of Communication Development–Revised.* Seattle, WA: University of Washington Press.

Henderson, R. W., Bergan, J. R., & Hurt, M. (1972). Development and validation of the *Henderson Environmental Learning Process Scale. The Journal of Social Psychology, 88,* 185–196.

Hess, R. D., Holloway, S., Price, G. G., & Dickson, W. P. (1982). Family environments and the acquisition of reading skills: Toward a more precise analysis. In L. M. Laosa & I. E. Sigel (Eds.), *Families as learning environments for children.* New York: Plenum.

Hingson, R., Alpert, J. J., Day, N., Dooling, E., Kayne, H., Morelock, S., Oppenheimer, E., & Zuckerman, B. (1982). Effects of maternal drinking and marijuana use on fetal growth and development. *Pediatrics, 70,* 539–546.

Hoffman, H. (1982). *Bayley Scales of Infant Development: Modifications for Youngsters with Handicapping Conditions* (revised). Commack, NY: Suffolk Rehabilitation Center, United Cerebral Palsy.

Hoffmeister, R., & Wilbur, R. (1980). The acquisition of sign language. In H. Lane & F. Grosjean (Eds.), *Recent perspectives on American Sign Language.* Hillsdale, NJ: Erlbaum.

Hoffmeister, R. J. (1988). Cognitive assessment in deaf preschoolers. In T. D. Wachs & R. Sheehan (Eds.), *Assessment of young developmentally disabled children.* New York: Plenum.

Holden, R. H. (1972). Prediction of mental retardation in infancy. *Mental Retardation, 10*(1), 28–30.

Holroyd, J. (1974). The questionnaire on resources and stress: An instrument to measure family response to a handicapped member. *Journal of Community Psychology, 2,* 92–94.

Holroyd, J. (1986). *Questionnaire on resources and stress for families with a chronically ill or handicapped member: Manual.* Brandon, VT: Clinical Psychology Publishing.

Holroyd, J., & Guthrie, D. (1979). Stress in family of children with neuromuscular disease. *Journal of Clinical Psychology, 35,* 734–739.

Holroyd, J., & McArthur, D. (1976). Mental retardation and stress on the parents: A contrast between Down's syndrome and childhood autism. *American Journal of Mental Deficiency, 80,* 431–436.

Holtzman, N. A., Morales, D. R., Cunningham, G., & Wells, D. G. T. (1975). Phenylketonuria. In W. K. Frankenburg & B. W. Camp (Eds.), *Pediatric screening tests.* Springfield, IL: Charles C Thomas.

Honig, A., & Lally, R. (1970). *Piagetian infancy scales.* Unpublished manuscript.

Hops, H., Guild, J., Fleishman, D. H., Paine, S., Street, A., Walker, H., & Greenwood, C. (1979). *Peers: Procedures for establishing effective relationship skills.* Eugene, OR: CORBEH.

Horn, J. L. (1985). Remodeling old models of intelligence. In B. Wolman (Ed.), *Handbook of intelligence.* New York: Wiley.

Horowitz, F. D., Sullivan, J. W., & Linn, P. (1978). Stability and instability in the newborn infant: The quest for elusive threads. In A. J. Sameroff (Ed.), Organization and stability of newborn behavior: A commentary on the Brazelton Neonatal Behavioral Assessment Scale. *Monographs of the Society for Research in Child Development* (Vol. 43, no. 5–6, ser. no. 177).

Horstmeier, D., & MacDonald, J. (1978). *Environmental Pre-Language Battery.* New York: Psychological Corporation.

House, L. I., & Rogerson, B. S. (1984). *Comprehensive Screening Tool for Determining Optimal Communication Mode.* East Aurora, NY: United Educational Services.

Howard, J. (1982). The role of the pediatrician with young exceptional children and their families. *Exceptional Children, 48*(4), 296–304.

Howard, J., Beckwith, L., Rodning, C., & Kropenske, V. (1989). The development of young children of substance-abusing parents: Insights for seven years of intervention and research. *Zero to Three, 9*(5), 8–12.

Howell, K.W., Kaplan, J.S., & O'Connell, C.Y. (1979). *Evaluating exceptional children: A task analysis approach.* Columbus, OH: Charles E. Merrill.

Huck, S., Cormier, W. H., & Bounds, W. G. (1974). *Reading statistics and research.* New York: Harper and Row.

Huer, M. B. (1983a). Comparing communicative interaction strategies of nonspeaking and speaking individuals. Paper presented at ASHA Convention, Cincinnati, OH.

Huer, M. B. (1983b). *The Nonspeech Test for Receptive/Expressive Language.* Lake Zurich, IL: Don Johnston Developmental Equipment.

Hunt, J. McV. (1975). Psychological assessment in education and social class. In B. Z. Friedlander, G. M. Sterritt, & G. E. Kirk (Eds.), *Exceptional infant,* Vol. 3: *Assessment and intervention.* New York: Brunner/Mazel.

Huntington, G. S. (1988). Assessing child characteristics that influence family functioning. In D. B. Bailey & R. J. Simeonsson (Eds.), *Family assessment in early intervention.* Columbus, OH: Merrill.

Hutchings, J. J. (1988). Pediatric AIDS: An overview. *Children Today, 17*(3), 9–14.

Hutton, J. B., & Roberts, T. G. (1986). *Social–Emotional Dimension Scale.* Austin, TX: Pro-Ed.

Ireton, H., & Thwing, E. (1974). *Minnesota Child Development Inventory.* Minneapolis: Behavior Science Systems.

Ireton, H., Thwing, E., & Gravem, H. (1970). Infant mental development and neurological status, family socioeconomic status, and intelligence at age four. *Child Development, 41,* 937–946.

Irwin, D. M., & Bushnell, M. M. (1980). *Observational strategies for child study.* New York: Holt, Rinehart and Winston.

Jackson, E. (1982). Environments of high-risk and handicapped infants. In C. T. Ramey & P. L. Trohanis (Eds.), *Finding and educating high-risk and handicapped infants.* Baltimore, MD: University Park Press.

Jenkins, J. R., Fewell, R., & Harris, S. R. (1983). Comparison of sensory integrative therapy and motor programming. *American Journal of Mental Deficiency, 88*(2), 221–224.

Jenkins, J. R., Odom, S. L., & Speltz, M. L. (1989). Effects of social integration on preschool children with handicaps. *Exceptional Children, 55*(5), 420–428.

Jenkins, J. R., & Sells, C. J. (1984). Physical and occupational therapy: Effects related to treatment, frequency, and motor delay. *Journal of Learning Disabilities, 17*(2), 89–95.

Jennings, K. D., Connors, R. E., Stegman, C. E., Sankaranarayan, P., & Mendelsohn, S. (1985). Mastery motivation in young preschoolers: Effect of a physical handicap and implications for educational programming. *Journal of the Division for Early Childhood, 9*(2), 162–169.

Johnson, B. H., McGonigel, M. J., & Kaufmann, R. K. (Eds.). (1989). *Guidelines and recommended practices for the individualized family service plan.* Chapel Hill, NC: National Early Childhood Technical Assistance System, and Association for the Care of Children's Health.

Johnson, L. J. (1988). Program evaluation: The key to quality programming. In J. B. Jordan, J. J. Gallagher, P. L. Hutinger, & M. B. Karnes (Eds.), *Early childhood special education: Birth to three.* Reston, VA: Council for Exceptional Children.

Johnson, R., & Mandell, C. (1988). A social observation checklist for preschoolers. *Teaching Exceptional Children,* winter, 18–21.

Jones, K. L., & Smith, D. W. (1973). Recognition of the fetal alcohol syndrome in early infancy. *Lancet, 2,* 999–1001.

Jones, R. R., Reid, J. B., & Patterson, G. R. (1975). Naturalistic observation in clinical assessment. In P. McReynolds (Ed.), *Advances in Psychological Assessment* (Vol. 3). San Francisco: Jossey-Bass.

Kahn, J. V. (1988). Cognitive assessment of mentally retarded infants and preschoolers. In T. D. Wachs & R. Sheehan (Eds.), *Assessment of young developmentally disabled children.* New York: Plenum.

Kaufman, A. S., & Kaufman, N. L. (1983). *Kaufman Assessment Battery for Children.* Circle Pines, MN: American Guidance Service.

Kazak, A. E., & Marvin, R. S. (1984). Differences, difficulties and adaptation:

Stress and social networks in families with a handicapped child. *Family Relations, 33,* 67–77.

Kazak, A. E., & Wilcox, B. L. (1984). The structure and function of social support networks in families with handicapped children. *American Journal of Community Psychology, 1,* 645–661.

Kazdin, A. E. (1982). Observer effects: Reactivity of direct observation. In D. P. Hartman (Ed.), *Using observers to study behavior.* San Francisco: Jossey-Bass.

Kearsley, R. (1979). Iatrogenic retardation: A syndrome of learned incompetence. In R. Kearsley & I. Sigel (Eds.), *Infants at risk: Assessment of cognitive functioning.* Hillsdale, NJ: Erlbaum.

Kekelis, L., & Andersen, E. (1982). *Blind children's early input: Mother accommodations.* Unpublished manuscript. Los Angeles: University of Southern California.

Kephart, N. C. (1971). *The slow learner in the classroom.* Columbus, OH: Merrill.

Kieran, D. W., & Dubose, R. F. (1974). Assessing the cognitive development of preschool deaf-blind children. *Education of the Visually Handicapped, 6,* 103–105.

Knobloch, H., & Pasamanick, B. (1974). *Gesell and Amatruda's developmental diagnosis: The evaluation and management of normal and abnormal neuropsychologic development in infancy and early childhood* (3rd ed.). New York: Harper and Row.

Knobloch, H., Stevens, F., Malone, A. Ellison, P., & Risemberg, H. (1979). The validity of parental reporting of infant development. *Pediatrics, 63,* 873–878.

Koch, R. (1963). A longitudinal study of 143 mentally retarded children (1955–1961). *Training School Bulletin, 1,* 4–11.

Kogan, K. L., Tyler, N., & Turner, P. (1974). The process of interpersonal adaptation between mothers and their cerebral palsied children. *Developmental Medicine and Child Neurology, 16,* 518–527.

Kogan, K. L., Wimberger, H. C., & Bobbitt, R. A. (1969). Analysis of mother–child interaction in young mental retardates. *Child Development, 40,* 799–812.

Kohn, M. (1986). *Kohn Social Competence Scale—Revised Edition.* New York: Psychological Corporation.

Koop, C. E. (1986). *Surgeon general's report on acquired immune deficiency syndrome.* Washington D.C.: U. S. Department of Health and Human Services.

Kopp, C. B. (1987). Developmental risk: Historical reflections. In J. D. Osofsky (Ed.), *Handbook of infant development.* New York: Wiley.

Krantz, P. J., & Risley, T. R. (1977). Behavioral ecology in the classroom. In K. D. O'Leary & S. G. O'Leary (Eds.), *Classroom management: The successful use of behavior modification* (2nd ed., pp. 349–366). New York: Pergamon.

Krug, D. A., Arick, J. R., & Almond, P. J. (1980). *Autism Screening Instrument for Educational Planning.* Austin, TX: Pro-Ed.

Lambert, N., Windmiller, M., Tharinger, D., & Cole, L. (1981). *AAMD Adaptive Behavior Scale—School Edition.* Monterey, CA: CTB/McGraw-Hill.

Landy, S., & Peters, R. D. (1990). Identifying and treating aggressive preschoolers. *Infants and Young Children, 3*(2), 24–38.

Langley, B. (1980). *Functional Vision Inventory for the Multiple and Severely Handicapped.* Chicago: Stoetling.

Laosa, L. M. (1982). Families as facilitators of children's intellectual development at 3 years of age: A causal analysis. In L. M. Laosa & I. E. Sigel (Eds.), *Families as learning environments for children.* New York: Plenum.

Leiter, R. G. (1948). *Leiter International Performance Scale.* Chicago: Stoelting.

Leiter, R. G. (1959). Part I of the manual for the 1948 revision of the Leiter International Performance Scale: Evidence of the reliability and validity of the Leiter tests. *Psychological Service Center Journal, 11,* 1–72.

Leland, H., Shoace, M., McElwain, D., & Christie, R. (1980). *Adaptive Behavior Scale for Infants and Early Childhood.* Columbus, OH: Ohio State University, Nisonger Center.

LeLaurin, K., & Risley, T. R. (1972). The organization of day care environments: "Zone" versus "man-to-man" staff assignments. *Journal of Applied Behavior Analysis, 5,* 225–232.

Lester, B. M., & Zeskind, P. S. (1979). The organization and assessment of crying in the infant at risk. In T. M. Field, A. M. Sosteck, S. Goldberg, & H. H. Shuman (Eds.), *Infants born at risk: Behavior and development.* New York: Spectrum.

Lewis, K. D., Bennett, B., & Schmeder, N. H. (1989). The care of infants menaced by cocaine abuse. *Maternal and Child Nursing, 14,* 324–329.

Lewis, M. (1987). Social development in infancy and early childhood. In J. D. Osofsky (Ed.), *Handbook of infant development.* New York: Wiley.

Lewis, M., & Michalson, L. (1983). *Scales of socio-emotional development.* New York: Plenum.

Lewis, M., & Wehren, A. (1982). The central tendency in the study of the handicapped child. In D.D. Bricker (Ed.), *Intervention with at-risk and handicapped infants: From research to application.* Baltimore, MD: University Park Press.

Lidz, C. S. (Ed.). (1987). *Dynamic assessment: An interactional approach to evaluating learning potential.* New York: Guilford.

Lidz, C. S., & Thomas, C. (1987). The preschool learning assessment device: Extension of a static approach. In C. S. Lidz (Ed.), *Dynamic assessment: An interactional approach to evaluating learning potential.* New York: Guilford.

Lieberman, A. F., & Pawl, J. H. (1988). Clinical applications of attachment theory. In J. Belsky & T. Nezworski (Eds.), *Clinical implications of attachment.* Hillsdale, NJ: Erlbaum.

Lillie, D. L. (1977). Screening. In L. Cross & K. Goin (Eds.), *Identifying handicapped children: A guide to casefinding, screening, diagnosis, assessment, and evaluation.* New York: Walker.

Linder, T. W. (1990). *Transdisciplinary play-based assessment: A functional approach to working with young children.* Baltimore, MD: Brookes.

McCall, R. B. (1982). Issues in the early development of intelligence and its assessment. In M. Lewis & L. T. Taft (Eds.), *Developmental disabilities: Theory, assessment, and intervention.* New York: Spectrum.

McCall, R. B., Hogarty, P. S., & Hurlburt, N. (1972). Transitions in infant sensorimotor development and the prediction of childhood IQ. *American Psychologist, 27,* 728–748.

McCarthy, J. M. (1989). Specific learning disabilities in preschool children. In L. B. Silver (Ed.), *The assessment of learning disabilities.* Boston: College-Hill.

McCarthy, D. A. (1972). *Manual for the McCarthy Scales of Children's Abilities.* New York: Psychological Corporation.

McCollum, J. A., & Stayton, V. D. (1985). Infant/parent interaction: Studies and intervention guidelines based on the SIAI model. *Journal of the Division for Early Childhood, 9*(2), 125–135.

McCarney, S. B., Leigh, J. E., & Cornbleet, J. (1990). *Behavior Evaluation Scale.* Austin, TX: Pro-Ed.

McConnell, S. R., Sisson, L., & Sandler, S. (1984). Category definitions for observational assessment of reciprocal social interactions. Unpublished observer training manual. University of Pittsburgh.

McDevitt, S. C., (1988). Assessment of temperament in developmentally disabled infants and preschoolers. In T. D. Wachs & R. Sheehan (Eds.), *Assessment of young developmentally disabled children.* New York: Plenum.

MacDonald, J. D. (1978a). *Environmental Language Inventory.* New York: Psychological Corporation.

MacDonald, J. D. (1978b). *Oliver: Parent-Administered Communication Inventory.* Columbus, OH: Merrill.

McDonnell, A., & Hardman, M. (1988). A synthesis of "best practice" guidelines for early childhood services. *Journal of the Division for Early Childhood, 12*(4), 328–341.

McEvoy, M. A. (1990). The organization of caregiving environments: Critical issues and suggestions for future research. *Education and Treatment of Children, 13,* 269–273.

McEvoy, M. A., & Brady, M. P. (1988). Contingent access to play materials as an academic motivator for autistic and behavior disordered children. *Education and Treatment of Children, 11,* 5–18.

McIntrye, M. (1974). *A modified model for the description of language acquisition in a deaf child.* Unpublished master's thesis. Northridge: California State University at Northridge.

McLean, M., McCormick, K., Bruder, M. B., & Burdg, N. B. (1987). An investigation of the validity and reliability of the Battelle Developmental Inventory with a population of children younger than 30 months with identified handicapping conditions. *Journal of the Division for Early Childhood, 11,* 238–246.

McReynolds, P. (1975). Introduction. In P. McReynolds (Ed.), *Advances in psychological assessment* (Vol. 3). San Francisco: Jossey-Bass.

McWilliam, R. A., Trivette, C. M., & Dunst, C. J. (1985). Behavior engagement as a measure of the efficacy of early intervention. *Analysis and Intervention in Developmental Disabilities, 5,* 59–71.

Madaus, G. F. (1988). The influence of testing on the curriculum. In L. N. Tanner (Ed.), *Critical issues in curriculum: 87th yearbook of the national society for the study of education.* Chicago: University of Chicago Press.

Mahoney, G. (1984). The validity of the Receptive–Expressive Emergent Language Scale with mentally retarded children. *Journal of the Division for Early Childhood, 9*(1), 86–94.

Maslin, C., & Morgan, G. (1984). *Manual for rating scales of child characteristics (Modified IBR).* Fort Collins: Department of Human Development and Family Studies, Colorado State University.

Meadow, K. P., Getson, P., Lee, C. K., & Stamper, L. (1983). *Meadow-Kendall Social–Emotional Assessment Inventory for Deaf and Hearing Impaired Students.* Washington D.C.: Outreach Gallaudet College.

Mearig, J. S. (1987). Assessing the learning potential of kindergarten and primary-age children. In C. S. Lidz (Ed.), *Dynamic assessment: An interactional approach to evaluating learning potential.* New York: Guilford.

Mehrabian, A., & Williams, M. (1971). Piagetian measures of cognitive development for children up to age two. *Journal of Psycholinguistic Research, 1,* 113–126.

Meier, J. H. (1976). Cognitive function normal development—Mental retardation. In R. G. Johnston & P. R. Magrab (Eds.), *Developmental disorders: Assessment, treatment, education.* Baltimore, MD: University Park Press.

Meisels, S. J. (1989). High stakes testing in kindergarten. *Educational Leadership, 46*(7), 16–22.

Mercer, J., & Lewis, J. (1978). *Adaptive Behavior Inventory for Children.* New York: Psychological Corporation.

Mercer, C. D., & Mercer, A. R. (1985). *Teaching students with learning problems* (2nd ed.). Columbus, OH: Merrill.

Milani-Comparetti, A., & Gidoni, E. (1967). Routine developmental examination in normal and retarded children. *Developmental Medicine and Child Neurology, 9,* 631–638.

Miller, L. J. (1988). *Miller Assessment for Preschoolers Manual* (revised ed.). San Antonio, TX: Psychological Corporation.

Minick, N. (1987). Implications of Vygotsky's theories for dynamic assessment. In C. S. Lidz (Ed.), *Dynamic assessment: An interactional approach to evaluating learning potential.* New York: Guilford.

Minuchin, S. (1974). *Families and family therapy.* Cambridge, MA: Harvard University Press.

Moog, J. S., & Geers, A. V. (1975). *Scales of early communication skills for hearing impaired children.* St. Louis, MO: Central Institute for the Deaf.

Moore, G. T. (1982). *Early Childhood Physical Environment Scale.* Center for Architecture and Urban Planning Research. P. O. Box 413, Milwaukee, WI 53210.

Moore, M. G. (1977). Program evaluation. In L. Cross & K. Goin (Eds.), *Identifying handicapped children: A guide to casefinding, screening, diagnosis, assessment and evaluation.* New York: Walker.

Moos, R. H., & Moos, B. M. (1981). *Family environment scale manual.* Palo Alto, CA: Consulting Psychologists Press.

Morgan, G. A., Harmon, R. J., & Bennett, C. A. (1976). A system for coding and scoring infant's spontaneous play with objects. *JSAS Catalog of Selected Documents in Psychology, 10* (ms. 1355).

Morgan, G. A., Maslin, C. A., Jennings, K. D., & Busch-Rossnagel, N. (1988). Assessing mothers' perceptions of mastery motivations: Development and utility of the Dimensions of Mastery Questionnaire. In P. M. Vietze & R. H. MacTurk (Eds.), *Perspectives on mastery motivation in infancy and childhood.* Norwood, NJ: Ablex.

Moriarty, A. E. (1972). Review of the Denver Developmental Screening Test. In O. K. Buros (Ed.), *The seventh mental measurement yearbook.* Highland Park, NJ: Cryphon.

Murphy, G. (1982). Sensory reinforcement in the mentally handicapped and autistic child: A review. *Journal of Autism and Developmental Disorders, 3,* 265–278.

Mutti, M., Sterling, H. M., & Spalding, N. V. (1978). *Quick Neurological Test—Revised.* San Rafael, CA: Academic Therapy Publications.

Naglieri, J. A. (1985). Use of the WISC-R and K-ABC with LD, MR, and normal children. *Psychology in the Schools, 22,* 133–140.

Neisser, U. (1976). *Cognition and reality: Principles and implications of cognitive psychology.* San Francisco: Freeman.

Neisworth, J. T., & Bagnato, S. J. (1988). Assessment in early childhood special education. In S. L. Odom & M. B. Karnes (Eds.), *Early intervention for infants and children with handicaps.* Baltimore, MD: Brookes.

Nelson, K. (1985). *Making sense: The acquisition of shared meaning.* New York: Academic Press.

Neeper, R., & Lahey, B. B. (1988). *Comprehensive Behavior Rating Scale for Children.* San Antonio, TX: Psychological Corporation.

Newborg, J., Stock, J., Wnek, L., Guildubaldi, J., & Svinicki, J. S. (1984). *Battelle Developmental Inventory (BDI).* Allen, TX: DLM/Teaching Resources.

Nihara, K., Mink, I., & Meyers, C. (1985). Home environment and development of slow learning adolescents. *Developmental Psychology, 21,* 784–794.

Nordquist, V. M., & Twardosz, S. (1990). Preventing behavior problems in early childhood special education classrooms through environmental organization. *Education and Treatment of Children, 13,* 274–287.

Odom, S. M., & McConnell, S. R. (1989). Assessing social interaction skills. In D. B. Bailey & M. Wolery (Eds.), *Assessing infants and preschoolers with handicaps.* Columbus, OH: Merrill.

Odom, S. L., McConnell, S. R., Kohler, F., & Strain, P. S. (1987). *Social interaction skill curriculum.* Unpublished curriculum manuscript. Pittsburgh: Early Childhood Research Institute. University of Pittsburgh.

Odom, S. L. & Warren, S. F. (1988). Early childhood special education in the year 2000. *Journal of the Division for Early Childhood, 12*(3), 263–273.

Office of Santa Cruz Superintendent of Schools. (1973). *BCP Observation Booklet.* Palo Alto, CA: VORT Corp.

Olswang, L. B., & Bain, B. A. (1988). Assessment of language in developmentally disabled infants and preschoolers. In T. D. Wachs & R. Sheehan (Eds.), *Assessment of young developmentally disabled children.* New York: Plenum.

Owens, R. E. (1989). *Language development: An introduction.* Columbus, OH: Merrill.

Parke, R. D., & Tinsley, B. J. (1987). Family interaction in infancy. In J. D. Osofsky (Ed.), *Handbook of infant development.* New York: Wiley.

Parten, M. (1932). Social participation among preschool children. *Journal of Abnormal and Social Psychology, 27,* 243–269.

Peter, L. (1967). *Prescriptive teaching.* New York: McGraw-Hill.

Petersen, N. S., Kolen, M. J., & Hoover, H. D. (1989). Scaling, norming and equating. In Robert L. Linn (Ed.), *Educational measurement* (3rd ed., pp. 221–262). New York: Macmillan.

Petersen, N. L. (1987). *Early intervention for handicapped and at-risk children.* Denver, CO: Love.

Phillips, D. K., Henderson, G. I., & Schenker, S. (1989). Pathogenesis of fetal alcohol syndrome: Overview with emphasis on the possible role of nutrition. *Alcohol Health and Research World, 13*(3), 219–226.

Popham, W. J. (1988). *Educational evaluation* (2nd ed.). Englewood Cliffs, NJ: Prentice-Hall.

Provence, S., & Lipton, R. C. (1962). *Infants in institutions.* New York: International Universities Press.

Quay, H. C., & Peterson, D. R. (1983). *The Behavior Problem Checklist—Revised.* Coral Gables, FL: Quay.

Ragozin, A., Basham, R., Crnic, K., Greenberg, M., & Robinson, N. (1982). Effects of maternal age on parenting role. *Developmental Psychology, 18,* 627–634.

Ramey, C. T., Trohanis, P. L., & Hostler, S. L. (1982). An introduction. In C. T. Ramey & P. L. Trohanis (Eds.), *Finding and educating high-risk and handicapped infants.* Baltimore, MD: University Park Press.

Ramey, C. T., & Brownlee, J. R. (1981). Improving the identification of high-risk infants. *American Journal of Mental Deficiency, 85,* 504–511.

Ramey, C. T., & Haskins, R. (1981). The modification of intelligence through early experience. *Intelligence, 5,* 5–19.

Ramey, C. T., & Smith, B. J. (1976). Assessing the intellectual consequences of early intervention with high-risk infants. *American Journal of Mental Deficiency, 81,* 318–324.

Ramey, C. T., Zeskind, P. S., & Hunter, R. S. (1981). Biomedical and psychosocial interventions for preterm infants. In S. L. Friedman & M. Sigman (Eds.), *Preterm birth and psychological development* (pp. 395–415). New York: Academic Press.

Raven, J. C., & Summers, B. (1986). *Manual for Raven's Progressive Matrices and Vocabulary Scales—research supplement No. 3.* London: Lewis.

Rescorla, L. (1989). The language development survey: A screening tool for delayed language in toddlers. *Journal of Speech and Hearing Disorders, 54,* 587–599.

Reynell, J., & Zinkin, K. (1979). *Reynell–Zinkin Developmental Scales for Young Visually Handicapped Children.* Chicago: Stoelting.

Richmond, B. O., & Kicklighter, R. H. (1980). *Children's Adaptive Behavior Scale.* Atlanta, GA: Humanics.

Riley, G. D. (1976). *Riley motor problems inventory.* Los Angeles, CA: Western Psychological Services.

Risley, T. R., & Cataldo, M. F. (1974). *Evaluation of planned activities: The PLA-Check measure of classroom participation.* Lawrence, KS: Center for Applied Behavior Analysis.

Ritter, D., Duffey, J., & Fischman, R. (1974). Comparability of Columbia Mental Maturity Scale and Stanford-Binet, form L-M, estimates of intelligence. *Psychological Reports, 34,* 174.

Rivera, C. (Ed.). (1984). *Communicative competence approaches to language proficiency assessment: Research and application.* Avon, England: Multilingual Matters.

Robinson, E. A., Eyberg, S. M., & Ross, A. W. (1980). Inventory of Child Problem Behaviors: The standardization of an inventory of child conduct problem behaviors. *Journal of Clinical Child Psychology, 9,* 22–29.

Robinson, H. R., & Robinson, N. M. (1976). *The mentally retarded child* (2nd ed.). New York: McGraw-Hill.

Rogers-Warren, A. K. (1984). Ecobehavioral analysis. *Education and Treatment of Children, 7,* 283–303.

Rogers-Warren, A. K., & Wedel, J. W. (1980). The ecology of preschool classrooms for the handicapped. *New Directions for Exceptional Children, 1,* 1–24.

Rogers, S. J. (1982). Techniques of infant assessment. In G. Ulrey & S. J. Rogers (Eds.), *Psychological assessment of handicapped infants and young children.* New York: Thieme-Stratton.

Rosenberg, S. A., Robinson, C. C., Finkler, D., & Rose, J. (1987). An empirical comparison of formulas evaluating early intervention programs. *Exceptional Children, 54*(3), 213–219.

Rosenblith, J. F. (1961). The modified Graham behavior test for neonates: Test–retest reliability, normative data and hypotheses for future work. *Biologia Neonatorium, 3,* 174–192.

Rosenblith, J. F. (1974a). Relations between neonatal behaviors and those at eight months. *Developmental Psychology, 10,* 779–792.

Rosenblith, J. F. (1974b). Relations between newborn and four-year behaviors. Paper presented at the meetings of the Eastern Psychological Association, New York City.

Rosenblith, J. F. (1975). Prognostic value of neonatal behavioral tests. In B. Z. Friedlander, G. M. Sterritt, & G. E. Kirk (Eds.), *Exceptional infant,* Vol. 3: *Assessment and intervention.* New York: Brunner/Mazel.

Rosenblith, J. F. (1979a). Relations between behaviors in the newborn period and intellectual achievement and IQ at 7 years of age. Paper presented at the meetings of the International Society for the Study of Behavior and Development, Lund, Sweden.

Rosenblith, J. F. (1979b). Relations between Graham/Rosenblith neonatal measures and seven year assessments. Paper presented at the meetings of the Eastern Psychological Association, Philadelphia.

Rosman, N. P., & Oppenheimer, E. Y. (1985). Maternal drinking and the fetal alcohol syndrome. In S. Harel & N. J. Anastasiow (Eds.), *The at-risk infant: Psycho/socio/medical aspects.* Baltimore, MD: Brookes.

Rossetti, L. M. (1986). *High risk infants: Identification, assessment, and intervention.* Boston: College-Hill.

Rossetti, L. M. (1990). *Infant-toddler assessment: An interdisciplinary approach.* Boston: Little, Brown.

Rossi, P. H. (1989). *Down and out in America: The origins of homelessness.* Chicago: University of Chicago Press.

Roth, F. P. (1990). Early language assessment. In E. D. Gibbs & D. M. Teti (Eds.), *Interdisciplinary assessment of infants: A guide for early intervention.* Baltimore, MD: Brookes.

Rotunno, M., & McGoldrick, M. (1982). Italian families. In M. McGoldrick, J. K. Pearce, & J. Giordant (Eds.), *Ethnicity in family therapy.* New York: Guilford.

Salvia, I., & Ysseldyke, J. E. (1979). *Assessment in special and remedial education.* Boston: Houghton Mifflin.

Sameroff, A. J., & Chandler, M. J. (1975). Reproductive risk and the continuum of caretaking casualty. In F. D. Horowitz (Ed.), *Review of child development research* (Vol. 4). Chicago: University of Chicago Press.

Sander, L. (1969). The longitudinal course of early mother–child interaction—cross-case comparison in a sample of mother–child pairs. In B. M. Foss (Ed.), *Determinants of infant behavior* (Vol. 4). London: Methuen.

Sattler, J. M. (1988). *Assessment of children* (3rd ed.). San Diego, CA: Sattler.

Schaefer, D. S., & Moersch, M. S. (Eds.). (1981). *Developmental programming for infants and young children.* Ann Arbor: University of Michigan Press.

Schaefer, E., & Bell, R. (1958). Development of parental attitude research instrument. *Child Development, 29,* 339–361.

Schlesinger, I. M. (1971). Production of utterances and language acquisition. In D. Slobin (Ed.), *The ontogenesis of grammar.* New York: Academic Press.

Schlesinger, I. M. (1974). Relational concepts underlying language. In R. Schiefelbush & L. Lloyd (Eds.), *Language perspectives: Acquisition retardation and intervention.* Baltimore: University Park Press.

Schlesinger, H. S. (1978). The acquisition of bimodal language. In I. M. Schlesinger & L. Namir (Eds.), *Sign language of the deaf.* New York: Academic Press.

Schneider, J. W., Griffith, D. R., & Chasnoff, I. J. (1989). Infants exposed to cocaine in utero: Implications for developmental assessment and intervention. *Infants and Young Children, 2*(1), 25–36.

Schoggen, P. (1978). Environmental forces on physically disabled children. In R. G. Barker (Ed.), *Habitats, environments, and human behavior.* San Francisco, CA: Jossey-Bass.

Scott, M. (1980). Ecological theory and methods for research in special education. *Journal of Special Education, 14*(3), 279–294.

Scriven, M. (1973). Goal-free evaluation. In E. R. House (Ed.), *School evaluation: The politics and process.* Berkeley, CA: McCutchan.

Scriven, M. (1974). Evaluation perspectives and procedures. In W. J. Popham (Ed.), *Evaluation in education: Current applications.* Berkeley, CA: McCutchan.

Searle, J. (1965). What is a speech act? In M. Black (Ed.), *The origins and growth of communication.* Norwood, NJ: Ablex.

Seligman, M., & Darling, B. R. (1989). *Ordinary families, special children: A systems approach to childhood disability.* New York: Guilford.

Sexton, D., Miller, J. H., Scott, R. L., & Rogers, C. (1988). Concurrent validity data for the Uzgiris and Hunt Scales and the Bayley mental scale: Additional evidence on the Dunst age norms. *Journal of the Division for Early Childhood, 12,* 368–374.

Sheehan, R., & Klein, N. (1989). Infant assessment. In M. C. Wang, M. C. Reynolds, & H. J. Walberg (Eds.), *Handbook of special education: Research and practice* (Vol. 3, low incidence conditions). New York: Pergamon.

Shere, E., & Kastenbaum, R. (1966). Mother–child interaction in cerebral palsy: Environmental and psychosocial obstacles to cognitive development. *Genetic Psychology Monographs, 73,* 255–335.

Shuster, S. K., Fitzgerald, N., Shelton, G., Barber, P., & Desch, S. (1984). Goal attainment scaling with moderately and severely handicapped preschool children. *Journal of the Division of Early Childhood, 8*(1), 26–37.

Sigel, I. E. (1982). The relationship between parental distancing strategies and the child's cognitive behavior. In L. M. Laosa & I. E. Sigel (Eds.), *Families as learning environments for children.* New York: Plenum.

Sigel, I. E., & Flaugher, J. (1987). *Parent–Child and Family Interaction Observation Schedule* (PCI). Princeton, NJ: Educational Testing Service.

Simeonsson, R. J. (1982). Intervention, accountability, and efficiency indices: A rejoinder. *Exceptional Children, 48*(4), 358–359.

Simeonsson, R. J. (1988). Assessing family environments. In D. B. Bailey & R. J. Simeonsson (Eds.), *Family assessment in early intervention.* Columbus, OH: Merrill.

Simeonsson, R. J., Huntington, G. S., & Short, R. J. (1982). Individual differences and goals: An approach to the evaluation of child progress. *Topics in Early Childhood Special Education, 1*(4), 71–80.

Simeonsson, R. J., Huntington, G. S., Short, R. J., & Ware, W. B. (1982). The Carolina record of individual behavior: Characteristics of handicapped infants and children. *Topics in Early Childhood Special Education, 2*(2), 43–55.

Simeonsson, R. J., & Wiegerink, R. (1975). Accountability: A dilemma in infant intervention. *Exceptional Children, 41*(7), 474–481.

Skeels, H. M., & Dye, H. B. (1939). A study of the effects of differential stimulation on mentally retarded children. *Proceedings and Addresses of the American Association on Mental Deficiency, 44,* 114–136.

Slobin, D. (1986). *The cross-linguistic study of language acquisition* (Vols. 1 and 2). Hillsdale, NJ: Erlbaum.

Smilansky, S. (1968). *The effects of sociodramatic play on disadvantaged children: Preschool children.* New York: Wiley.

Song, A., Jones, S., Lippert, J., Metzgen, K., Miller, J., & Borreca, C. (1980). *Wisconsin Behavior Rating Scale.* Madison: Central Wisconsin Center for the Developmentally Disabled.

Sostek, A. M., Quinn, P. O., & Davitt, M. K. (1979). Behavior, development, and the neurologic status of premature and full-term infants with varying medical complications. In T. M. Field, A. M. Sostek, S. Goldberg, & H. H. Shuman (Eds.), *Infants born at risk: Behavior and development.* New York: Spectrum.

Sparrow, S. S., Balla, D. A., & Cicchetti, D. V. (1984). *Vineland Adaptive Behavior Scales.* Circle Pines, MN: American Guidance Service.

Spitz, R. (1947). Hospitalism: A follow-up report. *Psychoanalytic study of the child* (Vol. 2). New York: International Universities Press.

Spring, J. (1988). *Conflict of interests: The politics of American education.* New York: Longman.

Squires, J. K., Nickel, R., & Bricker, D. (1990). Use of parent-completed developmental questionnaires for child-find and screening. *Infants and Young Children, 3*(2), 46–57.

Sroufe, L. A. (1979). Socioemotional development. In J. D. Osofsky (Ed.), *Handbook of infant development.* New York: Wiley.

Stallings, J. A. (1977). *Learning to look.* Belmont, CA: Wadsworth.

Stancin, T., Reuter, J., Dunn, V., & Bickett, L. (1984). Validity of caregiver information on the developmental status of severely brain-damaged young children. *American Journal of Mental Deficiency, 88,* 388–395.

Stedman, D. J., & Eichorn, D. A. (1964). Comparison of the growth and development of institutionalized and home-reared mongoloids during infancy and early childhood. *American Journal on Mental Deficiency, 69,* 391–401.

Stillman, R. (1978). *The Callier–Azusa Scale.* Dallas: Callier Center for Communication Disorders.

Stott, D. H., Moyes, F. A., & Henderson, S. E. (1984). *Test of Motor Impairment–Henderson Revision.* New York: Psychological Corporation.

Strenio, A. J. (1981). *The testing trap.* New York: Rawson, Wade.

Stufflebeam, D. L. (1971). The relevance of the CIPP evaluation model for educational accountability. *Journal of Research and Development in Education, 5*(1), 19–23.

Stufflebeam, D. L. (1974). Alternative approaches to educational evaluation: A self-study guide for educators. In W. J. Popham (Ed.), *Evaluation in education: Current applications.* Berkeley, CA: McCutchan.

Sutton-Smith, B. (1970). *A descriptive account of four modes of children's play between one and five years.* New York: Columbia University Teachers College.

Taft, L. T. (1982). Neuromotor assessment of infants. In M. Lewis & L. T. Taft (Eds.), *Developmental disabilities: Theory, assessment, and intervention.* New York: Spectrum.

Taylor, R. L. (1989). *Assessment of exceptional students: Educational and psychological procedures.* Englewood Cliffs, N.J.: Prentice-Hall.

Teti, D. M., & Nakagawa, M. (1990). Assessing attachment in infancy: The strange situation and alternate systems. In E. D. Gibbs & D. M. Teti (Eds.), *Interdisciplinary assessment of infants: A guide for early intervention professionals.* Baltimore, MD: Brookes.

Thoman, E. B., Becker, P. T., & Freese, M. P. (1978). Individual patterns in mother–infant interactions. In G. P. Sackett (Ed.), *Observing behavior,* Vol. 1: *Theory and applications in mental retardation.* Baltimore, MD: University Park Press.

Thomas, A., & Chess, S., (1977). *Temperament and development.* New York: Brunner/Mazel.

Thomas, A., Chess, S., & Birch, H. G., (1968). *Temperament and behavior disorders in children.* New York: New York University Press.

Thorndike, R. L., Hagen, E. P., & Sattler, J. M. (1986). *Stanford-Binet Intelligence Scale* (4th ed.). Chicago: Riverside.

Thurman, S. K. (1977). Congruence of behavioral ecologies: A model for special education programming. *Journal of Special Education, 11*(3), 329–333.

Thurman, S. K., & Widerstrom, A. H. (1985). *Young children with special needs.* Boston: Allyn and Bacon.

Thurman, S. K., & Widerstrom, A. H. (1989). *Infants and young children with special needs: A developmental and ecological approach* (2nd ed.). Baltimore, MD: Brookes.

Tjossem, T. D. (1976). Early intervention: Issues and approaches. In T. D. Tjossem (Ed.), *Intervention strategies for high risk infants and young children.* Baltimore, MD: University Park Press.

Touliatos, J., & Compton, N. H. (1983). *Approaches to child study.* Minneapolis, MN: Burgess.

Tourse, P., & Gundersen, L. (1988). Adopting and fostering children with AIDS: Policies in progress. *Children Today, 17*(3), 9–14.

Trembath, J. (1977). *The Milani-Comparetti Motor Development Screening Test.* Omaha: Meyer Children's Rehabilitation Institute, University of Nebraska Medical Center.

Turnbull, A. P., & Turnbull, H. R. (1986). *Families, professionals, and exceptionality.* Columbus, OH: Merrill.

Twardosz, S. (1984a). Environmental organization: The physical, social and programmatic context of behavior. In M. Hersen, R. M. Eisler, & P. M. Miller (Eds.), *Progress in behavior modification* (Vol. 18, pp. 123–161). Orlando, FL: Academic Press.

Twardosz, S. (1984b). Behavioral–organizational consultation to day care centers: The process of implementing change. *The Behavior Therapist, 7,* 193–196.

Twardosz, S., & Risley, T. R. (1982). Behavioral–ecological consultation to day care centers. In A. Jeger & R. Slotnick (Eds.), *Community mental health and behavioral-ecology: A handbook of theory, research, and practice* (pp. 147–159). New York: Plenum.

Tyler, R. W. (1971). Accountability in education: The shift in criteria. In L. M. Lesinger & R. W. Tyler (Eds.), *Accountability in education*. Worthington, OH: Jones.

Tyler, R. W. (1974). Introduction: A perspective on the issues. In R. W. Tyler & R. M. Wolf (Eds.), *Crucial issues in testing*. Berkeley, CA: McCutchan.

Tzuriel, D., & Klein, P. S. (1987). Assessing the young child: Children's analogical thinking modifiability. In C. S. Lidz (Ed.), *Dynamic assessment: An interactional approach to evaluating learning potential*. New York: Guilford.

Ulrey, G. (1982). Assessment considerations with language impaired children. In G. Ulrey & S. J. Rogers, *Psychological assessment of handicapped infants and young children*. New York: Thieme-Stratton.

Ulrey, G., Schnell, R., & Hosking, K. (1978). Cognitive stimulation for handicapped infants based on Piagetian scales. In G. Lubin, M. Poulson, & J. Magary (Eds.), *Eighth annual Piagetian conference proceedings*. Los Angeles: University of Southern California Press.

Uzgiris, I. (1976). Organization of sensorimotor intelligence. In M. Lewis (Ed.), *Origins of intelligence: Infancy and early childhood*. New York: Plenum.

Uzgiris, I., & Hunt, J. M. (1975). *Assessment in infancy: Ordinal Scales of Psychological Development*. Urbana: University of Illinois Press.

VanBiervliet, A., Spangler, P. F., & Marshall, A. M. (1981). An ecobehavioral examination of a simple strategy for increasing mealtime language in residential facilities. *Journal of Applied Behavior Analysis, 14,* 295–305.

VanderLinden, D. (1985). Ability of the Milani-Comparetti developmental examination to predict motor outcome. *Physical and Occupational Therapy in Pediatrics, 5*(1), 27–38.

VanderVeer, B., & Schweid, E. (1974). Infant assessment: Stability of mental functioning in young retarded children. *American Journal of Mental Deficiency, 79,* 1–4.

Vernon, P. E. (1950). *The structure of human abilities*. New York: Wiley.

Volkmar, F. R., Cicchetti, D. V., Dykens, E., Sparrow, S. S., Leckman, J. F., & Cohen, D. J. (1988). An evaluation of the Autism Behavior Checklist. *Journal of Autism and Developmental Disorders, 18*(1), 81–97.

Vygotsky, L. (1962). *Thought and language*. Cambridge, MA: MIT Press.

Vygotsky, L. S. (1978). *Mind in society: The development of higher psychological processes*. Cambridge, MA: Harvard University Press.

Wachs, T. D. (1979). Proximal experience and early cognitive–intellectual development: The physical environment. *Merrill-Palmer Quarterly, 25*(1), 3–41.

Wachs, T. D. (1984). Proximal experience and early cognitive–intellectual development: The social environment. In A. W. Gottfried (Ed.), *Home environment and early cognitive development*. Orlando, FL: Academic Press.

Wachs, T. D. (1988). Environmental assessment of developmentally disabled infants and preschoolers. In T. D. Wachs & R. Sheehan (Eds.), *Assessment of young developmentally disabled children*. New York: Plenum.

Wachs, T. D., Francis, J., & McQuiston, S. (1978). Psychological dimensions of the infant's physical environment. Paper presented to the Midwestern Psychological Association, Chicago.

Wachs, T. D., & Gruen, G. (1982). *Early experience and human development*. New York: Plenum.

Wahler, R. G., & Fox, J. J. (1981). Setting events in applied behavior analysis: Toward a conceptual and methodological expansion. *Journal of Applied Behavior Analysis, 14,* 327–338.

Washer, R. W. (1984). *Washer Visual Acuity Screening Techniques*. Bensenville, IL: Scholastic Testing Service.

Washington, V. (1985). Social and personal ecology influencing public policy for young children: An American dilemma. In C. S. McLoughlin & D. F. Gullo (Eds.), *Young children in context: Impact of self, family, and society on development*. Springfield, IL: Charles C Thomas.

Waters, E., & Deane, K. E. (1985). Defining and assessing individual differences in attachment relationships: Q-methodology and the organization of behavior in infancy and early childhood. In I. Bretherton & E. Waters (Eds.), *Growing points of attachment theory and research. Monographs of the Society for Research in Child Development* (Vol. 50, Nos. 1–2 ser. no. 209, pp. 41–65).

Watson, J. S. (1976). Early learning and intelligence. In M. Lewis (Ed.), *Origins of intelligence: Infancy and early childhood*. New York: Plenum.

Wechsler, D. (1958). *The Measurement and Appraisal of Adult Intelligence* (4th ed.). Baltimore, MD: Williams and Wilkins.

Wechsler, D. (1989). *Wechsler Preschool and Primary Scales of Intelligence—Revised*. New York: Psychological Corporation.

Wehman, P. (1977). *Helping the mentally retarded acquire play skills*. Springfield, IL: Charles C Thomas.

Wender, P. H. (1987). *The hyperactive child, adolescent, and adult: Attention deficit disorder through the lifespan*. New York: Oxford University Press.

Werner, E. E. (1990). Protective factors and individual resilience. In S. J. Meisels & J. P. Shonkoff (Eds.), *Handbook of early childhood intervention*. New York: Cambridge University Press.

Willems, E. P. (1977a). Chapter Two. In A. Rogers-Warren and S. F. Warren (Eds.), *Ecological perspectives in behavior analysis*. Baltimore, MD: University Park Press.

Willems, E. P. (1977b). Steps toward an ecobehavioral technology. In A. Rogers-Warren & S. F. Warren (Eds.), *Ecological perspectives in behavior analysis*. Baltimore, MD: University Park Press.

Wing, L., & Gould, J. (1978). Systematic recording of behaviors and skills of retarded and psychotic children. *Journal of Autism and Childhood Schizophrenia, 8*(1), 79–97.

Winton, P. J. (1988a). Effective communication between parents and professionals. In D. B. Bailey & R. J. Simeonsson (Eds.), *Family assessment in early intervention*. Columbus, OH: Merrill.

Winton, P. J. (1988b). The family-focused interview: An assessment measure and goal-setting mechanism. In D. B. Bailey & R. J. Simeonsson (Eds.), *Family assessment in early intervention*. Columbus, OH: Merrill.

Winton, P. J., & Bailey, D. B. (1988). The family-focused interview: A collaborative mechanism for family assessment and goal-setting. *Journal of the Division for Early Childhood, (12)*(3), 195–207.

Wodrich, D. L., & Joy, J. E., (Eds.) (1986). *Multidisciplinary assessment of children with learning disabilities and mental retardation*. Baltimore, MD: Brookes.

Wolery, M. (1983). Proportional change index: An alternative for comparing child change data. *Exceptional Children, 50*(2), 167–170.

Wolery, M., & Bailey, D. B. (1984). Alternatives to impact evaluations: Suggestions for program evaluation in early intervention. *Journal of the Division for Early Childhood, 9*(1), 27–37.

Wolff, P. H. (1982). Theoretical issues in the development of motor skills. In M. Lewis & L. T. Taft (Eds.), *Developmental disabilities: Theory, assessment, and intervention*. New York: Spectrum.

Woodruff, G., & Sterzin, E. D. (1988). The transagency approach: A model for serving children with HIV infection and their families. *Children Today, 17*(3), 9–14.

Worobey, J., & Brazelton, T. B. (1990). Newborn assessment and support for parenting. In E. D. Gibbs & D. M. Teti (Eds.), *Interdisciplinary assessment of infants: A guide for early intervention professionals.* Baltimore, MD: Brookes.

Worthington, G. B., & Berring, M. E. (1988). Use of the K-ABC in predicting achievement among students referred for special education services. *Journal of Learning Disabilities, 21,* 370–374.

Yang, R. K. (1979). Early infant assessment: An overview. In J. D. Osofsky (Ed.), *Handbook of infant development.* New York: Wiley.

Yang, R. K., & Bell, R. Q. (1975). Assessment of infants. In P. McReynolds (Ed.), *Advances in psychological assessment* (Vol. 3). San Francisco: Jossey-Bass.

Yarrow, L. J., Rubenstein, J. L., & Pedersen, F. A. (1975). *Infant and environment: Early cognitive and motivational development.* Washington, D.C.: Hemisphere.

Yoder, P. J. (1987). Relationship between degree of infant handicap and clarity of infant cues. *American Journal of Mental Deficiency, 91,* 639–641.

Zeaman, D., (1973). One programmatic approach to retardation. In D. K. Routh (Ed.), *The experimental psychology of mental retardation.* Chicago: Aldine.

Zeaman, D., & House, B. J., (1963). The role of attention in retardate discrimination learning. In N. R. Ellis (Ed.), *Handbook of mental deficiency: Psychological theory and research.* New York: McGraw-Hill.

Zeitlin, S. (1985). *Coping Inventory.* Bensenville, IL: Scholastic Testing Service.

Zeitlin, S., Williamson, G. G., & Szczepanski, M. (1988). *Early Coping Inventory.* Bensenville, IL: Scholastic Testing Service.

Zelazo, P. R. (1979). Reactivity to perceptual–cognitive events: Application for infant assessment. In R. Kearsley & I. Sigel (Eds.), *Infants at risk: Assessment of cognitive functioning.* Hillsdale, NJ: Erlbaum.

Zelazo, P. R. (1982a). An information processing approach to infant cognitive assessment. In M. Lewis & L. T. Taft (Eds.), *Developmental disabilities: Theory, assessment, and intervention.* New York: Spectrum.

Zelazo, P. R. (1982b). Alternative assessment procedures for handicapped infants and toddlers: Theoretical and practical issues. In D. D. Bricker (Ed.), *Intervention with at-risk and handicapped infants: From research to application.* Baltimore, MD: University Park Press.

Zelazo, P. R., & Weiss, M. J. (1990). Infant information processing: An alternative approach. In E. D. Gibbs & D. M. Teti (Eds.), *Interdisciplinary assessment of infants: A guide for early intervention professionals.* Baltimore, MD: Brookes.

Zelle, R. S. (1983). Meeting developmental and habilitative needs of infants and toddlers. In R. S. Zelle & A. B. Coyner, *Developmentally disabled infants and toddlers: Assessment and intervention.* Philadelphia: Davis.

Zelle, R. S., & Coyner A. B. (1983). *Developmentally disabled infants and toddlers: Assessment and intervention.* Philadelphia: Davis.

Zimmerman, I., Steiner, V., & Pond, R. E. (1979). *Preschool Language Scale.* Columbus, OH: Merrill.

Index